The New History of England

General Editors
A.G. Dickens and Norman Gash

10

The New History of England

*In preparation; all other titles already published

Wars and Welfare

Britain 1914–1945

Max Beloff

Edward Arnold
A division of Hodder & Stoughton
LONDON NEW YORK MELBOURNE AUCKLAND

© 1984 Max Beloff

First published in Great Britain 1984
Reprinted 1989

Distributed in the USA by Routledge, Chapman and Hall, Inc.
29 West 35th Street, New York, NY 10001

British Library Cataloguing in Publication Data

Beloff, Max
   Wars and welfare. — (The New history of
   England; 10)
   1. Great Britain — History — 20th century
   I. Title   II. Series
   941.083   DA566

ISBN 0-7131-6164-7 Pbk

Typeset in 11/12 Baskerville Compugraphic by Colset Private Ltd,
Singapore. Printed and bound in Great Britain for Edward Arnold, the
educational, academic and medical publishing division of Hodder and
Stoughton Limited, 41 Bedford Square London WC1B 3DQ by
Athenaeum Press Ltd, Newcastle upon Tyne.

Contents

Preface

I am deeply indebted to the editors of this series and to the publishers not merely for asking me to write this volume but for their exemplary patience in waiting for it. Professor Norman Gash has also devoted great care to eliminating errors and infelicities.

Since I have had to write the book at home I have been very dependent upon libraries which allow one to borrow books. I must therefore thank the librarians and staffs of the Codrington Library, All Souls College, the Library of St Antony's College, the Library of the House of Lords and above all of the London Library, my unfailing standby for almost half a century.

Where I have referred to original documents these come from material collected for the second volume of my work in progress, *Imperial Sunset*, and I must again thank my research assistants in that enterprise and in particular Mrs Mary Brown.

Dr John Ramsden has read the manuscript much to its benefit, and Dr J.C. Clarke performed the same service for the proofs. Delia Twamley typed the final version with speed and skill and Mrs Margaret Croft has once again displayed her talent as an indexer. Any errors of fact and eccentricities of opinion are of course my responsibility.

Max Beloff
Brighton, August 1983

1 Introduction

The writing of all history, and more especially of political history, is beset by one particular and inescapable intellectual problem. The makers of that history were not privy to the future. They might be inspired by hope and believe that by their actions they were contributing to one particular kind of future rather than another, but they could not have known for certain how things would in fact work out. The historian is normally in a different position; depending on his distance from the events he is describing he knows something that the subjects of his narrative could not know. If he allows this knowledge to dominate his account and to lead to judgements about the wisdom or lack of wisdom of policies pursued he may distort the reality of the mental world he is attempting to recapture. Yet to eliminate from his mind all that happened later is to make it hard to distinguish the important aspects of his period from the passing trivia.

Although other aspects of the historian's task are harder when he is dealing with more remote times, in this respect his task is much easier. It presents indeed a lesser problem for ancient historians than for medieval historians and for medieval historians than for modern historians. The most difficult task of all is that which confronts historians of the recent past, not, as is so often believed, primarily because some possible sources of information remain closed, but precisely because the angle of vision constantly alters as the events described become more remote and their more indirect consequences more apparent. The difficulty is even greater when the historian himself was a witness of at least part of the period described – the present writer was one year old in 1914 when this volume opens.

The historian of England – or of Britain as we should say of the eighteenth and nineteenth and the twentieth centuries – has a particular difficulty where the post-1914 decades are concerned. The framework of historical writing about Britain as it was set in the Victorian era was by and large what has come to be know as 'Whig'.[1]

[1] See for instance, P.B.M. Blaas, *Continuity and Anachronism: Parliamentary and Constitutional Development in Whig Historiography and the anti-Whig Reaction between 1890 and 1930* (The Hague, 1978) and J.W. Burrow, *A Liberal Descent: Victorian Historians and the English Past* (Cambridge, 1981).

The story is one of continuous though not of unbroken success, whether that success be measured in the development of popular institutions, in greater and more widely diffused material prosperity or in the painting red – the old colour of the Empire – of wider and wider stretches of the earth's surface.

In such circumstances the historian's task was much aided by the definite nature of his mandate. He would assume that the institutions of his own time were, if not the best that could be devised – since progress was to be continuous – at least better than what had gone before and direct his attention to discovering their origins and tracing their development or evolution. There might of course be minority views on the part of writers outside the academic mainstream – Catholic and occasionally Tory historians on the one hand and dissenting radicals on the other – but these did not have much impact on the central core of British political history as then defined.

So dominant was the effect of this tradition, and not only upon those temperamentally given to orthodoxy, that the books written about the period with which we are concerned at the time it ended were still much influenced by it. Although as early as the 1950s it was clear that the territorial extent of British rule and the economic and political influence of Britain in the world were very much less than in 1914, historians then and even later contrived to balance these facts by devoting more attention to other aspects of the story where progress could still be perceived – rising incomes, greater provision for private misfortunes, constantly extending public services.[2] A mere quarter of a century later this degree of optimism hardly appealed to any serious student of the contemporary scene.

Not merely had the reduction of Britain's world position to one of minor importance gone on at an ever accelerating pace, but there was also now found a parallel decline in Britain's internal well-being, falling standards of living, in some cases in absolute as well as relative terms, serious doubts about the stability of the currency, increasing dissatisfaction with the existing constitutional and governmental arrangements, growing conflicts between classes and groups, more internal violence, and threats to the unity of the United Kingdom itself.[3]

In the light of these preoccupations, the history of the preceeding period takes on a new aspect. We can no longer accept the comfortable Whig view that the party of progress or of change is always in the

---

[2] See e.g. C.L. Mowat, *Britain between the Wars 1918–1940* (London, 1955); A.J.P. Taylor, *English History 1914–1945* (Oxford, 1965).
[3] For the British political scene at the time this book was being written, see Max Beloff and Gillian Peele, *The Government of the United Kingdom: Political Authority in a Changing Society* (London, 1980).

long run vindicated as against the party of resistance, that all 'reforms' are positive in their consequences; we must give greater weight to the sceptics, even to the 'die-hards'; we must take account of the possibility that the seeds of decline were sown in those decades, perhaps even earlier. If despite such an approach we still find the condition of England in the inter-war period materially, and during the Second World War morally, at a high level we must still ask whether or not this is a mere illusion disguising deeper and less favourable trends that would with time appear. The warmest of 'Indian summers' masks but does not delay the advent of winter.

The political leaders who took part in making the history of those years did not know what was going to happen, and for the most part believed as their Victorian predecessors had done in the inevitability of progress, seeing setbacks as only temporary reversals of fortune. Indeed for a variety of reasons the general optimism was greater on the morrow of the Second World War than it had been after the First. For this fact, which helps to explain the tendencies in the historiography of the period to which we have already referred, many reasons might be adduced, perhaps the most obvious being the difference in the outcomes of the general elections of 1918 and 1945, the first returning if under a radical leader a government dominated by traditonalist attitudes, the latter giving unimpeded power for the first time to the political representatives of organized Labour.

It is the purpose of this volume as of others in the series of which it forms part to concentrate on the country's internal political history and not in any detail upon its relations with its overseas possessions or associates, nor upon its relations with foreign countries in war or peace.[4] Neither military nor diplomatic history can be given the weight to which they might in general terms seem entitled. For this approach there would seem to be some good reasons, notably the fact that in the processes through which the British chose their rulers, general elections in particular, priority was almost always attached to the internal rather than external records and promises of the rival parties. The idea that internal and external affairs are interdependent, that a country's prosperity may depend upon its power and prestige as much as its power and prestige depend upon its prosperity is one that democratic electorates find it difficult to entertain. Nevertheless there is an obvious artificiality about such a treatment in the case of Britain in the period with which we are dealing, since it was precisely her participation in the two world wars, and the losses human and material sustained in them, that were among the

---

[4] The period 1914–21 from this point of view is covered in the concluding part of the first volume of my *Imperial Sunset: Britain's Liberal Empire 1897–1921* (London, 1969). I hope in a second volume to take the narrative to the beginning of 1942.

most important political factors not merely during the war years but also afterwards. Yet even a cursory attempt to narrate the history of the wars themselves in which Britain was only one of many countries involved would completely destroy the balance of the history. The important thing is to be conscious of the distortion involved in a domestic perspective.

In similar fashion it is difficult to ignore the fact that during the reign of Elizabeth II, the area under the direct rule of the British Crown and Parliament was reduced once more to not much greater territorial extent than under Elizabeth I. It has been fashionable in recent historical writing on the British Empire, in reaction no doubt to the simplicities of the Hobson–Lenin school, to deny that the possession of overseas territories was itself a source of economic strength and so of political stability. In a world where there was general freedom of trade and investment and a general assurance of non-discrimination such arguments might be more readily upheld. The durability of such conditions was already being called into question at the time of the Boer War. But whether or not it be accepted, it can hardly be denied that a political system that had adapted itself to the management, whether by direct rule or through informal leadership of the concerns of a large portion of the earth's surface, was bound to feel the impact of the reduction in the scope of its responsibilities that set in with such rapidity on the morrow of the Second World War.

Nor was the impact of these changes limited to the country's political and administrative institutions and to the ways in which their personnel was recruited. They also raised in an acute fashion the very nature of the British economy and of the social structure to which it gave rise. What had been a persistent theme in English history and (after the Union with Scotland) of British history had been the importance of external commerce, finance and eventually investment. The Victorian anti-imperialist free-traders might argue that dominion overseas was wasteful and unnecessary, of benefit only to a small section of the ruling class; they did not deny the importance of the economic ties themselves. By 1914 the great days of British industrial pre-eminence were over; Britain was slipping downhill in the tables of industrial performance in the share of her products on the world's export markets. But to a great extent the decline had been compensated for by the growth in invisible exports, by the importance of her shipping and allied services, by the returns on overseas investment inside or outside the Empire, and above all by the rôle of London as the undisputed financial centre of the world. As one studies the earliest days of war in August 1914, nothing is more striking than the attention paid to its possible repercussions on the City. By 1917 the forebodings had proved accurate.[5] And even as late as the disputes over the scale of rearmament in the late 1930s the greatest importance was attached to doing nothing that might impede the ordinary workings of the financial markets, even though by this time it was New York rather than London which held the world's purse strings. It is only with the debates in the 1970s and 1980s over Britain's economic position, and the emergence of a school of thought prepared to contemplate a much more closed economy and a total concentration on the development of the island's own resources, that we can begin to put this earlier period into perspective and contemplate the possibility that like other mercantile-based polities in history, Britain's though long-lasting has had no guarantee of eternity. In this respect the crisis of 1931 has begun to take on a quite different aspect from that which dominated contemporary comment.

The vulnerability of a trading economy in strategic terms was foreseen by the prescient before the German submarine campaign of the First World War brought home to wider circles the stark reality of the position. Yet the instinct to return to the pre-war directions was too powerful to be gainsaid. Agriculture continued to decline and Britain continued to import a very high proportion of her foodstuffs from distant though cheaper sources of supply. Industrial prospects were sacrificed to financial considerations in the decision to return to the gold standard at the pre-war dollar parity. Meanwhile the shift from coal to oil as a principal source of energy created a new and dangerous form of dependence on external supply. In the Second World War the situation was only saved by an even more severe extension of rationing and through American assistance in policing the sea lanes even before the United States came into the war.

No persuasive theory connecting the changes in Britain's class structure – or failures to change – with the country's economic failings has yet been put forward. What actually happened can be broadly stated. The great innovations that used to go under the heading of the industrial revolution were the work largely of men outside the traditional ruling groups, whether of landed proprietors or of London-based mercantile wealth. The legislation that consolidated their position – the abandonment of protection, particularly of agricultural protection – was not as one-sided a bargain as might at first sight appear. For despite the changes in the franchise, the political tasks of ruling the country and the Empire, and the more intangible rôle of setting the society's basic values, were still largely in the hands of the traditional ruling class of the landed aristocracy and gentry,

---

[5] See K. Burk, ed., *War and the State: The Transformation of British Government 1914–1919* (London, 1982), chap. 4.

even though that class was constantly being recruited from those
newly enriched by industry and commerce or their offspring. In this
sense, the nineteenth-century State in Britain so far from being an
instrument of the middle classes (or bourgeoisie in Marxist terminology) lived in an uneasy relationship with it. And it has been suggested that it was because pre-industrial cultural values continued to
prevail, for instance in respect of education and of recruitment to the
public service, that Britain failed to adapt herself to the demands of an
increasingly competitive world.[6]

By 1914 the situation had already begun to change partly as a result
of the broadening of the franchise and the extension of educational
opportunities. The lower strata of the bourgeoisie and the upper
strata of the manual and clerical working population had now been
brought within 'the pale of the constitution'. Dissent had become
politically more active and the Labour movement was beginning to
throw up leaders capable of using the available political machinery in
ways outside the grasp of their predecessors in the age of the
Chartists. Britain by 1914 was in some respects a democracy as it had
not been in the classic age of the Constitution, in the mid nineteenth
century. The recruitment of the House of Commons, particularly in
the landslide election of 1906, and to some extent the recruitment to
the growing public services, as well as to the important new world of
the popular press, were drawn from wider social groups.

The bitterness of British politics in the years immediately preceding the war of 1914 was not only caused by the most obvious sources
of discord – Ireland, labour relations, female suffrage, the rôle of the
House of Lords – but also by the indignation of the political representatives of the former ruling classes, now increasingly concentrated in
the Conservative Party, at what they felt to be the challenge to traditional values on the part of the new majority, and of its leaders, many
of whom were still drawn from the same social strata as their opponents.

The war itself although temporarily putting some of the content-
ious issues into the shade accelerated the advent of full democracy by
making irresistible the demand for adult suffrage and for at least an
instalment of female suffrage. It was perhaps even more important
that it dealt a major blow to the prestige of the traditional ruling
groups. The fact that these had contributed exceptionally heavily to
the casualty lists did not atone for the fact that they were held guilty
both of having allowed Britain to drift into an unwanted war and for
not knowing how to conduct it when it came. It is not surprising,

---

[6] See Martin J. Wiener, *English Culture and the Decline of the Industrial Spirit 1850–1980*
(Cambridge, 1981).

given what was happening elsewhere in Europe, that the possibility of an actual revolution should have been widely entertained.

Once again however the views of contemporaries were too much coloured by what proved to be a series of passing conjunctures. Indeed by the mid 1920s, despite the unfashionableness of an older rhetoric, the actual political balance appeared to be not altogether different from that which had prevailed pre-war. For most of the inter-war period it was the Conservatives who seemed to be the natural majority party. For this phenomenon various explanations can be offered. The most obvious in parliamentary terms was that the exclusion of southern Ireland from the United Kingdom had meant that there was no longer in Parliament that solid bloc of Irish nationalist MPs who for tactical reasons had formed a permanent part of the pre-war anti-Conservative majority. The erosion of the Liberal Party's own strength had also benefited the Conservatives. While much has been made of the importance to the Labour Party of the drift into its ranks of radical Liberals in reaction against the record of Grey and Asquith, the Conservatives also found recruits, in their case among those for whom their historic enemies were less of a threat than the socialists with whom the surviving Liberal leaders appeared all too ready to collaborate. And this was true at all levels of politics, perhaps most notably at the grass roots. The Left while thus divided could not re-establish the victorious coalition of 1910 which had succeeded the Liberals' own majority of 1906, and the only stable governments of the period were those resting upon Conservative majorities. But it was a Conservatism more business-orientated and more business-like than its pre-war ancestry might suggest.

It is much harder to be certain as to what would have happened had the efforts to avoid a renewal of war been successful. Would there still have been that massive reversal of electoral fortunes witnessed in the general election of 1945? Or was it the degree of national mobilization of the war years and the breakdown of the remaining patterns of social deference as well as the new acceptance of collectivism that between them produced the landslide? Indeed the failure to avert war through 'appeasement' was one of the factors in the Conservatives' defeat, though no apparent distinction was made by the voters between the supporters and the opponents of the policy.

It is only in retrospect that we can see how great was the underlying shift in political power and social values that did not fully manifest itself for almost two decades after the 1945 election. It is now possible to assert that the election results of 1945 did not simply mean a reproduction of those of 1906 with Labour replacing the Liberals. The new majority was more class-based and in consequence more regionally differentiated. In particular Wales and Scotland produced

politics as different from those of England as those of Ireland had been
in the pre-1914 period. It is possible for the 1914–45 years to deal with
politics nationally, that is inevitably London-based. A future historian might well decide to allot more space to Scotland and Wales.
Indeed Scotland where the First World War was an even more important turning-point than in England, being followed by a long and
uninterrupted period of industrial decline, could be seen as
prefiguring the subsequent fate of much of England itself.[7]

In England as well as in Scotland and Wales the Labour Party was
shown to be still heavily anchored to the trade unions so that it was
inevitably a more sectional party than its Liberal predecessor. Despite
some of the language used in the 1945 campaign, the collectivism of
the then Labour leadership was of the gradualist variety. It was only
subsequently that importance was seen to attach to currents of
thought, partly though not exclusively of Marxist inspiration, which
were to divide British society in a more radical fashion than it had
been divided since the seventeenth century. The divisions were not
merely over the distribution of material goods or political power but
over the whole conception of what British society should be like and
how it should be directed. While none of the ideas were themselves
new and while all found some expression in the period covered by this
volume, it would be a distortion of reality to lay too much emphasis
upon them. Changes in the Conservative Party both in its leadership
and in the composition of its electoral support, so that it became in
fact the heir of both nineteenth-century liberalism and nineteenth-
century toryism, can also be traced to the inter-war period, though
the lines of division are still difficult to see clearly.

The increasingly collectivist aspects of British society after 1945
must not blind one to the unresolved arguments over the rightful
extent of State action in the inter-war period. Not until 1945 was there
a government with a parliamentary majority formally committed to a
preference for State as against other methods of framing and execu-
ting social and economic policy. Indeed the idea of the State as universal controller and provider was harder to entertain in Britain than
in other European countries where the State had assumed a more
definite rôle at a much earlier period, preceding the advent of democracy itself. What had been happening in the inter-war period in
Britain and at an accelerated speed during the war itself was that a
number of separate issues of economic and social policy were all
resolved in such a way as to increase the scope of State action. The

[7] No one has yet done for Scotland what Kenneth Morgan has done for Wales in his
magisterial *Rebirth of a Nation: Wales 1880–1980* (Oxford, 1981) but there is much material
particularly of an economic kind in Christopher Harvie, *No Gods and Precious Few Heroes: Scotland
1914–1980* (London, 1981).

failure to perceive the full consequences of this process taken as a whole, and the dismissal as mere reactionary alarmists of those who warned against its likely consequences, may in part be attributed to the very strength of individualism and voluntary action in the British tradition itself.

Much of the new rôle of the State and its servants arose from a new sensitivity to social ills and social needs and in public provision not just for primary poverty which had a long history behind it but also for the incidents and accidents of a working life: sickness, widowhood, unemployment, old age. The original instinct was to supplement voluntary provision whether made through insurance or philanthropy. But in many cases, culminating after 1945 in the creation of the National Health Service, what had begun in this way ended in a near monopoly by the State. Private provision was left only for those who could afford its full cost. In education from the nineteenth century considerations of the national interest in having a morally and intellectually educated work-force were supplemented by a more direct concern with the individual opportunities of children and young people. The basic decision to provide a fully State-financed system at the primary level alongside denominational and other privately financed establishments was carried on into the field of secondary education in R.A. Butler's Education Act of 1944.

The most important and controversial of the State's new or enlarged functions was in the sphere of housing where the provision of low-rent dwellings as a social service was given an additional impetus by the demands of the returning soldiers of the First World War. Although the political parties might differ in their attitudes to the scale of such provision, it was generally accepted that housing (unlike the provision of food or clothing) could not safely be left to market forces, nor to nineteenth-century-style philanthropic initiatives.

In other domains the First World War saw a great increase of public control, for instance in the field of transport and energy, that could and in some cases did result in a permanent commitment to public ownership whether national or municipal. But in many cases the reaction against excessive State intervention after the war led to a reassertion of the principle of private provision. The arguments for and against nationalization remained largely academic until after the Labour victory in 1945. Yet some of the steps taken between the wars, the creation of the BBC in 1926 and of the London Passenger Transport Board in 1933, were of great importance not only in relation to the service provided but also in the particular model for future nationalizations with which they furnished the incoming government.

The nationalization debate though given emphasis in some cases – the coal industry for instance – by the grievances of the work force was largely conducted in terms of efficient management for the general good. The alternatives were seen as direct management by the central government (as in the post office as then constituted) or by local and particularly municipal authorities, or through quasi-autonomous bodies intended to fulfil public purposes through structures modelled on those of private corporations. Ideas of direct participation by workers in the running of publicly owned enterprises which had earlier attracted some attention in socialist circles made no serious headway between the wars. The result was to make it likely that any addition to the public sector would be a source of further accretions to the central bureaucracy.

The transition from a relatively *laissez-faire* economy to one fully protectionist and interventionist also and inevitably led to a further growth of the governmental machine. And the need to spend much time dealing with government departments meant that the private sector itself had to develop appropriate instruments in the form of associations of various kinds each with its own bureaucracy. Britain thus became increasingly an administered and not merely a governed society with the two wartime experiences accelerating existing trends rather than diverting them.

What was notable given the British reputation as being the classic country of local self-government was the fact that the balance within government swung so heavily towards the centre. It was not that the units of local government, rationalized (outside London) on a consistent pattern in 1929, did not find their duties expanded, with housing and education as their principal fields, but that their work was increasingly monitored by central government and controlled as to policy through the financial dependence upon grants from the centre, made inescapable by the very uneven correlation between local rateable capacity and disparate burdens. And this feature of the situation tended in turn to politicize local government around the national parties and their policies, in itself a further factor in the growing dominance of London-based institutions.

The growth in the responsibilities of central government and in the complexities of the administrative machine had obvious and far-reaching consequences in the layout of the machine itself. Government departments and ministers multiplied; co-ordination at the official level beginning with the creation by Lloyd George of a cabinet secretariat became of increasing significance; discussion about the recruitment and training of government servants became a perennial topic of enquiry and discussion. The influx into Whitehall of non-professionals had some important consequences. The barriers between the official and non-official sections of the ruling élite were conspicuously though temporarily lowered.

What remained largely unaltered was the constitution itself and in particular Parliament which as the supreme legislator and authority for taxation was the main engine of change, even if the fuel for its operations was supplied externally through parties or pressure groups. The 1911 Parliament Act satisfied the Left in respect of the powers of the Upper House until the matter was raised again by the 1945 government.

Apart from the disappearance of the great majority of the Irish members after 1918, the House of Commons remained the same kind of body, elected, though with a much extended franchise, by the same methods; an attempt in 1918 to bring in proportional representation was unsuccessful. The rationale of a 'first past the post' system was challenged when after 1918 it looked as though a three-party rather than a two-party system had become the norm; but although the confused situation in the 1929 Parliament gave rise for a time to the possibility of change, the Liberals who would have been its principal beneficiaries were not strong enough to bring off the deal before the intervention of the 1931 crisis.

In the House of Commons itself two developments stand out. The first was that the multiplicity of new government offices meant that an increasing proportion of members in the governing party held some kind of post in the administration or could aspire to one and that the weight of back-bench opinion was correspondingly reduced. The large majorities that governments enjoyed for most of the period also had this effect. It is probable also that with the payment of members taking full effect for the first time, an increasing proportion of them regarded themselves as professional politicians. And this in turn made a difference both as to the nature of parliamentary proceedings and in relation to the construction of ministries. The other development was the sheer volume of legislation which although by no means uniform through the period as a whole, and much less for most of it than has since come to be normal, was already necessarily a vast one and manageable only through the acceptance of more delegated legislation, an increasing recourse to a close planning of the parliamentary timetable, and to the various devices for curtailing debate.

Apart from the two periods of minority Labour government (1923–4 and 1929–31), the administrations of the period all possessed an adequate majority and the House of Commons could thus be seen as fulfilling its prime modern function as the sustainer of ministries. It was thus an era to which the phrase 'cabinet government' most particularly and convincingly applied. Yet cabinets differed quite sharply one from another even if one omits the two very different experiments in the creation of wartime directorates headed by Lloyd George from 1916 to 1918 and by Churchill from 1940 to 1945, and the early period of MacDonald's 'National Government' in 1931 with its restricted cabinet membership.

The most notable feature of the ordinary peacetime cabinets of the period was their size. With many new ministries, some of them of considerable importance particularly in relation to public expenditure, it was hard to justify the exclusion for long of any departmental head. Cabinets were thus bigger than before, but also different in other ways. Many of the ministers were too fully absorbed in large-scale departmental activity to have much time to spare for general consideration of government policies; and this might lead power and influence to accrue either to the Prime Minister of the day, or on occasion to an inner cabinet, for which earlier precedents of course existed. Business was increasingly predigested by officials and dependent upon the efficiency of the cabinet secretariat and upon the work of a few powerful heads of departments. The lack of homogeneity in the social origins and aspirations of ministers and the change in social habits (particularly if we take the Labour governments into account) meant that the intimate personal links that often bound together members of earlier cabinets were largely lacking. The cabinet could no longer be seen as a homogeneous body of gentlemen coming together to settle the nation's affairs in a relatively relaxed and informal fashion. Both the cabinet itself and its network of committees with the inevitable circulation of minutes and conclusions were deeply embedded in the bureaucratic infrastructure.

If the period saw the consolidation of the power of the bureaucracy within the State, it also saw the establishment of the domination of the Treasury within the bureaucracy itself. The recognition in 1919 of the Permanent Secretary of the Treasury as head of the Civil Service was of more than symbolic significance. It helped to further the colonization of other departments from the Treasury, and the establishment of Treasury views as the orthodoxy of the whole of Whitehall. Because the Treasury in its management of the fiscal system and through its relations with the Bank of England, which were intimate long before the Bank's nationalization by the 1945 government, were thought to require maximum secrecy and confidentiality at all times, the insistence on secrecy and on remoteness from public attention, the strong emphasis on the anonymity of ministers' advisers were features common to the whole system. Public opinion was also nurtured on the mystique of the budgetary process; the isolation of the Chancellor of the Exchequer from his colleagues in his preparation of budgets, the drama of their presentation and the importance attached to their contents, made the chancellorship itself the most coveted post next to the premiership; of the Prime Ministers of the period 1914–45, only MacDonald (who had never served in a cabinet at all) became Prime

Minister without having been Chancellor.

What is perhaps most remarkable of all is that the system itself was unchanged even when the basic philosophy upon which it was operating was completely refashioned. The Treasury was as dominant in the inter-war period when it followed the classical prescriptions of limited government expenditure and balanced budgets as it was to be after the Second World War when its policies were dictated by the Keynesian conceptions of demand management that it had previously repudiated. From the point of view of national policy-making the chief feature of the whole period between the wars was the impermeability of government to externally generated ideas and opinions. To what extent this was assisted by the particular phase through which the party system was passing is an open question. On the face of it, the Labour Party committed to socialism by its 1918 constitution did offer a serious alternative approach to many economic and social issues. But because of its very radicalism on paper, it neither commanded a majority for its programme nor was at all clear as to the practical methods for carrying it out.

The timidity which is the common characteristic of most of the nation's political leaders during the inter-war period may perhaps be explained as can so much else by the national and international turbulence of the preceding decades, the sense of being a generation of survivors and a disinclination to see any further landmarks destroyed. Only two statesmen of obvious genius were present on the British scene – Lloyd George and Churchill. Much of British party history between Lloyd George's fall from power in 1922 and the outbreak of war can only be explained by the overriding determination of almost all the other political leaders to keep them out of office. The Conservatives it is true did try to keep Churchill within the fold following his return to their ranks in 1924 but after the government's defeat in 1929 he rapidly returned to the wilderness and was only reluctantly accepted by the party as its leader in the crisis of national survival in 1940.

The successful politicians of the period from 1922 onwards were those who could appeal above all to the deep desire for individual security and reasonable material comfort that in all welfare-conscious democracies has tended to be paramount in the voters' minds. Nor at a different level did entrepreneurs much differ from the attitudes of their employees. The fact that the 1929 election was lost by Baldwin with the slogan 'safety first' did not mean that safety was unappealing, but merely that it did not seem to have been forthcoming in sufficient measure, particularly in relation to security of employment.

It would be misleading therefore to think of the great growth of government control and intervention, and the scaling down of the rewards and prestige available to individual effort, as something forced upon a British people devoted to the sturdy virtues of independence. There was not even much attempt to check the growth of delegated legislation and administrative discretion that was the necessary concomitant of the new policies. Individual members of the judiciary might regret the failure to devise better legal protection for the aggrieved citizen, but on the whole the judges were content to be what had in the seventeenth century been termed the lions under the throne.

One is left with the clear discrepancy between the social history of Britain in the inter-war period and its political and economic history. On the social side, it would be hard not to accept a whiggish view. Although there still were notable black spots particularly in housing there can be no serious dissent from the view that the working population and its dependents were in nearly every way better off in 1939 than they had been in 1914, whether one considers diet, material comforts, assurance against misfortune, access to education, the possibilities of leisure or above all conditions of work. It is more difficult to be categoric about whether the middle class had seen a parallel advance in its standards, since against the greater mobility afforded by the automobile and the benefits of greater material comforts in the home, must be set the great reduction in the availability of domestic service. Yet here also there would seem to have some degree of consensus that things were improving, and some optimism that they would be bound to improve still further in the future.

Against this the economic historian must set the reflection that much of this increment in individual happiness was the product of redistribution rather than of the creation of new wealth, and that without some massive transfer of resources to the creation of such new wealth and an economic system and set of popular attitudes geared to such a process, the situation was only deceptively encouraging, as indeed it has proved to be. Finally the political historian must investigate the reasons for the failure of successive governments between the wars to come to terms with reality, the consequences at home and abroad of the dependence of Britain's rulers for the first time upon full adult suffrage, in respect to the quality of the leadership offered and of the policies adopted. To what extent did the notions of 'parliamentary sovereignty' and the 'rule of law' mask a situation in which neither could be taken at its face value and in which the traditional political institutions of the country corresponded less and less to the real location of the centres of power and influence?

2 Britain in the Great War

When Britain declared war on Germany on 4 August 1914, it was the first time she had fought against a European power since the end of the Crimean War in 1856, and the first time she had been involved in a war threatening the home islands since the final defeat of Napoleon at Waterloo in 1815. Neither the basic commitment to support France nor the consequences of a war fought with land armies on the European mainland had been fully grasped by more than a handful of ministers, soldiers, sailors and public servants; still less was the magnitude and duration of the necessary effort foreseen. The German invasion of Belgium helped those ministers who were first convinced of the need to fight to bring round the waverers of various brands and to reduce the number of resignations from the cabinet to two; it also helped to ensure that in the political world and among the public at large the out and out opponents of the war would for the time being be neither numerous nor influential. It is nevertheless difficult to explain the wave of patriotic enthusiasm which affected Britain as it did the other belligerents in the early weeks and months of the war, even allowing for the common expectation that a conflict on this scale could not be of long duration.

As the war went on and as the toll of losses and the drain on material resources continued it was tempting to lay the blame for what was happening on lack of preparation. Such a charge was largely misplaced. In almost all respects, Britain was better prepared for war than in any previous conflict in her history. The work of Haldane at the War Office, of McKenna and Churchill at the Admiralty and of the team around Maurice Hankey at the Committee of Imperial Defence now paid off in full; the mobilization of the fleet and its assembly at its war stations, the transport to France of the British Expeditionary Force, the measures at home to deal with internal security and with the financial aspects of the transition from peace to war – all these were carried through smoothly and expeditiously as soon as authority was given. What was lacking was not machinery nor detailed planning but a full appreciation of the kind of war it was going to turn out to be, and of the problems strategic and material that it would set.[1]

What turned out to have been principally lacking in the pre-war years was an adequate exploration of the way in which the balance of Britain's effort should be set as between land and sea operations, of the extent to which her course would be dictated in war by the rival pressures upon manpower of military and industrial requirements, and of the effect of both upon financial stability and long-term economic prospects. Neither armed service was guiltless in its pre-war appreciation of the impact of new technology. The army had not taken in the enormous advantages given to the defensive by a combination of the machine gun and field entrenchments nor the extent to which this would lead in turn to heavy demands for ammunition for the artillery whose barrages were (on the whole vainly) expected to prepare the way for the 'breakthrough'. As Churchill pointed out to his colleagues in June 1915, the allies had lost territory in Belgium and France before the possibilities of the defensive were fully apparent and now had to recover the ground they had lost. For its part the navy was wedded to the traditional doctrine of the supremacy of the capital ship. It failed to foresee that the submarine was the ideal weapon through which a naval power too weak to triumph in a set-piece battle could yet inflict terrifying blows upon a country so heavily dependent as was Britain upon the sea-lanes remaining open. Nor had it fully grasped the opportunities that the aircraft and wireless telegraphy could make in reconnaissance and the handling of the fleet. Although there had been staff talks with the French since 1906, the understandings reached about the disposition of naval forces and the position to be taken up by the British Expeditionary Force did not amount to a joint strategy.

One major reason for the failings in pre-war planning in the wider sense had been the lack of a national consensus. A divided government was hardly likely to share its dilemmas with an Opposition determined to force it out of office at the earliest opportunity. Opinions have differed as to the extent of Britain's internal crisis in the pre-war years but at the very least it is clear that divisions over industrial relations, the Irish question, the future of the second chamber and even female suffrage had been sufficient to divert most people's attention from the growing tensions on the European continent. To say that foreign war forestalled civil war is an extreme way of putting it; but the atmosphere of wartime politics cannot be fully appreciated without some attention to this prelude.

[1] For an insight into how the Prime Minister saw his problems from August 1913 to May 1915 see Michael and Eleanor Brock, eds., *H.H. Asquith, Letters to Venetia Stanley* (Oxford, 1982).

In considering the behaviour of statesmen other aspects of the immediately pre-war period needed to be taken into account. There was a feeling that money, particularly new money, had come to talk too loudly in the social and political life of Edwardian England. The 'Marconi' scandal during which only Asquith's resolute defence of his ministers – three of whom with the chief whip were alleged to have used their inside information to profit from share dealings in the Marconi company – and party discipline saved their careers, left an undercurrent of ill-feeling that could be exploited by the government's opponents. It also created, or helped to fortify in Asquith's own mind, a mistrust of businessmen and their motives which was not without effect when it came to considering the modifications of the supply system necessary if the demands of the forces were to be met. How to distinguish between a patriotic desire to help the country and the ambition to get quick profits out of fields hitherto monopolized by established firms with a privileged access to the service departments? Nor was it clear that the government could rely on being able to get the trade union movement to accept the changes in working practices that would be a necessary condition of accelerated production.

Free of anxiety about the parliamentary situation so long as the Opposition conceived it to be its patriotic duty to support the government in all that related to the conduct of the war, Asquith could attempt the task of meeting the emergency without any significant change in the structure or operations of central government. Controversial issues, notably Ulster, were put in cold storage for the duration. The only innovation was the choice of Lord Kitchener, the country's most distinguished professional soldier, for the office of Secretary of State for War which Asquith himself had temporarily taken over after the 'Curragh mutiny'.[2] Whether someone with no political experience and whose period as Commander-in-Chief in India had been marked by far from cordial relations with the Viceroy, Curzon, could fit into his new rôle was doubtful from the beginning. Asquith who would have preferred to see Haldane back in the position he had held from 1905 to 1912, appointed Kitchener largely with an eye to public opinion, and to satisfy the Opposition that party considerations would not be allowed to hamper military efficiency. It soon became apparent that the long years of peace had enabled the British to ignore the fundamental problems of civil–military relations which must always be a dominant element in the politics of a country at war.

---

[2] In this clumsily handled incident a number of officers stationed at the Curragh barracks near Dublin had announced that they would leave the army rather than take part in enforcing home rule against the Ulster loyalists and had received unauthorized guarantees that they would not be required to do so.

Although the political language of wartime was as usual over-simplified so that the contest was publicly represented as one between the forces of light and the forces of darkness, its international setting was the outcome of previous shifts in the alignments of the Great Powers. An alliance of France, Russia and Britain against the German and Austro-Hungarian empires was not however something that accorded with past experience, and its implications for diplomacy were not foreseen. In Britain, too little thought had been given to the rôle of neutrals, and to the incentives that might have to be provided to bring them in on the allied side or, at worst, to guarantee their continued non-belligerency. Still less was it appreciated how the growing number of political as well as military and financial commitments that the war would impose would impinge upon the possibility of finding a way out of the conflict that would justify the sacrifices made to win it.

The machinery available to tackle questions in which considerations of foreign policy were bound up with military and financial issues was not adequate, and in a war in which from the beginning the entire British Empire was involved and in which the home government made use of all its human and material resources, the channels of communication between Britain and the self-governing dominions were ill-suited to their growing sentiments of independent nationhood. Even more delicate were the wartime problems of the Indian Empire and the colonial territories.[3]

Britain's relations with her principal allies were never easy. French suspicions of Britain's willingness fully to commit herself could scarcely be allayed while the British contribution in manpower remained so much smaller than that of France. In a war in which all the belligerents incurred terrible losses, France's were in proportion to her population to be the greatest; in addition most of the fighting was on French soil and much of France's productive territory was in German hands almost throughout. The Entente had defined the respective imperial positions of Britain and France, but when the problem of war aims loomed up – as it did almost as soon as the initial shock was over – there were bound to be conflicting claims. With Russia, the area of agreement was even smaller; and the alliance with Tsardom was a stumbling block for the British Left. It was never a British desire that the German hegemony in Europe should be resisted only to give Russian expansionism free play. On the other hand, it was essential not to give encouragement to that section of court and official opinion in Russia that was doubtful of the wisdom of

---

[3] On these aspects of wartime government see Max Beloff, *Imperial Sunset*. Vol. I: *Britain's Liberal Empire 1897–1921* (London, 1969), chap. V.

fighting Germany and that might be tempted into a separate peace. The two Russian revolutions of 1917 changed much of the substance of the Russian problem; they did not resolve it.

In the earlier part of the war, British diplomacy was also largely concerned with those countries which had not yet declared themselves, whose stance varied from genuine neutrality to various degrees of non-belligerence. Turkey, Italy, the Balkan states, the northern neutrals – all required separate and careful handling. In each case and not unnaturally, their governments were concerned with the furtherance of their national interests and with a careful balancing of the prospective gains if they joined what proved to be the winning side with the possibility of disaster if they chose wrong. Their desiderata tended, in south-eastern Europe, and as between Japan and China in the Far East, to be difficult, and often impossible, to reconcile. Some countries had access in Britain to domestic pressure groups of different levels of effectiveness; none could be expected to see the conflict through British eyes.

Furthermore, in so far as the British found it necessary to employ naval and economic strength to weaken Germany's war-making potential and attack the morale of her home front through cutting off supplies, her interests and those of Germany's neutral neighbours were bound to conflict. This was the more true in that the development of the submarine had forced the Admiralty in 1911 to abandon the traditional 'close blockade' of the enemy's ports in favour of a 'distant' blockade. And at the beginning of the war, Britain's ability to use her maritime predominance came up against her own commitments to uphold some aspects of neutral rights. It had seemed better to preserve these when Britain could still hope that the next major conflict might see her able to remain aloof. By the time that British policy came round to a harsher view, and by the time that the machinery for controlling maritime commerce and communications was fully established, which was not until the summer of 1916, Germany's development of the submarine weapon had made the supply of the British home front equally vulnerable. It was only by a narrow margin, after the Admiralty's reluctant acceptance of a convoy system in April–May 1917, that the danger was averted. In their eagerness to destroy the German legend that their forces were never defeated and that the war was lost only through a 'stab in the back', historians may have underestimated the significance of economic pressure as one of the factors in Germany's ultimate surrender.

The most important and difficult aspect of the enforcement of limitations on German trade was its impact upon relations with the United States. In the early part of the war, when the likely need of American financial and other assistance was coming to be appreciated, the tendency was to treat American objections with some seriousness. Later on, American indignation over Germany's submarine warfare and the losses of American lives balanced the objections to Britain's violations of the 'freedom of the seas'. While it seemed unlikely that the United States would ever intervene on the German side, the possibility of American pressure leading the allies to accept something less than total victory was present from an early stage.

It was assumed and rightly that President Wilson's decisions in matters of foreign policy would reflect his susceptibility to various forms of internal pressure and his desire to ensure his re-election in November 1916. As the war went on the interests of Americans as the allies' creditors and suppliers increasingly balanced the specifically anti-British elements in the population – Irish-Americans whose leadership was much more extremist than that of Ireland's own Nationalist Party in the House of Commons, and German-Americans. But how far the balance allowed one to be tough with the Americans over neutral rights was something on which different judgements were formed by individual ministers and different government servants. In retrospect since it was the knowledge of America's capacities once she became a belligerent that made Germany's military leaders realize the hopelessness of their position, after their failure to achieve a knock-out blow in the spring and summer of 1918, one can say that Anglo-American relations proved the key to victory, and that those who were not prepared to take undue risks with President Wilson's cloudy sympathies were proved right in the end. Yet the likely presence at the peace-making of a country with a very different outlook on the war and its legitimate objectives was an additional question-mark hanging over the war aims debate.

On most issues of foreign policy in wartime there was no obvious line of division between the parties at least until the advent of the Bolsheviks. Mistakes or alleged mistakes were naturally attributed to the government of the day, and the failure first to keep Turkey out of the war and then to create a Balkan alliance against her were blamed upon the Foreign Secretary, Sir Edward Grey, and so contributed to weakening Asquith's position even though it was the military setbacks at the Dardanelles, at Salonika and in Mesopotamia that must be held largely responsible for the diplomatic débâcles. And the one positive success, Italy's adhesion to the allied side which was itself a product of *sacro egoismo* – her own self-interest – rather than of allied diplomacy, was not to prove an unmixed blessing from either the military, the economic or the diplomatic point of view. Where party questions did come in was over Anglo-American relations in so far as they were affected by the problem of Ireland.

In spite of the vague talk before 1914 of 'federalism all round', neither Scotland nor Wales reacted very differently to the war to the rest of the United Kingdom. In so far as labour disputes on the Clyde and in South Wales were to prove more intractable than those else-where, and in so far as the trouble on the Clyde carried political overtones, it was due to the particular history of labour relations in those areas, and to the particular demands made upon the engineer-ing and mining industries by the war rather than to any specific national viewpoints on the struggle against Germany. The same could not be, and was not, true of Ireland. By an agreed political truce both home rule and any separate arrangements for Ulster were put into cold storage. Most of the nationalist MPs at Westminster recognized the righteousness of resisting Germany and the propriety of taking up arms to do so, as many Irishmen did. It may be argued that the nationalist leader Redmond and his friends would have stood a better chance had Kitchener allowed Irish volunteers to enlist in specifically Irish brigades or given full public credit to the achieve-ments of Irish regiments. For the national movement in Ireland con-tained an element which took the old view that England's danger was Ireland's opportunity and saw nothing in itself wrong with seeking German assistance to that end if circumstances allowed.

Between their aim of a republic for the whole of Ireland (in the case of some leaders, of a socialist republic) and the Asquithian version of home rule, no reconciliation was possible. On the other side, even before the formation of the first coalition in May 1915 and the entry into the government of the Unionist leaders, the Unionists possessed a greater potential for influencing government policy than they had before the outbreak of war; and an Ulster division did exist and was to suffer heavily on the Somme. Given the views both of the traditional leaders of southern unionism such as Lansdowne, and the rather different views and interests of the spokesmen for Ulster Protes-tantism's own sub-brand of nationalism, it is understandable why no compromise was reached sufficient to buy off all but the most intran-sigent of the Irish, particularly when any solution had to be devised by harried politicians, deeply enmeshed in their country's life-and-death struggle with the enemy.

Nor could it be said that in this respect the British leadership was unrepresentative of its electorate. Once it was clear that, outside Ulster, recruitment in Ireland was not on the same scale as in the rest of the United Kingdom and that it was not going to have to endure compulsory service (whatever the government might say) when that solution to Britain's manpower problems was at last accepted by the government in December 1915, there was an inevitable gap between those who felt that they were making the sacrifices and those who were staying more or less comfortably at home. The tactics of the Irish revolutionary leaders were designed to widen the gap. The Easter Rising of 1916 achieved its purpose which was not to overthrow British rule, out of the question unless the Germans were to land in force, but to create a nationalist martyrology and thus envenom relations between the two countries so as to render untenable the positions of those who still believed in the possibility of a peaceful settlement. In the latter part of the war much of Ireland behaved like, and was perforce treated like, an occupied country, a net liability rather than a net asset to the empire of which it nominally formed part. And once President Wilson had made up his mind to intervene in the war so that American national sentiment was mobilized against 'hyphenated-Americans', the Irish leverage through America was much weakened. For the historic Irish party of Parnell and Redmond, no place remained in British politics. Its demise in the election of December 1918 registered the change in sentiment on both sides of the Irish sea. These events also meant that the coercion of Ulster which the Liberal government had proved unable to face in 1914, and which the strength of the Ulster element in the highest ranks of the British army made more than ever unthinkable, would now fail to commend itself as even a theoretical possibility to any British party.

Outside Ulster no one played an important rôle in Irish politics after 1918 who had played an important one before it. This was conspicuously not the case in the rest of Britain. Yet the changes in political sentiment and in the priorities attached to political issues were profoundly changed by the experiences of the war and are the primary explanation of both the advent of the first coalition under Asquith in May 1915 and of the creation of the second coalition formed by Lloyd George in December 1916 which clearly depended upon Conservative support in Parliament and in the country. The important thing to explain is not the extent of the changes, nor the 'death' of the Liberal Party or the 'rise' of Labour – labels matter less than what is in the bottles – but on the contrary the extent to which in spite of shifts in sentiment, reflected as these were in permanent changes in morals and manners, in ethical and aesthetic standards and in the habits of daily life, the fundamental institutions of a liberal democracy remained in being. Of the major European belligerents, Russia and Germany experienced revolution – much more far-reaching in the former than in the latter case – Austria-Hungary disappeared from the map; France only narrowly escaped collapse and was left in an invalid condition from which she had not fully emerged when in 1940 the collapse actually took place; Italy drifted into a revolutionary situation making possible the fascist coup of 1922; Britain came out changed but least changed of all.

Yet during the more than four years that elapsed between the outbreak of war and the armistice more was altered in Britain and for the British than during any such brief period of the country's history; indeed one of the historian's problems is to account for so much happening in so short a space of time. When one thinks of the normal peacetime delays in implementing some new domestic policy, in reshaping parts of the machinery of government, in habituating people to a new legal framework, the speed with which things were done during the war seems much more remarkable than the delays and rigidities against which the more ardent spirits protested. It is as though there was a major acceleration in the entire historical process.

Britain, a country which had for centuries relied wholly upon professional soldiers and sailors for fighting its wars and upon the operation of the voluntary principle, became a nation in arms, first through an extension of the voluntary principle itself backed by social pressures, and then by legal compulsion. It meant not merely a loss of life unprecedented in the country's history but also that large numbers of quite ordinary men had now undergone experiences of suffering and hardship and of a violation of moral sensibilties that set them apart from those too old, too young, too unfit or too indispensable to the civilian war effort to have been subjected to them. The question hardest to answer – it arises in different forms in the case of all the belligerent countries – is why men put up with it, and why majority opinion held in contempt those who refused to go along. It was argued at different times that to maintain morale at the front it was necessary to state war aims that could be defended in idealistic terms, or to promise that the war would be followed by great measures of social betterment. This would seem to be a rationalization. Social cohesion of a developed kind combined with a surviving and powerful element of deference in the country's social attitudes appear to have inhibited questions as to the reasonableness of the whole ghastly business, except in limited intellectual circles who made less impact upon their contemporaries than they were to make in retrospect on their successors.

It made a difference no doubt that the rest of the population not obliged to face the savagery and boredom of trench warfare had also to face departures from its customary ways of life. Air-raids though not reaching anything like the intensity of later wars, and bombardments from the sea meant that Britain's own soil and civilian population had lost their long immunity to the ravages of war, even though fanciful ideas that the Germans could mount an invasion without command of the sea were gradually abandoned. More

important was the extension of the industrial and agricultural and commercial work-force to include a high proportion of women both in the
interests of increasing production particularly of munitions and to
replace men enlisted in the services; for the first time also women had
a rôle in the armed services beyond nursing. For the main male
labour force, there were changes partly voluntary partly semi-
obligatory in the nature and place of their work. The free market in
labour and commodities was gradually replaced by a complex system
of controls. Consumption was regulated by rationing and some freedom of expression by censorship. The need to facilitate the mobility of
labour meant intervention in the provision of housing and the creation of new social services.

From living in a society in which most aspects of earning and
spending were related to market conditions, and in which state intervention in the control of working conditions and the provision of
services was severely limited and thought of as the exception rather
than the rule, the British had come to live in a society in which almost
everything was settled by government, and in which national needs
were automatically given priority over individual choice, and, where
politically possible, over vested interests as well. A vast expansion of
bureaucracy and of voluntary or semi-voluntary bodies performing
governmental functions transformed the centre of London and
affected provincial life. Perhaps because Britain was already to so
high a degree an industrial society with no important agricultural
hinterland, this high degree of organization was easier to bring about
and sustain than it was in the case of the other major belligerents. For
contemporaries again, the impression was one of hasty improvisation, false starts and much waste – a lack of central direction and
control at least until the creation of the Lloyd George war cabinet
system, and to some considerable extent even afterwards. In retrospect the impression is rather the other way – what is impressive as
has been said, is the speed of change as well as its depth. The response
to each new challenge and crisis whether over supply, manpower or
the provisioning of the civilian population appears to have been a
logical step forward to a situation in which the entire country could be
seen as engaged in total war.

In many of its aspects the new configuration of British society and
government was seen to be temporary and meant to endure only until
the end of the war. It was not thought that compulsory military
service would be appropriate for Britain's peacetime needs; such
inroads as had been made on the restrictive practices of trade unions
had been justified by wartime necessity and promises had been given
that their pre-war position would be fully restored. The TUC itself
was weakened by the war and largely replaced by the Labour Party as

the co-ordinator of the government's relations with organized labour.[4] The recovery by the Labour Party of its independence after Arthur Henderson's resignation from the war cabinet in August 1917 suggested that the idea of a continuing partnership between government and the unions to solve industrial problems would run into great difficulties; men of business and the rather fewer trade unionists recruited into government, whether at the ministerial level or in executive positions, would for the most part wish to return to private life; most restrictions on individual freedom would have to disappear very rapidly. On the other hand after so much destruction of life and after the annihilation of so much wealth could a newly impoverished and indebted Britain simply go back to the conditions of 1914? Should she even want to?

The extent to which previous conditions could be restored depended in large part upon economic and social developments that were in progress before the war, and were beyond the powers of government to halt. The relative decline of Britain's staple industries and the relative slowness with which she had responded to new industrial opportunities were evident by 1914 and had been much discussed; what the war did was to force the liquidation of overseas interests that had to some extent concealed the weaknesses in Britain's economic position and to bring about the transfer to New York of the decisive rôle in the world capital market. It could also be said that the extent of trade union power, at any event in the older industries and in public utilities, was fully apparent before the war and was merely made more obvious when it became clear that Britain's wartime needs could only be met if the movement could be taken into at least some temporary partnership. Positive state intervention for social provision had already been accepted as inevitable in a modern industrial society and the war merely gave greater scope to such activities. It is again unlikely that there would not have been a growth in the scope of employment available to women and in the concomitant extension to them of political rights. But these were things easier to perceive later on in a long-term perspective. The political events of the war years reflected more immediate pressures on the political system, and it was the legacy of these events that helped to make the political scene after 1918 very different from what it had been in 1914.

The decision to go to war would doubtless have been a more formidable hurdle for the government to cross had the Conservatives been in power opposed by a Liberal Party including a sizable pacifist or

[4] See Ross M. Martin, *TUC: the Growth of a Pressure Group 1868–1976* (Oxford, 1980), pp. 136ff.

near-pacifist element and a Labour Party where these trends were
even more pronounced. A Liberal government going to war could
rely on co-operation from the Opposition to give it the necessary
support for the measures it would have to take, although the closer
social connections between the Conservatives and the military meant
that the party cast a critical eye upon the government's actual dispositions and conduct of affairs.

Thanks to the German decision to follow the Schlieffen plan (by
which neutral Belgium had to be invaded as part of the attempt to put
France out of the war before Russian strength could make itself felt),
the cabinet itself went into the war much more united than at one time
seemed possible. The resignations of the veteran Morley and John
Burns, the former labour leader, were of no great significance, and
neither of them played any further rôle in British politics. Nevertheless there was from the beginning an element in the Liberal Party,
and among its Labour allies, that was unreconciled to the necessity of
war and that with some justification believed that the war could not be
fought except at the sacrifice of important Liberal values. To many of
them the principle of voluntary enlistment became the sticking point.
But while the ultimate split in the Liberal Party at the time of the
creation of the Lloyd George coalition was perhaps inherent in this
underlying disagreement over the proper respect to be paid to Liberal
principles, there was never any likelihood that a government determined to pursue hostilities until victory was achieved could be
brought down politically unless there were a large-scale and sustained
revolt by organized labour.

As against this fact one other aspect of the situation demands attention. Because victory was in fact won – indeed won sooner than most
people in 1917–18 thought possible – there is a natural tendency to
imagine that this outcome was throughout accepted as not only probable but inevitable. The leaders of a nation at war are unlikely to
indulge in public discussion of the alternatives to victory. The
Lansdowne letter of November 1917 is a solitary exception.[5] Nor
are they likely publicly to admit the possibility that their allies will let
them down. In a war in which the newspaper press reached the height
of its influence and in which newspaper proprietors and their editors
were more important figures in British politics than at any time before
or since, and one in which the great national and provincial dailies of
both parties were supporters of the war, the chances of doubts about
the outcome receiving much ventilation were minimal. All the energy
of the critics was used up in suggesting ways by which the war might

[5] Lord Lansdowne's letter proposing a compromise peace was published in the *Daily Tele-
graph*; it had earlier been refused by *The Times*.

be fought more successfully.

In private however the British ministers and others engaged in the higher planning and direction of the war were always aware particularly after the setbacks of 1915 that success could not be guaranteed and had always to contemplate (quite apart from the pressures in favour of peace exerted by the Americans until they themselves were drawn into the war) what terms might have to be agreed upon in the event of peace without victory. Such pressures might be internal – an inability to raise the troops or provide the necessary supplies, labour unrest, basic shortages of food and other supplies as a result of the submarine war – or they might be the result of one or other of the major allies finding it necessary or desirable to seek a separate agreement with the enemy. The losses of the French in 1916 and 1917 made the possibility of a fatal crack in French morale something that could not lightly be dismissed. Curiously enough when similar forebodings came true in respect of Russia with the failure of the provisional government to rally that sorely tried country for further efforts and the subsequent triumph of Bolshevism, it seems to have taken the British by surprise. With the arrival of American troops on the western front this blow was not as severe as it would have been at an earlier stage in the war, but it was severe enough powerfully to colour the subsequent history of relations between Britain and the new Soviet state.[6] Many of the military and political decisions taken during the war must be put down to publicly unavowed anxieties about the reliability of the home front and the solidarity of the alliance.

These dire possibilities helped to promote the movement towards turning the party truce of the early months of the war into a demand for an outright coalition so that the energies of all those capable of making a contribution to winning the war could be found a proper rôle in the national effort. As with so many other wartime developments the idea was not a new one. It had been mooted by Lloyd George in 1910 as a method of tackling the full agenda of social reform which had been largely set aside in the bitterness over home rule and the House of Lords. Without the Irish and without Labour, a Liberal–Conservative government of national unity could tackle such problems as housing, social insurance, drink, unemployment and the reform of the Poor Law.[7] These secret talks among a small number of

---

[6] In an account of British politics, the eastern front against Germany is bound to be neglected. For a full treatment of this important subject, see N. Stone, *The Eastern Front 1914–1917* (London, 1975).

[7] See the somewhat exaggerated account in R.J. Scally, *The Origins of the Lloyd George Coalition: the Politics of Social-Imperialism 1900–1918* (Princeton, 1975), p. 189, and John Grigg, *Lloyd George: the People's Champion 1902–1911* (London, 1978), pp. 264–5. Churchill had toyed with the idea of a centre party in 1901–2; there was also talk of bringing together Chamberlain and

party leaders could not then come to anything despite the wide interest in and discussion of, a policy of national efficiency.[8] By March
1915 Churchill was seeing the government's discussions with the
Opposition over a war aims agreement with the Russians as a possible
prelude to a war-waging coalition.

The problems that a British government of whatever complexion
would have to face were clear from fairly early on in the war.[9] The
initial phase of movement for which the general staffs and war col-
leges in all countries had been preparing was, on the western front, of
relatively short duration. After the battle of the Marne and the German failure to take Paris as a result in part of the withdrawal of
German formations to meet the Russian pressure in the East, there
came 'the race to the sea' and stabilization of the front with both sides
digging in. This had not been the intention of either side; the aim was
the historic one of rolling up the enemy's flank. But the fact
remained. By November 1914 the front was continuous from the sea
just inside the Belgian border with France to the frontier of
Switzerland. Until March 1917 the line never varied by more than 10
miles in any direction. The desperate allied offensives of that year
again ended in military stalemate. It was only with the first of Germany's successive attacks beginning in March 1918 that a war of
movement began once more; at first to Germany's advantage, later to
her undoing. From the late autumn of 1914 until the crisis of April
1918 what could be excluded was a British military defeat leading to
the capitulation or re-embarkation of her armies. During the entire
war on the other hand, the possibility of a naval defeat leaving open
the home islands to invasion and making the blockade unenforceable
was something that had to be taken into account. The balance
between fleets in terms of numbers of ships and firepower was easier
to calculate than that between land armies, and the necessity of keeping the Grand Fleet up to strength was as important a factor in the
mind of Admiral Fisher and his successors at the Admiralty as was
the unwillingness to divert troops from France among the leading
generals.

Rosebery on a platform of 'efficiency'. Between 1906 and 1909, Unionist Free Traders talked
of a Centre Party in conjunction with Rosebery on an anti-socialist foundation. See Alan
Sykes, *Tariff Reform in British Politics 1903–1913* (Oxford, 1979).

[8] See G.R. Searle, *The Quest for National Efficiency: a Study in British Politics and Political Thought
1899–1914* (Oxford, 1971).

[9] The emphasis of this history and its scale make it impossible to include the history of
military operations. Many attempts have been made to write the history of the First World
War. A work which in respect of balance and perspective and of clarity of exposition for the
layman has always seemed to me a model is C.R.M.F. Cruttwell, *A History of the Great War
1914–1918* (Oxford, 1934). An attempt to link the military and political history of Britain in the
war years is Paul Quinn, *British Strategy and Politics 1914 to 1918* (Oxford, 1965).

One possible way of breaking the deadlock would have been a total defeat of the German fleet which would have enabled the blockade to be made much more effective and troops to be diverted from home defence. It would also have permitted a major switch in the production of armaments away from the navy to the requirements of the land battle. It might too have made possible the opening up of the Baltic, a link with the Russians to replace that vainly attempted through the Dardanelles and the Bosphorus, and even landings on the German Baltic coast. On the other hand, the risks of a failure in a major naval engagement were greater for the British – the destruction of British naval power would be a blow much greater than Britain could hope to inflict by sea on the Central Powers whose strength lay on land.

In the event the battle of Jutland on 31 May 1916, which was made possible by a sortie by the German High Seas Fleet seeking to bring part of Britain's Grand Fleet to battle, was an inconclusive engagement, though in terms of tonnage lost and casualties inflicted the Germans had rather the better of it.[10] The failure to achieve another Trafalgar was a blow to morale and a subsequent source of controversy in which blame was divided between technical inadequacies in the British ships, over-centralization of command, lack of initiative by subordinate commanders and the over-cautious leadership of Admiral Jellicoe, as contrasted with the allegedly more aggressive attitude of his subordinate and subsequent successor, Admiral Beatty. On the other hand, the Germans found safety only in a retreat back to their bases, and ventured to sea only three times more during the entire war – in August and October 1916 and April 1918, on each occasion without being brought to battle. Losses incurred by the British fleet during the August operation through torpedo attacks imposed even greater caution for the remainder of the war. During the October 1916 sortie, the Grand Fleet did not put to sea.[11] Britain's control of the oceans was however confirmed and in that limited but important sense Jutland too was a success.

The effects of Jutland were two-fold. From the German side (since all her surface units outside European waters had been destroyed or cornered) it meant that all reliance at sea had to be placed on unlimited submarine warfare as a means of destroying Britain's ability to supply herself with food, raw materials and military supplies; and this involved the risk which in the end materialized of American belligerency which was to more than outweigh the defection of the Russians. On both sides it meant a return to the attempts to

[10] For Jutland and its aftermath see the balanced discussion in A.J. Marder, *From the Dreadnought to Scapa Flow: the Royal Navy in the Fisher Era 1904–1919*. Vol. III: *Jutland and After: May 1916-December 1916* (London, 1966).

[11] P.M. Kennedy, *The Rise and Fall of British Naval Mastery* (London, 1976), p. 217.

break through on the western front, the Germans at Verdun, the British and French on the Somme – ghastly and in the end fruitless expenditures of blood and treasure which damaged morale on both sides, and created new difficulties for governments that had got their countries into war and seemed to have no way of bringing the conflict to an acceptable end.

The battles of 1916 showed that the inclination of most British and French soldiers was to ignore the apparent triumph of the defensive and to continue battering away on the western front in the hope that greater weight of fire-power, or new tactical devices, would permit a breakthrough, or even that in a war of attrition the enemy's will to fight would give way sooner. A somewhat secondary rôle was assigned to the development of new weapons that might do away with the superiority of the machine-gun and barbed wire, and make up for the failure of artillery barrages to clear a way through the obstacles these represented. Eventually the 'tank' appeared as the British answer to the problem – and following them the French – but the length of time it took to develop and the failure to use it in such a way as to obtain the full value of surprise when first employed in significant strength at the battle of Cambrai in November 1917, prevented it from becoming the decisive weapon that its sponsors had hoped it might.[12]

Another road to victory which appealed more to statesmen, horrified by the losses incurred on the western front, and more aware than the soldiers of their impact upon the home front, appeared to lie in circumventing the enemy's strength on the primary front by finding alternative routes into central Europe from the east and south in the hope that by knocking out Germany's principal allies, Turkey (which joined the war on the side of the Central Powers at the end of October 1914) and Austria-Hungary, Germany itself might be brought to sue for peace. Secondary campaigns – 'side-shows' in the military parlance of the time – to capture the German colonies or to roll-back Turkey's empire in the Middle East from the Persian gulf or from Britain's base in Egypt might affect morale or secure territories of interest to the Empire; they could not hope to be decisive.

The alternative route to victory was for most of 1915 summed up in the one word 'Gallipoli'. It was a campaign that suffered both from confused conceptions of what could be achieved and from faulty execution. The idea of forcing the Straits and taking Constantinople in itself offered too many advantages to be the subject of critical appraisal. It could meet the appeal of the Russians for a diversion

---

[12] See B.H. Liddell Hart, *The Tanks: the History of the Royal Tank Regiment and its Predecessors*. Vol. I: *1914–1939* (London, 1959).

after the tremendous battering they sustained in the early months of the war; it would reopen communications between the western allies and the Russians by a warm water route; it would, it was hoped, decide in the allies' favour the wavering intentions of the Balkan countries and relieve the pressure on Serbia; it might push Germany's former ally Italy on to the allies' side from the neutrality she had adopted at the beginning of the war. It is not surprising that as late as 18 May 1915 Churchill, who had been one of the principal advocates of the enterprise, could still write: 'the shortest road to a victorious peace runs through the Dardanelles'.[13]

By this time however much had happened to make success almost unthinkable. The attempt in March to force the narrows through naval power alone, the original plan, had failed. The forces that landed at different points on the Gallipoli peninsula at the end of April did not exploit their initial success and came up against fierce resistance. The lines hardened and the campaign became yet another case of the superiority of the defensive, with the Turks far better placed to reinforce and supply their troops than were the British and Anzacs (Australian and New Zealand troops) on their limited beachheads. Whatever criticism could be made of the commanders and their decisions on the spot, it is clear that there was, in this as in other aspects of wartime government, an absence of clear direction and control. The large peacetime cabinet continued as the formal instrument of government; Asquith's 'war council' with its addition of service chiefs to a ministerial core blurred the lines of responsibility, and acted mainly as a way of registering decisions already taken by senior ministers or by the relevant departments.

Military failure was made more galling by the failures of British diplomacy.[14] The Russians who revived their ancient ambitions for the control of Constantinople and the Straits, and secured the assent of the allies in March 1915, were adamant against any arrangement with Greece, the only Balkan country prepared to consider joining in the war against Turkey. The Secret Treaty of London was indeed signed with Italy on 26 April, and Italy entered the war on 23 May, but she was not in a position to make an immediate impact upon the course of the main struggle. Bulgaria withstood all the allies' blandishments and entered the war on Germany's side by attacking

[13] Martin Gilbert, *Winston S. Churchill.* Companion Vol. III (London, 1972), pt. 2, p. 903.
[14] For wartime diplomacy until the fall of the Asquith coalition, see F.H. Hinsley, ed., *British Foreign Policy under Sir Edward Grey* (Cambridge, 1977). Lloyd George, strongly anti-Turk and pro-Bulgar, was a critic of Grey's diplomacy and this helped to separate him from Asquith. 'Grey's Balkan policy', he once said, 'is like a man trying to reconcile his wife to his taking a mistress'. M.G. Fry, *Lloyd George and Foreign Policy.* Vol. I: *The Education of a Statesman 1890–1916* (Montreal, 1977), p. 294.

Serbia in October 1915. Rumania preserved her neutrality until August 1916 and, having then entered the war on the allies' side, suffered a catastrophic defeat.

Although some of these disappointments lay in the future it was clear by May 1915 that the Gallipoli expedition had run into the gravest difficulties and that the question of dealing with them, whether through further naval action or through the allocation of still more troops, divided ministers, and in Churchill's case brought about a crisis in relations between himself and his principal service adviser, Lord Fisher, whom he himself had brought back as First Sea Lord. At the same time the shortages of shells on the western front exploited by Asquith's enemies in the press, were bringing further discredit on his government. In these circumstances the government's position in Parliament in the face of Opposition criticism became crucial. To have a parliamentary showdown even in secret session might scare off the Italians, and would make relations with the Conservatives even more difficult should agreement with them be needed later on. To carry on meant facing an election by the end of the year which in the mood of the country might well be hostile. On the other hand to legislate for postponing the election required Conservative consent not just out of feelings of constitutional propriety but because of the Conservative majority in the Upper House.[15] The alternative of a coalition which would keep Asquith himself at the head of the government, and avoid any disruption of such unity in the nation as existed, made an obvious appeal.[16]

The Conservatives for their part seem to have had no wish to fight an election even though they might win it. The divisions in the party had been bridged rather than eliminated by the election to the leadership of Bonar Law. The party's performance in the House of Commons was affected by the absence of a large number of members on war service; it had little ministerial experience to offer after a decade in the wilderness; above all a Conservative government in wartime would face a much more intractable opposition from both Liberals and Labour. After tortuous negotiations centering around personalities, Asquith succeeded in forming a coalition in which most of the important ministries went to the Liberals. Conservative successes were largely of a negative kind. Haldane was excluded – his alleged sympathies with Germany were too much of a burden for the government to sustain. Churchill, disliked by Conservatives for his earlier apostasy, reckoned as unreliable after his quixotic mission to beleaguered Antwerp in October 1914 and his commitment to the Gallipoli

[15] M.D. Pugh, 'Asquith, Bonar Law and the First Coalition', *Historical Journal* XVII (1974).
[16] C. Hazlehurst, *Politicians at War, July 1914 to May 1915* (London, 1971).

venture, was forced out of the Admiralty into the Chancellorship of the Duchy.

The political history of Britain during the war years is only to be understood if the major issue of how to achieve victory (or at least avoid defeat) is seen as superimposed upon the divisions of interest and ideology inherited from the pre-war period. The pursuit of any of the possible paths to victory carried with it its own demands, and called into question particular aspects of the governmental institutions and habits as they had existed in August 1914. It was the demands of the western front in terms of men and material that imposed the greatest strain. If Kitchener's new volunteer armies and their conscript successors were to be supplied adequately there had to be a vast expansion of munitions production which would need to draw upon a far wider range of firms and a far larger labour force than had been required to deal with the demands of Britain's relatively small professional forces in the past.

The actual production of the munitions of war needed support from the mining of coal, the making of steel, the revival of agricultural production so as to save imports and tonnage and the improvement of communications on land (especially the railways) and by sea. All these depended upon manpower and upon the skills required to make the best use of what was available. In these areas the government could not blame the admirals and generals for any failings. It was the supreme test of administrative and political skills.

It was essential to balance the demands of the forces for men with the need to retain, or at times recover from the army skilled men upon whom the productive process depended. The voluntary system dear to the hearts of British Liberals could not cope with these contradictory pressures. After a variety of expedients had been found wanting, a compulsory service bill was introduced for single men in January 1916 and for married men in May. Between that date and the armistice, Britain was a society almost wholly organized for war with few adults of either sex not directly or indirectly involved. In the second place, it was realized that the best use of skilled labour could not be obtained without the abandonment for the duration of time-honoured impediments to entry into skilled trades that it had been one of the major purposes of trade unionism to enforce.[17] And in turn it was evident that without the assent of the trade union movement 'dilution' would prove unacceptable. Its reluctance to give full assent to the necessary changes in the work force and in working practices was enhanced by the fact that during the early months of the war

---

[17] For relations between the government and the trade union movement during the war, see C. Wrigley, *David Lloyd George and the British Labour Movement: Peace and War* (Hassocks, 1976).

manufacturers were allowed to make very large profits so as to
encourage them to turn over their plants to munitions. Later in the
war, taxation was substantially increased and prices controlled. But
Lloyd George himself was surprised at the end of the war to discover
what fortunes had been made out of it.

Lloyd George as Chancellor of the Exchequer and with much pre-
war experience in dealing with labour questions was much involved
from the beginning in this aspect of the war. A first bargain with the
unions was struck in the 'Treasury Agreement' of March 1915. By
this agreement the unions agreed not to engage in strikes for the
duration of the war and to have referred to arbitration all disputes
about which no agreement could be reached. They also agreed to
recommend departures from trade customs but only until the end of
the war, and subject to the government imposing conditions on war
contractors and to the protection of the wages of skilled workers where
unskilled or female labour was introduced. Important elements in the
unions held out against the agreement and its impact was less than the
government had hoped.

Labour problems were not the only ones that affected the supply of
munitions. The pre-war practices of the War Office were designed to
deal with a limited number of recognized producers and were ill-
designed to make the most of other potential sources of supply. The
Admiralty insisted upon priority for its own needs – a priority the
harder to accept when there was little fighting at sea after the early
round up of German commerce raiders. It was even more difficult to
find room for the development of the new air arm whether under
army or navy auspices.

The creation of a Minister of Munitions and the acceptance of the
office by Lloyd George were perhaps the most important individual
features of the creation of the Asquith Coalition. It was a direct result
of the breakdown of the Treasury Agreement with the trade unions
owing to the government's unwillingness to control profits to the
satisfaction of the unions, and the unwillingness of the unions to do
away with the restrictions that were hampering production. The creation of the ministry was followed by the Munitions of War Act which
gave the new ministry sweeping powers over labour, outlawing
strikes and lockouts, and making a fresh effort to deal with the question of profits. The personnel of the new ministry was fortified by
bringing in figures from the business world foreshadowing Lloyd
George's new appointments in many areas when he eventually
became Prime Minister in 1916.[18]

---

[18] On Lloyd George's tenure of the Ministry of Munitions see R.J.Q. Adams, *Arms and the
Wizard: Lloyd George and the Ministry of Munitions 1915–1916* (London, 1978).

It was however clear that no system would be able to operate without at least the tacit assent of the leaders of labour, and that Lloyd George's negotiating skills would remain as important as his ability to enthuse his subordinates. Account had to be taken of the divided attitude of labour to the war. While the majority of the trade unions as well as of the political leadership was committed to the war effort, there were exceptions on both pacifist and extreme socialist grounds. The trade union leaders were always conscious of the need to avoid losing control of their members to militant elements whose position had been strengthened in the bitter clashes of the pre-war period. The unofficial disputes mainly centred on the Clyde and in South Wales were in part the fruit of political propaganda but were also explicable in terms of particular regional industrial and social problems.[19] For the rest of 1915 the underlying issue was that of conscription which the trade union leaders generally regarded as dangerous in that it might open the way to a more direct conscription of labour instead of relying on largely negative controls. In this opposition the Labour element was reinforced by many old-fashioned Liberals who took the view that compulsion under whatever guise struck at the very root of the Liberal society which Britain had gone to war to defend.[20]

It has been argued that the contribution of Lloyd George's tenure of the Ministry of Munitions to the solution of the army's supply problems has been exaggerated, and that the main lines of growth had already been laid down by the War Office and the main agreements with the unions already negotiated; even the measures taken to deal with restrictive practices under the Munitions of War Act were those unavailingly pressed upon the cabinet in October 1914. The shell crisis, it is claimed, was not the result of a supine lack of imagination but arose from genuine uncertainty as to the proper balance between shrapnel and high-explosive shell and to the difficulties of altering the use of lines of production without interfering with the immediate requirements of the armies in the field.[21] From the political point of view this issue is largely irrelevant. What mattered was that a new impetus had been given to dissociating the war effort from the ordinary lines upon which parliamentary politics divided. Lloyd George

[19] On the left-wing aspect of the British political and industrial scene, see Walter Kendall, *The Revolutionary Movement in Britain 1900–1921: the Origins of British Communism* (London, 1969).

[20] On the ideological split between the old-guard Liberals and those who eventually followed Lloyd George into alliance with the Conservatives, see M. Bentley, *The Liberal Mind 1914–1929* (Cambridge, 1977), pp. 26–44.

[21] See George H. Cassar, *Kitchener: Architect of Victory* (London, 1977). Even George Macaulay Booth, the archetypal 'Man of push and go' was an admirer of Kitchener and acted early in the war as a go-between to see that Runciman, the new President of the Board of Trade, was made aware of the army's needs for civilian-type supplies. See Duncan Crow, *A Man of Push and Go: the Life of George Macaulay Booth* (London, 1965), pp. 68ff.

had created a new partnership between government as embodied in a powerful minister, the representatives of existing industrial ownership and managements, acting under a greater or lesser degree of State control, and the accepted representatives of the labour movement. Labour's representation in the ministry itself was largely symbolic.[22] Lloyd George's handling of these developments both alienated him from most of those with whom he had worked in his pre-war radical phase and made him available as an alternative Prime Minister when the pressures on the Asquith coalition became too great to sustain.

Asquith himself contributed a good deal to the aggrandizement of the new ministry by weakening Kitchener's originally very powerful position. He took advantage of Kitchener's mission to look into the future of the Dardanelles expedition to replace Sir John French, the original commander of the Expeditionary force, by the more considerable figure of Sir Douglas Haig and transferred most of the War Office's supply functions to the Ministry of Munitions. It was agreed that the Chief of the Imperial General Staff should have direct access to the war committee of the cabinet, and when Kitchener returned he was forced to accept in that rôle Sir William Robertson, another powerful and popular soldier brought into the centre of affairs. The decision to evacuate Gallipoli and disappointments on the western front and in Mesopotamia had by the end of 1915 destroyed Kitchener's credibility with his colleagues, but the effort that had gone into building up his image with the public could not easily be put into reverse and he remained in office. The problem was only solved when in June 1916 Kitchener was drowned in the sinking of a ship taking him to Russia to look into that country's supply needs.[23]

Once the Ministry of Munitions was set up Lloyd George himself was removed from its day to day functioning. He could thus avoid the sensitive discussions about limiting the consumption of alcohol, proclaimed by the temperance lobby to be one of the main obstacles to greater productivity. Instead he was saddled with yet another, as it proved abortive attempt, to settle the Irish question, given a new urgency by the Dublin Rising of Easter 1916. Faced with the need to fill Kitchener's post, Asquith now asked Lloyd George to take over the War Office itself. Lloyd George was by now strongly critical of the professional military as represented by the Robertson–Haig axis. He therefore tried to get Asquith to agree to an arrangement which would give the cabinet war committee acting through the Secretary of State

[22] See Keith Middlemas, *Politics in Industrial Society: the Experience of the British System since 1911* (London, 1979), chaps. 3, 4, and 5.

[23] For a vivid appraisal both of Kitchener the man and Kitchener the legend, see Philip Magnus, *Kitchener: Portrait of an Imperialist* (London, 1958).

for War a much greater say in matters of military policy. Even when Lloyd George backed his request with a threat of resignation Asquith refused to endorse the proposal and Lloyd George decided to accept the offer as it stood.

For the rest of the year, Lloyd George had perforce to accept the view of the generals that top priority must be accorded to the western front and to put up with the appalling losses on the Somme which resulted from their offensive between July and November. At the same time there was a further blow to the allies' cause in south-eastern Europe; Rumania which had entered the war at the end of August was almost knocked out by the close of the year with three quarters of her territory under enemy occupation. Unable to affect general strategy, Lloyd George confined himself to seeing that the generals did not suffer from lack of manpower or technical resources. He insisted for instance that Haig employ a successful civilian railway manager to create a proper network of light railways behind the lines in France.[24] Meanwhile it was clear that the Asquith government could hardly hope to survive another year of disappointment; the only question in the latter half of 1916 was the form that the expected political upheaval might take.[25]

In a novel published just after the war and written by an author with an *entrée* into the political world, one of the characters, a member of Parliament, is depicted as saying in September 1916:

I'm sometimes surprised that these fellows lasted so long, but I think their days are numbered. If you throw your mind back, you'll remember a phase when Asquith's worst political enemies said he was indispensable, the only Prime Minister, the one man who could hold the Government and the country together. You don't hear that now; we've outgrown that phase. Now people are openly saying he's not master in his own house, that we shall never win the war so long as he's in the saddle, that they'll turn him out the moment they can find someone to put in his place. . . . Lloyd George would be in power today if his friends in Fleet Street could be sure he wouldn't hanky-panky with the Army. . . . To read the papers you'd think it was the cumulative effect of reverses like Gallipoli and Mesopotamia, the shortage of food, and the fact we've done nothing to increase home production, and our failure to grapple with submarines. . . . It's deeper and blinder than that. . . . It's because the Government *hasn't won* the war that it

[24] See Peter K. Cline, 'Eric Geddes and the "Experiment" with Businessmen in Government 1915–1922', in K.D. Brown, ed., *Esssays in Anti-Labour History: Responses to the Rise of Labour in Britain* (London, 1974).

[25] Subsequent feuds between Asquithian and Lloyd Georgian Liberals have tended to obscure the extent to which all the principal figures in the drama were responding to currents of popular opinion magnified in the press – currents that themselves were responses to the increasing gravity of the military and at times even the diplomatic situation. On the rôle of the press, see J.M. McEwen, 'The Press and the Fall of Asquith', *Historical Journal* XXI (1978). For a fair-minded summary of the main issues, see Peter Lowe, 'The Rise to the Premiership 1914–1916', in A.J.P. Taylor, ed., *Lloyd George: Twelve Essays* (London, 1971).

will fail; and any new Prime Minister will fall in exactly the same way unless he can win it.[26]

In Parliament itself, both Liberal and Conservative back-benchers had formed committees at the beginning of 1916 to press for a more forceful conduct of the war; the Liberal committee consisted of only 40 members and was less formidable than the Conservative war committee presided over by the Ulster Unionist leader Sir Edward Carson after his resignation as attorney-general in October 1916. Of the two party leaders, Bonar Law was in the weaker position; the Conservatives who supplied much of the government's parliamentary support were discontented with the distribution of offices which much favoured the Liberals and were suspicious of the Liberals' intentions about home rule as well as about the strength of their commitment to a total victory. With the emergence of Carson as a rival leader, Law had little option but to abandon Asquith when the crunch came.[27]

Carson was also in touch with Churchill who had resigned his ministerial post in November 1915 when Asquith excluded him from the war committee. After a period of active service in France, Churchill had returned to active politics in May 1916 and was another dangerous critic of the way the war was being run.

It was over the machinery for conducting the war that Lloyd George's break with Asquith came, and had Asquith been willing to accept the idea that the day-to-day running of the war might be left to a committee under Lloyd George's chairmanship, he would have been able to retain his office as Prime Minister and the general supervision of the home front. Unable to believe that the Conservatives would be willing to serve under Lloyd George and being himself unwilling to remain in the government as Lord Chancellor, Asquith found himself as leader of the Opposition in a Parliament which he had dominated as Prime Minister – an Opposition subsequently diminished in strength as members of it were drawn off into the new coalition.[28]

The Lloyd George coalition thus relied to a much greater extent upon the Conservatives than had its predecessor.[29] But it was also to a much greater extent a government of individuals rather than of

[26] Stephen McKenna, *Sonia Married* (London, 1919), p. 165. Stephen McKenna was the nephew and biographer of Reginald McKenna, Chancellor of the Exchequer in the Asquith coalition. His two novels, *Sonia* (1917) and *Sonia Married* (1919), give useful insights into the politics of the period, as does his autobiography, *While I Remember* (London, 1921).

[27] Barry McGill, 'Asquith's Predicament 1914–1918' *Journal of Modern History* XXXIX (1967).

[28] See Edward David, 'The Liberal Party Divided 1916–1918', *Historical Journal* XIII (1970).

[29] Conservatives had taken a leading rôle in constructing the new combination, especially Balfour and Lord Robert Cecil. See John D. Fair, *British Interparty Conferences: a Study of the Procedure of Conciliation in British Party Politics 1867–1921* (Oxford, 1980), pp. 150–6.

parties. The idea of war committee with delegated powers from a cabinet disappeared when Asquith refused to play the part allotted to him in the original scheme. In place of both, Lloyd George began with a 'war cabinet' originally of only five members: himself, Curzon as Lord President, Bonar Law as Chancellor of the Exchequer – the only departmental head – and two ministers without portfolio, Lord Milner and Arthur Henderson whose presence marked a further phase in Labour's ascent to a share in governing the country.[30] Other ministers, even those of cabinet rank such as Carson now at the Admiralty, were to attend the cabinet only when departmental matters of concern to them were under discussion. The rest of the business of government was consigned to a network of committees or delegated to departments including such new ones as national service, food control, pensions and shipping.

It was a government largely freed from the customary dependence of ministers on the House of Commons. Ministers were selected for their administrative reputations – public as in Milner's case, private as in the case of some businessmen. When the South African leader General Smuts joined the war cabinet in June 1917, he was and remained a member of neither House of Parliament. The new structure could not be combined with the lax business methods inherited by the Asquith government from peacetime. The establishment of a cabinet secretariat modelled on that of the Committee of Imperial Defence was an essential part of the political changes and 'draft rules of procedure for the war cabinet' including the use of the secretariat were drawn up by its head Maurice Hankey within a week of the new government's taking office. Both Hankey and his deputy, Thomas Jones, were more than mere cogs in an administration and must indeed be reckoned among the new Prime Minister's principal advisers.[31]

The cabinet secretariat seemed to the Asquithian critics to be less a necessary element in the co-ordination of the work of government, an almost inevitable consequence of the vast increase in the range of the government's responsibilities than proof of a dangerous accretion of power in the hands of the Prime Minister. Even more obloquy attached to his enlarged personal secretariat, conspicuously manned from outside the civil service, and showing some signs of Lloyd George's still living links with Welsh Liberalism, which both enabled

[30] On the significance of Milner's appointment see P.A. Lockwood, 'Milner's Entry into the War Cabinet, December 1916', *Historical Journal* VII (1964).

[31] J. Naylor, 'The Establishment of the War Cabinet Secretariat', *Historical Journal* XIV (1971). On Hankey's rôle, see Lord Hankey, *The Supreme Command 1914-1918* (2 vols., London, 1961); Stephen Roskill, *Hankey, Man of Secrets*. Vol. I: *1877-1918* (London, 1970). For Thomas Jones, see T. Jones, *Whitehall Diary*, ed. K. Middlemas (3 vols., London, 1969-71).

him to bypass official channels of communication and to maintain his links with the press and with opinion at large.[32] What none of these arrangements did was to resolve the tension between the civilian and military aspects of decision-making; the generals still felt excluded from ultimate decision-making and Lloyd George still felt that consideration of more promising paths to victory were being obstructed by professional obscurantism.

On the naval side the issue was the most clear-cut since Lloyd George was an advocate of a convoy system to cut down the dangerously accelerating scale of losses of merchant shipping to submarines. Some historians have followed Lloyd George himself in giving him credit for the Admiralty's turnabout on this subject in April 1917. The truth would seem to be that professional opinion was in any event moving swiftly in this direction for two main reasons. The first was that the mounting scale of sinkings cast doubt on the ability of the existing methods of anti-submarine warfare to deal with the problem before the food situation became critical and the second was the American entry into the war, to which of course the submarine campaign had itself made a major contribution. The advent of the United States as a co-belligerent meant that the assembly of convoys was now easier and more vessels were available to protect them. While pressure from Downing Street where Lloyd George had his own sources of information on this as on other matters may have stimulated the Admiralty's rethinking, the idea that a major policy was reversed in the course of one day spent by Lloyd George at the Admiralty must be treated as one of the war-time myths.[33]

The adoption of the new system took time and there was still a long wait before its full results were visible; but from September 1917 American warships became available for convoy duty. Meanwhile public discontent with the navy's performance and with its inability to find an offensive rôle was not allayed nor was the Prime Minister satisfied. Carson who had displayed no great talent in office was in July 1917 elevated to the war cabinet and replaced by Eric Geddes, already working at the Admiralty as controller. At the end of the year, Jellicoe himself, after differences with both Geddes and the Prime Minister, was dismissed from the post of First Sea Lord after holding

[32] The idea that the Prime Minister's secretariat was a centre of Milnerite influence linking the Lloyd George government to the earlier doctrines of 'efficiency' and imperial development has come under useful criticism from J.A. Turner in his article 'The Formation of Lloyd George's "Garden Suburb": Fabian-like Milnerite penetration?', *Historical Journal* XX (1977); see also J.A. Turner, *Lloyd George's Secretariat* (Cambridge, 1980), and 'Cabinets committees and secretariats: the Higher Direction of War' in K. Burk, ed., *War and the State: the Transformation of British Government 1914–1919* (London, 1982).

[33] The evidence on this matter which is abundant is surveyed convincingly in Marder, *Dreadnought to Scapa Flow*. Vol. IV: *1917: Year of Crisis* (London, 1969), chap. VI.

it for only a year.[34] But although no great victories were won in 1918 the situation at sea continued to improve and occasioned none of the anxieties of the war on land.

Before the strength of the United States was thrown into the war at sea on the allies' side, there were some difficult moments. Indeed on becoming Prime Minister Lloyd George found himself at once confronted by the gravest crisis so far in Anglo-American relations. President Wilson was still hoping to avert intervention by the United States through helping to bring about a general settlement, an ambition with which he had intermittently been concerned ever since the beginning of the war.[35] Britain's growing dependence on American supplies and financial aid made resistance to Wilson's pressure difficult to sustain, particularly in view of the prestige he enjoyed with liberal opinion. On the other side, Germany, needing to give the appearance of seeking peace to satisfy her Austro-Hungarian ally and requiring an excuse to return to unrestricted submarine warfare, was prepared to exploit the President's ambitions by offering plausible terms.

The German 'peace note' of 12 December 1916 was sent by way of the United States government, although Wilson made it clear that he was acting as an intermediary only and not endorsing its terms. But on 18 December Wilson himself sent a note suggesting that soundings should be taken to see what common ground might exist between the belligerents in whom he professed to see a similarity of aims.

Forestalling the publication of Wilson's note with its possible repercussions on war-weary opinion, Lloyd George made a speech on 19 December in which he made it clear that no peace would be acceptable that left Germany as strong as before the war.[36] On 20 December the allies rejected the German proposals and in a reply to Wilson's own note, sent on 10 January 1917, their own terms were set out in some detail. Wilson had not abandoned hope of getting terms from Germany that the allies could be induced to accept but the German announcement on 31 January of a return to unrestricted submarine warfare began a rapid deterioration in US–German relations leading inexorably to the US declaration of war on 6 April. But although this turn of events was of major political and psychological significance, the United States was not in a position immediately to bring help where it was most needed, on the western front. Not until March

[34] For Jellicoe's year as First Lord, see John Winton, *Jellicoe* (London, 1981), chap. 15.

[35] See Beloff, *Imperial Sunset* I, pp. 223–39 for a summary of Anglo-American relations at this time. For a sympathetic account of Wilson's gradual move towards war see P. Devlin, *Too Proud to Fight: Woodrow Wilson's Neutrality* (London, 1974).

[36] S. Kerner, 'The British Government's Reactions to President Wilson's "Peace" note of December 1916', *Historical Journal* XIII (1970).

1918 did the new American armies see action.

From his assumption of the premiership to the turning of the tide on the western front with the help of the Americans in July 1918, Lloyd George was in the difficult position of not agreeing with the basic premises of his military advisers yet without hope of finding other advisers who might fundamentally differ from them.[37] Indeed it is difficult to see how an eastern strategy could provide an alternative once the Russians had disappeared as an important fighting force. The Salonika expedition which had begun in October 1915 was never strong enough to affect the course of events while the Germans and Bulgarians were gaining their victories. The accession of Greece to the allied side in June 1917 as a result of extreme allied pressure was not an important contributory factor to the eventual allied success, though that country's presence as a victorious co-belligerent was to complicate the peacemaking process. But for the particular political reasons which impelled successive French governments to support the commander at Salonika, General Sarrail, the expedition might well have been wound up at an early stage. It was only in the last months of the war after the Italian victory on the Piave in June 1918 that the troops advancing from Salonika played an active part in the final downfall of Germany's allies. In Mesopotamia and Palestine victories in 1917 to which Lloyd George attached much importance were again more important for the complications they were to introduce into the peace settlement and into inter-allied relations than for their effects upon the military strength of the principal enemy.

The difficulties that Lloyd George faced in dealing with the military were also aggravated by his own political weakness, his consciousness of his dependence upon his Conservative colleagues in the absence of a coherent party of his own, his knowledge of the links that existed between the Conservatives and the soldiers and his awareness that he was unforgiven by the Asquith Liberals. The changes from his original ministry betrayed his anxiety to limit the numbers of those who might be enticed into a rival combination.

At the same time as Carson left the Admiralty in July 1917 Edwin Montagu who resigned with Asquith but had given the new government general support, replaced Austen Chamberlain at the India Office – the position of the latter having become untenable after the Report of the Commission on the disasters in Mesopotamia in 1915–16. Christopher Addison, one of Lloyd George's closest associates who had succeeded him as Minister of Munitions, left that

[37] The best analysis of the relationship between Lloyd George and the military remains Robert Blake's introduction to *The Private Papers of Douglas Haig 1914–1919* (London, 1952). For some reflections hostile to Lloyd George and sympathetic to the 'Westerners' see John Terraine, *The Smoke and the Fire: Myths and Anti-myths of War 1861–1945* (London, 1980).

ministry for the new post of Minister of Reconstruction and was replaced by Churchill. The return of Churchill to office against bitter opposition was obviously due at least in part to the fear that unless his restless energy was harnessed to the work of government, he might become reconciled to Asquith. In April 1918 when Austen Chamberlain was becoming prominent among the government's critics, he too was brought back. Lord Derby who as Secretary of State for War had supported Robertson and Haig almost, but never quite to the point of resignation, went to Paris as ambassador. Milner took over the War Office and Austen Chamberlain replaced him in the war cabinet.

In addition there were the political problems associated with war-weariness and the impact on British labour of the Russian Revolution. The British disaster of Passchendaele, the obvious inability of the French armies to move forward, the Italian rout at Caporetto and the Bolshevik Revolution combined with the length of time it was taking to make the American army a factor on the western front helped to create the mood of despondency which was widespread in the last months of 1917 and led to the Lansdowne letter. A possible peace-inclined coalition between Asquith and Lansdowne was despite its unlikelihood, seen by Lloyd George as yet another threat. In January 1918 Carson again resigned – this time because of suspicions over home rule. Weak in Government, but a dangerous force in opposition, Carson could not be ignored.

Lloyd George's ability to remain at the head of affairs and to devote himself to the task of galvanizing not only the country but the allies as well depended upon the partnership with Bonar Law; and that was incompatible with direct action against the military chiefs; there remained only indirect paths to the ultimate objective of imposing the Prime Minister's own policies. Since it was Lloyd George who held in his hands the threads of relations with the allies – he was constantly seeing French and Italian statesmen – he could attempt to exploit their needs and views against his recalcitrant generals even at the price of falling lower in their esteem. For Haig and Robertson relations with Asquith, who deferred to military opinion on military matters, were far more satisfactory, and it is not surprising therefore that it was to Asquithian Liberal as well as Conservative support that Haig looked.

The fall of Asquith coincided with the fall of Marshal Joffre from his almost unquestioned rôle as the planner of French military action.[38] In his place a new star, Nivelle, promised a decisive victory if

---

[38] For an outline of Anglo-French relations during the war see J.B. Duroselle, 'Strategic and Economic Relations during the First World War', in Neville Waites, ed., *Troubled Neighbours: Franco-British Relations in the Twentieth Century* (London, 1971). On the wartime problems of civil-military relations in France see J.C. King, *Generals and Politics: Conflict between France's High Command, Parliament and Government 1914–1918* (Berkeley, 1951).

allowed to dictate the place and method of a new attack. By an extraordinary series of political manoeuvres Lloyd George forced upon the British generals full subordination to Nivelle during the course of the coming offensive. The Calais Conference of 26 February 1917 at which this plan reached fruition destroyed any hope that Haig might put his trust in Lloyd George. Nivelle's offensive in April proved to be a resounding failure and for the rest of the year the French armies had to be nursed through a dangerous convalescence by Pétain, while the burden of fighting the Germans fell upon the British. It was Haig's decision that the British effort should take the form of an offensive in Flanders partly to avoid diversion of troops and guns to the Italian front where Lloyd George saw prospects of a major victory but more specifically because the navy had failed to curb the menace presented by the German possession of the Belgian ports and the submarine dangers in the channel of which the armies in France were very conscious.

The terrible losses and eventual failure of the Passchendaele offensive as well as the Italian collapse at Caporetto at the end of October 1917 helped to set Lloyd George once more on the road to circumventing his own military advisers. At the Rapallo Conference at the beginning of November, Lloyd George and the French premier agreed to set up an Allied War Council with permanent military representation. Here Britain's representative was to be Sir Henry Wilson, a general who, although on the record another convinced 'westerner', was thought to be more susceptible to the Prime Minister's political preferences.[39]

The problems crowded in on the Prime Minister and his government in the winter of 1917–18. The Bolshevik Revolution finally removed Russia as a fighting force and made it likely that important German forces would be transferred to the western front by the spring; for their part the Americans appeared to be taking their time, and were unwilling to merge their effort fully with their 'associated powers' as they persisted in styling them. The inability of the British army at Cambrai in November 1917 to take advantage of a tank break-through because Haig had no reserves left increased scepticism about the ability of the British military leadership to find any alternative to the costly and hopeless pitting of flesh and blood against fixed defences. At home labour unrest and war-weariness were added to by shortages and rationing and the other irritations of domestic life in wartime.

[39] A vivid picture of some aspects of the Lloyd George government in the last year of the war is given in Arnold Bennett's novel *Lord Raingo*, published in 1926. Bennett himself had served in the Ministry of Information and the political content of the novel was checked with his close friend Lord Beaverbrook.

In a speech on 5 January 1918 Lloyd George produced a statement
of the objectives of the war which was accepted by a wide section of
national opinion. There were some cheering signs. The Italian front
was stabilized on the Piave. In the Middle East, the forces nurtured in
Egypt were now successfully on the offensive; Jerusalem had fallen to
General Allenby on 9 December. But the heart of the matter still lay
on the western front. Here Lloyd George was determined that there
should be no new offensive the burden of which would again be borne
by the British, since the French even under the new leadership of
Clemenceau were in no state to engage in a major attack. To secure
his end, Lloyd George kept down the numbers of men going to
reinforce Haig's armies. There were of course other good reasons for
not going to the limits of manpower – the need for labour for the war
industries and for the general running of the economy which had still
to supply many of the financial sinews of the allied strength, despite
the relief given by the belligerency of the United States. The
impossibility of actually imposing conscription upon Ireland even if
such a measure were passed was a further limitation. But the essence
of Lloyd George's policy was to be found in the Prime Minister's
distrust of the Haig–Robertson conception of the war and of their
conviction that in a war of attrition the Germans would be the losers.

In January 1918 the struggle reached a new climax when Lloyd
George and Clemenceau agreed to give executive powers to the new
Versailles organization. Robertson refused to take up the post of
British representative or to accept a restriction of the rôle of CIGS to
what it had been in Kitchener's time. His resignation was accepted
and Wilson became CIGS. The new organization helped to produce
the highly controversial extension of the British front to assist the
French. The publicity attendant on these changes was further
envenomed when the government's own figures of British military
strength on the western front were publicly challenged by General
Frederick Maurice in a letter to the press on 7 May. Since Maurice
had only recently ceased to occupy a high military position, this could
only be regarded by the Prime Minister as yet another challenge to his
authority.[40] But although Asquith forced a division in the debate on 9
May – the only time during his leadership of the Opposition – the
challenge was a feeble one.

By now in any event, the military situation was all-important.
Once the Germans began their expected offensive in March, Haig's
position was secure. The German successes brought about that unity
of command which Lloyd George's various manoeuvres had not

[40] The case for Maurice is presented and fully documented in N. Maurice, ed., *The Maurice
Case: from the Papers of Major General Sir Frederick Maurice* (London, 1972).

succeeded in doing – no troops had ever been available for the Versailles organization to handle. When it looked as though Pétain by retreating on Paris would bring about a rupture in the allied front which had been unbroken ever since the Marne in 1914, Haig's concern was to find a way to over-rule him and the only way was to accept a French generalissimo for all the allied forces. On 26 March Foch was appointed to the post. In July, the German onrush was first stemmed and then turned. The increasing flow of fresh American troops forbade any hopes on the part of the Germans that they might recover. The questions at issue between politicians and generals and increasingly between the major allies related to the terms upon which armistices might be granted first to Germany's now faltering allies and then to Germany herself. Most people had expected the war to be brief; after the initial shock of finding that it would not be they had become used to planning for a conflict of much longer duration. Most plans had been made on the assumption that it would at least go on into 1919. Now the preparations made for the transition to peace would fall to be tested sooner than expected and would prove to be less smooth in their operation than had been the putting into effect in 1914 of the 'war-book', the advance instructions to departments on the measures to take when war was declared.

In part the reasons lay in the post-war situation abroad. The Bolshevik regime which had made Russia's peace with Germany at Brest-Litovsk in March 1918 was a challenge to the existing order widely recognized and widely feared.[41] The need to have a German government able to withstand the Bolshevik contagion had been a factor in leading people to seek a compromise peace or in any event one that the Germans could reasonably accept. But elsewhere in Europe, the collapse of the Tsarist and Austro-Hungarian empires had released passionate and insoluble problems of national rivalries upon which revolutionary feeling might batten. Further afield the collapse of the Turkish Empire had raised even more difficult issues both local and international. Closer to home, Ireland after the failure of every wartime attempt to square the circle between home rule and self-determination for Ulster was treated (and unavoidably) as an occupied country. The demands on British resources, even on British military resources, would not disappear with the proclamation of the Armistice. An inter-allied machinery for handling problems of shipping and supply might have been turned to the new tasks but national impatience and a weariness of controls made its future hard to envisage.

[41] For relations between Britain and the Bolsheviks see R.H. Ullman, *Anglo-Soviet Relations 1917–1921* (3 vols., Princeton, 1961, 1968, 1972).

By 1918 the domestic scene was very different to what it had been at the beginning of the war. The revelations of incompetence in the country's political and military leadership had, despite ultimate victory, damaged the credibility of the old military, political and administrative élites. Parliament itself had not played its customary rôle in the absence of the normal requirements of party discipline. Turnout in divisions was low partly because of the fact that by 1917 some 160 members were in the armed forces – though some of them with desk jobs at home did occasionally attend.[42] Nor did by-elections, given the existence of a *de facto* party truce, serve to throw the usual light on the movement of opinion in the country. Independent candidates, some favouring a negotiated peace and others of a jingoistic cast, did appear during 1917 and 1918.[43] But for the most part, Lloyd George had to rely in Parliament on his powers of persuasion and patronage to retain the support he needed rather than look to the wider constituency outside.

Feeling in the country was largely contradictory. On the one hand, wartime promises and the new power that had accrued to the labour movement created a general expectation of improvements in the standard of living and in social provision. On the other hand, the country's commercial and financial leaders were conscious of the economic cost of the struggles and of the extent to which the world rôle of the City had been taken over by Wall Street. On all sides it was appreciated that there had been a major growth in State intervention and that the direct representation of capital and labour at the centre of decision-making made an important change in the conventions of constitutional government.[44]

In political terms, the prestige that Lloyd George now enjoyed was generally acknowledged. How far it was due to his own real services, how far to the projection by the press of his personal rôle could be disputed. Despite the antagonism of the Asquithian Liberals and the newspapers they influenced, the *Westminster Gazette* and *Daily News*, and of the high Tories of the *Morning Post* variety, the initiative lay with the Prime Minister. But in November 1918 it was by no means easy to project his future course.

One possible solution to Lloyd George's dilemma was seemingly ruled out. He would not be able to return to his pre-war radical rôle as the leader of the Left because despite his successes in the handling of labour relations in the early part of the war, he had during his premiership come under much criticism from both the trade union

[42] M. Pugh, *Electoral Reform in War and Peace 1906–1918* (London, 1978), pp. 119ff.

[43] For a useful list of the by-elections of 1917 and 1918 see A.J.P. Taylor, *Politics in Wartime, and Other Essays* (London, 1964), p. 39.

[44] See Middlemas, *Politics in Industrial Society*, chap. 4 'National Disunity 1916–1918'.

and the political wings of the labour movement. The old dilemmas of reconciling the army's needs for men with the trade unions' worries over 'dilution' particularly in private work were intensified as the general position worsened. The creation of a Ministry of Labour did not mean that it possessed a monopoly in dealing with labour relations although both its wartime heads came from the Labour Party, while labour relations in general were the concern of the successive Labour members of the war cabinet – Arthur Henderson and George Barnes. For there were also the needs of the services as represented by the new Ministry of National Service (where Neville Chamberlain's unfortunate experiences as the first Director produced his lifelong suspicion of Lloyd George). The Admiralty and the Ministry of Munitions, the Committee on Production and the Ministry of Agriculture at a time of increasing food shortage all had their interests in the use of the limited pool of labour. Indeed so great were the problems of food supply in the last 18 months of the war that they assumed the same salience as had munitions at an earlier stage. One by-product of dissatisfaction with rising food prices and alleged profiteering was the creation by the Co-operative movement of a separate political party of its own.

The degree of industrial unrest in the later stages of the war owed much no doubt to the general war-weariness and to the uncertainties over war aims and the purpose of the struggle itself – political critics of Lloyd George on these grounds sought support from the unions. The pressure to limit exemptions from military service and the other discontents were naturally exploited by those elements in the labour movement that had from the beginning taken a Marxist view of the nature of the conflict and were now encouraged by events in Russia. While the labour movement as a whole continued to support the war effort, and while the official representatives of the trade unions were deeply involved in the structure of war production, the shop-stewards' movement was able to exploit the discontent of the rank and file. The agitation on the Clydeside where Russian political exiles had played some part continued and in the May Day procession in 1917 Russian sailors from a warship in the Clyde marched alongside the workers.[45] In 1917 however when there was a major strike of engineers in England, the Clyde remained quiet. The strike itself was met by various conciliatory steps enough in total to bring the men back to work; further concessions were made to the miners in order to avoid a strike in September and further piecemeal concessions were made later in the year and in 1918 to munitions workers, to the miners again and on the railways. The legal powers to deal with strikes were

[45] Kendall, *The Revolutionary Movement*, p. 128.

clearly insufficient and there were obviously limits to the authority of the trade unions themselves. However much Lloyd George might try to centralize authority in this sphere, the urgency dictated by the needs of the war was a powerful reason for securing settlements whatever the financial cost. Action against ringleaders of unofficial strikes was therefore very restricted and the number of men involved in stoppages and of days lost which had fallen in 1916 as compared with 1915 rose to more than double in 1917 and rose again in 1918.

The record was such as to make it unlikely that Lloyd George could present himself with much confidence as the friend of labour. On the other hand the immediate political consequences of the labour unrest in 1917 were fairly easily contained. In June 1917 the ILP and British Socialist Party combined to organize a Leeds Soviet Convention at which both MacDonald and Snowden spoke; and at a follow-up open-air gathering in Glasgow in August MacDonald was again one of the speakers. But thereafter the movement in favour of emulating the Russians made no progress.

For most of the shop stewards, the limit to which they were prepared to go was to protect the working conditions of the men they led and to restrict the unfettered use of the powers of conscription that the government legally possessed. They were not ready to take action which might result in the country being defeated, and the most the political leadership could do – even on the Left – was to make certain that the government overlooked no chances of bringing the war to an end by negotiation. But the connection between industrial action and left-wing political agitation was present in the minds of the government and explains Lloyd George's anger at Henderson's assumption that he could square his duties as a leader of the Labour movement with his war cabinet rôle. He had indeed been reminded of the difficulties of this rôle from the other side when attacked at the party conference in January 1917 for the government's more unpopular measures.

It is true that for much of the time after the call for an international socialist conference at Stockholm had come in April from the Dutch and Scandinavian socialists, Lloyd George was inclined to think that it could profit the allies particularly through helping to counter German propaganda among the Russians. But this attitude changed after Henderson following a visit to Russia seemed prepared to work with socialists like MacDonald, whose attitude to the war was quite different from his own. Other allied governments and the Americans were also increasingly opposed to the idea and by August it seemed possible that such a meeting might actually weaken the resolve of the Provisional Russian government under Kerensky. Despite Henderson's own intention of preventing a shift to the far Left in Russia his support for the proposed conference seemed sufficient reason for dispensing with his services. He was replaced by George Barnes, a Labour MP with a trade-union background who had been the first holder of the new office of Minister of Pensions. Had Henderson remained in the cabinet until the Bolshevik Revolution in November which completely altered the problem he might well have stayed in office until the end of the war and would have been unable to devote himself to the affairs of the Labour Party and to rebuilding the unity in its ranks which the war had destroyed.

Although for much of 1917 and 1918 victory and peace seemed a long way off, they had to be assumed and the government had to plan for 'reconstruction', the label given to all forward thinking about domestic policy. The extent to which plans made in wartime would prove practicable and the degree to which the limitations on the authority of the State even in wartime might be magnified once the threat had been removed were open questions. But 'reconstruction' proved both a way of harnessing to useful work some of the intellectual talent seeking public service and yet not easily utilizable for the war effort, and a useful way of keeping out of mischief political talent that the Prime Minister could not otherwise easily fit into his schemes.

The machinery for planning post-war Britain antedated the formation of the Lloyd George government. A cabinet committee on reconstruction problems was set up by Asquith in the spring of 1916 and began to collect views from individuals involved in the new and extended functions of government such as William Beveridge who had been a leading figure in the pre-war organization of social insurance and in wartime labour and food questions.[46] In March 1917 Lloyd George set up a new committee with himself as chairman and Beatrice Webb among its members. And this in turn gave way to the Ministry of Reconstruction which had Christopher Addison as its first political head. During the remainder of the year and with a greater impetus in 1918 the ministry produced a stream of proposals in relation to housing, land-settlement, the establishment of a Ministry of Health to co-ordinate medical and insurance services, the abolition of the Poor Law in favour of a new structure of public assistance committees, the extension of unemployment insurance to the whole working population, a new structure of labour relations and major proposals in the field of technical and secondary education.[47]

[46] See José Harris, *William Beveridge: a Biography* (Oxford, 1977), pp. 250ff; P.B. Johnson, *Land Fit for Heroes: The Planning of British Reconstruction 1916-1919* (Chicago, 1969).

[47] See Kenneth O. Morgan, *Consensus and Disunity: the Lloyd George Coalition Government 1918-1922* (Oxford, 1979), pp. 23-5; K. and J. Morgan, *Portrait of a Progressive: the Political Career of Christopher, Viscount Addison* (Oxford, 1980).

A by-product of this activity was the Haldane Committee on the Machinery of Government in which a leading part was played once more by Beatrice Webb. While this was in form an enquiry into the way in which government business might in general most usefully be distributed between departments, and was also a vehicle for Haldane to express his belief in a forward planning organization as a necessary part of each department – a belief fortified by his war office experience from 1905 to 1912 – it served to keep up the pressure for the most controversial of the ministry's ideas, the creation of a new Ministry of Health to replace the routine-bound Local Government Board. The report, published just after the armistice, was in a sense overtaken by the urgency of events but remained as a pointer to some future developments.

Most important proposals for 'reconstruction' required legislation and for this little opportunity existed under war conditions. The exception was the Education Act of 1918, the achievement of H.A.L. Fisher whom Lloyd George had brought into his government direct from his Vice-Chancellorship of the University of Sheffield. Important advances were made in the central financing of education and opportunities for secondary education and for entrance to universities were extended.

Without minimizing the interest that Lloyd George and some of his close associates showed in the possibilities of domestic 'reconstruction' and in creating an agenda for post-war governments that should take full account of the weaknesses in some aspects of social provision, and of the new demands voiced by Labour, it is equally true that the change in the franchise, another piece of wartime legislation, imposed upon all political parties the need to take account of such matters. The Representation of the People Act passed early in 1918 considerably enlarged the electorate, first by removing all vestiges of property requirements – other than the second votes for business premises important in only a few constituencies – so that adult male suffrage became the general rule; second by enfranchising women – though only over the age of 30 – and third by simplifying the system of registration. In all the electorate was more than doubled. Redistribution on the principle of equalized constituencies also affected party fortunes. But after much discussion there was to be no change in the electoral system.[48]

For Lloyd George himself however it was the world stage that increasingly made an appeal and part of this concern about Britain's international future was manifest in the interest he showed in

[48] See Pugh, *Electoral Reform*. For changes in the franchise during the period covered by the present volume see D.H.E. Butler, *The Electoral System in Britain since 1918* (2nd ed., Oxford, 1963).

improving the machinery for co-operation with the self-governing Dominions in ways that might extend into the Peace. The old Radical now adopted, if in a partly new guise, the goals of the imperialist sector of British politics. Between March and May 1917 there were meetings not merely of an Imperial Conference of a kind for which pre-war precedents existed but also of a new body, an Imperial war cabinet, that is to say meetings of the British war cabinet attended by the Dominion premiers. Further such meetings took place in June and July 1918 and soon after the Armistice in order to discuss problems of peacemaking. It is true that it was made clear by some Dominion representatives, and notably by Smuts, that there was to be no covert federalism – no idea of an Imperial Parliament or Imperial Executive. It was rather a recognition of the full international status that the Dominions had acquired. But from the point of view of the outside world it was still possible to think of the British Empire as a single entity and for Lloyd George to speak for it if only as *primus inter pares*. The Prime Minister's position was of particular importance since it was agreed that communications between Prime Ministers would in future be direct and not through the Colonial Office whose standing was thus diminished. Despite the nervousness shown by some Dominions about the creation of any machinery which might suggest commitment to a general imperial foreign policy and despite the fact that the hopes of the advocates of imperial preference ran up against both British free-trading sentiments and the inter-allied commitments and machinery that existed by the end of the war, the war seemed to have given the imperial theme a new lease of life.[49]

The impact of the war on the British public mind was so profound that it is not surprising that it generated historical controversies which lasted well beyond the Second World War. Much of the controversy related to the problem of the causes of the conflict; could it have been avoided, could Britain have remained outside? But there was also the question, given point and poignancy by the tremendous losses sustained, as to whether the grand strategy had been correct. Had there been any alternative to the wearing down of the enemy by the bloody process of attrition on the western front? If more resources had been devoted to other theatres could Russia have been sustained and Germany's allies knocked out, leaving Germany itself weakened by blockade with no option but to seek peace? The upholders of the orthodox view can point to the fact that the war was in fact won, and won on the western front, despite the relief to Germany brought about by the Bolshevik Revolution and the subsequent separate peace. Furthermore they can point to the lack of success of many of

[49] See Beloff, *Imperial Sunset* 1, pp. 212–28.

the sideshows – against Allenby's successful campaign in Palestine must be set the disasters at Gallipoli and in Mesopotamia and the long-drawn out futility of the Salonika expedition. Furthermore the near-success of the German spring offensive of 1918 lends point to the persistent objections of the generals to the diversion of troops to other theatres. Again it might be arguable that while the concentration of force on the western front was justified, there was a lack of tactical skill to make the best of the strategic decision.

These questions cannot be settled by looking at purely military considerations. As in previous wars in Europe, Britain was fighting as part of an alliance. Once it had been decided that Britain's national interest demanded that France should be preserved from defeat much of the military decision-making was pre-empted. It was necessary to incur extra burdens if France's own forces required relief; hence the Somme offensive was to give France the opportunity to recover from the losses at Verdun. Once Italy was an ally, and was in danger, forces had to be allocated to her defence. Gallipoli itself arose from the wish to assist the Russians. To separate the military argument from the diplomatic one is ultimately artificial. Given the enemy and the actual or prospective allies, the war was probably fought in the only way it could be; but this did not lessen the desire to find some way of avoiding its repetition. And this was as true of those who had given the war effort their full support as of the dissident minority.

The Great War: a Chronology of Military Operations

	Western Front	War at Sea	Other Fronts
1914			
June			28 Assassination of Archduke Ferdinand at Sarajevo.
July			28 Austria declares war on Serbia.
			29 Russia mobilizes.
August			1 Germany declares war on Russia.
	3 Germany declares war on France.		
	4 Britain declares war on Germany.		
	7 British Expeditionary Force lands in France.		
			26-9 Russia defeated at Tannenberg.
		28 Action in Heligoland Bight.	
September	6-9 German advance halted at the battle of the Marne.		
			9-15 Russia defeated at battle of the Masurian Lakes.
October	12 (to 17 November). German advance on Channel ports halted at first battle of Ypres.		
			29 Turkey enters the war.
November		1 Battle of Coronel.	
December		8 Battle of Falkland Islands.	
1915			
January		24 Action off Dogger Bank.	

The Great War: a Chronology of Military Operations

	Western Front	War at Sea	Other Fronts
February			19 (to 19 March). Failure of Anglo-French attempt to force Dardanelles.
April	22 (to 14 May). Second battle of Ypres; first use of gas.		
			25 Landing at Gallipoli.
May		7 Sinking of *Lusitania*.	
			23 Italy enters the war.
October			5 Allied landing at Salonika.
			14 Bulgaria enters the war.
December			8 Evacuation from Gallipoli begins.
	15 Haig replaces French as C. in C.		15 Austrians complete conquest of Serbia.
1916			
January			5–26 Austria conquers Montenegro.
			9 Gallipoli evacuation completed.
February	21 (to 18 December) Battle of Verdun.		
		29 Germany starts unlimited submarine warfare.	
May		31 (to 1 June) Battle of Jutland.	
June			4 Arab revolt begins.
			4 (to 7 September). Russian (Brusilov) offensive.
	25 (to 1 July) Battle of the Somme.		
August			27 Rumania enters the war.
December			6 Germans take Bucharest.

The Great War: a Chronology of Military Operations

	Western Front	War at Sea	Other Fronts
1917			
March			12 First Russian Revolution.
April			6 United States enters the war.
	9 (to 3 May) Battle of Arras.		
		27 Convoy system introduced.	
July	13 (to 6 November). Third battle of Ypres (Passchendaele).		
			19–28 Russian retreat in Galicia.
August			21 (to 24 October). German Baltic offensive.
October			24 (to 12 November). Italian defeat·at Caporetto.
November			7 Bolshevik Revolution.
	20 (to 3 December) Battle of Cambrai.		
			29 Russia ends hostilities.
December			9 British capture Jerusalem.
			15 Russia signs armistice.
1918			
March			3 Peace of Brest-Litovsk.
	21 (to 4 April). Second battle of the Somme.		
	26 Foch becomes allied Generalissimo.		
May	27 (to 3 June) Third battle of the Aisne.		
June			15–24 Battle of the Piave.

The Great War: a Chronology of Military Operations

	Western Front	War at Sea	Other Fronts
August	8 Second battle of Amiens. 'Black Day' of German Army.		
September			15 (to 29). Allies' Salonika offensive.
	18 (to 7 October). Allies break Hindenburg line.		
			19 Battle of Megiddo.
			30 British take Damascus.
October	8–19 Allied advance.		
			24 (to 4 November). Italian victory of Vittoria Veneto.
			30 Turkey signs armistice.
November			3 Austria signs armistice.
			9 Revolution in Berlin.
	11 Armistice signed.		

3   Lloyd George and the Peace

> The generation which ended with the Peace of Versailles in 1919 is likely to be cut off from all that follows more completely than any of which we have record; a higher proportion of its youth has been destroyed and of those who remain hardly one has been left in the place that he filled before the war; the standard and distribution of wealth have changed; and former lines of social demarcation have been obliterated. Though the old forms continue, the life that inspires them is new: the schools and universities, the learned professions and the public services, the government itself are manned from a different class and actuated by different ideals.[1]

These lines written in a preface to a work of autobiography and dated 31 January 1921 may be taken as representative of much that was felt by members of the upper and upper middle classes in the years that immediately followed the war. Subsequent historians have also tended to treat the war as a great divide in British history during which major landmarks were obliterated. Not for nothing is a deservedly popular study of the home front in wartime entitled *The Deluge* .[2] Yet this can hardly be taken as the whole truth. For half a century and more after the Versailles Treaty, critics of Britain's economic and social and governmental habits were still talking in language which would have been familiar to their counterparts in an earlier generation – the indifference of the national leaderhip to industry and the technology upon which industrial advance is based; the excessive influence of the public schools and the ancient English universities; the narrowness and amateur outlook of the central bureaucracy; insularity and the persistence of imperial illusions; the excessive weight of the metropolis and its environs and the consequent neglect of northern industrial England and the Celtic periphery, even despite the advent of female suffrage the inadequate opportunities open to women in public life – all these would seem to be the constants of social criticism then and much later.

Wartime had been a period of considerable innovation in many

---

[1] Stephen McKenna, *While I Remember* (London, 1921), p. 13.
[2] Arthur P. Marwick, *The Deluge: British Society and the First World War* (London, 1965).

areas but the improvisations intended to deal with immediate enemy threats did not indicate a major conversion of opinion. On the contrary, as after all great upheavals, the prevailing instinct was to go back. Despite the heavy losses that Britain had sustained, the survivors were only four years distant from the world of 1914. Much had been crowded into those years even for the non-combatants but wherever one looks, whether at the political and administrative élite, at the principal figures in the economy or in thought or in literature and the arts, the names are the familiar ones. The citadels of power and influence had not been stormed by new men. The institutions were the same. If there was a new social balance it was not easily visible on the surface of everyday politics. Of course aspects of the old order were under threat and the threat was taken seriously because the Russian Revolution was there to show that in certain circumstances a full-scale transfer of power between classes was possible. The problem for those who did not welcome such a prospect was what aspects of wartime innovation they could safely discard, and where concessions had to be made to prevent the demands for change getting out of hand.

Before these questions could be tackled, there had to be a decision upon the kind of government under which Britain would face the problems of the immediate post-war period both domestic and foreign. In the absence of an organized party following, Lloyd George's position was an unusual one. How to deal with this situation had been a preoccupation of himself and his closest advisers from almost the beginning of his premiership.[3] At no time during the war had all Liberals been reconciled to the necessity of the struggle still less to the measures deemed necessary to win it. Towards the end of 1916 Lord Loreburn – a former Lord Chancellor – emerged as the voice of that section of the party which would have preferred to seek a compromise peace. When the Lansdowne letter was published in November 1917, it was widely believed that some prominent Liberals (though not Asquith himself) were in contact with him and that an alternative government might emerge requiring a wartime election to confirm the authority of the existing coalition. An anti-government vote of 131 on the Military Service Bill of April 1918 was large enough to cause some apprehension. A hard core of some two dozen Liberals went into the anti-government lobbies on a number of other occasions.

The question was the form which such an election might take. The electoral truce formally established at the beginning of the war was

---

[3] Roy Douglas, 'The background to the "Coupon" election arrangements', *English Historical Review* LXXXVI (1971).

not renewed when Lloyd George became Prime Minister; its continuance as far as Liberals and Conservatives were concerned was tacitly assumed although Labour was uncommitted. The problems of by-elections could be solved as they arose; they were indeed largely matters within the Liberal Party; for while the Liberal Party in the country was still a single body, its parliamentary membership was now divided into two groups handicapped by the mutual hostility of their leaders. The situation was far from clear-cut with many cross-currents and with the unwillingness of Asquith and most of his followers to enter into active opposition which might hinder the war effort.[4] In May 1917 soundings were made to see whether Asquith would enter the Lloyd George cabinet as Lord Chancellor, an idea to be mooted again just before the general election of 1918. But the rift remained unhealed.[5]

While the war was still being fought the Conservatives were primarily concerned to maintain the authority of the war cabinet. Milner had hoped when entering the war cabinet that a new patriotic Labour formation might emerge to assist the break with the past and that the government might even in wartime hold a general election to give itself a new mandate. But Bonar Law feared the consequences for his own leadership of the Conservatives.[6] In the quarrels between Lloyd George and the generals the Conservatives' sympathies were with the latter but when the matter came to a head in the Maurice debate in May 1918, they gave no support to Asquith for fear that the government might fall and be replaced by a new Asquith government prepared to seek a compromise peace.

Despite all the difficulties of a wartime election the Maurice debate did suggest that the government needed to refresh its authority through elections. The *Representation of the People Act* had become law in February 1918 and this provided a further argument for going to the country. Most important of all was the growing evidence that the House of Lords would be reluctant again to sanction a postponement which would now constitute a breach of the Septennial Act as well as of the Parliament Act of 1911. Lloyd George therefore began talks with his coalition partners to prepare for an election and together a list of Liberals was agreed whose fidelity to Lloyd George and support for the war effort was held to justify the Conservatives in abstaining from putting up candidates against them.

[4] For an account of the Liberals' internecine warfare see Trevor Wilson, *The Downfall of the Liberal Party 1914–1935* (London, 1966).

[5] See P.A.Lockwood, 'Milner's entry into the war cabinet, December 1916', *Historical Journal* VII (1964).

[6] See Roy Jenkins, *Asquith* (London, 1964), pp. 466ff; Stephen Koss, *Asquith* (London, 1976), pp. 234–6.

The sudden arrival of the Armistice made no difference to the situation this respect and it was Lloyd George's need to get the election over so as to attend to the crucial problems of peace-making that helped to consolidate the understandings arrived at. Indeed a week before the Armistice, Lloyd George had proposed to Bonar Law that they should fight the election in partnership and on the day after the Armistice Bonar Law replied accepting the suggestion.[7] In defending his decision, Bonar Law referred to the need to solve the pressing problems of the nation in a non-revolutionary way and to the requirement that the government should have a clear mandate to represent the country at the Peace Conference. It was clear also that the Labour Party would fight the election independently – Labour withdrew its ministers from the coalition at the behest of a special party conference on 14 November; in these circumstances and in the light of the recent resurgence of industrial agitation and the powerful impact of events on the continent, it seemed important not to divide the anti-socialist vote.

For dealing with the problem of the seats that were to be allotted to the Lloyd George–Liberal wing of the coalition, the lists drawn up in the summer, themselves largely based on taking the Maurice debate as the test of fidelity to the coalition, were by and large accepted with the result that of the approximately 600 candidates supporting the coalition and receiving the endorsement of letters signed by both Lloyd George and Bonar Law, the so-called 'coupon', about 150 were Liberals. In the light of this disproportion which reflected the weakness of the Lloyd George following it is not surprising that the coalition manifesto of 22 November stressed Conservative rather than radical themes.

The election, the first to be fought on the new extended franchise and after a redistribution which favoured the Conservatives, took place on 14 December but the votes were only counted a fortnight later to allow for the collection of service votes. Besides the Coalition parties proper, there was support for the government from the National Democratic Party, the outcome of efforts by Milner and others to create a 'patriotic' Labour party capable of winning working-class seats.[8] There was also a number of non-couponed Conservatives. Against them were the Asquithian Liberals, Labour and (in Ireland) Sinn Fein, as well as some extremists of different varities. The campaign was marked by the strong opposition to Lloyd George

---

[7] See Robert Blake, *The Unknown Prime Minister: the Life and Times of Andrew Bonar Law 1858–1923* (London, 1955), chap.24.

[8] See J.O. Stubbs, 'Lord Milner and Patriotic Labour', *English Historical Review* LXXXVII (1972). All the members elected under this banner joined the Coalition Liberals in 1922 but only one survived the election. The Party was formally wound up in 1923.

in the columns of *The Times* and *Daily Mail* , inspired by Lord Northcliffe their proprietor. Northcliffe who was in poor health had wished
to go to Paris as part of the British delegation to the Peace Conference
with responsibilities for government publicity, a rôle which largely fell
to Lloyd George's confidant Sir George (later Lord) Riddell, proprietor of the *News of the World* . But there were also differences of
policy dividing Northcliffe from Lloyd George. He had wanted the
Prime Minister to fight the election as an individual at the head of a
Ministry of All the Talents and deplored what he saw as his surrender
to reactionary 'torysim'. On the other hand, he feared that the terms
offered Germany would be too soft because of what he regarded as an
exaggerated fear of Bolshevism. The Labour Party was allotted a
daily column for its spokesmen in the *Daily Mail* and after the result
had been declared, Northcliffe was still emphatic on the need for
ministers with a Labour background to deal with the legitimate grievances of the working-class and of the returning servicemen.[9]

The election campaign itself largely and inevitably took the form of
a personal plebiscite in favour of the Prime Minister.[10] Lloyd George
and his colleagues have been criticized for their failure to warn the
country of the economic problems that must arise after the war and
the damage it had done to Britain's trading and financial position.
Above all, it has been objected that the voters were too easily given the
impression that the economic position could be repaired through
reparations from a defeated Germany, thus making the government's
task more difficult when it came to the Peace Conference. 'Hang the
Kaiser' and 'make the Germans pay' seemed out of tune with the
professions of idealism that had been made at the outset of the conflict. But the urge to allow the man who had 'won the war' to make
the peace was bound to be a powerful one. Intellectuals might feel that
the country's politics were being debased but there can be no doubt
that the government was in tune with much uninformed opinion and
that the pressures from below made for an even harder line than the
government offered at the beginning. Against the government's
exploitation of victory, the Liberal remnant had little to offer, while
Labour found it difficult to live down the equivocations that had
marked its own attitude to the war sufficiently to capitalize on the
impetus it derived from wartime industrial troubles, and the exten-

[9] For Northcliffe's rôle and views, see *The History of the Times* . Vol.IV. part I (London, 1958),
chaps. 7 and 8; also Reginald Pound and Geoffrey Harmsworth, *Northcliffe* (London, 1959),
pp. 673ff. Unlike the French government which retained war censorship throughout 1919, the
British government dispensed with any control of the press after hostilities ceased.

[10] The Coalition Manifesto was itself a restrained document emphasizing the need for
domestic reform. It is printed together with the Labour and (Asquith) Liberal Manifestos
in F.W.S.Craig, *British General Election Manifestos 1900–1974* (London, 1975).

sion of the vote to sections of the population from which it might hope
to derive additional support.

The results at a time of some confusion of parties were not easy to
tabulate but the extent of Coalition victory and of the predominance
of the Conservatives in the new House of Commons could not be
denied. The best calculation gives 473 supporters of the Coalition – 332 Conservatives, 127 Liberals and 14 other independents or
National Democrats who had received the coupon. They could rely
on general support from 47 uncouponed Conservatives and 3 Ulster
Unionists. The largest opposition group was in fact Sinn Fein whose
73 members never took their seats; the Labour figure was 60 while the
Asquithians numbered only 36 of whom a number accepted the Coalition whip after election. About 17 independents normally voted with
the Opposition.[11]

The Labour Party which now assumed the rôle of Official Opposition had clearly been the principal long-term beneficiary of the
unhealed Liberal split, since the massive Conservative gains obviously owed a great deal to the circumstances of the moment. As soon
as the impact of victory faded and the unresolved problems of peacetime recovered their normal saliency, the balance between right and
left in British Politics was likely to swing closer to equilibrium; the
Labour Party was now in the best position to benefit by this swing
when it came.

It was however a different party from that of the pre-war years. The
42 members elected in December 1910 had largely owed their seats to
the electoral pact with the Liberals. For the most part they had merely
been an appendage of the Asquith government's majority; unlike the
Irish National Party they did not make much use of their nominal
ability to exercise bargaining power. There has been much controversy over whether but for the war and the Liberal split that it brought
about, the Labour Party would have advanced to the centre of the
political stage. It has been argued that no important advance was
made in the years between 1910 and 1914 despite the prevalence of
industrial unrest. The by-elections of the period were not encouraging and there seemed little prospect that Labour could afford to do
without a renewal of the electoral pact when the next election arrived.
Against this must be set the evidence of progress at the local government level, a wider diffusion of socialist ideas and the greater attrac-
tiveness of the party to trade unionists.[12] On balance the belief of most

[11] Here and in dealing with other elections, national and local between 1918 and 1929, the
analysis is that of Chris Cook in his *Age of Alignment: Electoral Politics in Britain 1922-1929*
(London, 1975); further detail is available in F.W.S. Craig, *British Parliamentary Election Statistics* (London, 1969).

[12] Ross McKibbin, *The Evolution of the Labour Party 1910-1924* (London, 1974), chap.4.

Labour leaders that a political breakthrough was unlikely seemed supported by the facts.[13]

Against this view must be reckoned the fact that these were also years of great advance for the trade-union movement and ever since the miners had in 1908 decided to seek election for their representatives under the Labour Party's aegis, it had been clear that it was as a trade-union based party that Labour's future looked brightest. Of the 42 members elected in 1910, it has been reckoned that all but three were union-sponsored though not all of them of course had worked in the industries concerned.[14]

The advance of trade unionism marked by the rise in the number of trade unionists from 1,972,000 at the beginning of the century to 4,145,000 in 1914, of whom 1,600,000 were affiliated to the Labour Party, had owed much to the legislation of the Liberal governments of Campbell Bannerman and Asquith.[15] The Trade Disputes Act of 1906 which the Conservatives, anxious not to oppose directly measures clearly desired by Labour, did not seriously attack nullified the decision of the House of Lords in the Taff Vale case of 1901. The Act made union funds immune from suits for damages for actions of their officers and not open to injunctions for acts unlawful though not criminal. The building-up of union funds was as important as were to be the legal immunities of the unions unshared by any other bodies. It looked however as though the political utility of union funds had been put in jeopardy by the Osborne judgement of December 1909 in which the House of Lords held that their use for political purposes were *ultra vires* . Although there were elements within the trade unions themselves who took the same view, the Labour Party itself was naturally upset at this major blow to its finances, Asquith pledged himself before the election of December 1910 to remedy the situation, and Labour members after the election were in a position to exact fulfilment of his pledge. Asquith's proposals went only part of the way to meeting the demands of the trade unions because they provided for separate political funds in each union; individual members could 'contract-out' of that part of their subscriptions that went into them. The legislation was therefore delayed for a couple of years but in the end the Labour Party and the trade unions agreed to accept the bill as an instalment towards restoring the position to what they wished it to

[13] See Roy Douglas, 'Labour in Decline 1910-1914, in K.D. Brown, ed., *Essays in Anti-Labour History: Responses to the Rise of Labour in Britain* (London, 1974).

[14] On trade unionists in Parliament see F.D. Muller, *The 'Kept Men'?: the First Century of Trade Union Representation in the British House of Commons 1874-1975* Hassocks, 1977).

[15] For the pre-war history of trade unionism see E.H. Phelps Brown, *The Growth of British Industrial Relations: a Study from the Standpoint of 1906-1914* (London, 1960), and H.A. Clegg, A. Fox and A.F. Thompson, *A History of British Trade Unions since 1889* . Vol.1 : *1889-1910* (Oxford, 1964).

be, and it became law as the Trade Union Act of 1913. Further assistance to the Labour Party by minimizing the burden of maintaining its members in Parliament had already been given in 1911 when the Asquith government successfully carried through the House of Commons a measure giving members of Parliament a salary – something that Asquith himself had advocated for many years.

The contribution of the war years to the rise of Labour had not merely been its damaging impact upon the unity of the Liberal Party,[16] nor the further growth of trade union membership to 6,533,000 by 1918. It also precipitated a movement from Liberalism to Labour of a middle-class element including a number of distinguished figures in the academic world and journalism.[17] And it gave Labour figures experience of government and of co-operation with government, at both the national and local level. Once there had been Labour ministers the possibility that Labour would become a governing party could not be ruled out.

A principal vehicle for the movement of middle-class intellectuals into the Labour Party arose from the criticism of the decision to enter the war and to subsequent aspects of the government's war policies where they shared their position with part of the Labour Party, namely the ILP. The principal vehicle for this brand of criticism was the Union of Democratic Control created in the early months of the war.[18] Its principal founders were Charles Trevelyan, a junior minister who resigned on the declaration of war, and Arthur Ponsonby, the chairman of the Liberal Foreign Affairs group in the pre-war House of Commons. Another Liberal, a publicist of note, E.D. Morel became the secretary and main driving force of the organization.[19] The UDC also benefitted from the adhesion of the widely known writer on international matters Norman Angell, another Liberal. As the Liberal Party became a mainstay of the war effort with even pre-war opponents of the anti-German coalition aspects of British policy like C.P. Scott, the editor of the *Manchester Guardian* , fully committed to it, support to Labour increasingly appeared to be the only way in which the members of the UDC could secure their objectives.

The formation of the first Coalition seemed to the UDC to portend

[16] See Wilson, *Downfall of the Liberal Party* ; Edward David, 'The Liberal Party Divided 1916–1918', *Historical Journal* XIII (1970).

[17] An account of this process over a longer period is to be found in Peter Clarke, *Liberals and Social Democrats* (Cambridge, 1978).

[18] See Marvin Swartz, *The Union of Democratic Control in British Politics during the First World War* (Oxford, 1971).

[19] Morel's rôle has been seen as so crucial that the chapter on this period in A.J.P. Taylor's study of radical dissent over foreign policy is entitled: 'The Great War: the triumph of E.D. Morel'. *The Troublemakers: Dissent over Foreign Policy 1792–1939* (London, 1957).

a policy of fighting for a total victory which they believed might take years, and they insisted that the government should at once make known its war aims and so bring about negotiations. The conscription issue added to the support the government's critics were obtaining. The position of the UDC was based on the supposition that the Germans would be willing to negotiate on reasonable terms, though they had no specific reasons for supposing this would be so. They inevitably (like the conscientious objectors with whom some of them were associated) tended to be branded as pro-German by the government and by public opinion at large.

After the formation of the Lloyd George government there was an important influx of Liberals into the ILP as the most obvious political vehicle for their opposition to the war. The departure of Henderson from the war cabinet in August 1917 and the movement within the Labour Party towards the idea of a negotiated peace brought the UDC and the ILP out of their isolation. The reaction of the government was twofold. There was a more vigorous campaign against internal anti-war propaganda leading to the arrest of Morel himself for sending publications illegally to the French pacifist Romain Rolland then in Switzerland. On the other hand, as has been seen, Lloyd George himself moved nearer to the Labour Party's stance on war aims in his speech of 5 January 1918. But by this time, those who had cast in their lot with Labour were unlikely to withdraw their support.

The Labour Party had thus come a long way from the pre-war situation when it was not even obvious that it was a socialist party despite having been admitted to the Second International in 1908.[20] It had however become clear by the outbreak of war that it felt itself sufficiently strong to intend to face the electorate in the next general election independently of any arrangement with the Liberals – in April 1914 Lloyd George's overtures for a new radical alliance were rejected, partly because of the Labour leaders' conviction that the Liberals would in any event be defeated. The belief in the over-riding need to preserve and develop the party as an independent political entity was shared by its two dominant figures, the leader, Ramsay MacDonald and the Secretary, Arthur Henderson.[21] But their interpretation of what this implied differed, once war had broken out. MacDonald had hoped to see a major alliance in favour of Britain's

[20] For the impact of the war on the Labour Party and its philosophy, see J.M. Winter, *Socialism and the Challenge of War: Ideas and Politics in Britain 1912–1918* London, 1974). On the evolution of the Party and in particular of its organization, see McKibbin, *Evolution of the Labour Party* .

[21] See Christopher Howard, 'MacDonald, Henderson and the Outbreak of War, 1914', *Historical Journal* XX (1977).

neutrality develop between the Labour Party and the radical elements in the Liberal Party. But the German invasion of Belgium
made the same impact on most Labour supporters as on the rest of the
political spectrum. Between 3 and 5 August, the attitude of the party
in the House of Commons swung round completely and on 6 August
MacDonald resigned the leadership although remaining in the
party's inner councils in his capacity as Treasurer. The bulk of the
party supported the war and its members and the party machinery
was used in the recruiting campaign. On 29 August the party agreed
to take part in the electoral truce already in force between the
government and the Opposition.

Quite apart from its susceptibility to the national mood, the
Labour Party had good reasons of its own for fearing the alternative
prospect of a wartime election and for preferring a bargain with the
government. There was in the early months of the war a widespread
belief that the disruption of trade would mean massive unemployment and in default of government action for its relief, the trade union
leaders were worried about its impact on their own funds. Henderson
therefore believed that the policy of co-operation with the government
would best serve the long-term interests of the party and would
meanwhile do most to assist Labour's immediate objectives. It was
the same conviction that led the party in May 1915 to join the first
Coalition. MacDonald on the other hand believed that the energies of
the party should be devoted to exposing the secret diplomacy of the
Foreign Secretary, Grey, which was in his view the main reason for
Britain's entry into the war. While attempts were made to bring him
back into the fold, the publication on 11 October 1914 of a manifesto
signed by many prominent figures in the Labour movement and
blaming the war on the aggressiveness of the German Junkers made
such a reconciliation impossible and MacDonald henceforward found
his most congenial environment in the UDC.[22]

The decision of the Labour Party on 5 August 1914 to concentrate
on practical measures through a 'War Emergency Workers National
Committee', a body of which Henderson was chairman until he
became a minister, was to prove of decisive significance for the
party's future, since it provided the main organ for the Labour
movement as a whole and was largely an extension of the party's
national office. Its dominant provider of ideas in respect both of
policy and machinery was Sidney Webb who unlike his wife Beatrice

---

[22] Ramsay MacDonald's unhappy war years when he continued to withhold support from
the war without actively opposing it are sympathetically treated in David Marquand, *Ramsay
MacDonald* (London, 1977). A picture of him ill at ease among middle-class pacifist intellectuals
and conscientious objectors emerges from *Ottoline at Garsington: Memoirs of Lady Ottoline Morrell
1915–1918* , ed. Robert Gathorne Hardy (London, 1974).

had no qualms about supporting the war effort. Nevertheless some of the more 'patriotic' trade union leaders were somewhat suspicious of the 'pacifism' of the assistant secretary of the party, J.S. Middleton, who was the committee's principal executive, and of the miners' leader, R. Smillie, who became its chairman in September 1915. As fear of unemployment diminished, the primary concern of the committee was the rise in prices and it had become an important advocate of the control of food supplies and agricultural production before the establishment of the Ministries of Food Control and Shipping in December 1916. Webb also pressed the case for treating the wartime emergency as an occasion for the permanent extension of State control and the committee opposed the Corn Production Bill of 1917 on the ground that State assistance to any industry including agriculture should be conditional on State control.

Smillie himself refused to become Food Controller after Lord Devonport's departure from the government in the spring of 1917 since he wished to continue from within the committee his campaign for the nationalization of coal distribution if not of the mines themselves. Another sphere of activity was in relation to rents where Labour pressure helped to bring about the Rent Restriction Act of December 1915 and the further legislation of July 1917. While the committee opposed both the 'Derby scheme'[23] and conscription (thus aligning itself with MacDonald's original position), there was no attempt at active opposition. The argument was used to demand 'conscription of wealth'. Webb had come to appreciate the administrative difficulties of wholesale nationalization and was looking to redistributive taxation as a principal means of advancing the cause of socialism. There was again some tension with the TUC leaders who were opposed to any diversion of interest from the prosecution of the war to more long-term objectives, and the centre of Webb's interests now shifted from the committee to the Labour Party itself where he found himself aligned with the former BSP leader H.M. Hyndman to give it a strong push in a socialist direction.

Of importance for the future was the concentration of some active party members upon the local government level. At a meeting in May 1914, representative of all strands within the movement, a decision had been reached to set up a London Labour Party and its first annual conference was held in November that year. In May 1915 Herbert Morrison, a young member of the ILP close to MacDonald in his general preference for parliamentary activity over 'direct action' and like him an opponent of the war though not a pacifist, was chosen as

[23] Intended as a compromise between the growing clamour for conscription and a marked antiphathy in many quarters to the idea of compulsion. Under the scheme, men of military age simply attested their willingness to serve when called upon.

its secretary. London was to figure largely in Labour local electoral successes in November 1919 when the number of Labour borough councillors rose to 572 out of the 1,362 seats (as compared with 46 in November 1912). It now had an overall majority in 12 of the 28 boroughs.[24]

The events of 1917 accelerated the changes in the Labour Party and in the outlook of its leadership. After the Russian Revolution, the socialist anti-war convention at Leeds in June 1917 and the forced resignation of Henderson from the war cabinet, Henderson became the focus of the effort to prepare the party for an independent post-war rôle, which would include a set of specific attitudes in the sphere of foreign policy. MacDonald who held similar views about the future of the party was also convinced that the over-dependence of the party on its trade union side would be a handicap and that it must be prepared to give a welcome to middle-class supporters. Henderson worked closely with Webb who had in July 1917 drafted a statement of war aims and a new party constitution. The draft of the new constitution which now included provisions for individual member-ship and an organization on a constituency basis similar to that of the other parties was circulated to the National Executive Council in October and ratified in February 1918.[25] The suspicion still attaching to the ILP's 'pacifism' led to a reduction being made in the NEC representation of socialist societies but 'intellectuals' like R.H. Tawney and G.D.H. Cole who came to play an important rôle in the framing of party policy could now be directly associated with the party's work. The socialist commitment of clause 4 of the party's new constitution was adopted partly because of the influx of new men, partly as a result of the respectability given to State control and ownership by wartime experience, and partly as a means of making it clear that Labour was no longer an appendage of Liberalism but a competitor for power in its own right.[26]

Yet the most important factor in giving the Labour leadership confidence in the party's electoral future was the change in the com-position of the electorate in 1918. By the changes then made it has been reckoned that quite apart from female suffrage some four and a half million men more would have been on the register in 1910 if the 1918 provisions had operated then.[27] The great majority of the new electors were working-class and the effect of the changes was particu-

[24] The fortunes of Labour in London are explored in Bernard Donoughue and G.W. Jones, *Herbert Morrison: Portrait of a Politician* (London, 1973).

[25] See A.M. McBriar, *Fabian Socialism and English Politics 1884–1914* (Cambridge, 1962).

[26] The Constitution is reprinted in Peter Stansky, ed., *The Left and War: the British Labour Party and World War I* (New York, 1969), pp. 326ff.

[27] H.C.G. Matthew, R.I. McKibbin and A. Kay, 'The Franchise factor in the rise of the Labour Party', *English Historical Review* XCI (1976).

larly dramatic in urban areas. While, as has been seen, the consequences of the extended franchise were overshadowed in the 1918
election by the direct impact of the war, it has been argued that the
growth in the Labour vote from 1922 onwards was due to its attrac-
tion for the new voters rather than to the winning over of former
Liberals. It has also been powerfully argued that the Liberals lost
ground not only owing to their own internal divisions but also because
the money available to them as the result of the sale of honours by
both Asquith and Lloyd George led them to neglect constituency
organization and the need to maintain an efficient party organization
at the centre.[28]

It has been suggested that the Liberal Party, by its neglect of the
tactics of mass politics in the pre-1914 period and by its reliance on the
rational presentation of policy, was particularly ill-equipped to deal
with the new electorate, and that the more simplified even vulgar
electioneering of Labour and the Conservatives was better suited to
its requirements. Against this the expectation of some socialists that a
predominantly working-class electorate would naturally accept the
message of socialism if presented to it, and that an overall majority for
Labour could thus be expected in the immediate future proved over-
optimistic. And the appeal of the Labour Party was certainly
intended to be as rationally based as that of the Liberals.

The Conservatives for their part had feared the worst if manhood
suffrage came about without believing that it could in the long run be
avoided. The prospects for a retention of plural voting based on
business premises was also thought to be in jeopardy. On female
suffrage the Conservatives (like the Liberals) were divided though it
was generally accepted that in the event party fortunes would be little
affected, since women would tend to follow the voting patterns of the
men in their families. During the war some Conservatives including
Carson believed that an extension of the vote to all servicemen might
introduce a 'patriotic' element which would counterbalance the influence of the trade unions. But the government was forced into the
position of considering the electoral system as a whole and the Speaker's Conference of 1917–18 after the resignation of the die-hard Conservative members plumped for manhood suffrage, a limited female
franchise and some restrictions on plural voting. There was strong
opposition among Conservatives in Parliament and in the country to
these proposals which were unaccompanied by any counterbalancing
advantages such as a reform and strengthening of the Upper House or
the reduction in the over-representation of Ireland. The leaders of the

---

[28] Michael Pinto-Duschinsky, *British Political Finance 1830–1980* (Washington D.C., 1981),
pp. 92ff.

party, concerned above all to maintain the unity of the government, did not give their backing to these objections though some amendments were made slightly in the Conservatives' favour. The House of Lords did however remove the provision for the 'alternative vote' which might have facilitated a new Liberal–Labour alliance, but failed to get the Conservatives in the House of Commons to agree to proposals for proportional representation in the main cities. Conservatives after 1918 accepted pessimistically what Labour looked forward to hopefully – a House of Commons with a Labour majority. Yet on the possible safeguards – House of Lords reform, the referendum – there was no measure of agreement among them.[29]

The other important result of the 1918 Representation of the People Act was in the sphere of local government which also acquired a much expanded franchise. This extension made it possible for Labour to make gains in borough council elections and in the London County Council elections, providing both a base for the parliamentary effort and possibilities for resisting national policies to which Labour was opposed.[30] The most immediate impact was that caused by the removal of the disfranchisement of persons in receipt of relief from voting for members of the Boards of Guardians. In response to growing unemployment in 1921, the Guardians of Poplar in east London gave relief on scales which went beyond the normal rate. They were supported in this by the borough council which tried to get an evening-out of rate expenditure between the London boroughs by refusing to levy rates to meet the precept they were obliged to pay over to the LCC. Some of the borough councillors were imprisoned for contempt of court and then released by ministerial intervention. But this was not the end of the matter. By the Local Authorities (Financial Provisions) Act of 1921 concessions were made on rating but on condition that scales of benefit should be such as the minister approved. The Poplar Guardians refused to accept this limitation and in particular the lesser eligibility principle by which relief was supposed not to exceed the wages obtainable for unskilled work.

The battle over Poplarism went on for some years after the fall of the Coalition. John Wheatley, the Minister of Health in the first Labour government, refused to challenge the Guardians, but after that government's fall the District Auditor imposed surcharges on local councillors for paying excessive wages to their employees. In

[29] D.H. Close, 'The Collapse of Resistance to Democracy: Conservatives, Adult Suffrage and Second Chamber Reform 1911–1928', *Historical Journal* XX (1977). Close does not point out that there was a great measure of agreement on a possible reform of the House of Lords at the Speaker's Conference. See John D. Fair, *British Interparty Comferences: a study of the Procedure of Conciliation in British Party Politics 1867–1921* (Oxford, 1980), chap.9 and p. 327.

[30] See Chris Cook, 'Liberals, Labour and Local Elections', in Gillian Peele and Chris Cook, eds., *The Politics of Reappraisal 1918–1939* (London, 1975).

1927 Neville Chamberlain at the Ministry of Health secured an Act giving the minister the power to remit such surcharges (which the councillors could clearly not pay) but disqualified persons who had been surcharged from serving on local authorities. Poplar was not alone among local authorities in acting in this way – other socialist local authorities and Boards of Guardians behaved in the same manner, especially during and after the miners' strike in 1926, in an endeavour to relieve the hardship in the mining communities. In some cases it was clear that generosity shaded off into extensive corruption – for instance in West Ham. By the 1926 Boards of Guardians Default Act the minister was empowered to replace such Boards with his own nominees. But this was only a temporary device. By the 1929 Local Government Act the work of the Boards of Guardians was handed over to local authorities and the voting disqualification of those in receipt of relief was reimposed. It was to last in respect of local government until the National Assistance Act of 1948 formally put an end to the remnants of the Poor Law.[31]

The Coalition government felt its hold on real authority to be precarious. Local government and administration was only one of the spheres in which it could not take it for granted that its policies would be accepted and implemented. In retrospect these anxieties may seem to have been overplayed, certainly once the demobilization crisis had been overcome. Yet whenever there was a major industrial conflict, gloomy prognostications were forthcoming. In October 1919 Lord Riddell, chairman of the *News of the World* , noted in his diary that for the first time the printers in the newspapers had objected to printing matter of which they disapproved – attacks on the railwaymen who were then on strike.[32] In January 1920 there were fears that the failure to solve another railway strike would bring about industrial action by the whole Triple Alliance, the arrangement for joint consultation during periods of industrial strife which since 1915 had linked the railwaymen to the miners and transport workers. Union objections seemed to preclude the enrolment of a volunteer 'Citizen Guard'; though large numbers of special constables were recruited in 1920 and 1921. Meanwhile as has been seen the military strength available to the authorities had been dwindling rapidly. In 1920 the authority for conscription ended and the expense of creating an all volunteer army had to be faced.

The politics of the period were not therefore dominated merely by a wish to put off the acquisition by the Labour Party of a parliamentary

---

[31] The subject is dealt with at length by Bryan Keith-Lucas and Peter G. Richards in *A History of Local Government in the Twentieth Century* (London, 1978), chap. 4 'Poplarism'.

[32] *Lord Riddell's Intimate Diary of the Peace Conference and After 1918–1923* (London, 1933), pp. 129–30.

majority.[33] This objective had been given priority as early as 1905 by so far-sighted a statesman as Balfour. By 1918 it was widely accepted that sooner or later Labour was bound to form a government. What seemed more immediate was the threat of direct action by-passing the somewhat ineffective Labour Opposition in the House of Commons.

It is only in the light of these internal fears that the attitude of the British government (as indeed of the other western allies) to the Bolsheviks can be properly assessed. The fluctuating struggle of the Bolsheviks against their fellow-Russians in 1919 and subsequently against the peripheral nationalities and in particular the Poles in 1920-1, was felt as something directly relevant to the British domestic scene. And there was a constant struggle within the ranks of the government and its supporters between those who believed that Britain's strength should be cast in the balance against the Bolsheviks and those who believed that hostility to the Revolution would merely exacerbate class conflict at home. An episode such as that in May 1920 when Labour dockers supported by their union refused to load munitions for Poland, seemed to confirm the views of the latter. The Hungarian revolution of March–August 1919 and the Bavarian Revolution of April–May 1919 showed the capacity of communism to seize power if not to hold it and had their impact on British attitudes.

Subsequent historians have tended to treat Churchill's constant pressure for action against the Bolsheviks and Curzon's reluctance to treat with them as equals as aberrations in their careers. Yet the result of allowing the command of the resources of a great empire to remain in the hands of adherents of a doctrine implacably hostile to the social order of the western world has fully justified Churchill's dark forebodings. It was of course the belief of Lloyd George and of those who supported him that one way of securing the abandonment of the doctrine was to bring about renewed contacts between Russia and the West. If such contacts, above all trade, were to be given time to have their effect and if meanwhile the Russians were to be prevented from developing an exclusive and dangerous relationship with Germany, it was necessary to accept the ambiguities inherent in the position.

The fact that the British government pursued negotiations with Bolshevik emissaries from May 1920 to March 1921 while knowing (through radio intercepts) that they were busy intriguing with left-wing elements and doing their best to stimulate revolutionary activity in Britain itself is only the most paradoxical element in a wholly abnormal situation which caused continual frustration in the highest

---

[33] For this interpretation of the politics of the period, see Maurice Cowling, *The Impact of Labour 1920-1924: the Beginning of Modern British Politics* (Cambridge, 1971).

political, administrative and military circles.[34]

Yet it would appear in retrospect that in Britain as elsewhere, the immediate efforts of the Russians were counterproductive. The dominant voices in the Labour Party and most of the trade union leaders had no intention of interrupting the steady build-up of the Labour movement and their pursuit of the goal of a Labour government. While individual trade unions were prepared to use industrial strength to shelter their members from the onslaught of depression or to secure improved conditions, they were not prepared to surrender the initiative to unofficial groupings whose tactics were dictated from abroad. In 1919 the left-wing groupings concentrated upon exploiting the discontents in the armed services over the rate and methods of demobilization; and the heavy demands upon the country's military resources made by Ireland, by Europe and the Middle East meant that for a time it looked as though the authority of government might indeed prove difficult to uphold. The police strikes of 1919 brought another element of uncertainty into the situation. The Police Act of that year disallowed police membership of trade unions. There was however no major confrontation on the industrial front in that year, and no direct link between service or police discontent and industrial unrest. In August 1920 the organization by Herbert Morrison of a Council on Intervention to prevent British help going to Poland in the crisis of the Russo-Polish war awakened very serious fears as to how industrial action could be contained and the crisis was only resolved when the Poles defeated the Russian invasion without such assistance. The miners' strike in October with the threat of the railwaymen joining in to support their claims produced both an Emergency Powers Act and a settlement going some way to meet the miners' demands, and to give the government a further breathing space.

It would however be a mistake to see the general opposition in the Labour movement to intervention in the Russo-Polish conflict as indicating widespread sympathy with the Soviet regime; postwar pacifism and post-war isolationism played their part. It is true of course that quite apart from the core of pro-Soviet enthusiasts who were to form the nucleus of the British Communist Party there was and remained in being a much larger element in the Labour movement which stressed the fact that the Russians were after all socialists and hence on the right side and that any imperfections in their practice of socialism could be attributed to Russia's unfortunate heritage or to the Soviet government's need to cope with the hostile forces of

[34] See R.H. Ullman, *Anglo-Soviet Relations 1917–1921* . Vol. III : *The Anglo-Soviet Accord* (Princeton, 1972).

world capitalism. In so far as the Labour leadership was concerned it was easier to accept the insistence of the Soviet government on maintaining its external propaganda apparatus, in that much of the propaganda of which the government complained was directed against Britain's imperial positions, particularly in India and on her borders. This could be reconciled with the anti-imperialist strain in the Labour Party which had received a considerable accretion of strength through its middle-class converts from Liberalism. While political considerations were perhaps uppermost in Lloyd George's mind when the Russian trade negotiations were initiated in May 1920, the collapse of the brief post-war boom in the autumn of that year made the alluring (and imaginary) prospects of Russian markets appealing not only to Labour leaders concerned about mounting unemployment but also to a section of the business community itself. By the time the coalition fell the hollowness of the belief that Europe's economic problems could be solved by bringing the Russians back into the ordinary currents of international commerce had been demonstrated in the series of international conferences culminating in Genoa in April 1922. But the pressures to try again were always present in both Labour and business circles.[35]

The Soviet rulers for their part faced a tripartite problem of priorities. To cope with their desperate economic situation and to enable them to pursue the reconstruction (if within restricted borders) of the centralized Russian state, they required agreements with major foreign governments and in particular with Britain. Looking to an ultimate overthrow of these governments and to the advent of socialists to power, they wished to exercise the maximum influence over European socialist parties and Labour movements. But, in the third place, in obedience to Leninist philosophy it was necessary to create in each country a party committed to revolution and ready to accept the constraints of combining illegal conspiratorial activity with participation in ordinary politics. In most industrial countries this objective produced a scission in the socialist movement resulting in the creation of communist parties affiliated to the Third International alongside socialist or 'social-democratic' parties loosely linked in the Second International. In many cases there was a similar split in the trade union movement. In Britain the latter never took place although individual communists continued to play a significant rôle in particular unions. On the political side, the principal feature of the

[35] An important contribution to the understanding of the domestic background of Anglo-Soviet relations has been made by Stephen White in his book, *Britain and the Bolshevik Revolution: a Study in the Politics of Diplomacy 1920–1924* (London, 1979). But he somewhat overemphasizes the differences within the Conservative Party: industrial circles as against landed, finance or imperialist elements. Such abstractions conceal a more complicated reality.

Communist Party was its numerical weakness compared with the big battalions of Labour.[36]

The negotiations to form a Communist party began with a direct call from Moscow in late May or early June 1919 to form such a party out of the existing left-wing organizations including the British Socialist Party (the old SDF). The only other left-wing party of importance the ILP was excluded since its hostility to the Bolsheviks was already apparent. By May 1920 all the groupings other than the BSP had withdrawn or disappeared, and the decision in May 1920 to call a Communist Unity Convention to found a British Communist Party was the work mainly of the BSP. The Convention duly met on 31 July–1 August 1920 in the presence of a representative of the Third International (Comintern) and the new CPGB was born. An attempt to link the new party with the shop stewards' movement in the trade unions active at a time of depression and rising unemployment was made with the encouragement of the Russians and possibly with the help of Russian funds. And a further unification of left-wing forces under the banner of the CPGB was achieved in a conference at Leeds in January 1921. The pre-war guild socialist movement which had fallen on difficult times split in 1921–2 and contributed another and quite important element of the new party's membership. Closely associated with the party was the Labour Research Department, an offshoot of the Fabians. In Scotland finally, where the radicalism of the Clyde might seem to have held out hopes for a communist party, its recruitment was hampered both by the strength of the ILP and by the insistence of John McLean that Scotland should have its own party ready to emphasize (on the Irish model) a nationalist as well as a revolutionary message.

The new Communist Party had by 1921 achieved a shape that was not to alter very much in the entire inter-war period. It was small – 3,000 to 5,000 members in all (at a time when trade union members numbered over eight million and those affiliated to the Labour Party through their unions over four million, and when even the ILP was around 37,000 strong). It was professionalized in its organization and on policy matters committed to acting in conformity with the decisions of the Comintern. This conformity was a natural outcome of the fact that the party itself had been created at the bidding and under the guidance of the Comintern, and with the aid of material subsidies from it. In its objectives it mirrored the familiar dilemmas of such parties. It was at one and the same time to work for revolution and to seek representation in Parliament; to supplant the

---

[36] See L.J. Macfarlane, *The British Communist Party: its Origins and Development until 1929* (London, 1966); Walter Kendall, *The Revolutionary Movement in Britain 1900–1921* (London, 1969); R. Challinor, *The Origins of British Bolshevism* (London, 1977).

Labour Party but in the meanwhile to seek affiliation to it.

On both the Right and Left in British politics it was seen to be an imported and alien element in a way which had not been true of previous parties on the far Left. It faced some direct repression in 1921, and in 1922 was reorganized with substantially the leadership that would guide it over the next two decades.

Communists as individuals could still take part in Labour Party affairs and in the general election of 1922 while one Communist was elected as such, another, Saklatvala, was elected as a Labour candidate. Moscow saw this penetration by individuals as insufficient and pressed upon the party the need to seek for affiliation to the Labour Party – a proposal already rejected by the Labour Party at its conference in June 1922. In the 1923 Labour Party conference, 30 communists took part as delegates. In the election that year, five communists stood as Labour candidates and were all defeated, as were four others standing under their own colours. Further restrictions upon Communist participation in Labour Party activities were now introduced and by 1925 the separation between the two parties was complete; although Communist attempts to penetrate the unions continued. Meanwhile, in 1924 Saklatvala had returned to Parliament as its sole Communist MP; he held his seat until 1929.

Between December 1918 and October 1919 when the ordinary cabinet system was restored, Lloyd George's main activities were connected with the Peace Conference and he relied upon his colleagues and notably Bonar Law to handle the House of Commons and the more immediate press of domestic business – though after the signature of the Treaty with Germany on 28 June, negotiations with the other enemy powers were largely left to Balfour and Curzon. In assessing the outcome of the Peace Conference it must be remembered that the public mood embodied a series of logical contradictions which were largely reflected in the people's elected representatives. It wished to see the British Empire retain its new acquisitions and yet resented the military effort that this would require; it looked to see major advances in social provision and yet was highly susceptible to advocates of 'antiwaste'; it demanded a punitive peace and safeguards against a future revival of a militarist Germany and was yet strongly tempted to return to a policy of no continental commitments. In parliamentary terms the pressure on Lloyd George was from the Right rather than the Left.

For the time being, the Conservatives in whose ranks there persisted the latent possibility of a reawakening of the old freetrade versus protection issue that had so damaged the party's unity in the pre-1914 decade, were prepared to benefit from Lloyd George's popular appeal; but it was clear that this situation was not one that would endure. What should follow the coalition was an ever-present question.

Lloyd George's own attitudes fluctuated. Although the Coalition Liberals were numerically so weak they occupied many important places in government – seven sat in the reconstituted cabinet of October 1919 apart from Lloyd George himself, and further Liberals were appointed in 1920 and 1921. Churchill on foreign, defence and imperial matters in particular, and H.A.L. Fisher on domestic questions in 1919–20 were very close to the centre of decision-making. On the other hand, the Coalition Liberals were not successful in opposing all moves towards protection. They blocked 'anti-dumping' measures in December 1919 but failed in December 1920 to prevent a bill being passed dealing with the importation of dye-stuffs which had important defence as well as economic overtones. The Safeguarding of Industries Act of August 1921 was again a defeat for the free traders, and there were other signs that they were not strong enough to resist their powerful allies. It was equally true that while the Coalition Liberals had been the mainstay of the government's activist policies they could only put up a rearguard defence against the 'Geddes Axe', the name given to the cuts in public expenditure recommended by a com-mittee under Sir Eric Geddes whose report was published in February 1922.

The weakness of the Coalition Liberals was not in personnel at Westminster but in the country at large where, outside Wales, Lloyd George failed to build up an organization of his own despite success in collecting funds – largely through the sale of honours, a practice which was to contribute to his ultimate discrediting. The constituency parties remained in the hands of the Asquithians and when seats held by coalitionists fell vacant, it was usually Asquithian candidates who were chosen to succeed them. In these circumstances the desire for fusion with the Conservatives or the bulk of them in order to found a new centre party, which much tempted Lloyd George from the autumn of 1919 to the spring of 1920, had little prospect of success. Of his close colleagues only Churchill and (for rather different reasons) Addison were ever keen on the idea. Most of the party still felt the historic antipathy to the Tories and looked forward to ultimate reunion with the Asquithians. When Lloyd George met his parlia-mentary followers on 20 March 1920, he found them hostile to fusion and although there was further desultory talk about it during the remainder of the coalition's life, the idea was virtually dead. By 1922 Lloyd George had almost detached himself from any serious interest in the fortunes of his party and preferred to think of himself as an individual leader outside the party battle.[37] Suggestions for another leader of a 'Centre Party' – Lord Grey or Lord Robert Cecil – had no strong backing.

The political activity mirrored in the political correspondence of the time and dwelt upon by a still highly political newspaper press should not lead one to neglect the process by which in those years the traditional institutions of the British state were steadily being blended with the wartime innovations. The restoration of the old large cabinet including most departmental heads was partially ineffective in the sense that Lloyd George himself still spent much time abroad or out of London, so that decisions had to be taken by particular groups of ministers or even by individuals. But the framework of the new cabinet secretariat was sufficient to prevent these personal habits of the Prime Minister from impeding the course of business. Its importance was enhanced by the virtual dissolution of the Prime Minister's personal office, the 'Garden Suburb', although, first Philip Kerr and after his departure into private life in May 1921, Edward Grigg played important parts in Lloyd George's conduct of foreign policy to the vast annoyance of the Foreign Office, and of Curzon as Foreign Secretary.

The administrative problems of an enlarged area of governmental responsibility were gradually solved as areas of activity were returned to the operations of the market; the Ministry of Shipping which had been of vital importance in the immediately post-war years as well as in wartime was abolished in March 1921. On the other hand the Ministry of Health which had absorbed the old Local Government Board and acquired other functions was now an important office as was the new Ministry of Labour. While the wartime expansion of domestic agriculture was not maintained, the Ministry of Agriculture came to represent an important client interest in this and successive cabinets. What became of greatest importance of all was the further ascent of the Treasury as the key to government policy in all fields – a product in part of the salience of the problems of wartime finance.

The Treasury had for a long time been able to insist upon detailed control of departmental expenditure as the price of its approval for the necessary expenditure. It had in the eyes of some ministers an inherent tendency to deal with individual items of expenditure according to conventions of its own making without sufficient concern for overall policy.[38] Its traditional rôle was now much enhanced by moves

---

[37] Kenneth Morgan, 'Lloyd George's Stage Army: the Coalition Liberals 1918–1922', in A.J.P. Taylor, ed., *Lloyd George: Twelve Essays* (London, 1971).

[38] Churchill's correspondence as Secretary of State for War and later at the Colonial Office is full of complaints about the Treasury. In May 1919 the Treasury sanctioned the transfer of hundreds of thousands of superfluous rifles to the 'White' Russian army of Denikin but refused

towards the unification of the Civil Service.[39] The Permanent Secretary to the Treasury was styled Head of the Civil Service from October 1919 – the significance of this development was enhanced by the fact that the incumbent of the post, Warren Fisher, was to hold the position until September 1939. The Head of the Civil Service had the power of advising the Prime Minister on the appointment of senior officials in all departments; departments were obliged to appoint officers to standardize their staffing and accounting arrangements and after 1924, no new policy entailing increased expenditure could be submitted to the cabinet by a department without prior Treasury consent. The external control of the Treasury had now become an internal one.

But the new arrangements were not important only in enforcing standards of economy. The Treasury had its own policy views which led for instance in the post-war period to the running down of the wage-fixing activities of the Ministry of Labour, to the abandonment of the conception of a national minimum wage and to a general shift away from interventionism.[40] While these views were certainly in harmony with the national mood at the time, the domination of the Treasury was to become an even more significant and controversial factor later on.

The war had also left a legacy in the shape of greater governmental recognition of Britain's weakness in many of the newer and technologically advanced industries – 'safeguarding', i.e. protection, could not be the answer unless positive steps were taken to bring Britain's own industries up to date. Anxieties on this score and inquiries into scientific education and research had been set on foot before the war. Divisions of interest between university science in its various branches, scientific societies and the trade associations delayed for some time the emergence of a national policy. A committee of the Privy Council responsible for the spending of public money on research was establised in July 1915, and on 1 December 1916 Lord Crewe, the Lord President of the Council, announced that a fully fledged administrative department, the Department of Scientific and Industrial Research, would be set up. This machinery was carried over into peacetime. Although its creation was an important step, the achievements of the DSIR depended very heavily upon the willingness of the research associations set up by industrial groups;

to sanction the transfer of the 'pull-throughs' that went with them. The rifles were worth £7 each; the pullthroughs 4d.

[39] See Max Beloff, 'The Whitehall Factor: the Rôle of the Higher Civil Service 1919–1939', in Peele and Cook, eds., *Politics of Reappraisal* .

[40] See R. Lowe, 'The Erosion of State Intervention in Britain, 1917–1924', *Economic History Review* , 2nd ser. XXXI (1978).

industries were uneven in their interest in these matters, and there were inevitable problems about the effect of co-operative research upon the fortunes of individual firms.[41] The successive holders of the office of Lord President were not all equally interested in this aspect of their responsibilities though a favourable impetus was given to its work by the former Prime Minister Balfour who held the Lord Presidency from 1919 to 1922 and again from March 1925 until the fall of Baldwin's government in June 1929. Balfour's interest in scientific matters was of long standing and had been developed during his tenure of the Admiralty in 1917. A Committee on Civil Research established by the MacDonald government in 1924 was preserved from extinction largely through Balfour's efforts and in 1930 evolved into the Economic Advisory Council, having previously had a largely scientific and technical bias.[42]

Basic research was seen as primarily a responsibility of the universities but one which they were unable to provide for on the scale needed without an injection of public funds. Yet there was a strong suspicion of government finance in this field where the record of continental and in particular German universities appeared to be one of undue subservience to the demands of the State. The University Grants Committee established in 1919 was intended to be a buffer between the State and the universities since its composition would be non-official and mainly drawn from academics themselves. Scientific and technological advance could only prosper with a more highly educated people, and H.A.L. Fisher's Education Act of 1918 had been intended to go a long way to meet this requirement.[43] No exemptions were to be permitted from compulsory education up to the age of 14 (15 if local authorities so chose) and there was to be part-time continuation education on a large scale for those whose full-time schooling finished before the age of 16. Despite strong resistance from Fisher much of his educational programme took a severe cut during the 1921–2 drive for lowering public expenditure. Using their newfound power through unionization the teachers successfully resisted inroads upon their salaries which had risen dramatically since before the war with the establishment of the national 'Burnham' scale.

The main victim of the economies was Fisher's plan for continuing education which was indeed never implemented; the powers given to local authorities in respect of secondary education and of care

[41] For the origins and later history of the DSIR see the brief but illuminating account in Ian Varcoe, *Organizing for Science in Britain* (London, 1974).

[42] See Max Egremont, *Balfour: a Life of Arthur James Balfour* (London, 1980).

[43] To feel the full force of the expectations placed upon the Fisher Act, see for instance the article by Professor W.G.S. Adams formerly of the 'garden suburb': 'Education – the United Kingdom' in the 1922 supplementary volumes to the *Encyclopaedia Britannica* .

for the physical development of school children provided a
framework for future action but depended very heavily upon the
interests and attitudes of the local authorities themselves.

Room was also made for financial assistance to adult education
with which the universities were increasingly associated. While by
comparison with the pre-war period educational opportunities were
greater, the advance made was insufficient to satisfy either those still
worried about national efficiency, or the larger number, particularly
identified with the Labour Party, who regarded the extension of
educational opportunity to all as an essential attribute of a truly
democratic society. What was striking was the absence in discussions
of the Fisher Act or in the later debates over education in the inter-war
period of that preoccupation with the rôle of religion in the schools
which had been so marked a feature of the discussions over the Acts of
1870 and 1902.[44] Whether this indicated a general secularization of
British society or merely the weakening of organized nonconformity
is a subject for speculation.[45]

Not the least of the problems that confronted Lloyd George in his
relations with his coalition colleagues was what to do about Ireland.[46]
The nature of the problem had not been changed essentially by the
war and its outcome, despite changes in the Irish scene itself as the
unusual prosperity of the early part of the war gave way to the shortages and uncertainties that Ireland shared with the rest of the British
isles in 1917–18. The crisis of 1914 had dissipated whatever hopes
there might have been that a settlement of the land question would
suffice to create a united nation out of the disparate cultures that
clashed within it. Outside Ulster, Irish nationalism seeking to base
the nation's identity on linguistic, cultural and in practice religious
grounds, could not hope to recruit the whole-hearted support or
indeed make room for the Protestant heirs of the 'ascendancy' with
their essentially Anglo-Irish culture. The fact that a few individual
Protestants threw in their lot with the nationalists could not conceal
this fact, any more than the French or Russian revolutionary movements were robbed of their essential content by the presence in the

[44] The Coalition found no difficulty in putting through the disestablishment of the Welsh
Church enacted in 1914 though some financial concessions were made to it. It provoked the
resignation of Lord Robert Cecil from his under-secretaryship at the Foreign Office but this
was simply an echo of far off things. For the social and political attitudes of the Anglican
Church, see E.R. Norman, *Church and Society in England 1770–1970: a Historical Study* (Oxford,
1976).

[45] On nonconformity see Stephen Koss, *Nonconformity in Modern British Politics* (London,
1975).

[46] For a narrative of Anglo-Irish relations from 1906 to 1921, see George Dangerfield, *The
Damnable Question: a Study in Anglo-Irish Relations* (London, 1977); for the period 1914–1922 as
seen from the Irish point of view, see F.S.L Lyons, *Ireland since the Famine* (London, 1971), part
III 'The Union Broken'.

ranks of the revolutionaries of the occasional aristocrat or Tsarist officer.[47]

What was clear after 1914 was that in the last resort the Protestants of Ulster would rather seek their own salvation and rule over their own divided province than transfer allegiance with whatever safe-guards to a government in Dublin, which would of necessity be Catholic-dominated. In England the war strengthened the cause of unionism politically by the return of the Unionists to the ranks of government in the two wartime coalitions, through the influence of the professional military so heavily Anglo-Irish in its recruitment, and emotionally through resentment at the Irish acceptance of German aid, Irish immunity from conscription, and the constant anti-British pressure on President Wilson of Irish-Americans.[48]

In Ireland itself, as the election of 1918 showed, the main victim of the war had been the historic Irish Party dedicated to the pursuit of home rule through parliamentary pressure at Westminster. The underground workings of the conspiratorial and violent elements of the nationalist movement had culminated in the Easter Rising of 1916; its repression had been exploited by the revived Sinn Fein seeking an independent republic and looking to a Peace Conference that would, it expected, be dominated either by Germany or by the United States to impose separation. Interlocking with the political leadership of Sinn Fein were bodies that hoped to bring about the same end by the use of military force. The new wave of Irish national-ism, young and lower middle class in its leadership, thus resembling nationalist movements on the European continent that were also threatening the structure of the established empires, could exploit economic discontent without necessarily a commitment to social revolution. Irish labour which had shared in the pre–1914 unrest was involved by its principal leader James Connolly in the Easter Rising and remained subservient to the nationalist leadership, seeking no independent rôle.

The efforts made during the war to find a solution on the basis of the settlement plans suspended in 1914 – home rule with some special arrangements for Ulster – had come to grief on the familiar obstacles. The negotiations in 1916 between Lloyd George and Redmond cul-minated in an agreement that the 1914 Home Rule Act should be brought into effect as soon as possible with the six counties of Ulster

[47] For a cultural interpretation of the Anglo-Irish conflict, see F.S.L. Lyons, *Culture and Anarchy in Ireland 1890–1939* (Oxford, 1979); for an important contribution to understanding the historical roots of the Ulster problem, see A.T.Q. Stewart, *The Narrow Ground: Aspects of Ulster 1609–1969* (London, 1977).

[48] See F.M. Carroll, *American Opinion and the Irish Question 1910–1923: a Study in Opinion and Policy* (Dublin, 1978).

excluded – Redmond being led to believe that the exclusion would be temporary, Carson having received a pledge that they would be permanent. While Ulster could be persuaded to accept this situation, and while concessions were also made to Britain's strategic requirements, it offered nothing to southern Unionists who also feared that the credit for home rule would go to the extremists and be a prelude to further pressures for full independence. It was therefore understandable that it was the principal southern Unionist in Asquith's cabinet, Lord Lansdowne, who should have torpedoed the plan both by his opposition in cabinet and by a speech in the House of Lords which spelled out the limitations of the agreement from the Irish point of view.

The second initiative was due largely to American pressure after the Americans entered the war to furnish President Wilson with arguments to enable him to disarm the Irish-American lobby. It took the shape of a Convention of Irishmen meeting in Dublin under the chairmanship of the distinguished but non-political Sir Horace Plunkett, the apostle of co-operation and agricultural improvement, to try to find some new formula for a settlement.[49] From the beginning, the enterprise was doomed. It was not representative since neither Sinn Fein nor organized Labour agreed to be represented while the Ulster Unionists remained adamant in their demands for exclusion. Redmond's attempt to find common ground with southern Unionism even to the extent of abandoning or limiting the right of a future Irish Parliament to levy its own customs duties met with no response, and further weakened the cohesion of the Irish Party. Although the very existence of the Convention which sat from July 1917 to the spring of 1918 helped to remove the pressure on Lloyd George and on Redmond, it proved as unable to square the circle as any of its predecessors along the road to seeking agreed solutions to the Irish problem. Nor in the military crisis of early 1918 were the Unionists ready to accept Lloyd George's final offer of a home rule bill in return for Irish conscription. Irish conscription, passed into law in April but never implemented, provided yet another incentive to the Irish to accept nationalist leadership and the authority of the paramilitary bodies speaking in its name. The 1918 House of Commons was more unsympathetic to Irish aspirations than any House of Commons since Gladstone's conversion to home rule and Lloyd George himself neither trusted the Irish nor was trusted by them.

During 1919 the position remained somewhat frozen at least as seen from outside. Ireland was subject virtually to military government, at least outside Ulster, while the newly elected Sinn Fein MPs formed their own parliament, the Dail and its shadow ministry pro-

---

[49] See R. B. McDowell, *The Irish Convention 1917–1918* (London, 1970).

ceeded to build up or co-ordinate the underground activities of other shadow institutions in central and local government, and in the judicial sphere. It was a paradoxical situation with two conflicting demands made upon each individual citizen, but so long as the position could be contained at a relatively peaceful level, the British government had more urgent matters on the agenda.[50] The Peace Conference proved a disappointment to those in Ireland who had placed their hopes on internationalizing the Irish problem. No opportunity was provided for the provisional government to present its case and President Wilson refused to embrace the Irish cause, having clashed with some of the Irish-American leaders over other aspects of his policy, notably his commitment to the creation of a League of Nations. It had been shown that what Irish-Americans could offer was not political leverage but money; and with money in a post-war world it was always posible to procure arms.

The political rebuff to Ireland's claims and the availability of weapons led to violence taking the form largely of attacks upon the police which in turn made it possible to acquire further arms. Beginning towards the end of 1919 much of the country was the scene of intermittent guerrilla warface. Waged on the Irish side by small groups not in uniform and easily blending with the civilian population it is understandable that counter-action took on ugly forms. The battered Royal Irish Constabulary – the principal victims – were rapidly reinforced by English ex-soldiers – the 'Black and Tans' – and by a shock force of ex-officers – the Auxiliaries. The army itself – despite the calls upon its depleted forces for other duties overseas – was rapidly reinforced.

By the latter part of 1920, the British counter-measures had begun to have their effect and on both sides violence reached a new intensity in the closing months of the year. In 1921 the Irish developed tactics of ambush and assassination whose dreary toll continued until a truce was arrived at in July 1921. The truce came as the culmination of a series of contacts designed to explore the possibilities of a peaceful settlement, bedevilled throughout not merely by the familiar problems of the content of such a settlement but also by uncertainty as to the nature of the authority responsible for the Irish violence and of its capacity to make binding undertakings. Nor, as events proved, was this uncertainty unwarranted.

In the meantime, the government had to some extent tied its own hands through the passage of the Government of Ireland Act in 1920 purporting to set up separate parliaments in southern Ireland and in

[50] An inside view of the British government's wrestling with the Irish problem is available in the private diaries of the assistant secretary of the cabinet: Thomas Jones, *Whitehall Diary* , ed. K. Middlemas. Vol. III: *Ireland 1918-1925* (London, 1971).

Ulster with a somewhat shadowy Council of Ireland to form a link between them. And in May 1921 the new Ulster parliament was in fact elected with its inevitable and entrenched Unionist majority. The southern Irish used the machinery provided in order to elect a new and enlarged Dail. What the truce amounted to was then a willingness to negotiate with the Sinn Fein leadership in order to see whether by giving a greater measure of independence in fact as well as in theory to a southern Irish parliament, it was possible to exact acceptance of the Ulster status quo.

As so often in the history of Britain's imperial retreat of which this was to prove the first stage, the decisive factor was not the military one.[51] Despite initial disadvantages owing to poor planning, inadequate intelligence and the uneasy relationship between the three strands of civil administration, the police and the military, there is every reason to believe that the guerrilla fighters could have been crushed as the Boers had been. Indeed the Republican leaders were themselves to confess after the event that they had been on the verge of defeat. What brought about the acquiescence of the cabinet to what many conservatives saw as parleying with treason was the effect of the violence upon opinion at home, and to a lesser extent abroad. While Unionists such as Bonar Law, Balfour, Walter Long, Field Marshal French, the Lord Lieutenant, and Sir Henry Wilson, who on retirement from the post of Chief of the Imperial General Staff in December 1921 became military adviser to the new government in Ulster, believed that the Union was justified by Britain's strategic needs and had no qualms about the use of force to defend it against a people for whom they had something like contempt, the Liberals were more reluctant to abandon their home rule commitment – though they were appalled by the self-identification of Sinn Fein with terrorism. It was the concentration of the Liberal press upon the evils of the British reprisals that shook their resolution, and Irish propaganda made the most of their moral qualms.[52]

The negotiations that followed the truce and which occupied the attention of Lloyd George and his senior colleagues between October 1921 and the signature of the Anglo-Irish treaty on 6 December were long and painful, illustrating the uncertainties on both sides.[53] Yet

---

[51] The British military dilemma is fully explored in Charles Townshend, *The British Campaign in Ireland 1919–1921: the Development of Political and Military Policies* (London, 1975).

[52] For the propaganda war see D.E. Boyce, *Englishmen and Irish Troubles: British Public Opinion and the Making of Irish Policy 1918–1922* (London, 1972).

[53] The account of the negotiations given by Frank Pakenham (later the Earl of Longford) in his *Peace by Ordeal* first published in 1935 (London; 2nd ed. Cork, 1951) has not been superseded. The volume includes the text of the treaty itself. Lloyd George's skill in negotiation is well brought out (chap. 12).

their outcome was a fair reflection of the limits to which the two sides could go. British opinion – even Liberal opinion – while now aroused against the coercion of Ireland by England would not countenance the coercion of Ulster. In the last resort Britain could renew the war. To some extent the issue was fudged by the provision that the Six Counties' boundary would be subject to revision by a boundary commission, and the Irish belief that their recommendations if they took account of Catholic and hence nationalist enclaves might be such as to render the separate existence of the Ulster government unviable.[54] For the rest of Ireland after the rejection of the idea that it might be a republic associated with but outside the Commonwealth, agreement was reached on what amounted to Dominion status for an Irish Free State with particular provision made for Britain's defence needs through the retention of certain naval facilities – a provision to which the Irish negotiators rather curiously made little objection at the time.

The treaty was not the end of the story. Although it was eventually ratified by the Dail, its opponents led by de Valera, sole survivor of the leaders of the 1916 uprising, embarked upon a civil war against the new Free State which caused much more bloodletting before ending in a truce in May 1923 and which at moments overflowed into violence against the new government in Ulster. On the British side, the treaty gave relief to the pressures upon the British army and budget. It meant also the final eclipse of Southern Unionism as a force in British politics and with the personal eclipse of Carson, for a time of Ulster Unionism as well. On the other hand, it was not easy for English adherents of the Conservative and Unionist party to forgive those who had finally acquiesced in the destruction of the Union, and who had gone well beyond the home rule which it had been part of their political creed to reject. The four principal negotiators on the government side, Lloyd George himself and Churchill for the Liberals, Austen Chamberlain and Birkenhead for the Conservatives were to be the principal political victims of the Conservative uprising against the coalition in the autumn of 1922.

An added reason for the withdrawal of Conservative confidence in the Lloyd George coalition was the sentiment that the government had embarked upon, and was persisting in, a forward policy in the Middle East which had left Britain isolated without even the certainty of Dominion support. This new isolation was not entirely of Britain's making. The hopes expressed during the war and powerfully surviving in certain sections of British opinion that the participation of the United States in the final victory would presage a continued

[54] For the self-delusion of the Irish negotiators on this point see Boyce, *Englishmen and Irish Troubles* , p, 168.

period of close Anglo-American co-operation had been rendered untenable by three developments in American opinion reflected in the conduct of the American government.

It was soon clear that in pushing the claims of the new idea of a League of Nations as the central feature of a peace settlement it was not President Wilson's intention (nor would it have been within his power) to commit the United States to defending the new territorial settlement in Europe. The failure of the United States Senate to ratify the Treaty and the consequent absence of the United States from the new world organization was only a confirmation of the basic American position, not the turning point that it is sometimes made out to be. In the second place for reasons of Pacific rather than Atlantic security as well as because of the historic American dislike of the uses of British sea-power – encapsulated in the American phrase 'the freedom of the seas' – the United States was prepared to enter into a period of competitive naval building which in Britain's straitened circumstances it would be hard to match. In the third place, while the United States shared Britain's wish to see the renewal of world trade and a regime of stable exchanges and commercial non-discrimination, it was not prepared to take action to prevent the burden of war debts from playing its part in frustrating this common objective. The war debts owed by the allies were to be treated as though they were ordinary commercial transactions and it was up to the allies to meet their difficulties by the exaction of reparations from the defeated foe or at each other's expense, since money had been channelled through Britain to meet the requirements of the other allies.

No diplomacy however skilful could have dealt with the first of these issues. The strength of isolationism in the United States, confirmed by the withdrawal from intervention in Russia and by the ending of the American participation in the occupation of German territory in 1922, was a fact that had to be taken into account by successive British governments until after the outbreak of the Second World War. A solution for the war debts problems was not arrived at until after the fall of the coalition and then on unfavourable terms. On the other hand, Lloyd George's government seemed to have secured a major success on the naval side.[55] At the price of sacrificing the Anglo-Japanese alliance and of accepting purely consultative multinational arrangements for Pacific security the British achieved by a treaty concluded at Washington on 6 February 1922 a 10 year naval holiday in capital ships on the basis of a five-five-three ratio with the United

[55] On the developments leading up to the Washington Conference, see Max Beloff, *Imperial Sunset*. Vol. I: *Britain's Liberal Empire 1897–1921* (London, 1969), pp. 330–6.

States and Japan, with France and Italy accepting parity with each other at a lower figure.[56] Although the agreement was incomplete with neither cruisers nor (on France's insistence) submarines being included, the Washington Treaty did take the heat out of the Anglo-American confrontation, and renewed a unity in outlook among the countries of the British Commonwealth which had shown up deep divisions particularly over the Anglo-Japanese alliance during the Imperial Conference of the summer of 1921. Nevertheless some critics at the time pointed to the fact that Britain had effectively abandoned its three centuries of maritime supremacy, and was now in the last resort dependent upon American goodwill in the future vicissitudes of world politics. Although the participation of the Conservatives' elder statesman Balfour in the Washington negotiations helped to prevent a Conservative outcry against their results, a party very susceptible to service opinion cannot wholly have ignored these developments in assessing the government's record.

The unwillingness of France to see submarines limited by treaty because for a lesser naval power submarines were an essentially defensive weapon while for Britain, remembering their use against wartime commerce, they were essentially offensive, was only one aspect of the rift between the two former allies that developed during and after the Peace Conference.[57] In some respects a measure of disagreement over the terms of the Peace was to be expected. The experience of the two countries had been totally dissimilar. Heavy as had been Britain's losses in manpower, the French had been even harder hit and with a traditionally low birthrate would find the losses harder to make good. In addition while Britain's only important material loss had been in merchant shipping – a loss largely and quickly made up by acquiring German ships as part of reparations – France had suffered the devastation of war on her own soil so that sheer physical reconstruction was her primary need. France's fear for her security in the event – which seemed inescapable – of a German revival was enhanced by the disappearance of the Russian counterweight which had probably saved France in the autumn of 1914; Poland was a poor if necessary substitute, credible only so long as Russian power was also in abeyance. The imperative for French statesmanship was to create a new system of security primarily

[56] For the Washington Conference and Treaties, see F.S. Northedge, *The Troubled Giant: Britain among the Great Powers 1916–1939* (London, 1966), pp. 284–90.

[57] A major study of Anglo-French relations in the post-war period is badly needed, taking into account the economic and military as well as the diplomatic elements of the subject as has been done so thoroughly for Franco-German relations in J. Bariéty, *Les Relations Franco-Allemandes après la Première Guerre Mondiale: 10 Novembre 1918–10 Janvier 1925: de l'execution à la negociation* (Paris, 1977).

against Germany. The reasonableness of this approach to the problem of peacemaking was not denied by responsible opinion in Britain; though those who had sought a compromise peace during the war carried over to the peace their predilection for giving the Germans the benefit of the doubt. And even in France there were those who while more constrained in their political activities did not rule out for good an alternative policy of seeking a continental accommodation with Germany as being less burdensome and as ultimately safer than reliance upon the 'Anglo-Saxons'.[58] In some British service quarters it was believed that France's insistence on a large submarine fleet and a large air force was directly anti-British in intent.

During the Peace Conference itself, the discord between the allies revolved round methods rather than objectives. In the French view, the only safe guarantee would be a territorial one. The restoration of Alsace-Lorraine did something to redress the balance but not enough. Was it not possible to separate for good the Left bank of the Rhine, now under allied occupation as a result of the Armistice terms, and without proclaiming French sovereignty gradually to build up a Rhenish buffer-state as a protection for France's frontiers and as a permanent guarantee of access to the heart of Germany's industrial strength if the disarmament or reparations clauses of the Peace should be violated? Did there exist in the Rhineland elements of antipathy to Prussian rule and to imported Prussian bureaucrats which could be utilized to promote separatism? This point of view – that embraced by Marshal Foch who divided with Clemenceau the support of French public opinion and of President Poincaré – was in the end abandoned under pressure from Britain and America. Britain was in no position to underwrite a settlement that presupposed an indefinite occupation for which troops were and would be hard to find; nor did the British believe that the permanent separation of the Rhineland from Germany was possible or even desirable. What France received instead – though Lloyd George somewhat disingenuously denied the *quid pro quo* element – was an Anglo-American guarantee to come to her aid in the event of renewed German aggression. The occupation was to be for 15 years only with phased withdrawals at earlier dates, though with the loophole that the question of evacuation could be reconsidered if the guarantees against German aggression should come to seem insufficient or if the Germans defaulted on reparations. The Rhineland itself while politically part of the German republic was to be 'demilitarized'.

[58] Public opinion in the two countries was equally far apart in its assessment of the Peace. See R. B. McCallum, *Public Opinion and the Last Peace* (London, 1944) and the much more detailed and systematic study, Pierre Miquel, *La Paix de Versailles et l'opinion publique française* (Paris, 1971).

Clemenceau's defence against his French critics was that the continued co-operation of the allied powers and the United States was and should be the main objective of French foreign policy; but he may well have believed that Germany would in fact behave in such a way that the escape clauses could be invoked. On the British side it was perhaps more surprising that such a departure from the principle of no continental commitments should be accepted despite obvious Dominion uneasiness. The fact that when the guarantee treaties lapsed in March 1920 with the failure of the American Senate to ratify the Peace Treaty, the news should have been greeted with relief in Whitehall, suggests that from the British point of view the guarantee was not so much a radical departure in foreign policy as a way of getting round an awkward impasse in the negotiations at Paris.

Meanwhile the French retained their power to bring pressure on the Germans when required and the arrangements for the allocation of authority in the occupied zones gave the French and Belgians a built-in majority if such action seemed appropriate.

Over the settlement in eastern Europe, and the form of arms limitation to be imposed on Germany as well as over non-European questions, there was a good deal of friction but not such as to prevent an agreed text from being presented to the Germans. But that text while providing for German reparations and creating the legal grounds for them left the amounts and modalities of payment to be settled later by a Reparations Commission. And the question of reparations together with the other economic questions outstanding were at the centre of the feverish Conference diplomacy of the rest of Lloyd George's premiership. Here too differences of policy revealed differences of interest. For France, even when the heady notion that the Germans could somehow 'pay for the war' had been abandoned, there were precise needs; physical reconstruction and assistance to France's finances in order to avoid national taxation at a level which it was felt impossible to impose. Payments from the Germans were also supposed to assist in the liquidation of inter-allied debts. The French were prepared to consider direct participation of the Germans in reconstruction and in particular deliveries in kind – notably of coal in the light of the destruction in the French coalfields and the requirements of the steel industry in the newly recovered Lorraine. But arrangements of this kind threatened to compete with British coal exports, already deprived of Russian and other European markets, and this at a time when the centre of Britain's industrial unrest was in the mining industry. Indeed any arrangements for reparations other than cash seemed incompatible with the re-establishment of the 'normal channels' of trade.

It is true that for a brief moment during the war it had looked as though Britain and France might impose upon a defeated enemy a permanent position of economic dependence. This idea was reflected in the agreements reached at an inter-allied economic conference in Paris in June 1916 to prevent what was believed to be a German plan for an 'economic offensive' as soon as peace came. The most positive proposal had been to deny to the ex-enemies the 'most-favoured nation clause' common in commercial treaties.[59] Such an approach had been substantially abandoned by the British government before the end of the war, despite the hopes placed in it by the advocates of protectionism and imperial preference.[60] The French had however wished to retain the possibility of discriminatory commercial action in their armoury and had denounced all existing commercial treaties containing the most-favoured nation clause. By the Treaty of Versailles, the most-favoured nation clause was imposed unilaterally upon Germany for a period of five years.[61] But the British wish to see the old commercial order restored remained apparent.

In order to improve the British share of the claims made against Germany, the bill for war pensions had been included among her liabilities – thus swelling the total without solving the problem of the modalities of payment across the exchanges. The inter-allied conferences had to deal with ths question and that of the shares of the victor powers in whatever could be extracted which was settled at the Spa Conference in July 1920. Throughout the period the British took a largely economic view of the issues; the French were more concerned to keep Germany in a position of weakness, strong enough to resist the Bolshevik contagion but not strong enough to threaten France or her eastern neighbours. Germany was constantly suspected of not fulfilling the disarmament clauses of the Treaty. In 1920 the French appeared ready to go some way along the British road after the extension of the occupation area on the right bank of the Rhine. Plans for the extension of the occupation to include the Ruhr were ready when in April 1921 the total of Germany's obligations was settled by the Reparations Commission. In May the Germans accepted the proposed schedule of payments. Thereafter Anglo-French differences hardened. There was a crisis in July over Upper Silesia. An attempt by the French to come to terms with the Germans direct by the Wiesbaden agreements of 6–7 October 1921 broke down for reasons largely of French internal politics, and because the settlement of the Upper Silesia issue by the League of Nations went so far in favour of

---

[59] V. H. Rothwell, *British War Aims and Peace Diplomacy 1914–1918* (Oxford, 1971), pp. 267–9.

[60] See the importance attached to it by W.A.S. Hewins in his diary entries reprinted in Vol. II of *The Apologia of an Imperialist: Forty Years of Empire Policy* (London, 1929).

[61] Bariéty, *Les Relations Franco-Allemandes*, pp. 178–9.

France's ally Poland as to reanimate German suspicions of the French.

It was now Britain's turn to attempt an agreement with the Germans and during a long visit to London in December 1921, Rathenau, the German Minister of Reconstruction, seems to have received enough encouragement from Lloyd George to ask later in the month for a moratorium on Germany's payments.[62] The whole issue between reparations in kind favoured by the French and the British case for monetary settlements was again pushed into the limelight. The Cannes Conference of January 1922 neither improved Anglo-French relations nor saved the ministry of Briand which had been identified with a revisionist approach. The idea canvassed in the Foreign Office that France might be won over by a direct British alliance to replace the lapsed Anglo-American guarantees had been discussed by Lloyd George with Briand in December but France's unwillingness to separate her security from that of Poland and differences over the Middle East and the rest of eastern Europe were impediments to any progress along these lines.

The idea was revived in conversations with Poincaré, Briand's successor, but proved unattractive to the French in any form that Britain could contemplate. The Genoa Conference in April 1922 which was intended by Lloyd George to see Europe set out on a new road of reconciliation proved a fiasco. The Russo-German Treaty of Rapallo of 16 April could be seen as confirming Lloyd George's preference for a more lenient treatment of both countries; for the French it was an additional proof that the Germans were not to be trusted. The spectacular recovery of the German steel industry despite reparations added to their fears. The decline in the value of the German currency and the social strains this was producing in Germany did not appear to be weakening the great German industrial combines. German objections to reparation payments appeared economically implausible and hence politically sinister. Attempts to bring about a direct understanding between French and German industrialists met with strong opposition from Poincaré. By the summer of 1922 France's intention of occupying the Ruhr as soon as Germany was shown to be in palpable breach of its obligations was apparent to the British government, nor was it much consolation, given the isolationist mood of the United States, to know that such a move would be disapproved of in Washington as well as in London.

The principal legacy hitherto of the brief American intervention in

---

[62] Rathenau claimed that the allies had given insufficient recognition to Germany's rôle as a bulwark against Bolshevism and discussed the possibility of international action by industrialists to put Russia on her feet economically. Walter Rathenau, *Tagebuch 1907–1922* (Düsseldorf, 1967), pp. 263–73.

the European war and its settlement was the League of Nations which became very much a European affair, and with the exclusion of the ex-enemies and of Russia too, was inevitably dominated by Britain on the one hand and France and her east European associates on the other. Its ability to contribute to European security as the French saw it would depend upon the interpretations placed upon its Covenant. More immediately however it provided the machinery by which the defeated powers could be stripped of their empires without the victors incurring the guilt of annexation. The allocation of mandates was in fact determined by the wishes of the victors though in the case of those territories taken from the Turkish Empire it was provided that they should eventually graduate to full independence.

The disagreement with France over European policy was aggravated by a persistent rivalry in the Middle East where Britain had declared a Protectorate over Egypt in December 1914 and where her plans for a major rôle in the remaining Arab provinces of the former Turkish Empire ran up against France's long-standing claims particularly in Syria and the Lebanon. The first attempt to resolve these differences, the Sykes–Picot agreement of 16 May 1916, had been overtaken by the Russian Revolution, the Arab revolt and the British pledge to create a Jewish National Home in Palestine enshrined in the Balfour Declaration of 31 October 1917. Expectations had been aroused at home and abroad which were hardly capable of reconciliation.[63] In particular those imperial servants who felt that Arab nationalism offered the best security for the British presence were difficult to convince that there was room for another western power. The India Office, the War Office and the Admiralty all had their particular aims to satisfy and the oil-fields of Mosul gave a particular importance to Mesopotamia (Iraq) and its frontier with Turkey. If it had been possible to associate the Americans with the settlement as mandatories for Palestine or Armenia the direct confrontation with the French might have been easier to avoid. But by the end of 1919 it was clear that while the Americans might continue to display an interest, notably in the affairs of Palestine, they would not accept any form of direct responsibility.

The Treaty of San Remo in April 1920 kept fairly closely to the wartime dispositions.[64] Syria, where Faisal, a member of the Hashimite dynasty of the Hedjaz much favoured by the British and in particular by Colonel T.E. Lawrence, whose activities figured largely in France's suspicions, had declared himself king, was allotted to France along with the Lebanon; Palestine and Mesopotamia

---

[63] See Beloff, *Imperial Sunset* I, pp. 254–64 and 297–306.
[64] See Paul C. Helmreich, *From Paris to Sèvres: the Partition of the Ottoman Empire at the Peace Conference of 1919–1920* (Columbus, 1974).

including Mosul went to Britain. Faisal refused to accept the San Remo Treaty and was expelled by the French. At the same time the British had to face major troubles in Mesopotamia following a reduction in British strength – the presence of British forces in Mesopotamia was one of the main targets of the economizers at home. It was decided that the best hope was to try to harness the nationalist tide and Faisal himself accepted the throne of Iraq in December 1920.

This arrangement was confirmed at a conference in Cairo in March 1921, presided over by Churchill as Colonial Secretary – since it was that department that had come out on top as far as Whitehall's internecine warfare was concerned.[65] On 1 July 1920 Sir Herbert Samuel, the former Liberal Home Secretary and a Zionist sympathizer though not a Zionist, had taken over from the military government as the first High Commissioner of the mandated territory of Palestine. The question of its boundaries remained unsettled. Faisal had claimed the area east of the Jordan as part of his Syrian kingdom but in the Treaty of San Remo that area had been allotted to Britain. It was now decided to turn it into a separate emirate of Trans-Jordan for the benefit of Faisal's brother Abdullah, himself a former candidate for the throne of Iraq. Although his authority was subordinate to that of the High Commissioner for Palestine, Trans-Jordan was thus excluded from the area open to Jewish settlement. In May 1921 there took place the first outbreak of Arab violence against Jewish settlement in Palestine itself, giving an intimation of the enormous and perhaps insuperable difficulties that Britain would find in applying ideas of democratic rule to so deeply divided a society.[66]

Even more crucial for relations with France was the question of what should be done with the non-Arab parts of Turkey and above all with Constantinople and the Straits. Although there were Admiralty objections, Lloyd George himself would have been prepared to see the United States become the mandatory power at Constantinople (as well as in Armenia) but when this prospect disappeared, a clear divergence of view presented itself. The position had been complicated by the landing of Greek troops in Smyrna with the approval of the Supreme Allied Council and by the establishment in central Anatolia of a rival government to that of the Sultan – a regime inspired by

---

[65] See Aron S. Klieman, *The Foundations of British Policy in the Arab World: the Cairo Conference of 1921* (Baltimore, 1970).

[66] The difficulties of holding the balance were intensified by the conviction on the part of many of the soldiers and civil administrators on the spot that the Zionist commitment had been an error and by their personal inclinations towards the Arabs. See Bernard Wasserstein, *The British in Palestine: the Mandatory Government and the Arab-Jewish Conflict 1917–1929* (London, 1978).

nationalist sentiment and not averse to receiving help from the Russians if this were necessary to balance the pressure from the western powers.

In these circumstances, the British wished to see the Turks deprived of Constantinople and territorial concessions made to the Greeks. The French preferred to see the Sultan remain at Constantinople where he would be subject to allied pressure. In February 1920 Lloyd George accepted this view largely under domestic pressure – his phil-Hellenism was not widely shared – but got an agreement for some form of international control of the Straits. The peace treaty drawn up at the San Remo Conference and eventually signed by the Turks as the Treaty of Sèvres in August 1921 – the allies had been in occupation of Constantinople since March – was unrealistic in that it took no account of the gathering strength of the Kemalist movement. The French had suffered a military reverse in Cilicia in February 1921 and both they and the Italians who had also made territorial claims had decided not to get further embroiled with Turkish nationalism. On 20 October the French concluded an agreement with Kemal and finally separated themselves from the British pro-Greek stance.

By this time however the situation was no longer a matter of the Prime Minister's phil-Hellenism. For the re-establishment of the Turks at Constantinople in sovereign command of the Straits at a time when the intimate relations between the Kemalist movement and the Bolsheviks were common knowledge was bound to look like the abandonment of one of Britain's principal gains from the war. The losses at Gallipoli were also bound to weigh with Churchill who was along with Lloyd George the principal opponent of giving way to the Turks. Thus while France's withdrawal from the scene – and Italy's stepping aside in the final crisis – had been at least in part because of the repercussions they feared among their own Moslem subjects, the British government resisted the strong pleas from the government of India for a less anti-Turkish line. When this divergence was publicly pressed in March 1922 by Edwin Montagu, the Secretary of State, Lloyd George removed him from office.

It was true that Montagu had by now become a political liability. The rapid development of the movement towards greater association of Indians with the government of their country since his assumption of office in 1917, and the fact that the passage of the Government of India Act of 1919 which embodied the principles of the Montagu-Chelmsford report of the previous year had not dissuaded Indian political leaders from pressing the case for complete self-government to the point of civil disobedience and actual disorder, did not endear him to most Conservatives.[67] The dismissal of General R.E. Dyer after the Amritsar massacre of 13 April 1920 was denounced by a large number of Members of Parliament and by a majority in the House of Lords. The parliamentary debates in July 1920 were notable for the fierceness of the attacks upon Montagu personally and for the overt anti-semitism expressed by some of his adversaries.[68]

The crisis over relations with the Turks came in September 1922 after their destruction of the Greek army at Smyrna and the subsequent massacre of the civilian population when a small force of British troops at Chanak faced the advancing Kemalists. The question of how far to go in resistance was complicated by the discovery following an appeal by Churchill for Commonwealth troops that on this issue the unity of the Commonwealth simply did not exist. It was complicated by an error in timing that meant that the Canadian Prime Minister first read of the appeal in the press.[69] The 'freedom of the Straits' might mean something to New Zealanders and Australians, but even the Australians were hesitant to commit themselves and the Canadians and South Africans saw no relevance in the crisis to their own needs. The good sense of the commander on the spot, General Harington, and Kemal's unwillingness to take on the British as well as the Greeks gave the government time. Conversations with the French and Italians brought about a readiness to revise the Treaty of Sèvres in Kemal's favour and by the Convention of Mudania on 11 October hostilities were brought to an end on terms substantially favourable to the Turks, but allowing the allies to remain at Constantinople and on the Straits until a new peace settlement had been arrived at to replace the ill-fated Treaty of Sèvres.[70]

By this time, however, the prospect of a peaceful settlement was too late to assist the Coalition. On 7 October Bonar Law, the former Conservative leader who had retired from the cabinet on health grounds in March 1921, had returned to the political fray with a letter

[67] An important study of the rôle of India and its army in the imperial system at this time and of the impact of the Montagu – Chelmsford ideas upon the viability of the Raj is to be found in Algernon Rumbold, *Watershed in India 1914–1922* (London, 1979).

[68] The Coalition government was regarded by its right-wing critics as too receptive to Jewish influences – some Jews prominent in business life were of course also seen as tainted by their German origins. Apart from Montagu, Sir Alfred Mond, Minister of Health from April 1921, was the only Jew to reach cabinet rank under Lloyd George; but the appointment of the Lord Chief Justice, Lord Reading, to be Viceroy of India in April 1921 following that of Sir Herbert Samuel to the High Commissionership in Palestine helped to fuel the agitation and revive memories of the pre-war 'Marconi scandal'. For the whole topic, see G.C. Lebzelter, *Political Anti-Semitism in England 1918–1939* (London, 1978).

[69] C. P. Stacey, *Canada and the Age of Conflict: a History of Canadian External Policies* . Vol. II : *1921–1948, the Mackenzie King Era* (Toronto, 1981), pp. 17–31.

[70] On the Chanak story see David Walder, *The Chanak Affair* (London, 1969). For its effects within the British cabinet see J. G. Darwin, 'The Chanak Crisis and the British Cabinet', *History* LXV (1980).

to the press declaring his belief that no action should be taken in the Middle East without French agreement and that Britain could not 'act alone as the policeman of the world'. Its impact upon the gathering discontent within the party was weighty. Lloyd George and his principal associates were believed to be contemplating an early general election in order to prolong the life of the Coalition in its existing form. Austen Chamberlain, the successor to Bonar Law as Conservative leader, was prepared to accept this course as was Birkenhead. But Curzon, the Foreign Secretary, whose loyalty had been progressively strained did not follow them, and became one of the rebels whose obvious unwillingness to see the Coalition perpetuated obliged Chamberlain to call a party meeting to decide the issue.

On the morning of 19 October it was revealed that the Conservatives who had decided locally to fight the seat had won the Newport by-election, thus suggesting that the idea that only Lloyd George's continued leadership could hold off Labour was an illusion.[71] At the Carlton Club meeting that afternoon the Conservatives voted 187 to 87, after a debate in which Bonar Law's was the crucial voice, to end the Coalition and to fight the next election as an independent party. By the evening Lloyd George had resigned and the Coalition was at an end.

Somewhat ironically, the difficulties with the Turks renewed themselves after the fall of the government. Kemal denounced the Convention of Mudania and all treaties concluded by the Sultan's government and on 5 November the Kemalists seized Constantinople where the Sultan under allied protection still exercised a shadowy sovereignty. Again it appeared that the neutral zones held by British troops might be over-run, and the need to stand firm accepted by the new government received general support, and may indeed have helped its election campaign, though by polling-day with an agreement with the French achieved, the new crisis was more or less at an end.[72]

Too much should not be made of this postscript since although the Chanak incident did show up what some Conservatives found most alarming about the Lloyd George regime, its apparent willingness to take new and expensive risks in isolation and on this occasion even without Commonwealth support, the process of disentangling the party from its commitment to the Coalition had been gathering strength among ministers, particularly junior ministers, back benchers and activists in the country for quite a long time. A govern-

---

[71] Both the Conservatives and Labour had expected a Labour victory. Policy in the Near East was not an issue as all three candidates opposed the government line. See the article on the Newport by-election by John Ramsden in C. Cook and J.A. Ramsden, eds., *By-Elections in British Politics* (London, 1973).

[72] M. Kinnear, *The Fall of Lloyd George: the Political Crisis of 1922* (London, 1973), pp. 166–74.

ment which had presided over a period of depression, high unemployment and severe deflation, affecting both wages and social services and much labour unrest could not expect popularity and was almost certain to lose the favour of the electorate; during 1922 there were some ominous by-election swings against the Coalition. With the ordinary voter these reasons for distrusting the government may have been as important as the resentment closer to the political scene of what seemed the distant, self-seeking cosmopolitan life-style of the Prime Minister and his friends in politics and Fleet Street.[73]

An independent Conservative party seemed in these circumstances more likely to win the favour of the voters if enabled to repudiate the inheritance of the existing government. For Conservatives within the government who might aspire to promotion or those outside it who might hope for office, the prospect of sharing out the not inconsiderable number of posts occupied by the Coalition Liberals was attractive, even if one discounts the expectation that the removal of the latter from office might remove the impediment to full-scale protection with imperial preference which for some members of the party was still the cause they had most at heart.

The general view among historians has been the same as that of so many contemporaries, namely that the Lloyd George government in peacetime betrayed the hopes placed in it by failing to carry forward the massive reconstruction of the country's economic and social fabric, the need for which had been demonstrated by the war. It has been argued that Lloyd George's machinery for planning such changes was inferior to that which he had inherited from Asquith and that if controls had not been abandoned so soon and the much vaunted pledge of a great housing programme carried through, the alienation of Labour from the government might have been prevented.[74]

Recent research has taken a more positive view of the merits of the Coalition government and pointed to the fact that the inauguration of universal state insurance against unemployment, the measures taken on pensions and social security, the creation of the Ministry of Health, as well as the Education Act make up a formidable list of achievements. It is also claimed that to some extent the government was hampered by the unwillingness of local authorities to act on the new powers conferred upon them.[75] On the other hand, it is also the

[73] The fear that the Lloyd George style of government was stimulating hostility to the ruling classes among working people is effectively put by Cowling, *Impact of Labour* , pp. 242–3.

[74] See e.g. P.B. Johnson, *Land Fit for Heroes: the Planning of British Reconstruction 1916–1919* (Chicago, 1969).

[75] See Kenneth O. Morgan, *Consensus and Disunity: the Lloyd George Coalition Government 1918–1922* (Oxford, 1979).

case that much of the constructive work relates to the earlier years of
the government and that Addison's resignation as Minister of Health
after the curtailment of his housing programme in July 1921 did mark
the culmination of a swing towards less expansive policies.[76] Yet
again, as the election was to show, the swing reflected the balance of
electoral opinion and it was only in the longer run that Labour was
able to benefit from the ending of the last period of Liberal reform.

[76] K. and J. Morgan, *Portrait of a Progressive: the Political Career of Christopher, Viscount Addison*
(Oxford, 1980).

4   The Conservatives Return

The task of creating a Bonar Law administration did not prove difficult in spite of the omission of the senior Conservatives who had continued to support Lloyd George: Austen Chamberlain himself, Balfour, Birkenhead and Sir Robert Horne, Chancellor of the Exchequer since April 1921, who after a meteoric ministerial career now left office never to return. Bonar Law was able to use the services of a number of Conservatives with previous ministerial experience as well as the two senior ministers from among the rebels against Lloyd George, Curzon who remained at the Foreign Office and Stanley Baldwin, the President of the Board of Trade who became the new Chancellor.

The election that followed was fought on party lines except in Scotland where Conservatives proved reluctant to attack seats held by Coalition Liberals.[1] In England there were some constituencies where arrangements were made between Coalition Liberals and Conservatives – facilitated by the survival of a few two-member constituencies. Of the 615 seats, 483 were fought by the Conservatives, 162 by Lloyd George's National Liberals, 328 by Asquithian Liberals and no fewer than 411 by Labour. The final result which concealed some movements of political allegiance in opposite directions was a decisive victory for the new government with 344 seats. Labour made an expected advance to 142 seats; of the 115 Liberals, 62 followed the Asquith and 53 the Lloyd George banner. The apparent recovery of the Asquithian Liberals looked a hollow one when it could be seen that their gains lay very largely in rural seats where Labour had little chance of winning. It might thus be thought of as an anti-Coalition protest given added force by the government's failure to tackle the decline in farm prices which bore heavily on the large numbers of farmers who had bought farms between 1918 and 1922. In terms of the national vote, the Conservatives won 38.5 per cent, Labour 29.4 per cent and the Liberals 29.1 per cent.

[1] The election results are analysed in detail in Chris Cook, *The Age of Alignment: Electoral Politics in Britain 1922–1929* (London, 1975), pp. 17–26.

Labour's successes were highly concentrated in the mining areas, in Glasgow and on the Clyde and in parts of London. In some industrial areas including the textile districts of East Lancashire and West Yorkshire, it lost ground and it was obviously far from being able to make headway in rural areas or the smaller cities and towns of southern England. Against these geographical restrictions could be set the advantage that in many Labour seats there were clear and often large majorities over the other two parties, so that the party now had a solid core of support even if one heavily emphasizing the party's dependence upon the major unions.

In personal terms, the Conservatives were obviously the most successful. Only one minister, Griffith-Boscawen at Health, failed to retain his seat or to win another at a by-election, thus enabling Bonar Law to promote Neville Chamberlain into the cabinet in March 1923. Labour's ranks enjoyed a major infusion of strength. Side by side with the trade union phalanx there were for the first time a large number of professional people including university graduates; the party's range in Parliament was in this sense broader than its electoral base. Arthur Henderson had already been returned to Parliament in a by-election, he was now rejoined by MacDonald, Snowden, and Lansbury. Among former Liberal MPs now on the Labour benches were Arthur Ponsonby and Charles Trevelyan; with them was E.D. Morel; together they represented the core of the UDC. Other new members were Sidney Webb, Clement Attlee, Herbert Morrison, now emerging as the unquestioned boss of the London Labour Party, and among the Clydeside contingent, Emanuel Shinwell, James Maxton, and John Wheatley. It was clear that a party with a considerable and varied array of talents of this kind could be expected to act as an effective Opposition and to put itself forward as an alternative government. Its intention to fulfil these expectations was demonstrated when despite its normal tenderness to office-holders, it replaced as Leader in the House of Commons the somewhat ineffective Clynes with Ramsay MacDonald himself.[2]

The Asquithian Liberals were fortified by the return of Asquith himself, though they had lost Donald Maclean who had led the Asquithian remnant in the 1918–22 Parliament. The real disaster was that which befell the Coalition Liberals whose losses included the seats of Churchill, Hamar Greenwood, the last Chief Secretary for Ireland, and the Chief Whip F.E. Guest. Of the Liberal government that had taken England into the war, only Asquith, Lloyd George and John

---

[2] For the somewhat controversial aspects of MacDonald's election to the leadership, see David Marquand, *Ramsay MacDonald* (London, 1977), pp. 285–7.

Simon remained as members of the House of Commons.[3] Even to take part in a government it would be necessary to call on veterans in the House of Lords like Grey and Crewe; Haldane was by now clearly moving towards Labour.[4] The narrowness of the margins in popular votes and in seats between Labour and the combined forces of the Liberals did not represent the true ratio of strength. By and large those elements in the intellectual world who regarded themselves as on the side of progress were being attracted to Labour as the true party of movement as they had been attracted to Liberalism at an earlier time.[5] In part this was due to the alienation from Lloyd George of his erstwhile radical supporters; thus when the Liberals came together again in 1923 the radical journalist H.W. Massingham took the occasion of going over to Labour. The only obstacle to this movement towards Labour was the fear which Massingham himself shared that the dominance of the trade unions would still mean that Labour was a class party rather than one truly national in its makeup and outlook. It was this feeling that kept other intellectuals of the Left like the social historians the Hammonds, and the Greek scholar and propagandist for the League of Nations Gilbert Murray, in the Liberal camp where they were to be joined in the twenties by members of a younger generation such at J.M. Keynes. He suspected that Labour did not have the intellectual flexibility to deal with the economic problems that were increasingly to preoccupy the governments of the post-war world.[6]

In a longer retrospect one can see that the fall of the Coalition was the signal of a generational shift. Two of the senior statesmen who left office at this time – Austen Chamberlain and Balfour – were to hold office again and Curzon also represented continuity with an earlier age; Asquith was to be regarded briefly again as a possible Prime Minister and the party politics of the 1920s and 1930s are hardly to be understood without remembering the constant preoccupation of senior politicians with the possibility of Lloyd George's return to power and their determination not to let it happen.[7] But for the next quarter of a century Britain's place in the world would very largely depend upon the successes and failures in confronting the new problems of the age of 15 statesmen born between 1866 and 1885 and

---

[3] Asquith had lost his seat in the 1918 election but had been elected for Paisley at a by – election in 1920.

[4] For Haldane's shift in political sympathies, see Dudley Sommer, *Haldane of Cloan: his Life and Times 1856–1928* (London, 1960), pp. 373–5.

[5] On the identification of intellectuals with the Liberal Party in the 1860s, see Ian Bradley, *The Optimists: Themes and Personalities in Victorian Liberalism* (London, 1980), pp. 32ff.

[6] Peter Clarke, *Liberals and Social Democrats* (Cambridge, 1978), pp. 237–8.

[7] For a study of Lloyd George's career after 1922, see John C. Campbell, *Lloyd George: the Goat in the Wilderness* (London, 1977).

whose political apprenticeship had for the most part come in the Edwardian period.

In order of seniority they were Arthur Henderson (born 1863), Philip Snowden (born 1864), Ramsay MacDonald (born 1866), Stanley Baldwin (born 1867), Neville Chamberlain (born 1869), F.E. Smith (Lord Birkenhead) and John Simon (both born in 1873), Winston Churchill and J.H. Thomas (both born in 1874), Samuel Hoare (later Lord Templewood) (born 1880), Edward Wood (later Viscount Irwin and Earl of Halifax) and Ernest Bevin (both born in 1881) and Clement Attlee (born 1883). Churchill had been the first to enter the House of Commons (in 1900) and was the first and would be the last to hold office. Most of the others entered the House of Commons before 1911, though Chamberlain had to wait until 1919, Attlee until 1922 and Bevin, the dominant figure in the trade union movement, until he was found a seat on becoming a member of the war cabinet in 1940.

The statesmen of this generation spanned a wider social spectrum than their predecessors. The aristocratic element was reduced, though this was not the impression conveyed by Bonar Law's cabinet which could boast of a duke, two marquesses, an earl and two viscounts. It was the last cabinet in British history to contain a Derby and a Devonshire as well as a Salisbury. But among the future leaders named, most can best be described as middle class though with an element drawn for the first time from clearly proletarian origins. Age may often be a more important factor than class in determining attitudes towards policy, since ideas often harden early in life. This consideration is particularly true in relation to foreign affairs; politicians keep themselves more easily abreast of the domestic scene. In the year of the Bolshevik Revolution, the oldest of the group, Henderson, was 54, the youngest, Attlee, 34; when Hitler came to power, MacDonald was 66, Baldwin 65 and Neville Chamberlain 63.

It was unlikely that any deficiency in imagination or expert knowledge would be made up for by officials. Part of the impetus that carried Bonar Law to power was a product of impatience with the innovations that Lloyd George had introduced into the machinery of government. The rôle played by private agents in foreign policy on Lloyd George's behalf disappeared – all that was left by now of the 'garden suburb'. Even the cabinet secretariat was for a time under severe threat. It lost to the Foreign Office the responsibility for servicing international conferences and Hankey no longer acted as the Prime Minister's adviser on foreign policy. The Foreign Office also became responsible for Britain's participation in the Reparations Commission, but the actual representative, Sir John Bradbury, one of the wartime permanent secretaries to the Treasury, had very considerable influence. The biggest obstacle to the re-establishment of the authority of the Foreign Office was for the moment the War Office since policy in respect of occupied Germany was a matter for the Inter-Allied Military Commission.[8] But the future of the Foreign Office seemed assured by the fact that it avoided absorption into Warren Fisher's domestic civil service empire.

The war had produced proposals for more specialized training for officials, particularly in respect of Russian affairs, but nothing had been done. The linguistic expertise that diplomats were encouraged to acquire took second place in their postings to sheer administrative convenience. The only important change carried out before Sir Eyre Crowe succeeded Lord Hardinge as Permanent Under-Secretary in November 1920 was the amalgamation of the Foreign Office and the diplomatic service as recommended by the 1911–14 Royal Commission. And Treasury parsimony made even this reform incomplete.[9]

For the time being the Consular service remained separate, though with the decline of extra-territoriality in the Levant and the Far East, the old specialized services declined and were merged in the general consular service by 1935.[10] The foundation of the new Department of Overseas Trade in 1917 meant an increasing concern for trade promotion and the creation of a new Commercial diplomatic service, as well as increased work for consuls.[11]

The individual contributions of diplomats are harder to assess than those of ministers. The routine of official work makes it difficult to know the ultimate authorship of the dispatches for which they took formal responsibility and in their memoirs and those of their contemporaries, they all appear equally wise and benign. What one can say is that all the dominant figures from the time of the Peace Conference itself to the end of the Second World War had entered the foreign service between about 1888 and about 1907, that is to say in the years which saw the abandonment of isolation in favour of a more active and complex foreign policy of alliances and alignments.[12] Sir William Tyrrell (Lord Tyrrell) who had for eight years been Grey's private secretary succeeded Crowe as Permanent Under-Secretary in 1925 and then served as Ambassador in Paris from 1928 to 1934, when his contemporary as Ambassador to Germany (1928–33) was Sir Horace Rumbold who had been chargé d'affaires at Berlin in

[8] Alan J. Sharpe, 'The Foreign Office in Eclipse 1919–1922', *History*, New Ser. LXI (1976).

[9] C. Lerner, 'The Amalgamation of the Diplomatic Service with the Foreign Office', *Journal of Contemporary History* VII (1972).

[10] D.C.M. Platt, *The Cinderella Service: British Consuls since 1825* (London, 1971).

[11] Lord Strang, *The Foreign Office* (London, 1955), pp. 66–7; P. Byrd, 'Regional and Functional Specialization in the British Consular Service', *Journal of Contemporary History* VII (1972).

[12] There is no equivalent for the period after 1915 of Zara S. Steiner, *The Foreign Office and Foreign Policy 1898–1914* (Cambridge, 1969).

August 1914. He was succeeded as Permanent Under-Secretary by
Sir Ronald Lindsay, who after two years went as Ambassador to
Washington where he remained until the outbreak of war. His successor Sir Robert Vansittart (Lord Vansittart) was Permanent Secretary
from 1930 to 1938. His case was unique in that he had never held a
major embassy though he had served as principal private secretary to
two Prime Ministers. Baldwin and MacDonald.

Ambassadors were never fully to recover in an age of constantly
improving communications the importance which they had had in the
pre-war era. But this did not prevent the Foreign Office from making
sure that the coveted posts in the major capitals were reserved for the
professionals. Here as elsewhere Lloyd George had attempted innovation. Lord Derby had held the Paris Embassy for two years after
leaving the War Office in April 1918; the post returned to the hands
of the diplomatic service when Lord Hardinge was appointed in
November 1920,[13] although Bonar Law reverted to the Lloyd George
model by appointing the Liberal statesman Lord Crewe in December
1922. When full diplomatic relations were restored with Germany in
June 1920 Lloyd George appointed as Ambassador Lord D'Abernon,
who had had varied administrative, political and economic experience at home and abroad. He remained at Berlin until after the
conclusion of the Locarno Treaty and Germany's entry into the
League of Nations. To Washington where the wartime relationship
had been so important on the financial and commercial side, Lloyd
George had in January 1918 replaced a professional diplomat, Sir
Cecil Spring-Rice, with Lord Reading then Lord Chief Justice and he
in turn was succeeded in March 1920 by Sir Auckland Geddes, the
then President of the Board of Trade, who remained for a four-year
term. The immediate post-war years thus saw the three principal
embassies held by outsiders and only when D'Abernon was succeeded
by Lindsay in 1926 was the normal run of things fully resumed.

In so far as the new international organizations were of importance
in the post-war world, British representation in the conduct of their
business was significant. The first Secretary-General of the League of
Nations (from 1919 to 1933) was Sir Eric Drummond who came to the
post after serving as principal private secretary to the Foreign Secretary. The post of Director of the Economic and Financial Section
which had played a considerable part in post-war reconstruction, for
instance in Austria, was from 1919 to 1920 and again from 1922 to
1931, held by Sir Arthur Salter, who had been an important official
on various inter-allied wartime bodies, notably in respect of shipping.

---

[13] For Hardinge's contribution to limiting Anglo-French discord, see J. Douglas Gould,
'Lord Hardinge as Ambassador to France and the Anglo-French Dilemma over Germany and
the Near East 1920–1922', *Historical Journal* XXI (1978).

It is perhaps not surprising that the League of Nations should have seemed to the French a somewhat British affair.

What did not change once it was decided to retain the cabinet secretariat was the rôle of its head Sir Maurice Hankey, who combined that post with the secretaryship of the revived Committee of Imperial Defence and the more dignified rôle of Clerk of the Privy Council. Like Warren Fisher, he remained in office as successive governments came and went and was clearly much more than a cog in the governmental machine. Since Hankey, especially in the early 1920s, was inevitably much concerned with international developments and with the problems of the defence services, his deputy from 1916 to 1930, Thomas Jones, occupied a very important rôle in relation to domestic affairs enhanced by a range of personal friendships stretching from Baldwin to Geoffrey Dawson (né Robinson), who was editor of *The Times* from 1912 to 1919 and after the acquisition of *The Times* from Northcliffe's heirs by the Walter and Astor families again from 1923 to 1941.

The connection between Jones and Dawson shows how difficult it is to draw a contrast between the closed world of politics and administration and the open world of public debate. On the other hand, the position of *The Times* as the main organ of élite opinion was unique, and no other journalist in this period had as ready an access to government as Dawson; although C.P. Scott the editor of the *Manchester Guardian* remained an important figure in Liberal circles.[14]

Anxiety expressed during the period of the coalition government that too much influence was being exercised by the 'press barons', able it was assumed to manipulate opinion by the exploitation of the popular press, proved exaggerated. Northcliffe himself was a spent force by the time he died in August 1922. His brother Lord Rothermere as owner of the *Daily Mail* did espouse various right-wing causes in the 1920s and 1930s but was never the power that Northcliffe had been. Max Aitken (Lord Beaverbrook) was unusual in seeing his creation Express Newspapers as primarily an instrument of his political ambitions and also played an active part in the political arena himself.[15] His political fortunes had been much engaged with those of his fellow-Canadian Bonar Law but Law's accession to office did not imply a triumph for Beaverbrook's own version of the imperial creed.

[14] See *The Political Diaries of C.P. Scott 1911–1928*, ed. Trevor Wilson (London, 1970).

[15] Beaverbrook's own account of the history of the years between 1914 and 1922 can be found in his three books, *Politicians and the War 1914–1916* (London, vol. I, 1928; vol. II, 1932), *Men and Power 1917–1918* (London, 1956), *The Decline and Fall of Lloyd George. And Great was the Fall Thereof* (London, 1963), The main source for Beaverbrook's own role is A.J.P. Taylor, *Beaverbrook* (London, 1972).

In any event, the ability of the press to elevate or bring down politicians was dependent upon the monopoly they held of presenting the politicians to the new mass electorate. Their ascendancy fills the gap between the age of the platform and the new era in which the electronic media enabled politicians to project themselves more directly. By the end of the 1920s radio was already prefiguring the rôle that television would occupy after the Second World War.

The experience of the pre-war as well as of the war years was also understandably the principal formative element in the professional military who were to be the advisers of statesmen in the inter-war decades. Sir Henry Wilson was succeeded in 1922 as CIGS by the Earl of Cavan who held the post until 1926 when he was succeeded by Lord Milne. Retiring in 1933, Lord Milne was succeeded by Sir Archibald Montgomery-Massingberd who held the post until the eve of war in 1939. All three had fought in the Boer War and first achieved important commands in the Great War. It is not surprising that their influence should have been in favour of traditional men and methods.[16]

The navy was dominated by two sailors, Beatty who was First Sea Lord from 1919 to 1927 and Lord Chatfield who served from 1933 to 1938, when he was succeeded by Sir Dudley Pound, the First Lord for most of the Second World War.[17] The air force which had to fight for its independence as a service, particularly against naval jealousies, was also dominated by two men, Lord Trenchard, who as a soldier had also fought in the Boer War and was chief of air staff from 1918 to 1930, and Sir Edward Ellington, who after two shorter tenures of the post was chief from 1933 to 1937. In every case the professional's tenure was much more prolonged than that of the ministers whom they served – the three soldiers served under nine secretaries of state, the two sailors, Beatty and Chatfield, under 10 First Lords, four airmen under nine secretaries of state. The holders of service ministries like those of most other cabinet posts other than the most important were there in accordance with the immediate convenience of the Prime Minister of the day and as stepping-stones in their own careers. Given the pre-eminence attached to economy and the control exercised by the Treasury, it was unlikely that any great alteration of the country's dispositions for defence would be the result of the

[16] See Brian Bond, *British Military Policy between the Two World Wars* (Oxford, 1980). For a highly critical reaction to the military establishment of the inter-war period not uninfluenced by the author's own doctrinal convictions, see B.H. Liddell Hart, *The Memoirs of Captain Liddell Hart* (2 vols., London, 1965).

[17] The navy has attracted more scholarly attention than either of the rival services. See Stephen Roskill, *Naval Policy between the Wars* (2 vols., London, 1968, 1976); but the army's problems are well chronicled in Bond, *British Military Policy*.

initiative of a departmental minister – there was to be no Cardwell, no Haldane.

Where the professionals were concerned, their predominant attitude was based on the determination to avoid a repetition of the events and the losses of the war.[18] The defence policy which was pursued for as long as possible owed more to the ideas worked out in the pre-1914 years than to the major improvisations forced upon Britain during the war itself. Priority was given not to intervention in Europe but to imperial defence. Since it was hoped there would be no major conflict on land, not much attention needed to be paid to the way in which such a war would have to be fought or the demands it would make upon military technology. At sea, the case was somewhat different since the importance of the submarine as a commerce destroyer could not be gainsaid; and all naval planning had to take account of this fact. On the other hand, the effect of air-power upon naval warfare could not clearly be demonstrated on the basis of wartime experience and remained a debatable point until settled by the lessons of the Second World War. What most struck the imagination of those seriously concerned with defence was the vulnerability of civilian populations to aerial attack and the question of whether to deal with this threat by defensive measures or by the creation of a powerful bomber force capable of acting as a deterrent was one on which it proved possible to differ.

Navies and air forces could only be constituted and maintained on a professional basis. In Britain's case it was possible to argue that the largely imperial rôle envisaged for its ground forces also made conscription inappropriate and this reversal to the idea of a wholly professional army with only limited trained reserves coincided with the main weight of public opinion. Conscription had been only reluctantly accepted by the British Left – and then not universally – and there was strong resistance to maintaining it even during the turbulent period that followed the Armistice.

The fact that in Britain military doctrine and the prejudices of the public pointed the same way and in a different direction to that dictated by the needs and outlook of the continental countries must be appreciated if one is to understand the policies upheld by British statesmen in negotiations over disarmament and later over the plans for collective resistance to aggression. The main preoccupations of continental countries revolved around the question of the security of their frontiers and the maintenance and training of conscript forces. In the German case where there existed the prohibition of

---

[18] The argument is well set out in Michael Howard, *The Continental Commitment: the Dilemma of British Defence Policy in the Era of the Two World Wars* (London, 1972).

conscription embodied in the Peace Treaty, the accent was upon the
training, under the guise of a limited professional army, of the cadres
for its future expansion when compulsory service should be restored,
and the preparation with foreign collaboration of prototype weapons.
The differences in military perspective are above all important for
understanding the Anglo-French friction that with only a few short
interludes dominates the diplomacy of the inter-war years. From the
end of the Peace Conference until the resolution of the Ruhr crisis in
1924, France with its large air force and submarine fleet was thought
of as a potential enemy; later it was reluctantly accepted as an ally.
But neither at the level of statesmanship nor at that of opinion was the
Entente restored.[19]

The Bonar Law government was thus impelled, as had been its
predecessor, to devote a good deal of its time and energies to international questions. Law hoped that their solution might help to solve
the economic problems of the country which were highlighted by the
continuation of industrial unrest, if on a somewhat reduced scale. For
since the general opinion of business leaders and politicians alike was
that Britain could only prosper if the foreign markets could be recap-
tured and a regime of stable currencies restored, any strict separation
between domestic and foreign policy was hard to make. What was not
restored was any enthusiasm for social innovation; in so far as economies had not affected them too sharply it was mainly a question of
absorbing the Coalition's legislation into the working practices of
government, central and local.

Bonar Law's opportunity of imprinting a personal stamp upon the
new government was in any event soon ended by his own ill-health
which obliged him to resign the premiership at the end of May 1923.
He died in October.[20] Bonar Law had made no formal recommendation to the sovereign as to his successor so the question of who was to
be summoned to form a cabinet was an open one. Of the two candidates, Curzon had behind him a long and distinguished career in
some of the highest offices of state, Stanley Baldwin was a relative
newcomer to office although with considerable influence in the Conservative party, having been a major instrument in the downfall of the
Coalition. In the event, the advice received by George V from
Baltour who was consulted was that Curzon's membership of the
House of Lords was an over-riding objection. The primacy of the
House of Commons seemed the more clear-cut in that the Labour

[19] See John C. Cairns, 'A Nation of Shopkeepers in search of a suitable France 1919–1940',
American Historical Review LXXIX (1974).
[20] For a sympathetic assessment of Bonar Law, see Robert Blake, *The Unknown Prime Minister: the Life and Times of Andrew Bonar Law 1858–1923* (London, 1955).

Party, the official Opposition, was hardly represented in the Upper
House. But although Baldwin was duly summoned, the reasons for
the monarch's choice were not formally recorded, so that the possibility in other circumstances of a peer being chosen as Prime
Minister was left open. Baldwin's cabinet did not differ a great deal
from his predecessor's. Curzon retained the Foreign Office and
Baldwin himself remained at the Exchequer until August when he
was succeeded by Neville Chamberlain.[21]

The accession of Baldwin to the premiership ushered in one of the
longest periods of the dominance of the British political scene by a
single figure. From 1923 until 1937 whether in or out of office
Baldwin exercised a quite extraordinary influence for reasons which
are still much debated. Apart from his belief in the Conservative
Party and the necessity for preserving its unity intact, it is difficult to
connect any clear system of belief with the name of Baldwin or to be
certain as to the extent to which his professions of conciliation across
class barriers were tactical rather than heartfelt. At the most one can
say that his long-range purpose – very largely fulfilled – was to assist
in the acclimatization of the Labour Party within the existing political
system, and to avoid the polarization of society which the rise of
socialism seemed to have produced elsewhere in Europe. Coming like
Bonar Law from an unequivocally business background, if in his case
a more established one, Baldwin nevertheless presented the picture of
a man steeped in the traditional harmonies of English rural and small
town life. He was thus able to stand out not so much as a representative of the England of his own day but as the image of England as
people would like it to have been. He never fully commanded the
allegiance of his own party and on more than one occasion came close
to losing the leadership, but the appeal that he exercised to the electorate at large was too great for anyone to take the risk of putting forward
a substitute.

In another aspect of policy, he was all too representative of his
countrymen. Abroad as much as at home, he saw himself as a man of
peace, a peace to be attained as far as possible by the avoidance of
entanglements and of great armaments. He wished to be an insular
not an imperial, still less an international, statesman. When the
fallacies inherent in this position were revealed in 1940–1, his
countrymen turned against him and his record was generally reviled.
The balance remains hard to strike.

In the light of Baldwin's own main interests, it is ironical that his
first premiership like Bonar Law's was of necessity largely devoted to

[21] Baldwin has been the subject of many biographical studies, none of them wholly successful. The fullest is Keith Middlemas and John Barnes, *Baldwin: a Biography* (London, 1969).

unfinished business in foreign affairs.[22]

The most important of the new government's achievements was the settlement of the Straits question and the conclusion of a peace treaty with Kemalist Turkey. During the long drawn out Lausanne Conference (November 1922 to February 1923 and April to July 1923) Curzon was successful in getting Britain's substantial interests incorporated in the treaty, including provisions for the neutralization of the Straits and free passage into the Black Sea for warships as well as merchant shipping. The settlement of the boundary between Turkey and Iraq was delayed (though the disputed Mosul area went to Iraq by a further treaty in 1926). The attempt to revive the Gladstonian tradition of external care for the fate of Turkey's minorities was unsuccessful except in so far as Turkey's membership of the League of Nations might benefit them. From a wider point of view, the possibility of close association between Turkey and Soviet Russia which had been so prominent in the early years of the Turkish Revolution now appeared to be excluded.

While disagreement over the treatment of Turkey had been one of the issues in contention between Britain and France, the solution of the problem did not of itself end the friction between the two countries. The promise that Lloyd George's removal from office would mean an improvement in Anglo-French relations was not fulfilled and despite Bonar Law's efforts to create a new atmosphere, the substantive divisions particularly over Germany remained; nor was the new government itself wholly united on these matters. The question was how far Britain could go to meet French requirements so as to prevent the French taking matters into their own hands. At the end of 1922 France secured from the Reparations Commission a declaration that Germany was in default, and French and Belgian troops began in January 1923 the long-heralded occupation of the Ruhr. Passive resistance to French attempts to run the Ruhr mines and industries was encouraged by the German government, though the costs of this policy contributed to the massive inflation in Germany itself which had its effects upon other currencies as well.

France's critics in Britain – mainly on the Left but including some Conservatives – could readily argue that her aims went beyond the

---

[22] Baldwin himself was well aware that this would have to be the case: 'We've got to settle Europe' he told Thomas Jones on 28 May 1923, 'we can't wait for emigration and Empire development', T. Jones, *Whitehall Diary*. Vol. I: *1926–1930* (London, 1969), pp. 237–8. Despite his later reputation for insularity, Baldwin was in fact the most accomplished linguist among the Prime Ministers of the period. He had good French, passable German and a reading knowledge of Russian but he preferred to conceal these accomplishments. Middlemas and Barnes, *Baldwin*, pp. 33–4.

recovery of what was due to her and were ultimately political.[23] The development in the autumn of a separatist movement in the Rhineland seemed to bear out these suspicions; and quite apart from the genuine separatists, the local population was generally affected by antagonism towards the central government arising out of the sacrifices demanded of it in pursuing the policy of passive resistance. Anxieties about a possible break-up of the German republic were stimulated by events elsewhere in the country, notably by a challenge to Berlin from the right-wing Bavarian state government and from the Left in Thuringia, Saxony and Hamburg. The almost equally unpalatable alternative was that the Stresemann ministry which had taken office in August might be displaced by a right-wing coup, raising the spectre of a rebirth of German militarism. In the light of subsequent events, the attempted coup by Hitler on 8 November 1923 has naturally attracted most attention but at the time it was seen as only one of the long series of threats to German and European stability that French intransigence seemed to have provoked.[24]

Baldwin had originally hoped that on becoming Prime Minister he could come to an agreement with the French and in a frank discussion with Poincaré in September he explained the British position in an unaggressive fashion.[25] But as the situation inside Germany worsened, British anxieties increased. A hardening of Baldwin's attitude towards the French coincided with a meeting of the Imperial Conference in October. It was important to try to bring the Dominions into a consensus on foreign policy which had been far from existing at the time of Chanak.

One of the principal protagonists of leniency towards Germany over reparations and of opposition to French demands for further measures of security was in fact the South African Prime Minister, Smuts.[26] On 23 October 1923 while in London for the Imperial Conference he delivered a speech to the South Africa Club in which he called for a major initiative to settle the reparations question, declared the occupation of the Ruhr and the direct exploitation of German

[23] The British Left was much affected by guilt feelings over the alleged severity of the Versailles Treaty. For German contacts with the Asquithian Liberals, see Harry Kessler, *The Diaries of a Cosmopolitan: Count Harry Kessler 1918–1937*, trans. and ed. Charles Kessler (London, 1971).

[24] For an introduction to the German domestic situation in this period, see Gordon A. Craig, *Germany 1866–1945* (Oxford, 1978), chap. 20, 'Reparations, Inflation and the Crisis of 1923'. The extent to which foreign policy was dominated by domestic considerations including the fear of revolution in both France and Germany is discussed in C.S. Maier, *Recasting Bourgeois Europe: Stabilization in France, Germany and Italy in the Decade after World War I* (Princeton, 1975).

[25] Note of conversation of 19 September 1923 between Mr Baldwin and M. Poincaré. DBFP, 1 st series XXI, pp. 529–35.

[26] W.K. Hancock, *Smuts (Cambridge, 1962) I, pp. 132ff.*

resources to be a violation of the Treaty of Versailles (of which he had
been a signatory) and called attention to the signs of disintegration in
Germany which would be a major catastrophe for Europe as a whole.
Finally he uttered a warning against any proposal in respect of inter-
allied debts which might enable France to increase her armaments on
land and in the air and thus contribute to the further militarization of
Europe.[27]

In any event Smuts's declaration while deplored in Paris was welcome in Berlin. Stresemann the German foreign minister wrote on 29
October to thank Smuts both for making the speech and for a direct
message of support sent through a member of the German foreign
office.[28] Stresemann added that the same individual would be glad to
discuss the follow-up to Smuts's proposal and further meetings
between the two were held on 31 October and 3 November.[29] But with
the return of Smuts to South Africa, the initiative passed to Baldwin
himself.

As Smuts had made plain in his speech, the economic rehabilitation of Europe would have to take into account not only reparations
but also war debts. Solutions to these problems would depend in large
part on what the United States was prepared to do. Relations with the
United States during the last period of the Coalition government had
not been cordial. To the British government the policy expressed in a
note from Balfour of 1 August 1922 of not asking Britain's allies to

[27] *The text of the speech is in W.K. Hancock and Jean van der Poel, eds., Selections from the Smuts Papers*
(Cambridge, 1973) v, pp. 192–205. It is clear from the German archives that this was not an
initiative taken without preparation since Smuts was in contact with the German government
(Bariéty, *Les Relations Franco-Allemandes après la Premiere Guerre Mondiale: 10 Novembre 1918–10
Janvier 1925, de l'execution à la negociation* (Paris, 1977), p. 256 fn.). According to a German
historian the intermediary between Smuts and the German foreign minister Stresemann was
the historian Oswald Spengler (K.D. Erdmann, *Adenauer in der Rheinlandpolitik nach dem Ersten
Weltkrieg* (Stuttgart, 1966), p. 104). But this would seem to be an oversimplification. Spengler
himself was on the far right of German politics and no admirer of Stresemann. (See A.M.
Koltanek, *Oswald Spengler in seiner Zeit* (Munich, 1968).) Another German historian does
however indicate that the contacts which enabled the German government to be informed as
early as 18 October that Smuts was preparing a plan for settling the reparations question were
said to have been made possible through Spengler (W. Weidenfeld, *Die Englandpolitik Gustav
Stresemann: Theoretische und praktische Aspekte der Aussenpolitik* (Mainz, 1972), p. 212). What does
appear from Spengler's own correspondence is that he did in fact write to Stresemann on 26
September suggesting a personal meeting and indicating that he had a channel of communication with Smuts which could be used for the government's purposes. Smuts' opinions, he
indicated, had now veered in an anti-French direction though he was handicapped in
advocating a changed policy by his having been originally responsible for swelling the
reparations bill by the inclusion of war pensions. By the time Spengler got a favourable reply
from Stresemann on 6 or 7 October, it was too late for him to go to Berlin to see him, since
Stresemann had suggested 30 September as the appropriate date. He therefore did not carry
out his intention of going to London but a letter from an associate of his dated 2 October does
seem to have reached Smuts. See Oswald Spengler, *Briefe 1913–1936*, ed. A.M. Koktanek
(Munich, 1963), pp. 133ff.

[28] Stresemann to Smuts, 29 October 1923. Hancock and van der Poel, *Selections*, pp. 209–11.
[29] Weidenfeld, *Englandpolitik*, pp. 215–20.

repay her more than she needed to meet her own debt to the United States seemed a generous one. To the Americans this seemed to be linking together two quite separate issues. Despite the agreements reached during the Washington Conference, the United States was still suspected of trying to replace Britain as the world's major sea-power and to wrest from her commercial and financial supremacy.[30]

The Bonar Law government had tried to find a remedy to the war debts issue and in January 1923 Baldwin as Chancellor of the Exchequer reached an agreement with the Americans which formed the basis of a definitive settlement in June. The terms of the settlement were however too onerous in the opinion of some members of the cabinet and Bonar Law had to be dissuaded from resignation when they were first made known.[31] Even so he wrote anonymously to *The Times* to denounce the settlement.

The hopes that such a settlement might pave the way for a return to constructive participation in European affairs by the United States seemed justified when on 9 October 1923, President Coolidge announced that he would follow the policy agreed upon by President Harding (whom he had succeeded on 2 August) and participate in discussions on European recovery. On 19 October, that is to say before Smuts's speech, Curzon sent a note to Washington announcing that Britain would enlist the co-operation of her European allies in asking the United States to participate in an enquiry into reparations and related topics. And a few days later, Poincaré made it clear that France would welcome the appointment of such an expert inquiry in which the United States would participate.

On the more immediate question of the Ruhr however there was still no meeting of minds; Britain made it clear in a note to the French on 31 October that she was totally opposed to any moves that could lead to the break-up of the Reich. Ignoring the fact that the Belgians were now moving towards the British point of view which would mean that France would lose its majority on the Reparations Commission, Poincaré stood firm on the French position and an acrimonious exchange of notes followed. But at the same time despite some weakening in the American initiative for an expert committee, the French now took up and pressed forward this proposal as their own. Thus when in mid November Baldwin decided upon an early general election, the deadlock between the British and the French seemed no nearer resolution.[32]

These disputes were further aggravated by differences of approach

[30] See the outburst by Lloyd George in a cabinet meeting on 25 July 1922. PRO/CAB 23/30. Mtg 42.
[31] Blake, *Unknown Prime Minister*, pp. 490–6.
[32] Bariéty, *Les Relations Franco-Allemandes*, pp. 266–87.

to the perennial problems of disarmament and security under discussion at the League of Nations.[33] The proposed Treaty of Mutual Assistance seemed to suggest that further calls were to be made upon Britain's armed forces without any corresponding advantages from her own point of view. Baldwin had tried to suggest his government's commitment to the League idea by bringing in Lord Robert Cecil as Lord Privy Seal with the special task of handling League of Nations affairs, but his chances of overcoming Foreign Office and service opposition to the latest proposals were diminished by the strong objections of the Dominions expressed at the Imperial Conference, particularly since it was known that the anti-League prejudices of the Canadian Prime Minister Mackenzie King were largely shared by the Conservative opposition under Arthur Meighen.[34]

In other respects, the Bonar Law–Baldwin government's record in foreign policy was a mixed one. It had come into office hoping to cut down expenditure by withdrawal from both Iraq and Palestine. The arguments for withdrawal in the case of Iraq did not stand up against the fears that Turkey might not only take the opportunity of recovering it but might go on to seek to recover Syria and Palestine as well. There was also fear that withdrawal might assist Bolshevik penetration of Persia. The success of air force policing operations had shown that the cost of retention was not as high as had been feared. As has been seen, Curzon had secured Turkey's recognition of Iraq's independence from her and paved the way for a frontier which would put the oil-wells on the Iraq side. At the same time a concession was made to the advocates of withdrawal by the provisions that the mandate should terminate four years after an agreement with Turkey had been reached.

The Palestine issue remained more complex and the divisions over it within Whitehall more acute. The Lloyd George government had, as has been seen, excluded Trans-Jordan from the area covered by the Balfour declaration but there was also strong opposition to Zionist claims being given preference within Palestine proper. On 27 June 1923 its future was referred to a cabinet committee. The Colonial Office with an eye to the concessions made to Egyptian nationalism felt that the security of imperial communications would for some time to come depend upon the retention of Palestine; the question of air

[33] The League of Nations did possess an appeal among some elements in the British intelligentsia whose support Baldwin would not wish to lose. The major apologist for the League idea was the Liberal classical scholar Gilbert Murray who was president of the League of Nations Union, the main pressure group, from 1923 to 1938. Sir Alfred Zimmern, successively professor of International Relations at Aberystwyth and Oxford and a familiar figure on the Geneva scene, was unusual in espousing both the League and the Commonwealth ideals.

[34] For the Canadian attitude, see R. McGregor Dawson, *William Lyon Mackenzie King: a Political Biography*. Vol. I (London, 1958).

routes was also important to the India Office. The military were less confident of its value. In the end the decisive factor proved to be the cabinet committee's conclusion that the existing policy could not be reversed without abandoning the mandate itself and that this would mean it being taken over by either Italy or France or else the return of the Turks. And this argument carried the day with the cabinet when it decided on 31 July to retain the mandate and to be guided by its basic principles.

In defending this decision however the government did not refer to the security considerations which were crucial to it. It was the obligation to the League that was stressed, and this made it possible to argue that British treasure was being spent and British lives being put at risk for the quixotic purpose of creating a Jewish National Home which could not be described as a British interest.[35]

The advent of a Conservative government was not calculated to improve Anglo-Soviet relations despite the belief in some business circles that recognition of the Soviet regime might help to encourage British exports. Apart from the clash at Lausanne where the Russians wish for a regime of the Straits that might keep them closed to foreign navies, there were no formal disputes between the two countries. But the issue of propaganda notably in India which had exercised the coalition government was still unresolved. On 8 May 1923 Britain threatened to denounce the trade agreement and recall its agent from Moscow unless the activities of the Comintern were curtailed. Subsequent negotiations produced a new agreement on 29 May embodying a British formula binding the Soviet government 'not to support with funds or in any other form persons or bodies or agencies or institutions whose aim is to spread discontent or foment rebellion in any part of the British Empire'.[36] Since such an agreement could in no way alter the basic position of the Soviet government further friction inevitably followed.

Setbacks in Europe were not compensated for by developments in the Empire and Commonwealth. The 1923 Imperial Conference showed how far apart were Britain and the Dominions on many vital issues. The idea of a single Empire foreign policy was repudiated and not only by the Canadians. In defence the British preference for central planning based on the notion of an integrated web of naval defence came up against the Dominions' concentration on local threats, while their strong reluctance to spend any money at all for military purposes pointed to a continued burden on the United

[35] The records of the committee are in PRO/CAB 23/46. See on the public debate, Christopher Sykes, *Crossroads to Israel* (London, 1965), pp. 93ff.
[36] On this phase of Anglo-Soviet friction, see E.H. Carr, *A History of Soviet Russia: The Interregnum 1923–1924* (London, 1954), pp. 165–72.

Kingdom taxpayer. On the other hand, the Dominions were sensitive
to any suggestion that Britain should act without consultation even
when the direction of British policy was in line with their own thinking, as in the case of Curzon's note to Washington of 19 October
about the proposed enquiry into reparations and related topics. Their
fear was always one of commitment through unilateral British action.

While the situation in India was somewhat easier after the temporary eclipse of Gandhi and the decision of the Swaraj party to contest
the provincial elections due in 1924, there was still anxiety on the part
of the Viceroy Lord Reading as to the sufficiency of the military force
available from Britain despite the conclusion of a further treaty with
Afghanistan in 1921.[37] Peel who retained the India Office under both
Bonar Law and Baldwin did his best to reassure the Viceroy, though
with Curzon dissenting the cabinet agreed to reduce the size of the
Indian Army itself, in the light of the financial situation of the Indian
government. The issue of the status of Indians elsewhere in the
Empire, notably in South Africa and East Africa, which had come up
at the 1921 Imperial Conference again created trouble at the 1923
Conference, though this was patched up, and the threatened walkout
of the Indian delegation did not occur. The question illustrated both
the anomaly of Indian representation at the Imperial Conferences
when ultimate political authority was retained in London, and the
extent to which all the Dominions now claimed so great a measure of
independence that the Crown increasingly appeared to be the only
link between them.

On economic issues there were also differences. All the Dominions
had some interest in the possibility of an imperial preferential system
and some concessions to them proved possible without going beyond
the government's existing commitment to free trade. The Indians for
their part wished to see not a general system of preference but a
recognition of their right to build up a protectionist system of their
own, while on the British side with unemployment so dominant in
ministers' minds preferences in the Indian market were still thought
to be of great importance.

The Conference was however most important because of the
opportunities it gave to question the free trade policy itself. The
Coalition had not been brought down solely by protectionists. Of
those who took a leading part in its overthrow, Bonar Law, Baldwin,
Neville Chamberlain, Amery, Bridgeman and Gretton were protectionists, but Salisbury, Devonshire and Derby belonged to the
free-trade wing of the party. And Baldwin's own devotion to pro-

[37] On Reading's Viceroyalty see Denis Judd, *Lord Reading: Rufus Isaacs, first Marquess of
Reading, Lord Chief Jurtice and Viceroy of India 1860–1935* (London, 1982), chap. 14.

tection had nothing of Joseph Chamberlain's crusading spirit. His move towards a protectionist policy must be seen as a concession to the pressures brought upon him during the autumn of 1923.[38] The Imperial Conference provided opportunities for discussions with the Commonwealth statesmen assembled in London, and at two week-end meetings at Chequers both Mackenzie King and Bruce of Australia were present. It was decided that Baldwin should at the Conservative Conference at Plymouth on 25 October announce his commitment to a policy of protection and imperial preference.

The policy was announced in very general terms with no commitment to particular measures or to an exact timetable. It would have been possible to develop the partial measures of protection that already existed. In 1915 the McKenna duties, an *ad valorem* tariff of 33 per cent had been introduced on a variety of so-called luxury items including cars, bicycles, clocks and musical instruments. But the House of Commons had been assured that their purpose was not to protect the home producer but to save shipping space and prevent the expenditure abroad on purposes not connected with the war. The Dyestuffs Act and the Safeguarding of Industries Act of 1921 had given protection avowedly to industries that had been shown to have direct relevance to national security; there had also been some 'anti-dumping' duties imposed. To have limited himself in this way would have enabled Baldwin to feel that he was acting within the scope of Bonar Law's pledge not to introduce a major change in the fiscal system.[39] But seemingly Baldwin prefered to free his hands through an election fought on the general theme.[40]

The original idea had been to delay an election until June 1923, by which date a protectionist budget could have been presented and public opinion given time to accept the change. One version still widely circulated is that Lloyd George who was in the United States at the time was preparing to campaign himself on an imperial platform which would recreate his links with the Unionists who had remained loyal to the Coalition. His failure earlier in the year to bring about a Liberal reunion perhaps makes the suggestion more plausible. But there is no evidence that he seriously entertained such an idea; indeed the crowded circumstances of his American tour would seem to have precluded any close attention to the development of British politics.[41]

In any event Baldwin did dissolve in November and in his election

[38] See the material in Robert Rhodes James, ed., *Memoirs of a Conservative: J.C.C. Davidson's Memoirs and Papers 1910–1937* (London, 1969).

[39] Blake, *Unknown Prime Minister*, p. 468.

[40] Maurice Cowling, *The Impact of Labour 1920–1924: the Beginning of Modern British Politics* (Cambridge, 1971), pp. 278–9, 304, 308.

[41] Campbell, *Lloyd George*, pp. 64–71.

address drafted by Amery affirmed his adherence to the doctrines of imperial preference as the best hope of promoting industrial revival at home.[42] Baldwin thus over-rode those Conservatives who believed that the old free trade argument still carried weight with the electorate particularly in Lancashire, and who also felt in some cases that the argument for preference would only be convincing if combined with a more positive policy for the promotion of emigration to the Dominions.[43]

The decision was thus a personal one of Baldwin's and illustrates the rapidity with which a new Conservative leader could establish his authority. Baldwin tried to balance possible defections by free-traders by attempting to bring Austen Chamberlain back into government as if to emphasize the link with the Chamberlain imperial tradition. But Chamberlain would not accept office without Birkenhead and Birkenhead was still anathema to some traditional Conservatives who apart from personal objections felt that he had become identified in the public mind too ostentatiously with the cause of the 'haves' against the 'have nots' to be anything but an electoral liability.[44]

The Conservatives entered upon the election, against which the leading Party officials had warned Baldwin, with some handicaps. While Lloyd George's swift espousal of the free trade cause made it inevitable that the Conservative coalitionists would soon return to the fold, the position of the free-traders was a difficult one and at least 20 Conservative candidates fought the election on a free trade platform.[45]

For the Liberals the opportunity seemed a golden one. While Lloyd George did not wholly abandon his contacts with Chamberlain and Birkenhead, Alfred Mond had already prepared the way for a new attempt at Liberal reunion even before Lloyd George's return to England. It was achieved at a meeting on 13 November between Asquith and Simon on the one side and Lloyd George and Mond on the other.[46] Asquith thus resumed leadership of an ostensibly united party though one with very grave weaknesses in organization and in finance where Lloyd George remained in control of his separate

[42] *The Leo Amery Diaries*, ed. John Barnes and David Nicholson. Vol I: *1869-1929* (London, 1980), pp. 351–6. L.S. Amery, *My Political Life*. Vol. II: *War and Peace 1914–1929* (London, 1953), p. 296. Julian Amery, *The Life of Joseph Chamberlain* (London, 1969) VI, pp.1013–14.

[43] See, e.g., Derby to Baldwin, 22 October 1923, in Randolph Churchill, *Lord Derby, 'King of Lancashire'. The Official Life of Edward, Seventeenth Earl of Derby 1865-1948* (London, 1959), pp. 523–4. Under the Empire Settlement Act of 1922, the government had undertaken to provide up to £3,000,000 per annum for 15 years to assist emigration. In the course of the succeeding decade nearly half a million people did in fact emigrate from Britain to Commonwealth countries.

[44] John Ramsden, *The Age of Balfour and Baldwin 1902-1940* (London, 1978), pp. 179–80.

[45] Cook, *Age of Alignment*, pp. 114ff.

[46] Campbell, *Lloyd George*, p. 72.

fund.[47] What was lacking also (as the results when analysed were to show) was a clear constituency in the country. The Liberal appeal was local and fragmented; it could neither appear to the solid trade union core of the Labour Party nor to middle-class suburbia. It had also suffered through the decline in the political importance of religious nonconformity. On the whole the nonconformist leadership had accepted the war and took pride in the achievements of Lloyd George the first nonconformist Prime Minister. But his failure to fulfil their hopes of striking a decisive blow for the cause of prohibition helped to strengthen their disillusion with him after his increasing identification with the Conservatives. While some nonconformists remained faithful to the Asquith wing of the party and while traditional areas of rural nonconformity, for instance in the south-west of England, continued to return Liberals to Parliament for some time to come, an important section went permanently over to Labour, particularly in industrial towns.[48]

These strategic weaknesses were to some extent overshadowed by the exhilaration of a campaign for the old style of Liberal economic policy. Even Churchill who had been out of politics since his defeat in October 1922 succumbed to a revival of his old free-trade enthusiasm, though he disappointed his wife who feared the influence over him of Lloyd George and Beaverbrook, by preferring to fight a seat where Labour would be the principal opposition rather than one of the Manchester seats that the Liberals now hoped to recapture from the Conservatives.[49]

The omens looked much brighter for Labour which had much improved its organization and which had been shown in by-elections to be making inroads on the Liberal vote. It too had its weaknesses particularly the absence of a strong financial position at the centre. Local parties depended too heavily on trade unions for both members and finance and the weakness of this position was particularly strong in more rural areas. The opportunity of individual membership provided by the new party constitution was not widely taken up and the ILP was now in decline. The London Labour Party modelled by Herbert Morrison on continental social democracy, by trying to provide a network of socialist cultural and leisure facilities did provide one new element of strength alongside the mining areas and other concentrations of heavy industry but Party headquarters were reluc-

[47] Trevor Wilson, *The Downfall of the Liberal Party 1914-1935* (London, 1966), pp. 243-63.
[48] See Stephen Koss, *Nonconformity in Modern British Politics* (London, 1975).
[49] Martin Gilbert, *Winston S. Churchill*. Vol. v: *1922-1939* (London, 1976), pp. 15-21. Clementine Churchill's struggle to keep her husband closer to his pre-war Liberalism and away from what she regarded as the corrupting influences of Lloyd George, Birkenhead and Beaverbrook is clearly set out in Mary Soames, *Clementine Churchill* (London, 1979).

tant to subsidize it and it remained short of funds.[50] The Co-operative movement was another possible source of funds but had aims of its own which prevented it from merging its identity with the Labour Party. It was however able to find room for itself by putting forward 'Labour and Co-operative' candidates in a number of winnable seats.

The difficulty of combining the attitudes of a class party, on which much of the enthusiasm of its militants depended and which was necessary to preserve it against Communist inroads on its strength, with a wider national appeal remained formidable. It was true that as has been seen there had been the important accretion of ex-Liberals from the middle-classes but these were significant rather for their individual talents than for their numerical strength. It was also true that not only nonconformity but even the Established Church was in part open to Labour views, and the social doctrines espoused by many active clerics and laymen were more collectivist than *laissez-faire*. When after the 1922 election Labour became the official Opposition MacDonald received the formal congratulations of 510 Anglican priests of whom 10 later became bishops.[51]

From the point of view of Labour not as the official opposition but as a prospective party of government, its pool of potential ministerial talent was though reinforced still a restricted one. In part this was due to a conscious decision by the leadership of the trade union movement to remain aloof from the parliamentary side of Labour's activities. In the pre-war Labour Party a dominant position was held by general secretaries of the major unions. But after 1918 the standing orders of the Party prevented simultaneous membership of the National Executive Committee of the Party and of the TUC Parliamentary Committee, which changed its name to General Council in 1921.[52] Unions also changed their rules to prevent their general secretaries and other full-time officials from holding parliamentary seats. Union-sponsored members remained very important, particularly in the safer seats, which meant their proportion of the parliamentary party increased when it was at its numerical weakest. Only once in the inter-war period – after the major surge forward in 1929 – did MPs sponsored by trade unions account for less than half of the Labour representation. It has been held that MacDonald's victory over Clynes in the 1922 contest for the leadership was due to the influx then of non-sponsored MPs. Since trade unions increasingly used their sponsored seats to reward retired officials who could be relied upon to put the interests of the unions and even of their own union in front of every-

[50] Ross McKibbin, *The Evolution of the Labour Party 1910–1924* (London, 1974). p. 171.

[51] E.R. Norman, *Church and Society in England 1770–1970* (Oxford, 1976), p. 316.

[52] See Ross M. Martin, *TUC: the Growth of a Pressure Group 1868–1976* (Oxford, 1980), pp. 152ff.

thing else the changes did limit the options available to a leader looking for effective colleagues.[53]

The Labour Party in the election held on 6 December had the advantage of a unity more genuine than the Liberals were able to contrive or than the Conservatives could muster in respect of the issue of Protection[54] The number of candidatures as compared with 1922 was only slightly up at 427; the Liberals fielded rather more candidates but often in a very improvised fashion. The issue of resistance to socialism cut across the free trade commitment of both Labour and Liberals and in some areas notably in Scotland and the North there were local and informal anti-socialist pacts. The Conservatives fought only 536 of the 615 seats – 53 more than in 1922. The failure of the Liberals to propose a constructive policy for dealing with the industrial recession and agricultural distress and their self-limitation to fighting the old free trade battle again, helped the Labour Party to mount an attack against them which was extremely bitter. The MacDonald strategy of destroying the Liberal Party so as to make British politics a straight fight with the Conservatives in which Labour it was assumed as the party of the people would ultimately be triumphant, had obviously been unaffected by the re-emergence of the fiscal issue.

Yet the only question to which the electorate seemed to have returned a clear answer when the results were declared was precisely this one. The Conservatives lost 108 seats (and made only 20 gains); their losses were to Labour in the cities, to the Liberals in rural seats and middle-class suburbs. Labour gained 63 seats but lost 16 and the Liberals made 80 gains but lost 36. These net figures conceal many cross-currents, for instance some measure of Liberal–Labour co-operation in rural areas. On the whole it would appear that the Liberals had gained from the Conservatives sometimes rather surprisingly while they had further lost ground to Labour which could be said to vindicate the Labour strategy. Had more Labour candidates fought, the Liberals would have lost more to the Conservatives. Within the Liberal Party itself the individual results strengthened the Asquithian at the expense of the Lloyd George faction. Churchill and Hamar Greenwood failed to get back into Parliament and among other Coalition Liberals defeated was Mond.

The situation within the Liberal Party and its own assessment of its rôle were of crucial importance when the state of affairs in the new Parliament was taken into account. The Conservatives having won

---

[53] See W.D. Muller, *The Kept Men?: the First Century of Trade Union Representation in the British House of Commons 1874–1975* (Hassocks, 1977).

[54] For the 1923 election see the account in Cook, *Age of Alignment*, part 3.

30 per cent of the popular vote had 258 MPs; Labour with 30.7 per cent, 191 and the Liberals with 29.7 per cent, 158. It looked as though the Liberal position was a strong one. The Liberals mainly because of the free trade issue had enjoyed major support in the popular press including that of the two strongly anti-Baldwin proprietors, Rothermere and Beaverbrook. Having obtained a total vote so close to Labour's it was hard for the Liberals to see themselves as a perpetual third party remote from all hopes of power. Because the Liberal Party had large central funds, under Asquith's control from the sale of honours under his administration and under Lloyd George's control from his own traffic on an even more extensive scale, the organization in the constituencies was being allowed to wither away, but this was not yet obvious.[55] It was not at once clear how the Party would take advantage of this situation but since the Conservatives did not at once repudiate protectionism it would have been difficult for it to sustain Baldwin in office.

[55] Michael Pinto-Duschinsky, *British Political Finance 1830–1980* (Washington D.C., 1981), p. 92.

5 The First Labour Government

Conservatives reacted to their defeat in a variety of ways. Baldwin decided to meet the new Parliament and place the onus of dismissing him from office on the Liberals. Neither Asquith nor Lloyd George doubted the wisdom of voting for a no-confidence amendment to the address. While it was clear that Baldwin would have no truck with ideas of bargaining with the Liberals, there was an appeal from some quarters to Asquith to put himself forward as a possible candidate for the premiership with Conservative support. But for the leader of the third party to do this before any other combination had been tried might seem unconstitutional; nor was Asquith willing to incur the obloquy of creating a 'bourgeois' coalition with the sole purpose of keeping the socialists out in a way which might harden the class division in British politics. A government depending on the Liberals for their parliamentary majority could hardly indulge in much revolutionary legislation; it was therefore a good moment to make the experiment. If Labour proved unequal to the challenge of governing, the Liberals' time would come.[1]

It is hard to see how any other decision would have been possible. What Asquith and Lloyd George may have underestimated was the determination of the Labour victors and especially MacDonald not under any circumstances to admit being beholden to the Liberals or to seek for any formal arrangement with them. With the abandonment by the Conservatives of protection after they left office the defence of free trade was no longer an issue bringing Labour and the Liberals together. Asquith might not wish to form part of a 'bourgeois coalition' but Labour was not prepared to differentiate between bourgeois parties. Labour's parliamentary tactics would turn out to be based upon the desire to get rid of the encumbrance of Liberal support and

[1] Asquith's most recent biographers do not substantially disagree in their interpretation of his actions at this time. See Roy Jenkins, *Asquith* (London, 1964), pp. 499–501; Stephen Koss, *Asquith* (London, 1976), pp. 263–6. See also Maurice Cowling, *The Impact of Labour 1920–1924: the Beginning of Modern British Politics* (Cambridge, 1971), pp. 341ff.

to make at some point a challenge for individual power.[2] Meanwhile in the country and particularly at the municipal level the task of building up Labour strength could continue and the basic weaknesses of the Liberals be exposed.

The time between the election and taking office on 22 January 1924 was filled by MacDonald partly in the task which proved not too difficult, of persuading his party and the trade union movement that to decline the opportunity would set the Party back, and partly in surveying the somewhat exiguous material available in the Party and among its sympathizers for cobbling together a ministry.[3] The only serious difficulty was the position of Henderson who had been so largely responsible for the Party's growth but who had himself failed to be returned to the new Parliament. MacDonald toyed with the idea of not including him, and allowing him to concentrate on building up the party machine for another election which no one believed could be very long delayed. But the idea could not be sustained and Henderson took office as Home Secretary, returned to Parliament at a by-election in February; of the other stalwarts, Clynes became Lord Privy Seal, Snowden, Chancellor of the Exchequer, Thomas, Colonial Secretary and Webb, President of the Board of Trade. For Lord Chancellor, MacDonald turned to Haldane whose breach with the Liberals had hardened. Lord Chelmsford at the Admiralty was a former Conservative, and the Lord Advocate, Hugh Macmillan, was a Conservative who was to hold office under Neville Chamberlain in 1939–40. Other ex-Liberals, trade unionists and members of the ILP filled the remaining cabinet and non-cabinet positions. The Foreign Office which was likely to be of key importance was also held by MacDonald – the first Prime Minister since Salisbury to attempt the double task. Given the material to hand and the differences that remained within the Labour movement, it was, despite some obvious weak spots, a not undistinguished administration. But its lack of experience of high office including the Prime Minister's, naturally gave additional weight to the civil service and in particular to Hankey and Thomas Jones in the cabinet secretariat, though Jones was not as close to Macdonald as to Baldwin.[4]

Since the lack of a parliamentary majority precluded any major instalment of socialism it was in foreign affairs that the new government appeared to have the best opportunity of striking out on its own;

[2] Much light on this aspect of the situation is thrown by *The Political Diaries of C.P. Scott, 1911–1928*, ed. Trevor Wilson (London, 1970).

[3] The most detailed and important account of MacDonald's first premiership is that in David Marquand, *Ramsay MacDonald* (London, 1977), chaps. 14–16.

[4] Although much new material has become available since it was published, R.W. Lyman, *The First Labour Government, 1924* (London, 1957) still provides a useful introduction to its work.

it was here also that some of the Party's views came closest to those of at least a segment of the Liberals upon whom the majority in Parliament depended. What was not clear was how far the attitudes that Labour had expressed in Opposition would prove the foundation for policy in office.

The most vocal group had been that of the ex-Liberals who had come to the Labour Party via the Union of Democratic Control and the ILP, notably Arthur Ponsonby, the new Under-Secretary for Foreign Affairs and E.D. Morel who was much put out at not receiving office. The main contribution of this group was to express the widespread anti-war feeling that played so powerful a part in shaping public opinion in this period; since they were also bitterly anti-French and had direct contacts with circles in Germany for whose aspiration for a revision of the Versailles Treaty they had total sympathy.[5] They were therefore opposed to the League of Nations which they saw as an instrument for upholding the *status quo*; in Morel's case this was combined with a strong antipathy to the Foreign Office and indeed to all the traditional instruments of diplomacy.[6] The French occupation of the Ruhr gave an added impetus to their convictions. Morel himself who had come into the public eye through his exposure of imperialist exploitation in Africa had been in 1920 notable for his attacks upon the conduct of French colonial troops in the occupied zone in which every device of racialist rhetoric was employed.[7] Other doctrinaires of the ILP arrived at much the same position by a different intellectual route, regarding the League of Nations as a pillar of the capitalist world system as well as of existing frontiers; in many cases the League was also seen as a potentially anti-Soviet device. The most important figure from the ILP although he was not particularly pro-Soviet was the Chancellor, Philip Snowden, a man of invincible

---

[5] See Henry R. Winkler, 'The emergence of a Labour Foreign Policy in Great Britain in 1918–1929', *Journal of Modern History* XXVIII (1956).

[6] See C.A. Cline, 'E.D. Morel and the Crusade against the Foreign Office', *Journal of Modern History* XXXIX (1967).

[7] Morel's campaign had dwelt in particular on the alleged unbridled sexual appetites of Africans and on the hideous fate of German womanhood at the hands of the coloured troops. His assessment of the Africans' proclivities was supported by another socialist with claims to expertise, C.B. Thomson, later, as Lord Thomson, MacDonald's Secretary of State for Air. Among the socialist women who flocked to give Morel their support were many notable figures including Ethel Snowden, the redoubtable wife of the future Chancellor. MacDonald was among those who took the chair for Morel at one or other of his meetings. Since the charges could not be substantiated, the campaign more or less collapsed by 1921, though Morel went on remorselessly. See Robert C. Reinders, 'Racialism on the Left: E.D. Morel and the 'Black Horror on the Rhine', *International Review of Social History* XIII (1968). See also John C. Cairns, 'A Nation of Shopkeepers in search of a suitable France 1919–1940', *American Historical Review* LXXIX (1974). Since the *Daily Herald* was the main vehicle of such anti-French propaganda, it is not surprising that the French Ambassador called it 'A German newspaper published in English'. A.F.C. de B. Saint-Aulaire, *Confession d'un vieux diplomate* (Paris, 1954), p. 586.

antipathies, with the French coming top of the list. Since the main issues which the incoming government faced – reparations, war debts – were in part Treasury matters, Snowden's prejudices were not unimportant. Many of the trade union leaders took an ultra-Left point of view stressing in their pronouncements the impossibility of building a more peaceful world while capitalism continued.

Other cabinet ministers, Clynes, Thomas and after some hesitation, Arthur Henderson, took a more moderate line with particular emphasis on building up international organizations. Henderson relied in particular on the Advisory Committee for International Questions set up by the National Executive in 1918 – a body which brought together Labour MPs, some of the Party's intellectuals including Morel and experts on international questions from outside the Party's ranks. Its stance had become a more moderate one after a fairly radical beginning and it provided a framework within which particular problems could be studied and assessed.[8]

MacDonald himself in this as in other respects remained an ambiguous figure. He had moved some way away from his earlier pacifist and left-wing stance and was inclined to give greater value to the tasks of conciliatory diplomacy. While still on the whole anti-French and rejecting the view that German aggression had been an important if not the most important single cause of the war, he did not share Snowden's acute prejudices. Indeed his view of himself (and of Britain) was of an impartial arbiter between contending blocs. He did not share the enthusiasm in some quarters for 'collective security' under the auspices of the League.[9] But like many Liberals and socialists he cherished the goal of general disarmament.

From the beginning MacDonald made it clear that he would not share policy-making in this field with the cabinet at large, certainly where relations with France and Germany were concerned.[10] The Russian issue was left very much in Ponsonby's hands. For the rest, MacDonald found it congenial to work closely with Hankey and with Crowe, now Permanent Secretary at the Foreign Office. Positive successes might serve to demonstrate that the gibe that Labour could not rule was a false one.[11] MacDonald was also able to use the by now

---

[8] See Vol. IV of the autobiography of Leonard Woolf, an important figure in this Committee, *Downhill all the Way* (London, 1968).

[9] In 1923 MacDonald refused to become an Honorary President of the League of Nations Union which, he claimed, had kept itself clear of him and his political friends at a time when they were unpopular. See exchange of letters with Gilbert Murray in July 1923. Gilbert Murray Papers.

[10] See e.g. Beatrice Webb's diary entry, 15 May 1924, in M. Cole, ed., *Beatrice Webb's Diaries 1924-32* (London, 1956), pp.13–14.

[11] See e.g. J.H. Grainger, *Character and Style in English Politics* (London, 1969), chap. 8 'Labour's Lost Leaders'.

familiar argument of British Prime Ministers that Dominion consent was required before any binding commitments could be made, even though his record of actual consultation of Dominion governments was not regarded by them as above reproach.[12]

The Colonial Secretary, Thomas, was certainly concerned to maintain that the Labour Party was fully determined to preserve the British Empire and did not even share the theoretical anti-imperialism of the Secretary of State for India, the former Colonial Governor Lord Olivier. But where the Dominions were concerned the awkward point was the commitment reached at the Imperial Conference in respect of imperial preferences. Lord Arnold, Thomas's under-secretary, almost at once put up a memorandum arguing that the government was not bound by the action of its predecessor and putting the straight free trade case.[13] In this he was supported by Snowden whose commitment to free trade was total, although when telling the House of Commons in his budget speech that the preferences would not be proceeded with, Snowden was at pains to add that the new government was 'not one whit behind the Opposition in their desire to promote the best interests of the Empire'.[14] The procedural dilemma was solved by the government putting forward the agreed proposals and recommending the House to reject them.[15]

The diplomatic inheritance was also complex. At the time MacDonald took office it looked as though the advent of the proposed expert committee, the Dawes Committee as it came to be called might permit a new arrangement on reparations, which would be sufficiently attractive to the French to lead them to abandon their hold on the resources of the Ruhr and permit the reunification of the German economy and the withdrawal of their occupying forces. Yet it was clear that so long as Poincaré was in power, France would insist on tangible guarantees for the future. The more general problem of giving security to the French and their east European allies through a strengthening of the League mechanism was also unresolved. The Draft Treaty of Mutual Assistance put before the League Assembly in September 1923 had been designed to encourage disarmament by

[12] It is perhaps rather hard to say of MacDonald as one Canadian historian does that 'his blundering in imperial relations verged on genius'. H. Blair Neatby, *Mackenzie King* (Toronto, 1963) II, p. 39, The reference is to Canada's exclusion from the London Conference of August 1924.

[13] The memorandum is printed in Ian M. Drummond, *British Economic Policy and the Empire 1919-1939* (London, 1972), pp. 174ff.

[14] The draft of the budget speech including this phrase in particular had been approved by the Cabinet that morning. PRO. CAB. 23/48.

[15] In the event, the Government only defeated the increases in existing preferences very narrowly. Nearly all the Lloyd George Liberals voted with the Conservatives as did one or two Labour members 'while the Clyde showed their dislike of both sides by abstaining'. P.J. Grigg, *Prejudice and Judgement* (London, 1948), p. 139.

making provision for assistance to the victims of aggression and con-
ferring on the Council additional powers to designate an aggressor
and decide upon appropriate sanctions.[16]

The opposition of the Dominions to such commitments was known
but the decision as to whether to accept them now rested with the new
government. MacDonald showed little personal interest in the matter
and entrusted the conduct of affairs at Geneva to the Lord President
of the Council, Lord Parmoor, whose attitude did not commend itself
to partisans of the League.[17] By June all the reports from Geneva
indicated that MacDonald had no intention of involving the League
machinery in any important matters.[18] Lord Cecil of Chelwood did
his best in a memorandum submitted to MacDonald on 23 June to
argue the case for the Draft Treaty and to contest the doctrine that the
Dominions now had a veto on British foreign policy irrespective of
what the British government might feel to be in the Empire's best
interests.[19] Cecil was not optimistic about the possibility of converting
MacDonald to a more pro-League position, believing that the Prime
Minister's own scepticism was reinforced by that of the permanent
officials, notably Crowe and Hankey.[20] In fact the cabinet had already
turned down the Draft Treaty at a meeting on 30 May although the
League was not informed until 5 July and the British note published
only on 19 July. The negotiations with the French over the Dawes
plan and future security had thus been in progress for some time
before the French became aware that MacDonald would not accept
the current League version of collective security.

In considering these negotiations two additional elements in the
situation remain to be assessed.[21] In the first place, the Bank of
England, still nominally a private institution, or rather Montagu
Norman its governor (1920–44) increasingly felt able to play an
almost independent rôle. And this was not merely to offer advice on
the technical aspects of international finance but to indulge in what

---

[16] See F.S. Northedge, *The Troubled Giant: Britain among the Great Powers 1916–1939* (London,
1966), pp. 232ff.
[17] 'Alas for Parmoor. He seems unteachable'. Cecil to Gilbert Murray, n.d. Gilbert Murray
Papers: Cecil Correspondence.
[18] Eric Drummond to Cecil, 27 June 1924. Cecil of Chelwood Papers. B.M.Add. 51110.
[19] Cecil of Chelwood Papers. B.M.Add. 51081.
[20] Cecil to Drummond, n.d. Cecil of Chelwood Papers. B.M.Add. 51110.
[21] Stephen A. Schuker, *The End of French Predominance in Europe: the Financial Crisis of 1924 and
the Adoption of the Dawes Plan* (Chapel Hill, 1976), pp. 242–3. The work by Schuker is the most
important treatment of MacDonald's European policy in 1924 although the main theme is the
change in the French position. J. Bariéty's book *Les Relations Franco-Allemandes Après la Premier
Guerre Mondiale: 10 Novembre 1918–10 Janvier 1925, de l'execution à la négociation* (Paris, 1977)
again gives much material on British policy despite its more restricted title. No British historian
has been into these matters in the same detail nor assimilated the economic issues so effectively
into the diplomatic narrative. Valuable also is Walter A. McDougall, *France's Rhineland Diplomacy 1914–1924: the Last Bid for Balance of Power in Europe* (Princeton, 1978).

might almost be described as a parallel international diplomacy of his own.[22] The weight of the bank's influence was thrown heavily on the side of Germany, in part because Norman saw in Schacht the dominant figure in German finance someone to whom he could give unstinted admiration. The second point was that the return of the Americans to the international scene was largely made inevitable by the general conviction that the new era in reparations could only be started if Germany could receive an international loan to which the American banks would have to be the main subscribers. While the American bankers were less interested in seeing that Germany's political demands were met, and while J.P. Morgan and his colleagues who had helped to finance the allied war effort were if anything largely French in their sympathies, Norman managed to manipulate them into joining in his insistence that the loan could not be floated unless the conditions of the new settlement were such as to be acceptable to the Germans. Meanwhile the French possibility of resisting these pressures was much weakened by the financial crisis in the early months of 1924 which made France itself heavily dependent upon American goodwill.

MacDonald was thus both inclined to try for a settlement on a new basis and being pushed towards it by an incongruous combination of the Labour Party, Whitehall and the bankers.[23] In his early period in office MacDonald showed himself relatively conciliatory especially since it was clear that any French ideas of encouraging separatism in the Rhineland or the Palatinate had been abandoned. Poincaré used the eminent French socialist Albert Thomas as an intermediary and it was agreed that he should visit England in June. It is however clear that in part at least MacDonald was awaiting the outcome of the French elections due in May in the hope that a move to the Left and a victory of the 'Cartel' would assist him in getting his way. Whether the allegations made by some Frenchmen that British secret funds were channelled to the pro-Cartel press were well-founded is difficult to confirm. But the victory of the Cartel and the emergence of Herriot as the new premier, with socialists supporting his government though not taking posts in it, were developments undoubtedly welcome to MacDonald and his advisers.

[22] On Norman's role at this time see Henry Clay, *Lord Norman* (London, 1957), pp. 212–3 and Andrew Boyle, *Montagu Norman: A Biography* (London, 1968), pp. 167–77. Neither biographer brings out the full extent of Norman's direct negotiations with the Germans on which see Bariéty, *Les Relations Franco-Allemandes*, p. 610. See also R.S. Sayers, *The Bank of England 1891–1944* (Cambridge, 1976) I, pp. 153–211.

[23] MacDonald may have been aware of the incongruity since he is reported to have said at one meeting of the London Conference that he would have been much blamed as head of a Labour government if it appeared that he allowed his handling of affairs to be dictated by capitalists. Paul Schmidt, *Statist auf diplomatischer Bühne 1923–45: Erlebnisse des Chefdolmetschers in Auswärtigen Amt mit den Staatsmännern Europas* (Bonn, 1949), p. 59.

It was thus Herriot who visited MacDonald at Chequers on 21 and 22 June. Herriot's hopes that this meeting might inaugurate a new era of close Anglo-French co-operation were rapidly shown up as fallacious. His hopes that in return for the evacuation of the Ruhr he might get some new security guarantees and some relaxation of the British claims for debt repayments proved equally wide of the mark. It became clear that putting the Dawes plan into effect would mean abandoning any serious possibility of renewing sanctions if Germany should default again. German goodwill was the assumption upon which the administration of these proposals were based; nor could German failure to meet the disarmament obligations of the Versailles Treaty be used as a reason for retaining physical guarantees.[24] So obvious was Herriot's retreat that his own position in France became precarious leading to a visit to Paris by MacDonald on 8 July which was largely intended to help Herriot keep the support of the French socialists. The formulae accepted at Paris papered over the realities which took shape in the London Conference in August. In the latter part of the Conference the Germans for the first time since the war came to an international gathering on terms of full equality with the victors. A visit to London during the Conference by two French socialist leaders, Léon Blum and Vincent Auriol, did not influence the outcome in France's favour. In return for accepting the British point of view on the major issues, the reduction in reparations payments, the abandonment of the important rôle of the Reparations Commission and the setting of a date for the evacuation of the Ruhr and the three Rhineland towns occupied in 1920, Herriot got merely a vague undertaking from the Germans about future commercial relations and an even vaguer one from the British about the war debts.

It was therefore not difficult for MacDonald to regard this aspect of his tenure of the Foreign Office as a success. He certainly resisted any pressure from outside his immediate circle to alter his position. The Dawes plan was criticized by the Miners' Federation and by the textile manufacturers as likely to benefit their German competitors; but this criticism seemed to have made little impact.[25] In an interview after the Conference, Snowden actually criticized the new arrangements as being too favourable to the French and as still putting too much of a burden on the Germans.[26] Even this clear breach of cabinet

---

[24] The first account of the Chequers meeting was published in 1928 by a French journalist, Georges Suarez, basing himself on Herriot's documents and recollections. This work, *Une nuit chez Cromwell* was republished in 1932 with additional material by Poincaré as *Herriot (1924–1932)*.

[25] Schuker, *End of French Predominance*, p. 315

[26] Colin Cross, *Philip Snowden* (London, 1966), p. 221.

solidarity was not taken up by the Prime Minister. It is however fair to say that even if one dates the beginning of the 'appeasement' of Germany to MacDonald's premiership, he was on the whole in this respect supported from far outside Labour's own ranks.

Although the General Staff believed that British and French security were still intimately connected, suspicion of France was still powerful in naval and air force circles.[27] Many Conservative politicians were also persuaded that France's best hope lay in being conciliatory to Germany and in not relying upon her east European allies. Churchill himself believed that the best way of getting France to behave in this way was to deny her a British guarantee, and was prepared for the sake of peace to see changes made on Germany's eastern frontiers.[28]

MacDonald himself was now prepared to see the League in a more favourable light and the September meeting of the Assembly was attended by both himself and Herriot – the first two heads of government of major powers to take part.[29] MacDonald's speech on 4 September advanced the idea that a country's readiness to submit to arbitration should be the test of 'aggression'. This principle was the foundation of the 'Geneva protocol' which emerged from the Assembly's deliberations on 2 October. A main difference from the rejected Draft Treaty of Mutual Assistance was the scaling down of the duty of individual countries to comply with a call for sanctions. Even so the indications are that the Dominions and the government of India which were fully consulted about the Protocol were no keener on it than on its predecessor.

'Appeasement' in Europe reflected not merely Labour's own ideas but a general sense of the gap between Britain's resources and her obligations. In imperial matters, the Labour government did little to mark itself off as very different from its immediate predecessors. In India, the Viceroy Lord Reading was encouraged to hold the line against the increasing radicalism of the national movement. Despite Lancashire's worries, protectionist measures by the Indian government were not disallowed. In the colonial sphere there was no important change. In regard to Iraq the government insisted that the Anglo-Iraqi Treaty concluded by the Bonar Law government be ratified despite nationalist objections. In Egypt there was some reason

---

[27] Schuker, *End of French Predominance*, p. 254.

[28] Schuker, *End of French Predominance*, p. 389.

[29] The theatrical nature of the occasion did not escape comment: 'It was the year when that queer vain simulacrum of a Statesman, Ramsay MacDonald was posturing with poor Herriot as his rather abashed protagonist. MacDonald played to an imaginary audience, a Victorian audience that had been dead five and twenty years'. H.G. Wells, *The World of William Clissold* (London, 1926) II, p. 568.

to expect a change in policy since MacDonald had when passing through Cairo in 1922 voiced his sympathy for the nationalist leader, Zaghlul. But when Zaghlul came to London in September 1924 he found himself completely at odds with MacDonald both on the future of the Sudan and on the remaining elements of the British presence in Egypt proper.

The degree of continuity in foreign and imperial policy was matched by a lack of any revolutionary impulse where defence policy was concerned. To the disgust of Beatrice Webb former pacifists were quite prepared to take a conventional view of their duties when called upon to take up ministerial posts in the service departments.[30] As a general guide on defence matters, the government looked to Haldane who presided over the Committee of Imperial Defence as Mac-Donald's deputy.[31] The Admiralty was instructed to draw up a memorandum about possible measures of naval disarmament but no use was made of it.[32] The only major change was the decision made against the wishes of the Admiralty and the Colonial Office and the expressed views of Australia and New Zealand to abandon the Singapore base. It was argued that to do otherwise would be incompatible with a foreign policy based upon a strengthened League of Nations.[33] It was the best example of MacDonald's belief that so far from the League requiring an infusion of British strength if it was to guarantee the peace, it could in some undefined way act as a substitute for such strength and provide reasons for economy in the defence budget.

Lavishness was not indeed a characteristic of the first Labour government. Whatever the depth of his socialist convictions, Snowden as Chancellor of the Exchequer in a non-socialist state was fully Gladstonian in his outlook. He demonstrated his free trade convictions not only, as has been seen, in respect of imperial preference but also by abolishing the wartime McKenna duties and allowing the safeguarding duties to expire. Business was assisted by abolishing the corporation profits tax and the ordinary citizen by abolishing the inhabited house duty and various taxes on commodities. His adherence to the temperance cause also led Snowden to lower the entertain-

---

[30] For those (unlike the Webbs) gifted with a sense of humour, there was some amusement to be gleaned from this situation: 'Our new secretary of war – a miner – opened his first Army Council with the words: "Well, gents, I hope we shall pull well together for our King and country and the dear old flag" '. Harold Laski to Justice Holmes. M. de Wolfe Howe, ed., *Holmes–Laski Letters* (London, 1953), p. 590.

[31] F.A. Johnson, *Defence by Committee: the British Committee of Imperial Defence 1885–1959* (London, 1960), p. 194.

[32] Stephen Roskill, *Naval Policy between the Wars.* Vol. II: *1919–1929* (London, 1968), pp. 428–9.

[33] Roskill, *Naval Policy* II, pp. 419–22.

ments duty so as to assist attractions rival to the public house.

In domestic matters the combination of financial orthodoxy and the lack of a parliamentary majority made it obvious that not a great deal could be done to improve the lot of Labour's own natural constituency in the industrial working class; MacDonald had to be prepared for attacks from the Left in the Labour movement that he was not implementing socialist policies. It was clear from the beginning that despite the trade union preponderance in the Party, MacDonald was not prepared to treat union demands from any point of view but that of the national interest as the government saw it. A dock strike early in the government's life was avoided by a settlement which favoured the dockers, but not before it became evident that the government would if necessary use troops to keep essential supplies moving. A threatened strike of London transport led to the actual proclamation of a state of emergency, though a settlement was in fact arrived at before drastic measures needed to be taken.

The two main issues were housing and unemployment. After a shaky start in handling the difficult problems of rent control and the evictions of unemployed men for failure to pay rent, John Wheatley the only MP from the 'Red' Clyde who attained ministerial office was successful with a housing bill following Neville Chamberlain's Act of 1923 which produced an important expansion in publicly provided housing over the next few years. Unemployment was more difficult. MacDonald put some hopes in electrification schemes and in afforestation where the rural areas were concerned. But these proposals could not have a rapid impact; it was clear that the government, like its predecessors, saw no real hope except in revival of trade, especially exports, and would not divert resources in such a way as to hamper private industry. What was done for the unemployed was to improve the scale and conditions of benefit; but even here the government had to face revolts among its own supporters. By the end of the session, public works had virtually been abandoned as an important element in ministerial planning, and given Snowden's financial conservatism this was hardly surprising. It was clear that Labour's preparation for office had not included any serious consideration of the rôle of finance or indeed of the relationship of possible policies to economic theory of any school.

When Parliament rose there was however no evidence that the uneasy relationship between the government, the left wing of its own supporters and the two Opposition parties would soon reach a crisis; by-elections suggested that the government was not losing ground and that the Liberals in particular had no reason to seek an early election. What was overlooked was the time-bomb in the shape of the negotiations with the Russians.

The pressures for recognition of the Soviet government were various. In the trade union movement, the struggle against communist infiltration was not over and had produced a considerable degree of suspicion of the Russians which was shared by most of the leading figures in the Labour party.[34] On the other hand, the former Liberals who were so powerful in the Advisory Committee were much more favourably inclined to the Russians. In addition, those business circles which had tried in vain to persuade the Conservatives to seek agreement with the Russians could now press their case once more. The idea that Russia could provide a major market for British manufactures and cheap foodstuffs to bring down the cost of living had an obvious appeal.[35] Both the Liberal and the Labour parties had included recognition in their election manifestoes and it thus appeared to be something for which a clear majority existed in the new Parliament.[36]

The question was whether or not anything could be got in return – either in the matter of the Tsarist debts or in respect of Soviet propaganda – the subjects at issue between the two governments ever since their first tentative contacts on the morrow of the Revolution. The Russians were however adamant that recognition must be unconditional, and after some hesitation, the note of recognition was sent on 1 February. It was however understood that there would be a conference to deal with the question outstanding, and this met in London on 14 May – its conduct being left to Ponsonby. From the beginning it was clear that the Russians' willingness to make concessions on the points to which the British and particularly the City attached importance depended upon British willingness to extend a loan, which they regarded as essential for their own industrial and agricultural reconstruction, and of export credit facilities to firms trading with them.

The negotiations proved protracted and were more than once threatened with a breakdown particularly over the question of compensating the bond-holders. MacDonald himself was persuaded to withdraw his original veto on a loan. But when the cabinet were confronted in July with a memorandum drawn up by Ponsonby it became clear that there was significant opposition to further concessions. Snowden in particular was sceptical of the proposed economic advantages to Britain, and could see no reason to allow the Russians

---

[34] See Roderick Martin, *Communism and the British Trade Unions 1924–1933: a Study of the National Minority Movement* (Oxford, 1969).

[35] See Stephen White, *Britain and the Bolshevik Revolution: a Study in the Politics of Diplomacy 1920–1924* (London, 1979), part III 'Labour, Business and Recognition'.

[36] For relations with the Soviet Union during the period of the Labour government, see G. Gorodetsky, *The Precarious Truce: Anglo-Soviet Relations 1924–27* (Cambridge, 1977), chap. 1.

to repudiate their debts.[37] But when it was made clear that the loan was conditional on the debts issue being settled, the cabinet instructed Ponsonby to conclude a treaty before Parliament rose early in August.

At a plenary session of the Conference on 4 August some measure of agreement was registered, but the Russians refused to make the other parts of the treaty dependent upon an agreement over the claims upon them and on 5 August the cabinet was informed that the negotiations had broken down. They were reopened after the intervention of a group of back-benchers among whom Morel took a leading part, and after some hectic proceedings a treaty was actually signed on 8 August. Neither the formula about claims nor the suggestion of a further treaty to embody a loan were regarded as satisfactory in financial and commercial circles, and the desirability of a loan was contested even within the Labour Party.

Since the treaty would not enter into effect without parliamentary approval it was parliamentary opinion that mattered most; and it soon became clear that the Liberals increasingly disillusioned with their rôle in the House of Commons and worried about the unity of the party if it should be prolonged were ready to separate themselves from the government on this issue. Lloyd George now took the lead in rallying Liberal opinion to oppose the treaty, though it was agreed with Asquith that the attack should be directed primarily at the loan provision. The Liberals tabled a motion for the rejection of the treaty on 1 October, the day after Parliament reassembled.

The vote was never taken since another matter had arisen which seemed to MacDonald in the end to provide a more favourable issue on which to court defeat and go to the country. It arose out of the suspicions attached to Soviet propaganda and to the Soviet Union's relations with the British Communist Party.[38] On 5 August a Communist journalist, J.R. Campbell, was charged under the Incitement to Mutiny Act. On 13 August the prosecution was withdrawn, and MacDonald was accused of having brought pressure to bear on Patrick Hastings the Attorney-General at the behest of his own left wing. The Conservatives who had intended to table a vote of censure decided instead to back a Liberal motion for a select committee to enquire into the affair. After some uncertainty, MacDonald decided

---

[37] Colin Cross, *Philip Snowden*, p. 220.

[38] It has recently become known to what an extent intelligence sources enabled successive British governments to be informed about Soviet propaganda and subversion both in the United Kingdom and in the Empire. Many earlier judgements on Anglo-Soviet relations in this period must be revised to take account of the new material. See Christopher Andrew, 'The British Secret Service and Anglo-Soviet Relations in the 1920's.' Part 1: 'From the Trade Negotiations to the Zinoviev Letter.' *The Historical Journal* XX (1977).

that the Liberal motion would be treated as one of confidence. The vote – 359 to 198 – was decisive. On the following day, 9 October, MacDonald saw the King who reluctantly granted a dissolution.

The campaign found the Labour government in a difficult position in that their handling of the Russian treaty had destroyed any hopes of capitalizing on MacDonald's apparent success at the London Conference and at Geneva. For the Liberals the prospects were even gloomier, since a bill for electoral reform which if passed might have served to renew their hopes of playing a leading rôle again had been defeated on a free vote of the House after the government had refused to give it any official backing. Nearly all the Conservatives and an overwhelming majority of Labour members voted in the negative. The indiscipline of the party at Westminster which may have owed something to the still difficult relationship between Asquith and Lloyd George was shown up by the failure of 40 Liberals to vote at all.

In the country the collapse of morale was indicated by the failure to prepare candidatures for a fight which could not be long avoided, again partly because of Lloyd George's unwillingness the release funds and the lack of other financial resources.[39] The 10 by-elections of the Parliament had all been discouraging for the Liberals. In every constituency the Liberal vote dropped, often to Labour's advantage. The Conservatives had managed to use the tactics which were to prove so effective in the general election campaign of branding the Labour Party as conniving with communism and rallying the voters to themselves as the only sure bulwark against the threat of socialism. Some Liberals found it necessary to match them in this respect.[40]

In these circumstances, it is still difficult to see why the Liberals chose to precipitate an election at this time although it is also clear that MacDonald could have postponed his fate if he had so chosen, and could even have found a compromise formula to prevent a majority of Liberals voting against the Russian treaty. These are however questions of tactics and of personality; MacDonald was now by all accounts a very tired man. What was clear was that the Liberals had failed to get the Labour Party to treat them as any kind of partner and had under-rated the determination of the Party and of MacDonald himself to destroy them as an effective force even where putting forward Labour candidates in a Liberal area might hand the seat over to the Conservatives.[41]

[39] From the point of view of party politics the most useful account is that in Chris Cook, *The Politics of Alignment: Electoral Politics in Britain 1922-1929* (London, 1975), part 3.

[40] See Chris Cook, 'The By-Elections of the First Labour Government', in C. Cook & J.A. Ramsden, eds., *By-elections in British Politics* (London, 1973).

[41] The problem is well treated in Trevor Wilson, *The Downfall of the Liberal Party 1914–1935* (London, 1966), chaps. 14 and 15.

Despite the inherent weakness in the government's position given the issues on which the election would most likely be fought, the Labour Party entered on the campaign in an optimistic frame of mind. Almost everywhere its organization had improved and it was able to field candidates where it had not sought to previously.[42] The total was 514, up 87 on the previous election. The Conservatives were also in a high state of preparedness and confident of success. The number of candidates went down by 2 compared with 1923, but the divisions in the Party had almost all been healed with the dropping of protection, and Baldwin now led a united team. The Liberals could not hope to make up for their weak showing during the year. In some cases they withdrew as a result of anti-socialist pacts; in others they simply failed to field a candidate. Instead of 457 candidates, the number slumped to 340. A party fighting on so narrow a front was not a credible competitor for political power.

Labour fought on its record and on a variety of promises for future action in the economic and social field, none of them startlingly radical. The Conservatives were successful from fairly early on in concentrating attention upon the issue of Communism and the need for stable government after the uncertainties of the recent Parliament. MacDonald's speaking campaign which was the core of the Labour riposte had the disadvantage of further highlighting the issues upon which the government was most vulnerable. Nor was it easy for him after beginning with strong attacks on the Liberals to end up by appealing for progressive Liberal and nonconformist votes. It was into a campaign already faltering that the curious episode of the 'Zinoviev letter' was injected.

This document purported to be a letter signed by Zinoviev, the President of the Comintern and a member of the three-man triumvirate then in power in the Soviet Union, and was addressed to the Communist Party of Great Britain calling upon the Party to campaign for the ratification of the Russian Treaty. More important it went on to call for agitation in the factories, and to instruct the 'military section of the party' to form cells in the army which 'might be in the event of an outbreak of active strife, the brain of the military organization of the Party'.[43]

This document came into the hands of the Foreign Office via the Special Intelligence Service on 10 October, the day of the dissolution. There was no division in the Foreign Office over its authenticity but some division as to whether in addition to a protest, there should be publication which would clearly embarrass the government. Crowe

---

[42] On the election of 1924 see Cook, *Age of Alignment*, part 4.
[43] See Gorodetsky, *The Precarious Truce*, pp. 35ff.

was however adamant that the 'Russian machinations should be exposed' and the violations of the 1921 Trade Agreement in respect of propaganda called to the attention of the Soviet government. The document reached MacDonald on 16 October and he agreed to Crowe's proposals provided the document was known to be genuine. The preparation of the protest and the strengthening of the draft by MacDonald himself all took time since MacDonald was campaigning out of London. On 24 October Crowe possibly misinterpreting MacDonald's wishes, as the Prime Minister was later to claim, sent off the note of protest, and handed both it and the offending letter to the press.

In fact the decision of the Foreign Office about publication had been pre-empted by the fact that the 'Zinoviev letter' itself had come into the hands of the *Daily Mail* in complicated circumstances in which officials of the Conservative Central Office played some part. It was circulated to the rest of the press and published on 25 October four days before polling day. Labour ministers unaware of the contacts between MacDonald and the Foreign Office over the past fortnight were confused and ordinary Labour candidates even more so. It seemed easy enough to blame Labour's defeat on the injection into the campaign of this new piece of evidence that the government had gone too far in tolerating Soviet intervention in Britain's internal affairs and that the Russian Treaty would only add to the Communists' opportunities.[44]

---

[44] It was obvious that the explanation that the letter was a forgery would commend itself to Labour circles since it would bolster a claim that the electorate had in fact been deliberately deceived for party reasons. After some fairly heated exchanges between MacDonald and the Soviet ambassador, the Cabinet seems to have come round to this view and MacDonald instructed the protest to be withdrawn. But on the same day, 6 November, the government resigned; owing to the absence of the king from London, this action had not been taken immediately the results of the election were known. Many historians have shared the view that the 'Zinoviev Letter' was indeed a forgery and the publication in 1967 of the book *The Zinoviev Letter* by L. Chester, S. Fay and H. Young seemed to indicate both how it was done and how the document came into the hands of the press. But the matter is not as simple as that if only because the various versions of the story do not tally. It has been argued that the Soviet government might even have wished to discredit the Labour government which had embarked upon a European policy that looked like reconciling Germany with the Western Powers and bringing about her membership of the League. See N. Grant, 'The "Zinoviev Letter" case', *Soviet Studies* XIX (1967) and a letter from W.E. Butler, *Soviet Studies* XXI (1970), which suggests that the matter remains an open one. An important contribution to the debate casting an adverse light on some of the 'forgery' argument is Sybil Crowe, 'The Zinoviev Letter: A Reappraisal', *Journal of Contemporary History* X (1975). Finally, Christopher Andrew points out that although conclusive evidence one way or another may now never be obtained, a committee of the subsequent Baldwin cabinet reached the conclusion that 'there was not a shadow of doubt as to the authenticity of the document' and that their view was shared by the principal officials of the Foreign Office and Cabinet Office. For this judgement to be set aside he writes 'stronger evidence of forgery is required than has so far been produced'. *The Historical Journal* XX (1977), p. 675. In the same volume, E.H. Carr upheld the forgery thesis. On the other hand the fact that the leak to the press was made for electoral purposes is clear. Further evidence for the

The results of the election seemed unequivocal.[45] In the new Parliament 412 Conservatives together with 7 'Constitutionalists' faced 151 socialists and a mere 40 Liberals. The Conservatives had gained 162 seats and lost only 7; Labour actually gained 22 seats of which 16 were from the Liberals but lost 64; the Liberals gained a mere 9, all but one as a result of electoral pacts with the Conservatives, and lost 123.

The Conservatives with two thirds of the seats in the House of Commons seemed to have won a landslide victory on a par with that of the Liberals in 1906. But in terms of votes cast, the position appeared in a rather different light. The Conservative share of the vote had increased from 38 per cent to 46.8 per cent but Labour's share had also gone up, from 30.7 per cent to 33.3 per cent. It was the drop in the Liberal share of the vote from 29.7 per cent to a mere 17.8 per cent which had made the difference. The defeat of Asquith himself in a straight fight with Labour was symbolic of the catastrophe. It was the penalty for 'putting Labour in'.

The election indicated that in industrial England the fight was now between Conservatives and Labour with Labour poised to take any advantage of the swing of the pendulum. In most of the larger cities the Liberals had disappeared as a fighting force. To some extent this strength of Labour in the industrial areas was balanced by their weakness in rural England and London suburbia. There were also specific factors that exaggerated the Conservative triumph – the fall in the number of unopposed returns, particularly in Ulster, and the increase in the turnout. And it was the increase in turnout, particularly in middle-class constituencies, that may have been the most tangible consequence of the Zinoviev letter.

What was clear was that the brief transitional era of three-party politics was over. Britain would be governed either by Conservative or Labour governments; what was less clear was whether either party had the capacity to find solutions to the problems the country faced. It was the Conservatives with their huge majority who would first have to face the test. Less than a year after leading his party into what many of his followers believed to have been an unnecessary disaster, Baldwin was back at the helm.

forgery thesis, connecting the forgery with the British spy Sidney Reilly, is contained in Michael Kettle, *Sidney Reilly: the True Story* (London, 1983).

[45] For a detailed analysis, see Cook, *Age of Alignment*, chap. 19.

6 The Baldwin Years

The second Baldwin government was in many ways the most effective administration of the inter-war period. It witnessed what appeared to be the culmination of Britain's efforts to secure the pacification of Europe and a largely successful resolution of the problem of relations between Britain and the newly assertive Dominions; at home it brought about a more effective system of social administration looking to the final elimination of the old Poor Law and a major consequential reform in local government; it faced and emerged successfully from a major challenge, or what appeared to be a major challenge from the trade union movement, and despite legislative changes to the detriment of some trade union privileges seemed able to count upon a new and relatively peaceful period in industrial relations. Serious and persistent weaknesses in parts of the economy were balanced by advances in newer industries, particularly automobiles and consumer durables. The return to gold suggested that Britain had recovered its pre-war financial standing. The stresses of the war and post-war periods were in the past, the impact of the slump was yet to come.

The new cabinet contained an unusually large number of members who retained their places and their original offices throughout its life; notably Churchill at the Exchequer, the Marquess of Salisbury as Lord Privy Seal, Austen Chamberlain at the Foreign Office and his half-brother Neville Chamberlain at the Ministry of Health; Leo Amery as Secretary of State for the Colonies, to which title the new designation of Dominions Secretary was shortly added; Lord Eustace Percy at Education, Sir Philip Lloyd Greame shortly to become Sir Philip Cunliffe-Lister at the Board of Trade, Sir Arthur Steel-Maitland at Labour; Sir William Joynson Hicks at the Home Office. The same was true of the three service ministers: W.C. Bridgeman at the Admiralty where he fought hard for the navy against Churchill back in his economy mood; Sir Samuel Hoare at the Air Ministry at the time that the potentialities of inter-imperial air routes were beginning to be recognized, and Sir Laming Worthington-Evans at the War Office.

Such changes as there were were made mainly for non-political reasons. Curzon returned to office but Baldwin's desire to carry on with what appeared to be a bettering of relations with France precluded his appointment to the Foreign Office, and he was appointed Lord President; when he died in April 1925 his place was taken by an even more senior Tory figure, Balfour, who thus returned for his last spell of office at the age of 76; when the Lord Chancellor, Cave, died in 1928 he was succeeded by the Attorney-General Douglas Hogg who took the title of Viscount Hailsham; Birkenhead who went to the India Office resigned for personal reasons in 1928 and was succeeded by Viscount Peel who had held the office in the previous Bonar Law–Baldwin government. The only resignation on political grounds was that of Viscount Cecil (the former Lord Robert Cecil) whom Baldwin had reluctantly included once more to satisfy pro-League of Nations opinion and who, much disillusioned with the government's handling of affairs at Geneva, finally broke with it over the question of naval disarmament.

The cabinet represented a wide spectrum of Conservative opinion and drew both from those who had opted for independence in 1922 and from the coalitionists. The most surprising appointment was that of Churchill whose career since leaving office had not done much to endear him to main-line Conservatism. In particular in March 1924 he had stood unsuccessfully against an official Conservative candidate in a by-election, as an independent anti-socialist still angling for Liberal as well as Conservative support. In the general election he had however been encouraged to stand as an independent 'Constitutionalist' supporting Conservative policies from outside the Party's ranks. It was clear that he was regarded as safer inside than outside the fold; nevertheless even with Neville Chamberlain preferring to return to the Ministry of Health, the appointment surprised almost everyone including Churchill himself.[1]

It was of course not the case that the cabinet was in agreement on every issue; but it is not easy to classify its members in any regular way. The most obvious distinction was between those who like Churchill had turned their backs on protection and imperial development and preferred free trade, government economy and progress in social provision and the more imperially – and defence-minded.[2] Such considerations would put Churchill on the 'Left'; yet as the General Strike was to show his sympathy for the plight of the miners

---

[1] Churchill's career between 1922 and 1939 is fully dealt with in Martin Gilbert, *Winston S. Churchill*. Vol. v: *1922–1939* (London, 1976).

[2] 'It really is a disaster that Stanley put him at the Exchequer where he intensifies all the "little Englandism" of the Treasury'. Amery diary entry 10 March 1926. *The Leo Amery Diaries*, ed. John Barnes and David Nicholson. Vol. I: *1869–1929* (London, 1980), p. 445.

did not lessen his determination to preserve the authority of the State, particularly where the spectre of Soviet-inspired communism was still a factor. What was however most important at least until the government began to run into difficulties towards the end of its life, was the ascendancy of the Prime Minister himself over his colleagues, in the House of Commons and in the Party in the country, where his close associate J.C.C. Davidson was responsible for major improvements in organization and finance.[3]

The position in the House of Commons where MacDonald once more led the Labour Opposition was sufficiently secure for the government to be able to pursue its policies without serious difficulty. Indeed MacDonald had to face the inevitable attacks upon a party leader who could be accused of being responsible for a major defeat – attacks largely from the Left. But with no alternative leader in sight except Snowden, himself unpopular on the Left, the challenge to his leadership was fought off without too much trouble. What was more important was a shift to the Left in the trade union movement and a greater activism already noted in 1924. For the essence of the position at which MacDonald had arrived was that Labour was henceforward to fulfil unquestioningly the parliamentary rôle of an alternative party of government which it had been the object of his strategy to achieve.[4] But for a party which so heavily depended for men and money on the trade unions it was a rôle which demanded their willing assent.

In any event, the crushing of the Liberals had been severe enough to make their rôle in the new Parliament a minor one. It was the Asquithian wing that had proportionally suffered the most and over half the small band of Liberal MPs were now ex-coalitionists. On 2 December 1924 Lloyd George was elected to the leadership in the House of Commons, but at once a small group was formed under Runciman which refused to accept the decision; the rivalry between the two wings of the party seemed unabated by disaster. Asquith himself entered the House of Lords early in 1925 but remained leader of the Party until his retirement in October 1926 after further differences centering around the General Strike, and after further losses in by-elections had brought Party morale even lower.

It was now with his leadership of the main body of the Party secured, that Lloyd George undertook what was to prove his final effort at rejuvenating the Liberal Party, bringing about much needed

[3] On the Conservative party in this period see Ramsden, *The Age of Balfour and Baldwin*, chaps. 10–12. On Davidson's rôle see Robert Rhodes James, ed., *Memoirs of a Conservative: J.C.C. Davidson's Memoirs and Papers 1910–1937* (London, 1969).

[4] A motion at the 1925 party conference that the party should not again take office without a majority of its own was heavily defeated. Alan Bullock, *The Life and Times of Ernest Bevin* (London, 1960) I, pp. 258–60.

improvements in the organization with the aid of the former Liberal minister Sir Herbert Samuel, who agreed to become its head. It looked for a time as though these efforts might also profit from the spadework put in at creating an active body of Liberal intellectuals who could furnish the Party with policies more suited to the felt needs of the hour than the shibboleths of former times. At a juncture when the Labour Party's commitment to socialism seemed to deprive its leaders of any distinctive policies pending the advent of a socialist society, the opportunity seemed inviting. The economists Keynes and Hubert Henderson and the historian Ramsay Muir were among the leading figures involved in this aspect of Liberal activity culminating in the two celebrated documents *Britain's Industrial Future* (The Liberal 'Yellow Book') published in January 1928 and *We Can Conquer Unemployment* (March 1929).

Industrial questions – above all the persistent high levels of unemployment – were the key to political success and failure.[5] How far government action could affect the situation was a matter of dispute among economists and businessmen alike. The government was increasingly involved with sounding outside opinion and with seeking areas of agreement. In this respect it is no doubt significant that both the trade union movement and the employers' organizations had become more representative and better organized during the post-war period. To some extent indeed their progress can be seen as a single feature since each side of industry was affected by its view of the other.[6]

Before 1914 the trade unions' strength resided almost wholly in the individual unions.[7] The Parliamentary Committee of the Trade Union Congress which was the only organ of co-ordination was supposed to deal with legal questions affecting the movement, electoral reform, and inter-union disputes. But although its ambitions grew during the war with the involvement of the trade unions in so many aspects of the war effort a body of 17 members with one secretary was unable to do a great deal. The idea that unions might give each other

[5] The number of unemployed fluctuated very markedly from year to year throughout the 1920s. As a percentage of the insured workers it jumped from 2 per cent during the post-war boom in 1920 to 17.1 per cent in 1921; it fell back to 13.6 per cent in 1922, 11.2 per cent in 1923 and 10 per cent in 1924. The figure rose to 11.1 per cent in 1925 and 12.3 per cent in 1926 but fell again to 9.4 per cent in 1927 – the best year for employment between 1920 and the war – and then rose to 10.5 per cent in 1928 and 10 per cent in 1929. See D.H. Aldcroft, *The Inter-War Economy: Britain 1919-1939* (London, 1970), p. 352.

[6] In his *Politics in Industrial Society* (London, 1979), Keith Middlemas calls his chapter on the 1923-31 period 'Journey to the Centre', seeing the balance between the Conservatives and their links with the employers and the trade unions with their links with Labour as making possible a series of bargains to avoid the harsher clashes visible on the European continent.

[7] V.L. Allen, 'The Reorganization of the Trade Union Congress 1918-1927' *British Journal of Sociology* XI (1960).

mutual support was enshrined in the General Confederation of Trade Unions founded in 1899; but that body never fulfilled the hopes originally placed in it, and gradually faded from the picture.

Industrial muscle seemed to be the prerogative of the unions representing the three main groups of workers upon whom the rest of industry depended; the coal-miners, the railwaymen and the transport workers. The Triple Alliance was set up in 1915 and the mediation of the other unions helped to settle the rail strike of September 1919. Discussions during and after the war in which Ernest Bevin of the transport workers played an important rôle led to the acceptance by a special Trade Union Congress in December 1919 of the idea of setting up a General Council to replace the old Parliamentary Committee. The form the new institution might take was of course crucial for relations with the Labour Party and the final scheme as presented to the 1920 Congress by G.D.H. Cole, at the time a leading figure among Labour intellectuals despite his somewhat unorthodox 'guild socialist' background, provided for the new body to share in the management of new research, legal and publicity departments with the Labour Party and the Co-operative movement. From 1920 the TUC and the Labour Party were housed in the same building.

The first General Council was elected by the Congress in September 1921 but its membership did not differ significantly from that of the old Parliamentary Committee, nor was there an important shift of power towards the centre. What did develop was an administrative machine of increasing size and complexity under the aegis of the first General Secretary, Fred Bramley, and after his departure from the scene through failing health in 1925 of Walter Citrine, first as acting Secretary and then from September 1926 as General Secretary – a post which he was to retain until 1945.

The idea of joint activities appealed to the Labour Party which was always short of funds but the trade unions were less enthusiastic. A National Joint Council to handle the joint activities was agreed to in January 1922 and research, press and publicity, and international departments were created under its supervision. No legal department was in fact set up. Trade union dissatisfaction with the work of the joint bodies was enhanced by MacDonald's failure to consult the trade unions during the 1924 government and in March 1926 the joint departments were wound up. The trade union movement henceforward had its own research and publicity departments while the international department reverted wholly to the Party.[8]

During the lifetime of the Baldwin government and subsequently,

---

[8] See Ross M. Martin, *TUC: The Growth of a Pressure Group 1868–1976* (Oxford, 1980), pp. 189 ff.

the TUC was in a position to speak for its membership independently of political considerations, without however relaxing its primary rôle within the Labour Party. The annual meeting of the Trade Union Congress was thus an important indicator of the ways in which the Labour Party Conference was likely to move. And considerable political weight extending beyond the industrial sphere could accrue to a trade union leader such as Ernest Bevin who unlike some earlier leaders in the movement did not seek membership of the House of Commons.[9]

The major period for forming employers' organizations had been in the 1890s; the powerful Engineering Employers' Federation had been set up in 1896. In 1916 the Federation of British Industries was set up largely to counter what was seen as an increasingly dominant rôle for trade unions in the direction of national policy. Discontent with some aspects of its conduct led the Engineering Employers' Federation to sponsor the creation of the National Confederation of Employers' Organization in 1919. By the 1920s most firms belonged to trade associations or federations and these in turn were brought together in the FBI or NCEO. The NCEO claimed to speak for all employers as the General Council of the TUC claimed to represent all workers; in fact by 1928 its members employed about 60 per cent of the nation's work force. The FBI had by 1925 conceded to the NCEO the main rôle in relations with government and henceforward saw itself more as a supplier of services. A third body, the National Association of Manufacturers founded in 1916, was mainly the voice of the smaller firms and did not claim a say in the political arena. Nevertheless there was some overlapping between all three of the main employers' organizations, and given the importance also of particular trade associations and of some major firms individually, capital was even less integrated than Labour.[10]

It was however the banking world rather than industry that had the ear of the government in the major economic decision taken by Baldwin's administration, the return to gold at the old pre-1914 dollar parity. In a sense the decision to do this in Churchill's first budget in April 1925 was pre-ordained although Churchill made every effort to take opposing views into account.[11] When the export of gold had been prohibited by statute in 1920, it had been for a five-year period, and it had been the firm convictions of previous governments, including MacDonald's, that the return to gold should be made as

[9] Bevin was Secretary of the Transport and General Workers Union from 1921 to 1940. For a sympathetic account of his career in this period, see Bullock, *Ernest Bevin* I.

[10] In 1934 the NCEO changed its name to British Employers Confederation. The three organizations were amalgamated into the Confederation of British Industry in 1965.

[11] Gilbert, *Churchill* V, chap. 5 'Return to the Gold Standard'.

soon as the price levels obtaining in the United States and Britain should permit it. Montagu Norman himself and his associates in the British and American banking communities had no doubts about the wisdom of this course. But it is fair to say that the main advice upon which Churchill relied was that of Otto Niemeyer, then a Treasury official though later to join the Bank, and that the political responsibility was Churchill's and Baldwin's.[12]

There is now a general though not a unanimous consensus among economic historians that the critics of the decision – in particular Keynes – had the better of the argument, that the parity chosen did not represent the true position and that to maintain it demanded a regime of high interest rates and other deflationary measures which were a handicap to British industry and an obstacle to reducing the burden of unemployment. In respect of the export industries in particular, the over-valuation of the currency was an additional handicap in the struggle to reconquer traditional markets or find new ones, although it was argued that fixed exchanges should help exporters. Furthermore it was wrong to believe, so the critics argued, that the pre-1914 automatic operations of the gold standard would be allowed to operate by governments all of which had acquired a greater taste for intervention in the economy and greater means for implementing their wishes. The British economy would thus become under a fixed rate vulnerable to the speculative movement of foreign funds and to decisions taken elsewhere.[13] To some extent this aspect of the matter was concealed for the next few years by the revival in the European economies consequent on the massive influx of American funds particularly into Germany after the conclusion of the Dawes Plan. But the American crash of 1929 set in train events that fully revealed the precariousness of the situation.

Whether if industry had been as certain of a hearing in court and as effective at putting its views as the City, the decision might have been a different one it is not possible to say. What is clear is the curious detachment of the Treasury and the Bank from the problems of industry. Explanations have been sought in sociological investigations. A simpler explanation might be the continued and accelerating polarization of the country between London and its suburbs and satellites

[12] R.S. Sayers, *The Bank of England 1891–1944* (Cambridge, 1976) I, chap. 6. On the rejection of Churchill's suggested alternative of shipping gold to the US to pay war debts and by increasing US gold supply to increase American foreign loans and investments and so bring down the dollar, see M.J. Hogan, *Informal Entente: the Private Structure of Co-operation in Anglo-American Diplomacy 1918–1928* (Columbus, 1977), pp. 71–7.

[13] See S. Pollard, *The Development of the British Economy 1914–1967* (2nd ed., London, 1969), pp. 214–23. On the US factor in British financial policy, see C.S. Maier, *Recasting Bourgeois Europe: Stabilization in France, Germany and Italy in the Decade after World War I* (Princeton, 1975), pp. 598 ff.

and the older industrial areas on the periphery which was so marked electorally, and which would continue to make itself felt. The juxtaposition between Westminster, Whitehall and the City was mental as well as topographical. Nor was the Labour Party which might be held to represent industrial Britain able, for want of expertise and intellectual driving power, seriously to challenge Conservative administrations when in Opposition or implement new and more appropriate policies when in office. How indeed could a party believing that what was wrong was the location of ownership accept policies that suggested that amelioration could precede socialization?

The most immediate and far-reaching impact of the return to gold was upon the fortunes of the coal-mining industry which had been in constant crisis since the war owing to competition in overseas markets, technological changes, resistance to rationalization in a highly fragmented and poorly led industry, bad labour relations and a strong commitment on the miners' side to public ownership as the only way out. Successive governments had done their best to find solutions upon which the interests involved could agree but without success. Meanwhile the miners at times urged upon the rest of the trade union movement the use of industrial power to secure this objective.[14] The Royal Commission of 1919 (the Sankey Commission) failed to find a measure of agreement though it left the miners feeling that the government had tricked them when it refused to act upon either the nationalization of the industry recommended by the casting vote of the chairman or the nationalization of coal royalties upon which there was a fair measure of agreement.

The reduction of working hours in 1919 and the setting up of a coal mining division within the Board of Trade in 1920 did not prevent a strike that October. When wartime government control ended in April 1921 it was the prelude to a further bitter strike which was marked by the failure on 'Black Friday' of the two other members of the Triple Alliance to come to the miners' aid.[15] The fall in prices which followed decontrol and the insistence of the owners on lowering wages to meet competition from abroad caused much hardship and helped to make the mining areas the natural recruiting ground for the extreme Left in politics even though more moderate leaders retained control.[16]

[14] For the general strike and its prehistory, see G.A. Phillips, *The General Strike: the Politics of Industrial Conflict* (London, 1976).

[15] On 'decontrol' see Susan Armitage, *The Politics of Decontrol of Industry: Britain and the United States* (London, 1969).

[16] For the most important of the left-wing movements, see Roderick Martin, *Communism and the British Trade Unions 1924–1933: a Study of the National Minority Movement* (Oxford, 1969). For left-wing politics in two mining communities, see Stuart Macintyre, *Little Moscows: Communism and Working-class Militancy in Inter-war Britain* (London, 1980).

The Baldwin government thus faced a situation in which both sides in the mining industry were united only in rejecting the necessity for contraction in the new economic circumstances, and which faced each other as enemies in the class war, and the possibility, for which emergency preparations had to be kept in being, that other unions would on the next occasion give the miners the support they had refused in 1921. The temporary alleviation of the situation due to the French occupation of the Ruhr came to an end; the owners were not prepared to continue the higher wages then achieved and wished if possible to get rid of the two aspects of their position to which the miners attached most importance – the seven-hour day and the national minimum wage.[17]

By the end of 1924 the deadlock between the miners and their employers over the interpretation of the situation in the industry and the means of improving it was abundantly clear and further strike action appeared likely. The miners sought support from the rest of the trade union movement and in particular from their former partners in the triple alliance. The breakdown in relations in the industry itself came in the summer of 1925; an independent court of inquiry set up by the government produced a report which seemed to accept much of the miners' case. But even before it reported, the willingness of the General Council of the TUC to take some action in support of the miners in the light of the view that a general employers' offensive on the wage front was beginning had widened the prospective area of conflict.

With some reluctance the government were drawn into an attempt to avert the crisis by more direct intervention. It became clear that in order to avoid immediate and perhaps widespread industrial trouble for which emergency preparations were incomplete and the economic and financial repercussions of even an unsuccessful stoppage in transport as well as mining, it would be necessary to depart from the government's preferred stance of non-intervention and offer a subsidy to enable the existing level of wages to be paid while new efforts were made to find an acceptable long-term solution. The latter was to take the form of a new Royal Commission. This retreat by Baldwin, which came to be known as 'Red Friday' – 30 July – was criticized by some government supporters as well as by Lloyd George. It was also not wholly welcome to the official Opposition since the Labour Party leadership had not been involved by the General Council in its approaches to the government. The TUC General Secretary Citrine was alone among trade union leaders in seeing that a possible

---

[17] The vicissitudes of the South Wales mining industry and of the communities dependent upon it are treated in detail in Kenneth O. Morgan, *Rebirth of a Nation: Wales 1880–1980* (Oxford, 1981).

constitutional issue was involved in the apparent use of industrial power – going beyond the idea of a sympathetic strike – to coerce an elected government.

In any event the crisis had been postponed rather than averted. While the Commission sat and the subsidy was being paid, tensions within the industry remained unabated; the Left secured further support among the miners and the government continued to make its preparations to keep essential services going should the TUC again threaten action.

The Commission's chairman, the Liberal ex-Minister Herbert Samuel, and the other members of the Commission, none of whom had intimate knowledge of the industry but whose general approach was of a liberal non-radical kind, could not be expected to provide a solution over and above the various measures canvassed ever since the post-war crisis. The basic assumption of the report was that the international market for coal would recover and that the important thing to do was to improve the industry's productivity by amalgamating undertakings, by developing its by-products and by co-operative arrangements for selling coal particularly abroad. While government intervention would be necessary in the last resort to enforce amalgamations, nationalization was ruled out; the only concession was the recommendation that mineral rights should be taken over by the State.

To meet the existing impasse, the report accepted the contention that miners' wages would have to come down and the national minimum abandoned. How this was to be achieved was left vague; yet since the Commission were opposed to continuing the subsidy which upheld the existing wage structure, there seemed no alternative.

Despite the government's own objections to the nationalization of mineral rights, it was after some hesitation decided to accept the report, but the announcement by Baldwin to this effect on 24 March made it clear that this was conditional on both sides of the industry agreeing to its implementation. Since the owners did not believe that the reconstruction of the industry was the solution for its problems, and since the miners were opposed to any tampering with the existing wage arrangements, this approval was of largely academic importance. Of more importance was the fact that there were signs that the TUC did not share the miners' totally negative approach and that if there were to be a struggle – as now seemed inevitable – it might give them less than whole-hearted support. In principle, it was indeed prepared to give them help, but very little was done to decide on the nature of such assistance and the point at which it might involve a confrontation of a dangerous nature with a government, itself actively preparing the machinery required to ensure the nation's vital supplies. By April 1926 these preparations were far advanced.

The intransigence of both sides in the mining industry impelled the government to take a direct hand in the attempts to find a settlement but in the course of the discussions between 23 and 30 April Baldwin came close to accepting the owners' point of view. In these circumstances, the support of the TUC for the miners would be forthcoming and somewhat unco-ordinated activities took place with a view to supplying it. At the same time the TUC was drawn into a final effort to avert a stoppage through direct negotiations with the government. The government has been criticized for failing to perceive the possibility of getting the TUC to abandon its preparations for a general strike without at the same time settling the dispute in the mining industry itself. Within the cabinet differences of attitude and temperament naturally revealed themselves, as was indeed true of the General Council, torn as it was between a feeling of solidarity with the miners and its own preference for avoiding a crisis.

An attempt to bring in the Labour Party leadership – MacDonald and Henderson – came only after strike notices had been issued and when their withdrawal was one of the government's conditions for further efforts to seek an agreement. While the General Council felt that the government had done too little to press reorganization on the coal-owners, it did not at this stage press the argument for further financial aid. But the main factor in its attitude was a reluctance to face renewed charges of letting down the miners both on grounds of working-class solidarity and because of the fillip which this would give to extremist elements. On the government side, there was of course pressure from its supporters not to give way to a challenge to State authority and the feeling in contrast to that of the previous summer that if such a challenge came the government had the resources to defeat it; the government's own preparations helped to create this mood.

The general strike which began on 3 May followed a course which might have been predicted from its pre-history. The government proved able to keep vital services in being by the use of volunteers, and where necessary of the army. It also managed to present its case, despite the absence of a national press, in such a way as to enlist support for its view that what was at stake was a constitutional issue. In a sense the TUC were unlucky in the timing of their challenge. The level of sophistication the economy had reached, particularly in the vital areas of energy and transport, was not such as to make it vulnerable to the action of relatively small groups of workers as came to be the case after the Second World War – volunteers and servicemen without special training could be used more effectively than would later be the case. Radio broadcasting which was a relative novelty gave the government an instrument of action and propaganda which a generation earlier would not have been available. If the strike had been prolonged, it is possible that more extreme elements on the trade union side might have come to the fore and produced direct clashes with the authorities that would have brought about something nearer to the revolutionary situation that other European countries had confronted in the post-war period. But a revolution was not what the General Council had in mind, and as might have been expected, attempts to find a way of ending the strike began very soon after its shape and scope became clear.[18]

The effort while it lasted was a major one; a total of some 1,650,000 workers took part excluding the miners themselves and also most engineering workers and workers in ship-building who were brought out only on the last day of the strike, by which time others were going back to work. But to win a battle it is not enough to have willing troops. Since there was no serious plan for securing victory for the miners' cause and since the railwaymen in particular were anxious about their future, the only question was the source from which a successful peace initiative might come. An appeal to end the strike on terms which the Labour leadership found acceptable was made by the Archbishop of Canterbury, Randall Davidson, on 7 May after some pressure upon him from ecclesiastical quarters. His ability to evoke a large measure of public support was much diminished by the refusal of the Managing Director of the BBC to allow him to broadcast it.[19] Ending the strike thus became a matter for private behind the scenes negotiation and the instrument found was Samuel himself, who returned to London from abroad on 6 May. In his view the government had misinterpreted his report and gone too far in their acceptance of the case for massive cuts in wages. A proposal to link reorganization with a National Wages Board for the industry proved agreeable to the General Council although its details were rather vague; on the other hand, the miners, feeling that the proposal envisaged some reduction in wages, found the Samuel proposals an unacceptable basis for negotiation. In the course of further discussions an agreed set of proposals were worked out with Samuel and although there was no formal assurance that the government would make them its own, the General Council without feeling that they had reversed themselves called off the strike on 12 May.

[18] The course of events is well-handled in Patrick Renshaw, *The General Strike* (London, 1975).

[19] See G.K.A. Bell, *Randall Davidson, Archbishop of Counterbury* (London, 1935) II, chap. LXXX. It was Reith's own decision, influenced by his fear of the government taking over the BBC itself as some ministers wished. See Asa Briggs, *The History of Broadcasting in the United Kingdom* (London, 1966) I, pp. 360 ff.

The General Council had overestimated the degree of the government's commitment to Samuel's proposals and also the likelihood
that the miners would accept some such solution. The abandonment
of the strike left in being the lockout of the miners for refusing to
accept the owners' new terms and they continued to struggle along
alone for six more months, after which the increasing hardships they
were undergoing and the differing circumstances of the several
coalfields brought about a ragged but eventually complete abandonment of the stoppage. The government's suspension of the Seven
Hours Act in July and Mining Industry Act giving effect to some
measure of reorganization did not affect the basic situation; though
from November most workers did go back to an eight-hour day. The
settlements made over a large part of the industry adversely affected
miners' incomes and the whole picture was probably worse than it
would have been without the strike. Furthermore the Miners Federation of Great Britain was badly damaged by the struggle both financially and in its cohesion, losing members both to non-political unions
in some areas and to a rival left-wing organization in Scotland. Nor
did the fall in wages put the industry back on its feet; further markets
were lost during the six months of the strike and never recovered.
Between 1925 and 1928 Britain's share of the world market for coal
went on falling and a slight revival in 1929 was overtaken by the world
slump. By the time this hit the industry the owners themselves had
abandoned the attempt to recapture sales by cost-cutting and were
embarked upon the alternative policy of limiting competition combined with extensive pit closures. Embodied in the Labour Coal
Mines Act of 1930, this policy of rationalization was not strongly
pressed because of its effect of adding to unemployment.

But the general move towards a more interventionist policy was
displayed when the National Government of the 1930s strengthened
the working of that part of the 1930 Act dealing with common marketing arrangements to such effect that competition in the industry had
been virtually eliminated by the time war came in 1939. A feature of
this process was the growing influence of the Mines Department
within the Board of Trade which had been set up in 1920 and which
acted within Whitehall as a pressure group to counterbalance the
influence of the mineowners' organization.[20]

The mining industry with its special problems remained a world
apart. The rest of industry and government itself had to take account
of the fact of the General Strike and of the lessons that could be
learned from it. It was clear to the majority of trade union leaders that

[20] M.W. Kirby, 'The Mines Department of the Board of Trade', *Historical Journal* XXII
(1979).

a general strike was not an effective means of coercing a government unless its leaders were willing to go to extremes and contemplate the possibility of revolution. The result was that the Labour movement as a whole swung away from the idea that its industrial side could act on its own and the political leadership regained some of the authority it had lost in the 1924 debacle. The triumph of moderation was not welcomed in all quarters, but the left wing organized since 1924 in the Minority Movement found itself handicapped by the effects of Russian intervention in its affairs through the Communist Party; and its efforts to build up voting strength with the trade unions antagonized the existing leadership. The Minority Movement was wound up in 1932 and though there were other 'rank-and-file movements' during the 1930s in which Communists played some part there was no serious challenge to the authority of the TUC.[21]

A sign of the new atmosphere was the beginning of talks in 1928 between a group of prominent employers and the TUC – the so-called Mond–Turner talks. Although little that was concrete came out of these deliberations, particularly when they were put on a more formal basis with the employers' organizations and were overtaken by the onset of the depression after the return of the Labour government in 1929, they helped in the recovery of authority by the TUC and marked a further step in the long-drawn-out process of trying to improve industrial relations which was to be of much importance when war again put the existing system under strain.[22]

From the government's point of view, it was not possible to resist the pressure from its own supporters for changes in the law to deal with the dangers that the General Strike appeared to have revealed. The Trade Disputes and Trade Union Act of 1927 excluded from the protection afforded by the 1906 Act certain categories of strikes – those which had any object other than the furtherance of a trade dispute, or were designed or calculated to coerce the government. Penalties were prescribed for ring-leaders in such actions and new limitations were placed on picketing. Other changes in the law were less directly related to the experience of the General Strike. It was laid down that civil servants could not be members of unions which included non-civil servants, nor could they be affiliated to any outside body. It was thus recognized that despite the growth in unionism within the civil service since the war its members had a relation to society more like that of the armed services and the police than that of ordinary employees. Where local authorities were concerned, it was provided that they could not legally impose a closed shop either on their own employees or on the contractors with whom they might

---

[21] For the details see Martin, *Communism and the British Trade Unions*.
[22] See Bullock, *Ernest Bevin* I, chap. 15.

need to do business. Finally, the 1913 Act was amended in that those trade unionists wishing to pay a political levy should have to indicate their wish to do so in a positive fashion, thus substituting what was called 'contracting in' for 'contracting out'. Although the inclusion of this part of the bill had been opposed by some ministers as being merely provocative without having any practical importance, the available figures suggest that only between 55 per cent and 60 per cent of trade union members contracted in.[23] This suggests that the trade union–Labour Party tie was not as automatic a one in the minds of all trade unionists as the rhetoric on both sides of the Labour movement habitually claimed.

The passage of the Act was strenuously opposed by the Labour Party and the need for its total repeal became a fixed item in the Party's programme; yet the experience of the 20 years during which the Act was on the statute book gives no evidence for believing that the legal framework thus created was an impossible one. Indeed with all allowances made for the unemployment of the 1930s and for special conditions of wartime, they were in labour relations the quietest period of the century; nor did the Act prove an obstacle to the exploration of the common interests of all sides of industry in the Mond–Turner talks. Whether Baldwin and the cabinet would have done better to follow Neville Chamberlain's advice and included some provision for hearings by an industrial tribunal as a necessary prelude to legal strike action is a moot point.

The main domestic legislation of the Baldwin government was however in the field of the social services, and can be regarded as a continuation of the work of the 1905 Liberal government and of the Coalition since it was based on very similar views about the rôle of the State. That so much was achieved was due primarily to the key rôle of Neville Chamberlain at the Ministry of Health. He began his second tenure of this office with 25 measures that he wished to see passed in that Parliament and was successful in piloting through no fewer than 21 of them. Since most of them inevitably involved increased governmental expenditure, it was clearly necessary that the Treasury should co-operate in this programme, and although relations between Chamberlain and Churchill were never very easy, the differences were in temperament rather than in fundamental philosophy. Churchill found it easy to go back to the rôle he had played in the Asquith administration before his transfer to the Admiralty; he preferred spending money on social reform to spending it on armaments and, to the disgust of Amery, to spending it on investment within the colonial empire. Important measures were the Widows and Old Age

---

[23] Financially the effect was not very great. Michael Pinto-Duschinskey, *British Political Finance 1830–1980* (Washington D.C., 1981), p. 74.

Pensions Act of 1925 and the National Health Insurance Act of 1928. Health care was a matter of particular concern to Chamberlain and the cause of medical education (and incidentally of constructive imperialism) was forwarded by the creation of the London School of Hygiene and Tropical Medicine. There were no great changes in the arrangements for public housing but the number of houses built between 1924 and 1929 was very considerable. Much of this building took place in the areas of the new industries in the midlands and south-east and was indeed a precondition of the increasing employment they offered. It was in slum clearance in the areas of declining prosperity that the government's record gave most room for criticism.

The responsibility for social provision was still divided between central and local government and it was clear to Chamberlain that the rating system in its traditional form was inadequate for the new responsibilities undertaken by local authorities. The Rating Act of 1926, much disliked by rural Tories for its reduction in the number of separate rating authorities, was the first step. But it was only a step. What Chamberlain had in mind was something bigger: the extension to the local authorities of the separate social responsibilities of the old Poor Law, thus getting rid of the Boards of Guardians and moving towards a single national network of social provision. It was also his wish to stimulate local initiative by substituting block grants that could take into account the very different circumstances of different local authorities for percentage grants that had tended to favour the richer ones. Into this had to be fitted Churchill's wish to improve the prospects for industry and agriculture (and stave off the demands for protection – his opinions were no less free trade than they had been) – by relieving them of much of the burden of rates. Both elements were brought together in the Local Government Act of 1929, the most important of all the measures of the Baldwin government.

While there were Tory rumblings of disapproval of the Chamberlain–Churchill line, its protagonists did not endear themselves to the Labour Party either. Chamberlain in particular alienated the Opposition both by some of his actions and by the acerbity of his manner. For his reforms were accompanied by a steady campaign against what he saw as the excesses of 'Poplarism', the attempts by some Boards of Guardians to use public provision of relief not simply to alleviate distress but as an instrument for changing the distribution of income. And the departures from financial prudence were accompanied in some cases, as Chamberlain observed, by acts of political favouritism and sheer nepotism that could only be regarded as corrupt. Behind the attacks on spendthrift Boards of Guardians there existed of course a difference of political philosophy not exactly coincidental with party lines, since the Webbs too had always held that provision for the relief of unemployment and other forms of distress must not be of such a kind or on such a scale as to weaken the will to work.[24]

It is still difficult to assess when dealing with the government's domestic policies what precisely was the rôle of Baldwin himself.[25] Neither he nor indeed anyone else could see the nature of the problems in the round. It is not clear, as it would be to later historians looking back on the 1920s, that the unemployment of the period was not simply the result of a downward turn in the trade cycle but was the product of new difficulties in some of the principal exporting industries. These could scarcely be resolved both because of changes in the world markets and because of rigidities within the industries themselves, not least the power of the trade unions.

In the 1920s as was to be the case in the 1930s British citizens were enjoying rising real incomes and rising standards of living; many indices both economic and social could be quoted. But a large section of the population was excluded from sharing in this prosperity through unemployment and this section because of the location of the industries which had hitherto given it work was very heavily concentrated in Scotland and Wales, in the mining counties, in the northwest and parts of east London.

What Baldwin stood for was not an economic analysis of the country's problems but an approach which suggested that all would be well provided that the old values were retained and the bitterness between classes assuaged; he was the spokesman for national reconciliation and the success he had in portraying this image of caring for all citizens was the core of his value to the cabinet and the Party. Within the cabinet his rôle was also essentially that of a conciliator between colleagues of different views and often of strong personality. To have presided over it with the resignation on principle of only one colleague, and he a Cecil, was a remarkable achievement. He is the only major figure in modern British political history who reached his position of distinction without a single major legislative measure or diplomatic feat attached to his name.

The Baldwin government's position was strengthened by its successes in external relations. The question of imperial economic unity had been for the time being laid to rest by the election of 1923. In spite of Amery's appeals for a more active policy, efforts to make more of imperial economic relations were limited to some attention to communications, some assistance to emigration and the public relations efforts of the Empire Marketing Board. Exploration of the possibili-

---

[24] On the rôle of Chamberlain in the Baldwin government, see Keith Feiling, *The Life of Neville Chamberlain* (London, 1946) and Iain Macleod, *Neville Chamberlain* (London, 1961).

[25] On Baldwin's rôle in the 1924–9 government see especially Keith Middlemas and John Barnes, *Baldwin: a Biography* (London, 1969), chap. 18 'A New Style of Leader'.

ties of closer union between the three East African territories and between the two Rhodesias and Nyasaland revealed the gulfs between the attitudes of white settlers, Indian immigrants and the native population for whom most officials saw themselves as trustees. The Dominions pursuing their individual policies were more concerned with safeguarding their rights as independent members of the international community. The Imperial Conference of 1926 was thus largely taken up with the constitutional issue and was notable for the Balfour Declaration by which the separate sovereignties of the Dominions was given a verbal formulation which in turn after further negotiation and another Imperial Conference in 1930 was to lead up to the legal provisions of the Statute of Westminster of 1931.

On more specific issues, there were some ominous signs for the future. The Irish Free State was an uneasy member of the Commonwealth and its unease was exacerbated by the unresolved problem of the future of Ulster.[26] The Irish delegates had agreed to the 1921 Treaty in part because they believed that the proposed Border Commission would recommend such large changes in the existing line that Ulster would cease to be a viable unit. On the other hand, the Ulster Unionist leadership was adamant against any change and Craig the Ulster Prime Minister refused to appoint a representative to the Border Commission, leaving the UK government to name a substitute. The Chairman of the Commission, the South African Judge Richard Feetham, a former member of Milner's kindergarten, interpreted the Commission's mandate as meaning that no changes could be proposed which were incompatible with Ulster's survival as a separate entity. And no formal objection was made by the Free State member. The report (which was not made public until 1968) recommended therefore only minor changes in each direction. This fact, leaked to the press at the beginning of November 1925, produced reactions that induced all three Prime Ministers to drop the whole matter and leave the very awkward frontier unaltered.[27] The position of the Unionist majority in Ulster was entrenched; its representation at Westminster acted as part of the Conservative Party; and ending 'partition' remained the chief claim to be pressed by Irish political parties whether in domestic politics or in their relations with the United Kingdom.

If policy towards Ireland did not occasion any major differences of opinion within the Conservative Party the same could not be said of India.[28] Baldwin's choice as Secretary of State of Lord Birkenhead,

[26] See A.T.Q. Stewart, *The Narrow Ground: Aspects of Ulster 1609–1969* (London, 1977).

[27] See G.J.P. Hand, ed., *Report of the Irish Boundary Commission, 1925* (Shannon, 1969).

[28] For the impact of the Indian issue on Conservative politics from 1924 to 1935, see Gillian Peele, 'Revolt over India', in Gillian Peele and Chris Cook, eds., *The Politics of Reappraisal 1918–1939* (London, 1975).

the only Coalition minister who had opposed the Montagu – Chelmsford reforms, suggested a desire to consolidate the existing situation rather than proceed with further advances towards self-government. But Birkenhead himself decided that it might be better to pre-empt a future possible Labour government by instituting a constitutional inquiry before the expiry of the time provided for under the 1919 Act, and while he could still nominate its members. The Simon Commission's investigations were however boycotted by the Indian Congress Party on the ground that it was wrong that this body (which apart from Simon himself included as its only figure of note the future Labour Prime Minister Clement Attlee) should have no Indian member. Birkenhead's scepticism was shared by his successor as Secretary of State (in October 1928), Viscount Peel. But a more important decision had been made by Baldwin when as Lord Reading's successor as Viceroy he appointed in April 1926 Lord Irwin whose view was that a more flexible approach might serve to divide Indian opinion and permit agreement on the constitutional future with at least some sections of it.

The Middle East continued to present the British government with a series of unresolved problems. In Egypt the British High Commissioner Lord Lloyd had the choice of relying on the King and unrepresentative governments depending upon his personal favour, or of pressing for a more democratic regime which would be run by the Wafd, the main nationalist party and which would undoubtedly press for the abrogation of the special position that Britain occupied in relation to the country's defence, and for a change in the status of the Sudan which would give the Egyptians a say in its affairs. Lloyd's handling of this situation did not meet with the approval of Austen Chamberlain who regarded his methods as too abrasive, but no different policy was proposed.

In Iraq pressure was also exerted by Britain in favour of a constitutional form of government and a constitution embodying responsible government was actually promulgated in 1925, but neither the monarchy nor those elements in Iraqi society upon whose consent it rested were prepared to allow policy to be determined by a wider constituency; and elections as has been common in the Middle East were inevitably arranged. Since Britain's interest in Iraq was less deep-rooted than in Egypt the repercussion of events there, provided military expenditure could be kept down, were less significant in British politics than the Egyptian issue or than the even more tangled affairs of Palestine.

In Palestine the commitment to the Jewish National Home which had powerful supporters in all political parties had been balanced by the pressure particularly from within officialdom to do nothing locally that might alienate Arab and Moslem opinion over a wider area. The British administrators, though for the most part striving for balance between the rival claims, usually tended to feel more sympathetic to the Arabs, and to wish to follow the familiar colonial model of the time by providing the country with some form of representative institutions to which the Jews had always been averse, seeing that its likely effect would be to confirm their minority status.[29]

In the early years of the Baldwin administration with a firm High Commissioner in the person of the soldier Lord Plumer, things looked moderately hopeful from the British point of view. Jewish immigration was not very rapid, and the Arabs began to look towards more moderate leaders prepared to contemplate some compromise solution. But by the time Plumer's successor Sir John Chancellor announced on 1 January 1929 that negotiations were to begin, looking to the setting up of a legislative council, a new dispute beginning in 1928 over access to the Western Wall of the Temple (the so-called wailing wall) on the Jewish Day of Atonement, 24 September, had both envenomed relations between the two communities and enabled the extremist leader of the more extreme elements among the Arabs, Haj Amin al-Husseini, the Mufti of Jerusalem, to regain his authority. By the time that Baldwin's government gave way to MacDonald's second administration in June 1929 and Leo Amery who was sympathetic to Zionist aspirations was followed at the Colonial Office by Lord Passfield (Sidney Webb) who was personally strongly hostile to them, events in Palestine were rapidly moving towards a new outbreak of violence.

Challenges to Britain's position in the Middle East were however not such as Britain could not contain provided it could feel secure elsewhere. Austen Chamberlain's primary purpose as Foreign Secretary was to continue the search for pacification in Europe which primarily involved the question of the trade-off between French security and disarmament.[30] The cabinet was indisposed to accept the Geneva Protocol, the last fruit of MacDonald's efforts. Chamberlain who would himself have preferred a straightforward guarantee to France was obliged to settle instead for the idea of a Rhineland Pact advanced by Stresemann when it became clear that the western allies would not begin the evacuation of the Rhineland without further assurances.[31]

Chamberlain had his work cut out ot convince his colleagues to go forward, since Churchill, Curzon, Birkenhead and Amery would

[29] The best treatment of this period is Bernard Wasserstein, *The British in Palestine: the Mandatory Government and the Anglo-Jewish Conflict 1917–1929* (London, 1978).

[30] See Anne Orde, *Great Britain and International Security 1920–1926* (London, 1978).

[31] See Jon Jacobson, *Locarno Diplomacy: Germany and the West 1925–1929* (Princeton, 1972).

have preferred to wait until France embraced a more conciliatory policy towards Germany. It took a threat of resignation before Chamberlain got his way.

The Locarno Treaty by which Britain became a co-guarantor with Italy of the frontiers between France, Belgium and Germany and which reaffirmed the demilitarization of the Rhineland, was signed in London on 1 December 1925. Although it contributed to a sense of stability in Europe and so helped in the current improvement in the economic situation, the Locarno Treaty had a number of effects of a less positive nature, some of which were perceived by critics at the time. For continental Europeans, the most noteworthy aspect of the settlement was that it gave the western neighbours of Germany guarantees that were not extended to the countries on her eastern borders, and given the strength of German revisionism this was bound to have its effect. From the British point of view, the most significant feature was that the Dominions were not signatories of the treaty nor bound by its provisions; yet they feared that Britain could by fulfilling its terms at some time put them in a position when it would be hard for them to avoid being drawn in. More immediate was the effect of the treaty on Britain's defence policy. Since Britain could theoretically be drawn into a conflict on either side, prior consultations with one side seemed ruled out, and the military collaboration with the French which had survived the political disagreements of recent years was now allowed to decline. At the same time, the machinery for controlling Germany's own armaments was allowed to lapse. The 'Locarno spirit' provided an additional reason for economizing on Britain's own armaments.

One reason for the opposition to a too overtly pro-French stance had been the continued fear that a tough line would lead to Germany moving closer to the Soviet Union. This was also a motive for not being too hard on the Russians themselves despite the provocation caused by their activities during the General Strike, the continued friction over their propaganda in India, and their rôle in the Chinese revolution.[32] On the other hand, the pressure from within the Conservative Party spearheaded by the Home Secretary Joynson-Hicks was much increased as a result of the General Strike and did not abate even when the TUC Congress at its meeting in September 1926 exhibited a strong shift away from the pro-Soviet orientation of the past couple of years. What Locarno did was to remove Chamberlain's resistance to this pressure since it seemed for the time being to make it certain that Germany would look to the West rather than the East to

[32] Although somewhat more sympathetic to the Soviet position than the evidence warrants, the best description of the development of Anglo-Soviet relations at this time, is that in G. Gorodetsky, *The Precarious Truce: Anglo-Soviet Relations 1924–27* (Cambridge, 1977).

find its friends. The break of diplomatic relations which came on 26 May 1927 was publicly justified by documents found during a police raid on 12 May on the Soviet commercial company Arcos and other material giving more telling evidence of Soviet activities to Britain's detriment.[33] Despite the Soviet ambivalence towards the Labour Party and Communist attacks on the trade union leadership, the official Opposition criticized the break, giving rise to the expectation that relations would be restored when Labour returned to office. The most important practical reason for deploring the break was the continued belief in the importance of the Soviet market to the British economy despite the fact that the balance of trade was running much in the Russians' favour. In fact, trade relations were maintained after the breach which thus had a mainly symbolic importance.

No British government could ignore the importance of the United States which despite the predominance of the isolationist mood had performed an important rôle in sorting out the reparations controversy. But the only issue of direct Anglo-American importance was that of naval disarmament. Attempts to extend the Washington agreement on battleships to cruisers came up against the quite different needs of the two powers. The Geneva naval conference of 1927 broke up without agreement and the Anglo-American differences were widened when Britain and France agreed upon joint proposals in 1928. Britain remained anxious to limit the number of heavy cruisers which were the American favourites while retaining the right to build large numbers of light cruisers to protect her sea-routes; and the difference remained unresolved when Calvin Coolidge was replaced as US President by Herbert Hoover in March 1929.

To some extent the argument was an unreal one though pursued with vehemence by sailors on both sides. For it was by now an axiom of British policy that war with the United States was not an option available to it. Naval armaments although affected by considerations of French and Italian intentions were primarily a matter of the presumed threat from Japan. What this meant was that since questions of expenditure precluded the building of a separate Pacific Fleet, it would be necessary in time of war to send ships from home waters and the Mediterranean to the Far East. And this made a base in Far Eastern waters necessary; by 1921 it had been decided that the location of such a base would be Singapore.

The decision to build and equip the base was opposed from the

---

[33] The material found during the raid was considered insufficient to justify the government's action in breaking off relations. For the availability of Soviet documents to the British authorities see C. Andrew, 'The British Secret Service and Anglo-Soviet Relations in the 1920s', part I, *Historical Journal* XX (1977).

beginning by the Treasury.[34] The first MacDonald government suspended work upon it but it was resumed when Baldwin returned to office. The need for the base was widely accepted among Conservatives but there were repeated suggestions that since the main purpose of it would be to assist the Pacific Dominions, Australia and New Zealand should be ready to meet part of the financial cost.

On naval policy generally, the issue turned upon the interpretation of the one-Power standard to which Britain was committed since Washington. It was held that this need would be met provided there were sufficient local forces to maintain the situation pending the assembly of the main fleet. But Churchill took the view that the 10-year rule should not be interpreted to mean that Britain should acquire the capacity to fight Japan single-handed. He thus proposed that from 1928 the 10-year rule should be held to operate forward from day to day until the policy itself was abandoned. Against opposition particularly from Balfour, Churchill got his way and the same rule was held to operate in respect of air and land armaments as well. In the case of the army little opposition was to be expected. The army was not at this time a source of vigorous initiatives in military policy except for a few somewhat suspect enthusiasts for armoured warfare, and it was still organized and manned primarily for use in imperial defence, often in very small contingents.[35] It was still hoped that if there should again be war against a major power, Britain could return to the traditional policy of naval blockade supplemented by coastal raids.[36] Locarno did cause some rethinking in military circles since it was obvious that if the guarantee was to be taken seriously it could involve mobilization for a major war. But there was no important impetus behind such planning and a strong unwillingness on the part of the services to try to link their planning and budgets to particular scenarios in foreign policy.

In the distribution of the allocation for defence by the Treasury between the services, the army tended to do worst. The immediate post-war period saw some effort put in to the air force, mainly in order to guard against the effects of French preponderance in this arm. But in November 1925 a cabinet committee agreed to delay the completion of the programme for a whole decade. While the argument was largely a financial one, it is clear that by this time a rapprochment with France had taken place, and that while the danger of a direct

---

[34] For the role of the Treasury in respect of Singapore see Max Beloff, 'The Whitehall Factor: the Rôle of the Higher Civil Service 1919-1939', in Peele and Cook, eds., *Politics of Reappraisal*.

[35] See Brian Bond, *British Military Policy between the Two World Wars* (Oxford, 1980).

[36] Peter Dennis, *Decision by Default: Peacetime Conscription and British Defence 1919-1939* (Durham, N.C., 1972).

attack upon the United Kingdom was receding, more attention was being given to strengthening the route to the East. Yet in so far as the Royal Air Force had an important rôle in this respect, particularly in Iraq, this was not an argument for relaxing effort in this area. Nor did the better relations with France altogether reassure opinion in Britain, as Chamberlain pointed out to Briand in 1928. A suggestion for an agreement on metropolitan air forces limited to Britain, France and Italy was however turned down by the French on the ground that they had no air force separate from their army and navy.

The approach of the election of 1929 was faced with some confidence by the Conservatives. In particular the government felt able not only to set aside any further demand for House of Lords reform – for which pressure was in any event declining in strength – but also to proceed to another step in the democratization of the franchise which had figured in the Conservative manifesto, the lowering of the voting age for women from 30 to 21 – the so-called 'flapper vote' – enacted in the Equal Franchise Act of 1928. A backbench attempt to get an equal franchise at 25 was rejected. The 'flappers' showed no gratitude.

The Labour Party had meanwhile recovered from its defeat and increased its hold on local government particularly in London, While there had been some friction with the left-wing of the Party, particularly the ILP, MacDonald's authority seemed unimpaired, and his performance as leader of the Opposition, particularly in the field of foreign affairs, had been an impressive one. On the other hand, there seemed a possibility that any weakening in the government's support might be to the benefit of the Liberals who under the dynamic if sporadic leadership of a seemingly rejuvenated Lloyd George were capitalizing on the most evident of the government's failures – the still unacceptable level of unemployment. But the Liberal recovery shown in the by-elections was mainly in rural seats where Labour was weak, and the gains had been made at Conservative expense. In the urban areas the drain to Labour continued.

The Liberals nevertheless entered the election, fixed by Baldwin for the end of May, with high hopes – running candidates in 513 constituencies and arguing for a positive expansionist policy for dealing with unemployment against the Conservatives' somewhat dreary slogan of 'safety first'. The Conservatives remained the largest party in terms of votes cast with 38.2 per cent, but the vagaries of the electoral system put Labour which had secured 1.1 per cent less ahead of them in the new House of Commons with 287 seats against 260. The Liberals pushed up their percentage of the vote from 17.6 to 23.4, but in seats their total went up from 40 only to 59. For while they gained 35 seats which had eluded them in 1924, they had lost 19 of those they held, and 17 of these to Labour. With trade union organization buttressed by an increasingly powerful party machine, Labour now had an urban working-class following which appeared almost impregnable. For the time being the politics of class seemed more important than the politics of issues.

The importance of this remodelling of the electoral scene which corresponded to the very uneven distribution of the growth of prosperity in the late 1920s was however of more long-term than short-term significance. The Labour lead in the House of Commons was a convincing one and there was no thought as there had been after the 1923 election of trying some combination to keep Labour from office; indeed if there was one thing that united Baldwin, Chamberlain and the great majority of the cabinet it was their unwillingness to have anything to do with Lloyd George. Of the coalitionists only Austen Chamberlain and Churchill remained. But in the country the Labour Party's position was less secure. The fact that the Conservatives had secured more votes overall reflected in part the narrowness of many of the Labour victories. Many Labour seats had been won in three-cornered fights and 41 per cent of them against 21.9 per cent in 1923 on a minority vote. If the crushing set-back to Liberal hopes were to result in a further collapse of the Party, the Conservatives would be the more likely beneficiaries. Although there had been some movement from Liberal to Labour among prominent radicals, Alfred Mond (Lord Melchett) and Hilton Young (Lord Kennet) were powerful recruits from Liberal to Tory during the 1924–9 Parliament. It was an ominous portent.[37]

[37] For an examination of the electoral background to the second Labour Government, see John Stevenson and Chris Cook, *The Slump: Society and Politics during the Depression* (London, 1977).

7 The Second Labour Government and the Crisis of 1931

The second Labour government came into office at an unfortunate moment. The specific British problem of structural unemployment due to the decline of staple export industries was shortly made far worse by the onset of a world depression, the causes of which lay outside the control of any single government, although it was triggered off by the Wall Street crash of October 1929. In all countries the ultimate impact of the depression was to diminish the appeal of international solutions to their economic problems and to push them towards doing what they could with the resources under their own control, or in the case of the 'have-not' nations to seek to expand these by territorial acquisitions, or by reducing independent countries to a state of economic subordination through barter trade and clearing agreements. While all the major countries were signatories of the Kellogg–Briand Peace Pact of 1928 which had outlawed war as an instrument of national policy, the possibility of armed conflict could never be far from the minds of their rulers. It was a world which bore little relation to the ideals in which the leaders of the British labour movement had been nurtured.

The course followed by Britain while affected by its dependence upon foreign trade and the rôle of London as an international financial centre, was not radically different from that pursued elsewhere. All major countries began by attempting to meet the crisis through deflationary measures and were only later forced into a combination of autarky and employment creation through increased public spending. None of the latter were wholly successful though they were later regarded as examples of Keynesian economic theory in practice. Keynes himself had an opportunity to put forward his own remedies when he gave evidence to the Committee of Inquiry into Finance and Industry (the Macmillan Committee) – of which he was himself a member – set up by the Labour government in November 1929. But his views were challenged as impractical both by Montagu Norman, the governor of the Bank of England, and by the Treasury spokesman, Sir Richard Hopkins. While the report published in June 1931 largely drafted by Keynes made important suggestions on the management of the country's finances, it did not recommend either tampering with the gold standard or a massive programme of public investment.[1] The Economic Policy Committee set up by MacDonald in January 1930 which also had Keynes as a member failed to make any impact upon governmental thinking. But in the light of the orthodoxies then prevailing both at home and abroad, it seems unreasonable to single out the MacDonald government as particularly ineffective and obtuse.[2] What its short and unfortunate career was to show was that its socialist vision of a world in which production for use should replace production for profit was of no assistance when trying to remedy the ills of an existing capitalist economy. The dominant personalities on the economic side of the cabinet, Snowden at the Exchequer and William Graham at the Board of Trade, were as devoted to free trade and sound finance as any Gladstonian Liberal.

MacDonald's own instincts were not very different, though less indebted to theory of any kind. His pragmatic approach produced an attempt to take the unemployment question out of the mainstream of government policy by appointing the popular trade union figure J.H. Thomas to the position of Lord Privy Seal with special responsibility for dealing with unemployment and to back him up with a triumvirate of junior ministers, the left-wing apostle of 'poplarism' George Lansbury, as First Commissioner of Works, a Clydeside ILP figure, Thomas Johnston as Under-Secretary of State for Scotland, and Oswald Mosley a former Tory as Chancellor of the Duchy. Mosley, only 32 years of age, had been struck by the Keynesian ideas that Lloyd George had patronized, but even if he were successful in pressing them upon Thomas, there was little chance of such financial unorthodoxy making an appeal to Snowden.

The third leading figure in the cabinet was inevitably Henderson, the creator in so many respects of the Labour Party, and dominant in its national organization. He was appointed to the Foreign Office, MacDonald not wishing to repeat the experiment of combining that office with the premiership, but his control in this sphere was not by any means complete. MacDonald still kept an oversight in this field and was not always in accord with his Foreign Secretary.[3] On two

[1] See R.F. Harrod, *The Life of John Maynard Keynes* (London, 1951), pp. 397–8; 413–27.

[2] The important work by Robert Skidelsky, *Politicians and the Slump: the Labour Government of 1929–31* (London, 1967) suffers from the fact that it was written at a time when Keynesian economics had itself become the dominant orthodoxy, and before experience revealed its inadequacies, and from an over-estimation of the intellect and personality of Oswald Mosley, of whom Professor Skidelsky was to be the biographer; it also underestimates the appeal of tariffs to critics of government policy.

[3] See David Carlton, *MacDonald versus Henderson: the Foreign Policy of the Second Labour Government* (London, 1970).

crucial issues, relations with the United States including the vexed question of naval disarmament, and the handling of reparations and inter-allied debts, Henderson had to allow the lead to be taken by others – MacDonald in the former case and Snowden in the latter. On other issues there were also some differences between MacDonald and Henderson despite the fact that both of them were as convinced as their predecessors of the need to avoid foreign policy commitments which neither public opinion at home nor the Dominions were prepared to uphold. Henderson was closer to the doctrine of 'collective security' than MacDonald and thus more prepared to listen to French arguments and more suspicious of German revisionism.

Henderson and MacDonald were agreed in desiring the resumption of relations with the Soviet Union, and negotiations to this end began in July 1929 and were completed by the beginning of December, being followed by a temporary trade agreement in April 1930. The Soviet Union was the principal beneficiary of the renewed contacts since while trade grew, British exports to the Soviet Union were again much lower than the movement of goods in the opposite direction. Allegations about foreign-inspired (including British-inspired) sabotage which figured in a show trial in the Soviet Union, now undergoing the stresses of the first five-year plan, did not improve the atmosphere. And the leftward slant of the Comintern since 1928 with its repercussions on foreign communist parties meant that the Labour Party as a whole was less likely to press for closer relations with the Soviet Union than it had been during the lifetime of the 1924 government.

In general the new cabinet was not an impressive body, though this time MacDonald did not need to go outside Labour's own ranks to fill the various posts, except that for Attorney-General he called upon Sir William Jowitt who had been elected as a Liberal, and thus changed parties so as to take office. The cabinet had the distinction of being the first to include a woman, though Margaret Bondfield's undistinguished tenure of the Ministry of Labour did not add much weight to the feminist argument. As with Snowden, other portfolios went to those who had held them in 1924: Lord Parmoor as Lord President of the Council – his son, Stafford Cripps became Solicitor-General in October 1930 – Charles Trevelyan at Education, William Adamson at the Scottish Office, and Lord Thomson until his death in the crash of the R101 airship in October 1930 at the Air Ministry. Of other senior figures in the party, Sidney Webb, promoted to the Lords as Lord Passfield, made a very unimpressive Colonial Secretary and Clynes achieved promotion to the Home Office. Of those with their principal offices still ahead of them, A.V. Alexander, a leading figure in the Co-operative movement, became First Lord of the Admiralty, and Arthur Greenwood Minister of Health. Herbert Morrison, the boss of the London Labour Party, was made Minister of Transport from which vantage point he began the work which led in 1933 to the setting up of the London Passenger Transport Board – the model for many future measures of nationalization; but he did not enter the cabinet until March 1931; Clement Attlee got his first foot on the ministerial ladder at the same time when he became Postmaster-General in succession to H. Lees-Smith who entered the cabinet as Minister for Education in succession to Charles Trevelyan who resigned (after the failure in the House of Lords of his education bill) because of his objection to the movement already perceptible among his colleagues towards making cuts in public expenditure. Curiously, Christopher Addison whose career in politics had appeared at an end when he was thrown over by Lloyd George and had since moved into the Labour Party was given junior office at the Ministry of Agriculture before returning to the cabinet as head of the department in June 1930.[4]

For some aspects of government policy, it was possible to rely on a degree of national consensus, though it was never total. Naval talks with the Americans renewed almost at once and profiting from the goodwill of the new American President, Herbert Hoover, led to the calling of another five-power naval conference in London for January 1930. In the interim, MacDonald paid a successful visit to the United States – no British premier had ever visited that country while in office – which did much to end the endemic friction that had characterized Anglo-American relations since the Peace Conference. But European susceptibilities were wounded by the evidence of Anglo-American accord and although France and Italy signed part of the London Treaty of April 1930, they did not accept the ratios for overall strength which formed the core of the treaty where the three major naval powers were concerned. The agreement over cruisers with the United States and the postponement of battleship replacement were defended by the government on economy grounds, though attacked by the Conservatives and by the Earls Jellicoe and Beatty, for once in accord, as handing over maritime supremacy to the United States. Churchill, no longer Chancellor, could now reverse himself and join in the onslaught.

The closing period of the previous government and witnessed, as already noted, a distinct improvement in Anglo-French relations and this aspect of Austen Chamberlain's policy had come in for severe criticism from both Lloyd George and the Labour leadership and

⁴ See K. and J. Morgan, *Portrait of a Progressive: the Political Career of Christopher, Viscount Addison* (Oxford, 1980), Chaps. 6 and 7.

particularly from some Labour backbench MP's who urged unconditional evacuation of the Rhineland. But the French government refused to show the flexibility which Chamberlain suggested to them was necessary if the Baldwin government was to retain office.[5]

A new plan for reparations which if generally acceptable might lead to the evacuation of the Rhineland was worked out by an expert committee led by the American banker Owen D. Young and set up in February 1929. The plan was drafted by June, but the new government did not find the terms satisfactory from Britain's point of view and sought to seek its revision at a conference held at the Hague in August. Henderson while publicly urging an agreement on the simultaneous evacuation by the British, French and Belgians made it clear that if no agreement were reached he was prepared for the British troops to be withdrawn unilaterally. The possibility that the Young plan would not be accepted because of British opposition and that the French would therefore refuse to agree on evacuation had to be taken into account. It was the fear of Britain acting independently rather than Snowden's much trumpeted jingoistic firmness on behalf of the British taxpayer that secured agreement on a revised Young Plan. The British were out of the Rhineland by the end of the year and by 30 June 1930 the French and Belgians had followed them.[6]

The way now seemed clear for the British to pursue what was at the core of the new government's policy, and the matter closest to Henderson's heart, a measure of general disarmament which could align Labour's traditional pacifism with the realities of political responsibility. But while the Preparatory Commission set up in 1927 continued its labours to prepare for the projected world disarmament conference, the rising tide of German nationalism and the revisionism of both Italy and (in a different way) Soviet Russia meant that the old problem of whether disarmament should follow or precede arrangements for mutual security would be even harder to resolve. It was fitting in the light of his own share in the preparation of the conference that Henderson should be elected as its chairman when it met in Geneva in February 1932; but by then he was out of office.

There was no break in continuity as far as relations with the Dominions were concerned – although by the time J.H. Thomas who had become Dominions Secretary in June 1930 introduced the Statute of Westminster in the House of Commons in November 1931, he was occupying that post in the new National Government.

It was in fact Henderson at the Foreign Office who first

[5] Jon Jacobson, *Locarno Diplomacy: Germany and the West 1925–1929*, (Princeton, 1972), pp. 243–5.
[6] Jacobson, *Locarno Diplomacy*, pp. 281–363.

experienced the burden of the unresolved imperial problem.[7] He almost at once forced the resignation of Lord Lloyd as High Commissioner in Egypt. Since the previous friction between Lloyd and Austen Chamberlain prevented the Conservative front bench from using this event to attack the government, it was possible for Henderson to ride out the storm it created but the essential problem of reconciling British interests and Egyptian nationalism was brought no nearer solution, and indeed this was one more issue on which MacDonald and Henderson differed, since the former was much more hostile to the idea of any concessions over the Sudan. A new agreement offered the Egyptians a return to the pre-1924 situation but the victory of the Wafd party in the elections in December brought into office a new government which was determined to amend the agreement in Egypt's favour. Negotiations in London for that purpose were held in the following spring but without result. Some cordiality had been restored to Anglo-Egyptian relations but that Labour government had proved no more capable than its predecessor of finding an acceptable legal framework for them. The stumbling block had proved to be the Sudan and the government's military advisers may well have been pleased that it would not after all be necessary to pull back British troops from Cairo and Alexandria nor to make any concessions over the Canal Zone.[8]

Iraq which had wanted to replace the Treaty of 1927 did achieve its purpose; the lease of the base at Basrah was to be for only 25 years – the duration of the alliance, and after five years, British troops were to leave central Iraq.[9]

Egypt and Iraq were the concern of the soldiers and of that element in British opinion which took imperial affairs seriously – not a very large one. Palestine however continued to excite strong feelings and attract greater political attention. The sixteenth Zionist Congress held in the summer of 1929 with voices calling for a National Jewish State on both sides of the Jordan and for the repudiation of the 1922 White Paper, helped to stimulate Arab fears; violence broke out which the new High Commissioner Sir John Chancellor found it hard to contain with the reduced forces left at his disposal, after the withdrawals that had been found possible during Plumer's relatively peaceful rule. As a result, many Jews were murdered before reinforcements could be brought in from Egypt.

Weizmann the Jewish leader whose entire political career had been

[7] On Anglo-Egyptian relations during the period of the Labour government, see Carlton, *MacDonald versus Henderson*, pp. 163–73.

[8] S.P. Gupta, *Imperialism and the British Labour Movement 1914-1964* (London, 1975), pp. 164–5.

[9] Gupta, *Imperialism*, pp. 165–6.

based on the assumption that British and Zionist interests could be harmonized hurried to London to find in Lord Passfield the 'most anti-Zionist secretary of State with whom Zionists had to deal at any time'.[10] A Royal Commission under Sir Walter Shaw sent to investigate the disturbances took it upon itself to look at the whole question of the Mandate, despite assurances from MacDonald that this would not be the case. It concluded that the disturbances were 'unpremeditated', giving an almost clean bill of health to Haj Amin, the Mufti of Jerusalem, and saw the cause of trouble as lying in excessive Jewish immigration and the solution to lie in imposing curbs upon it. A further commission under Sir John Hope Simpson translated these general ideas into more specific recommendations which would effectively have crippled the National Home. A government White Paper published on 21 October 1930 accepted the Shaw–Hope Simpson doctrines and proposals and denied that the furthering of the Jewish National Home was the prime purpose of the Mandate.

The White Paper aroused a storm of protest not only as was to be expected among Jews but also in wider political circles – all the surviving members of the Coalition government that had issued the Balfour Declaration came out against it. And when the White Paper was debated in the House of Commons on 18 November, it was clear that it was also objected to by an important section of the Labour Party. A Jewish Liberal candidate at Whitechapel brought the Labour vote tumbling down at a by-election in December. Passfield was forced into negotiations with representatives of the Jewish Agency and MacDonald himself was persuaded by Weizmann to back the Zionist objections. A letter to Weizmann from MacDonald which was read out by him to the House of Commons on 13 February 1931, gave an 'interpretation' of the White Paper which amounted to its repudiation. For the time being the 1922 policy held. In achieving this success the Zionists owed something to Arab intransigence. The White Paper had included a proposal for a Legislative Council but the Arabs refused to attend a Round Table Conference to deal with the constitutional question when it was suggested by the government in December thus weakening Passfield's position and that of the pro-Arab officials in the Colonial Office.[11]

The developments in India were of much greater political significance to both the Labour and Conservative parties. As Secretary of State, MacDonald appointed William Wedgwood Benn, a prominent

[10] Christopher Sykes, *Cross Roads to Israel* (London, 1965), p. 140.

[11] MacDonald's very active rôle in this virtual reversal of government policy makes it curious that the episode goes unmentioned in David Marquand's biography of the Prime Minister.

Asquithian who had left the Liberals for Labour in 1927. A man more noted for effective waspishness in debate than for aptitude for high office, Benn left the Viceroy Irwin to make the running. During a visit to London after the new government took office, Irwin secured agreement on a declaration which was made public on 31 October 1929, stating that Dominion status was the goal of Indian constitutional progress. It was also agreed that a Round Table Conference should be held in London in 1930. While this appeared to be a considerable advance, the government's intentions and timetable were not sufficiently clear to win over most of the Indian nationalist leaders, nor did Benn and the Viceroy satisfy either them or the Labour Left by their stern handling of civil disobedience.[12]

It had been hoped that a further instalment of constitutional progress could be an all-party affair. And it appeared that Baldwin had agreed to the Irwin declaration. But this had been on the understanding that Sir John Simon would support it; in the event neither Simon nor Reading, important as a Liberal ex-Viceroy, were prepared to go along with the promise of dominion status.[13] Lloyd George also came out in opposition. The Indian question now served to focus the opposition to Baldwin's leadership within the Conservative Party. When Churchill (who had also defended Lord Lloyd) and Birkenhead took the lead in attacking the proposals, it is not surprising that Baldwin's intimates saw in this yet another attempt to revive the coalition around Churchill and Lloyd George.[14] The opposition to Baldwin was also fanned by the press magnates Beaverbook and Rothermere, who had other differences with him, and for a time he seemed in considerable danger of losing his hold. The pressure on Baldwin affected his choice of Conservative representatives to the Round Table Conference which was held from November to December 1930 and at which Gandhi was the only Congress representative, not a circumstance likely to endear it to Churchill. The debate on its proceedings on 26 January 1931 was the occasion for Churchill's resignation from the Conservative business committee (the shadow cabinet) and the beginning of his 10-year breach with the party which he had rejoined only six years before.

Conservative dissent over Indian policy was not merely a matter of the backwoodsmen or of individuals with service connections with India, it also had an appeal in Lancashire, where the textile industry

[12] Gupta, *Imperialism*, chap. 7 deals with the handling of Indian affairs by the second Labour government.
   [13] On the Irwin declaration see R.J. Moore, *The Crisis of Indian Unity 1917–1940* (Oxford, 1974), chap. 2.
   [14] See Gillian Peele, 'Revolt over India', in Gillian Peele and Chris Cook, *The Politics of Reappraisal 1918–1939* (London, 1975).

had already felt the effects of the fiscal convention of 1919 giving the Indian government control over its own tariffs. And Lancashire was important in being one of the few areas of the country in which there was still a strong Conservative working-class following. But the opposition to Baldwin on Indian policy was also linked with the more general revival of protectionist sentiment arising out of the increasing prominence of unemployment as the acid test of British political skills.

Protectionism as such did not have the support of all those who opposed the new moves in India; Churchill and the Liberals were still free-traders. The overlap came rather in the fact that the new protectionist impulse took on an imperial guise with the idea of the Empire as a self-sufficient economic system as a counterpoise to the increasingly autarkic policies of the other main industrial powers.[15] The 'Empire Free Trade' movement backed by Lord Beaverbrook appeared at one time to be an important rival to official Conservatism.[16] Launched in June 1929 the 'Empire Crusade' made important advances in 1930 culminating in a victory for its candidate over the official Conservative in a by-election in Paddington South on 30 October. Lord Rothermere's United Empire Party was also active and threatening to put up candidates.

The campaign against Baldwin came to a head when the death of the former minister Worthington-Evans in February 1931 forced the calling of a by-election in the strategically placed constituency of Westminster St George's.[17] The independent candidate chosen was more concerned with Indian and general tariff policy than with the Empire Crusade argument. After much hesitation, Alfred Duff Cooper, a rising young hope of the Conservative Party, was chosen as the official candidate, and he with some skill managed to steer the contest away from the divisive issues of India and Empire Free Trade and to make it a challenge to the right of the owners of the *Daily Mail* and *Daily Express* to decide who the leader of the Conservative Party should be. His victory by over 6,000 votes marked the beginning of a sharp decline in the fortunes of the Empire Crusade and the United Empire Party and freed Baldwin's hands to take full advantage of the growing domestic difficulties of the Labour government.

The fortunes of the Liberals during the lifetime of the Labour government followed a downward course. Although the government

[15] For the economic arguments see Ian M. Drummond, *Imperial Economic Policy 1917–1939: Studies in Expansion and Protection* (London, 1974). The author does not however deal with the political aspect of the question.

[16] The involvement of Beaverbrook is detailed in A.J.P. Taylor, *Beaverbrook* (London, 1972), chaps. 11 and 12.

[17] See Gillian Peele, 'St George's and the Empire Crusade', in C. Cook and J.A. Ramsden, eds., *By-Elections in British Politics* (London, 1973).

depended for its survival upon their votes they found it difficult to exact any price for their support; in particular the electoral reform that seemed the obvious answer to their now persistent under-representation again escaped them.[18] It is true that the government apparently without direct Liberal pressure set up a conference on the subject in which all three parties were represented and that this debated the issue from December 1929 to July 1930. But the interests of the parties were too divergent for there to be any prospect of agreement, although some Tories including Churchill were not wholly averse to change. After the failure of the conference there were some negotiations between the Labour leadership and the Liberals in the course of which Lloyd George made it plain that further Liberal support would depend upon the government introducing and passing a reform measure. The idea was highly unwelcome to MacDonald who saw it as a way of perpetuating the life of the Liberal Party when it had been his whole object to restore a two-party situation with Labour commanding all votes to the left of the Conservatives.[19] He was further embittered by the difficulties Liberals were making about current legislation, notably the Coal Bill. By the time the King's Speech for the new session was delivered on 28 October the promise of a measure of electoral reform had nevertheless been included. The method chosen was to be the alternative vote, not the system that Lloyd George or most Liberals preferred, though the best they could hope for from the existing government. One reason for the cabinet's change of heart was that it was hoped to get Liberal support for a measure repealing the 1927 Trade Disputes Act and the Liberals for the most part did at least abstain on its second reading in January 1931. The second reading of the Electoral Reform Bill was carried on a strict party vote by 295 to 230 on 4 February. The bill proceeded on its way with the aid of the whips, but the government was narrowly defeated over the proposal to abolish the university seats. The third reading was passed by 278 to 228 on 2 June. The Lords however now proceeded to delete from the Bill many of the points that the Opposition had contested in the House of Commons and restricted the application of the alternative vote to 174 constituencies in the larger boroughs where it was least likely to be of help to the Liberals. It was the government's intention to reverse the amendments in the House of Commons and if necessary to pass the Bill by using the machinery of the Parliament Act but the fall of the government in

[18] See D.H.E. Butler, *The Electoral System in Britain since 1918* (2nd ed., Oxford, 1963), chap. 3.

[19] For the contacts between the government and the Liberals, Dr Butler had to rely upon the account in Lord Snowden's memoirs; there is more material in David Marquand, *Ramsay MacDonald* (London, 1977), pp. 528–9; 583–5.

August put an end to this prospect.

The Liberals themselves had been divided over some aspects of the Bill and on other matters. The former Asquithians were now moving closer to the Conservatives. Lloyd George himself was generally regarded as a formidable political force in his own right rather than as the leader of a Third Party. The situation in the House of Commons was of course affected by what was going on in the constituencies. The politics of Britain were urban politics, and except in a few pockets where nonconformity was still a living if a declining force, Liberals now only counted for something in rural Britain.

The precarious parliamentary base of the MacDonald government could have propelled it to somewhat conventional solutions of its economic difficulties even had its own inclinations been different. But a full scale deflationary policy would mean spreading the burden of depression so as to affect those strata in the population who were its natural supporters, and to whom it was in any event tied through the organic links between the Labour Party and the trade union movement. Even moderate leaders of the trade unions could hardly do other than oppose policies which might otherwise be exploited against them by their left-wing rivals. On the other hand, even after Baldwin had recovered much of his hold upon the Conservative opposition, despite the estrangement of Churchill, there was no great incentive for him to seek to utilize the government's embarrassments in order to take office again, and bear the odium which was bound to accrue to any government pursuing deflationary policies during a deepening depression. The wider the responsibilities for such policies could be shared the less the long-term danger to the Party's prospects, and the less the damage to the nation's unity. The outcome of the 1931 crisis was thus inherent not merely in the country's economic situation but also in the existing prospects of the political parties.

The emergence of unemployment as the rock upon which the Labour government might founder can be dated from the presentation to the cabinet in January 1930 of a memorandum drawn up by Mosley as one of the group of ministers to whom the solution of the problem had been entrusted. It was a radical document in that it dealt not only with the short-term problems of job creation but with a long-term reconstruction of British economic policy on a near autarkic model, treating the recovery of export markets as unattainable, and with changes in the machinery of government to carry out the transformation.[20] In May the cabinet rejected the proposals, largely on the ground that the financial aspects were

[20] The setting of the Mosley memorandum and its contents are fully explored in Skidelsky, *Politicians and the Slump*, chap. 8 and in Robert Skidelsky, *Oswald Mosley* (London, 1975).

unrealistic, and Mosley resigned.[21]

Thomas who had shown no enthusiasm for Mosley's proposals but clearly had little else to offer was moved to the Dominions Office, now separated from the Colonial Office for the first time, and MacDonald himself became chairman of a cabinet committee to co-ordinate measures to deal with unemployment, served by a special secretariat.

Attempts to reach an agreement with the Liberals had, as has been seen, been embarked upon early in the government's life though with considerable reluctance on MacDonald's own part; but relations were never happy. Yet, with the weakening of their position in the country, the Liberals were in no position to fight the election which would be the likely consequence of bringing the government down. Discussions over policy including new Liberal proposals went on during the summer of 1930 but financial orthodoxy prevailed and the Liberal enthusiasm for embarking upon a major road programme to give employment did not sit well with their pleas, echoing those of the Conservatives, for reductions in public expenditure. Those Liberals who followed Simon were becoming less hostile to the idea of tariffs and thus both accentuated the division among the Liberals and strengthened the prospects of the Opposition.

When the Labour Party Conference met in October, unemployment was touching the 2,000,000 mark, and the expenditure on unemployment relief was beginning to preoccupy the government and its advisers. At the Conference, MacDonald successfully defended the orthodox view that the depression was due to international forces, and that only through measures taken internationally could solutions be found. Yet although he secured an easy victory over a censure motion, the decision not to remit the Mosley memorandum to the National Executive Committee was only made by a narrow margin; Mosley himself was triumphantly re-elected to the NEC – six months before he left the Party for good – and Thomas, the scapegoat for the government's failures, lost his seat.

It is not surprising that after Parliament reassembled and with no obvious upturn on the way, there should have been some talk about

[21] After the defeat of a motion at the Labour Party Conference in October 1930 to have the memorandum discussed by the National Executive Committee, a manifesto incorporating its main proposals and signed by 17 Labour MP's was published on 6 December. In March 1931 six of them including Mosley himself resigned from the Labour Party and formed the New Party though two of them resigned after the first day and John Strachey in June; one Conservative and one Liberal MP also joined. Mosley seeking a parliamentary rôle for the party made private contact with Churchill and Lloyd George, and when this brought no result tried to strike an electoral bargain with Neville Chamberlain, also to no effect. See Richard Griffiths, *Fellow Travellers of the Right: British Enthusiasts for Nazi Germany 1933–1939* (London, 1980), pp. 32–4. The party contested 24 seats in the ensuing General Election, but failed to win a seat. All its four MP's lost their deposits.

the possibility of a National Government to deal with the growing crisis – though of senior politicians only Lloyd George would seem to have looked at the idea with any enthusiasm. Some of the old coalitionists, including Churchill and Robert Horne, were willing to canvass such notions but the fact that this was so only made the leaders of the official Opposition more determined to have nothing to do with them. The divisions in the cabinet where not all ministers – and this included MacDonald himself – were as wedded as Snowden to the complete free trade position went on simmering and the possibility of the Liberals bringing the government down could not be excluded particularly in view of the poor prospects of electoral reform. But the crisis of August 1931 was not directly connected with the disagreements over economic policy nor due to a general desire to substitute a coalition government for the existing administration. It was fiscal not economic righteousness that came to be the issue, and the salience of this issue was partly the result of the general financial crisis which came to a head in central Europe in the summer of 1931 and which led to a run against the pound and partly the result of the government's own decision to tackle the rise in public expenditure.

The two issues were of course connected in that a major question was whether it was, as Keynes argued, impossible and unnecessary to retain the pound sterling at its existing level, or whether as the City and Treasury believed, the defence of the currency should be given priority. On 30 July a committee set up in March in response to Liberal pressure under the chairmanship of a prominent City figure, Sir George May, presented its report to the cabinet. It forecast a major budget deficit and recommended big economies of which some two thirds was to be at the expense of the unemployed. The report, published at once with no indication of the government's response, put the matter starkly before the country. Further procrastination was impossible and during August a number of ministerial meetings were devoted to the choices to be made. That some combination of additional taxation and some reduction in government expenditure would have to be faced was not disputed; but the relative proportions of the two, and above all the nature of the cuts, were clearly of great political significance.[22]

When the cabinet itself reached its preliminary conclusions on 19 August, there were essentially two questions remaining. Could a Labour government ask the unemployed to make a major sacrifice; and could the package that the cabinet had agreed upon secure the

[22] The main detailed treatment of the crisis is that by R. Bassett, *Nineteen Thirty-One. Political Crisis* (London, 1958); it is dealt with from further sources and from MacDonald's point of view by Marquand, and from the point of view of the Conservative Opposition by Keith Middlemas and John Barnes in *Baldwin: a Biography* (London, 1969).

Opposition support necessary to carry it through Parliament? The soundings taken of the two Opposition parties revealed that neither was satisfied with the economies proposed. On the former point, the rejection by a TUC deputation of the whole idea of the proposed economies was a poor augury for their reception by the Labour Party;[23] their opposition was echoed by the Consultative Committee of the Parliamentary Labour Party. At the same time the government was being told by the Bank of England that foreign holders of sterling were demanding major reassurance, that the Bank's reserves were melting away, and that the point at which sterling would have to be devalued was rapidly approaching.

On 21 August the cabinet agreed on a set of economies less far-reaching than those recommended by its committee largely because of a decision not to reduce the scale of unemployment allowances; this the Opposition parties clearly found unacceptable. The bankers also tightened the screw on the government by informing the Prime Minister and Chancellor that in order to save the pound they needed to raise an immediate loan in New York and Paris, and that the proposals would not meet the requirements of the potential lenders.

The position was reported to the cabinet on the morning of Saturday 22 August and during the weekend the Prime Minister tried to bridge the gap between the cabinet's thinking and what the bankers said the Americans would accept. On the morning of 23 August MacDonald saw the King who had arrived overnight from Balmoral to which he had just gone and told him that he was enquiring whether some additional economies would satisfy New York, but also warned the King that the proposals he had now submitted did not carry the full approval of the cabinet, and that it was possible that Henderson and other ministers might resign, which would make it impossible for the government to be carried on.[24]

With the possibility of the government's resigning, the King took the view that it would be right for him to consult the leaders of the other two parties. Hitherto the Conservatives had been represented at the talks with the government by Neville Chamberlain and Hoare; now Baldwin was summoned back from his annual holiday at Aix-les-Bains. Lloyd George was in hospital and out of action; the Liberal spokesmen were Samuel and Donald Maclean. Baldwin was however unavailable when the Palace tried to contact him, as he was consulting Geoffrey Dawson the editor of *The Times* at the latter's

[23] The Trade Union aspect has been dealt with from trade union sources in Alan Bullock, *The Life and Times of Ernest Bevin* (London, 1960) I, chap. 18.

[24] For the King's role in the crisis see Harold Nicolson, *King George V: his Life and Reign* (London, 1952) and Kenneth Rose, *King George V* (London, 1983).

home. It was Samuel who was the first to see the King, and his advice was that it would be best if the Labour government would stay in office to carry through the necessary economies. (Dawson had been of the same opinion.) But should the cabinet prove unwilling to do what was necessary then a three-party national government should be formed under MacDonald for the sole purpose of dealing with the financial crisis. A Conservative government would have less chance of winning popular support for what needed to be done.

Baldwin, when he saw the King in the afternoon, was asked whether he would be prepared to serve under MacDonald and agreed to do so; should MacDonald refuse to remain as Prime Minister, Baldwin himself would be ready to form a government if the Liberals would back him, but would ask for a dissolution once the crisis was over.

When the cabinet met that evening, word was received from New York that a short-term treasury operation was possible and that provided the economy proposals were thought acceptable to the Bank of England and City opinion generally, and were endorsed by the government, the necessary public loan could be successfully floated. MacDonald tried to persuade his colleagues to agree to the deal; but those who had objected originally to the terms MacDonald had been exploring with the bankers were now joined by others. Resentment against the cut in unemployment benefit was fortified by objections to the idea of American bankers imposing terms upon a British cabinet. With 10 resignations threatened from a cabinet of 21, MacDonald's continuance in office was impossible and he informed his colleagues that he would at once go to the Palace to resign, and recommend to the King that a conference of party leaders should be called to discuss the situation that had now arisen. The King however pressed him to remain in office.

MacDonald later returned to the cabinet meeting to indicate that the King had accepted his advice, and later that evening the three-party talks took place at Downing Street. Samuel, Baldwin and Chamberlain were present as well as for a short time representatives of the Bank. When the meeting broke up it appeared that MacDonald would not continue in office, and that Baldwin would have to form a government. But when the three leaders met the King on the following morning, the King again pressed MacDonald to remain Prime Minister and Baldwin and Samuel agreed to serve under him. The King then left the party leaders to work out an arrangement of this kind, and it was decided that the National Government to be formed should be a small cabinet of individuals formed for the purpose of dealing with the emergency, and that it should not be a coalition in the ordinary sense of the term, the parties being free to fight a subsequent election independently.

While Baldwin and Samuel experienced little difficulty with their colleagues, MacDonald's own position was less easy. At a cabinet meeting at noon, he informed his colleagues that he now proposed to tender the government's resignation and that he had agreed to accept the task of forming an emergency government. After formally resigning, and accepting the King's commission to form a new government, MacDonald met with the other party leaders to agree upon the allocation of offices. Snowden, Sankey and Thomas retained their existing posts, Thomas also taking over the Colonial Office; for the Conservatives, Baldwin became Lord President of the Council, Neville Chamberlain, Minister of Health once more, Cunliffe-Lister, President of the Board of Trade, and Samuel Hoare, Secretary of State for India. The Liberals were Samuel as Home Secretary, a post he had held under Asquith, and Lord Reading as Foreign Secretary. The remaining ministerial posts were left out of the cabinet and with MacDonald having few supporters of his own were mainly divided between the Conservatives and the Liberals; they included Austen Chamberlain who had begun his ministerial career under Salisbury, and Lord Crewe who had been a lord-in-waiting in Gladstone's third administration. It was thus a government which even with the exclusion of both Churchill and Lloyd George might well claim to embody much of the country's governing talent and thereby to deserve the designation 'National'. On the other hand, MacDonald himself realized that in forming the government he was dissociating himself from his own party, probably for good, and did not encourage more members of his former government to follow him than he needed to fill the quota of offices agreed upon. He made it clear that he thought the younger members of the Party should not risk their own future. The hostility that MacDonald expected was made amply clear at a joint meeting of the TUC General Council, the National Executive Committee of the Labour Party, and the Consultative Committee of the Parliamentary Party. MacDonald was invited to a meeting of the Parliamentary Party itself, called for the 28th, but did not attend; Henderson was elected leader with Clynes and Graham as his deputies. Whether MacDonald's presence would have made a difference to the Party's attitude or to that of some of its members is something that has been discussed, but the likelihood would seem to be that the divide was now too great for any bridge-building.

The events of this week in August were to have their effect long after the crisis itself was far in the past. Writers with Labour sympathies tended almost at once, as well as subsequently, to treat the creation of the National Government as the outcome of a long-matured plot of MacDonald's to find more congenial political partners. For that there is no evidence. Nor can it seriously be held that anything done by the King was unconstitutional or partisan. In any situation in which there is no clear majority in Parliament for a single party, it is bound to fall to the monarch to seek for a way in which the King's government can be carried on; and nothing was done without MacDonald's being informed and accepting responsibility. It must not be forgotten that MacDonald was Prime Minister throughout the crisis. It could be said that the King's influence must have been decisive in getting MacDonald himself to accept leadership in a new National Government rather than go into opposition. But the King's motives clearly had nothing to do with party politics. It is difficult because of MacDonald's declining stature and reputation in subsequent years to appreciate the strength of his position in 1931; it was based largely on his international standing which stood high particularly after his American visit. It was reasonable to believe that difficult and painful measures would more easily be accepted from an all-party government led by someone who had come to be regarded as a national leader emerging from the ranks of the people, than from Baldwin who had only just survived bitter attacks on his leadership from within his own party. Nor finally, is there any reason to believe that when the original agreement was drawn up, it was not sincerely felt on all sides that the new arrangement could be regarded as an emergency one for a limited period. It was the course of events not deliberate contrivance that brought about successive changes of heart and that prolonged the life of the National Government until 1940.

The attitude of the Labour ex-ministers is not difficult to understand. They had not in fact refused to follow MacDonald because they had any alternative policy to offer. The cabinet had rejected a revenue tariff as a method of balancing the books; they had not even contemplated accepting devaluation as an alternative. Above all a number of them had at one point in the cabinet discussions accepted most of the programme of cuts which MacDonald was proposing, though when it came to the crunch, their courage failed them. The essence of their argument was that deflationary measures were in essence Conservative measures, and that it would have been proper for a Conservative government to attempt them, with Labour bringing all its weight to bear in opposing them. What MacDonald and Snowden were suggesting by their presence in the government was that the economies were the only possible policy for the nation as a whole, and that it was opposition to them that was partisan and even sectarian. It was in this respect that MacDonald could be treated as having betrayed the Labour movement; and the vendetta that this brought about pursued him to and beyond the grave.

Ten days after the new government's formation it met the House of Commons; by this time it was clear that there would be strong objections to its measures from the Opposition and a campaign against those Labour members who had joined or were supporting the government. On the Conservative side, fears were being expressed that the chances of putting a Conservative policy embodying protection into effect might have been jeopardized, and that an election should follow in the very near future so that the government could claim a popular mandate. The debate in the House echoed these positions. In the end however the Conservatives voted almost solidly as did the Liberals in the division on a vote of confidence, which was carried by 309 votes to 249. Only 12 Labour members, all but three of them office-holders, voted with the government with five more abstaining. On 10 September Snowden's emergency budget embodying the cuts was adopted, after bitter Opposition attacks.

But the crisis was not yet over. Britain's credit had at first rallied with the formation of the new government but from early September the pound showed renewed signs of weakness. Widespread attention was aroused when crews of the Atlantic Fleet refused duty in protest against the cuts – the 'Invergordon mutiny'. Some concessions to the services followed and their general morale appears to have been unaffected, but the psychological damage had been done. It became clear that if Britain was to stay on the gold standard further foreign credits would be required; these were not forthcoming. On 21 September the bill needed to take Britain off gold was passed through all its stages.

With the departure from the gold standard, Britain entered a new era of economic policy no longer dominated by the attempt to get back to the pre-1914 world which had so manifestly disappeared. Nevertheless regaining international confidence in sterling remained important since there was no wish to see a further steep decline in its value, still less to face the precipitous inflation which had hit so many other countries in the 1920s. Political uncertainty at home would be an adverse factor, and the argument for arriving at a more stable state of affairs through holding a general election seemed a strong one. On the other hand, since a government formed to save the pound had failed to do so, there was no obvious reason for this formula of co-operation to continue.

The Conservatives remained, however, by and large of the opinion that a National Government enjoying the benefits of MacDonald's personal prestige was still the best thing to aim for, since it was certain that after an election they would form the dominant element in the government's following; Neville Chamberlain, Party chairman since March 1930, was set on getting a protectionist majority.[25] For the Liberals there was little real choice whatever their fears about the strengthening of protectionist forces. For MacDonald and his associates the question was a more open one. Henderson had not opposed the bill for leaving the gold standard; but 112 of his followers had gone into the lobby against his advice. Criticism of Henderson and other leaders by the left wing produced some signs that they might be prepared to come to terms with MacDonald in return for some concessions to the unemployed. If this were to happen, this further accretion of Labour support would turn the government into a truly National one and obviate the need for an election in which Labour looked like doing very badly. But before MacDonald had made up his mind as to whether such a development was worth attempting, he and his supporters had been expelled from the Labour Party by the National Executive Committee.

With the possibility of a Labour reunion thus pre-empted, the only question was that of the terms for continuing the agreement between the three constituent parts of the government's following and the nature of its appeal to the country. The negotiations were by no means easy since the Liberals fought a last ditch campaign to obviate a joint commitment to protection. On 5 October the cabinet agreed that while the government as such would ask for a 'doctor's mandate' to do what was necessary to restore the economy, each party would be free to argue its own case and put forward its own remedies. On 6 October it was announced that MacDonald had been granted a dissolution. Polling was fixed for 27 October.

The gloom of Labour and of the Samuelite Liberals – Simon's group were closer to the Conservatives and this ensured that most of their candidates were unopposed by them – at the electoral prospects is fully understandable.[26] Labour's vote in by-elections during 1931 had been sagging ominously, bearing out the conclusions drawn from its municipal setbacks in November 1930. The Liberals' share had fallen much more disastrously. Labour's own internal divisions had not been healed by the departure of MacDonald and his followers and in the constituencies held by National Labour MP's, Labour's own organization was at risk. It took some effort to put up as many as 516 candidates. Labour's only potential allies were the small Lloyd

[25] The key rôle of Chamberlain in the formation of Conservative policy is well brought out in John Ramsden, *The Making of Conservative Party Policy: the Conservative Research Department since 1929* (London, 1980), chaps. 3 and 4.

[26] The best analysis of the 1931 general election is in John Stevenson and Chris Cook, *The Slump: Society and Politics during the Depression* (London, 1977), chap. 6.

George group of Liberals; Lloyd George back in the fray had come out strongly against the National Government, and two members of his family resigned the junior posts they had received when the government was formed. Apart from losing the prestige conferred by Lloyd George's leadership, the Samuelite Liberals had not got the support of his fund and were much handicapped in fighting the election. Only 118 candidates were nominated, and of these 81 faced Conservative opposition, 26 in straight fights. By contrast of the 41 candidates following Simon, 35 faced no Conservative opposition. When one recollects that the Liberal Party had put up 513 candidates in 1929, one can see the effect of the two and a half years during which they had been supporting the minority Labour government. They were no longer a serious contender for power. Even less could MacDonald's pledged supporters offer a serious counterweight to the Conservative preponderance, putting up only 20 candidates in all - six less than the communists and four less than Mosley's New Party.

To some considerable extent the pattern of the nominations decided the outcome of the election before a single vote was cast. In 1929 there had been 447 three-cornered fights which, given the distribution of Liberal strength, gave a clear advantage to Labour. In 1931 there were only 99. In other words, in the vast majority of contests the voters were asked to make a clear choice between supporting the National Government and opposing it. The fact that MacDonald and Snowden were in a position to taunt the Opposition with having run away from their responsibilities added to its difficulties, and diverted attention from the split over protection within the coalition itself.

The result was even more disastrous for Labour than had been foreseen. They lost 215 of their seats and retained a mere 52 with four allies from the Lloyd George group. On the government side, National Labour had a mere 12 seats; the Liberal Nationals (as Simon's group were now called) 35 and the Samuel Liberals 33. The bulk of the government's supporters in the new Parliament was made up of the 471 Conservatives returned. No government in British peacetime history had ever enjoyed so overwhelming a parliamentary majority.

The distribution of seats in the new House of Commons did not of course accurately reflect the outcome of the voting.[27] The total government vote was just over $14\frac{1}{2}$ million (67.1 per cent), of which just under 12 million was Conservative; the Opposition secured just

---

[27] See D.H. Close, 'The Realignment of the British Electorate in 1931', *History* LXVII (1982).

over seven million (32.9 per cent), of which well over six and a half million were Labour votes. Labour was down from its high point of 1929 when it had secured 37.1 per cent of the votes; but with 30.8 per cent had still a powerful base upon which to build, and in many properly working-class areas, there was no collapse at all. It was the lost three million Liberal votes that had made the great difference; and these had clearly gone overwhelmingly to the Conservatives despite Lloyd George's advice to the contrary. Not merely was there a correlation between the strength of the Labour vote and the local level of unemployment; it was also the case that the fears of financial collapse and governmental improvidence while powerfully affecting middle-class voters did not to any marked extent bother the working class. The Labour Party's own immediate reaction which was to blame the nature of the campaign waged in particular by Snowden, ignored the underlying realities. In one sense one could say that the basic strategy of Labour under MacDonald which was to annihilate the Liberal Party and force the electorate to choose between Labour and Conservative had been only too successful. The Liberals had been mortally wounded; but their voters had not come flocking to the Labour standard but had gone over to the Conservatives. A Labour recovery would mean winning them back. It was going to take 14 years to do so; and by then British society and British politics would be very different, and most of the protagonists of 1931 would have passed from the scene.

8 Britain under the National Government (1931–1935)

The general election of 1931 inaugurated an unusual period in modern British political history, so much of which has been concerned with the struggle between political parties. The new Parliament was dominated by its huge Conservative majority. Not only had the Opposition been deprived of a membership in the House of Commons large enough to play a serious rôle, but what was left was leaderless. Among the victims of the anti-Labour swing from the former cabinet were Henderson, Clynes, Dalton, Greenwood, Addison, Johnston and Morrison. Lansbury a respected but by now scarcely dynamic figure was the only survivor and hence inevitably the new leader. Two junior ministers just held their seats, Attlee and Stafford Cripps. Attlee who as deputy leader much enhanced his reputation was nevertheless regarded as a stop-gap choice when he succeeded Lansbury in October 1935. Of the defeated, Henderson was returned at a by-election in September 1933 but he was already in poor health and his energies were devoted to presiding over the World Disarmament Conference to whose chairmanship he had been nominated while Foreign Secretary; Graham died in 1932. Addison got back at a by-election in 1934 only to lose his seat again at the general election in the following year. The others had to wait for that general election before returning to Parliament, and some of them including Margaret Bondfield, Susan Lawrence and Wedgwood Benn failed even then.

During the lifetime of the Parliament there was some recovery, Labour winning in all 10 by-election seats from the government, but this hardly affected the balance of forces in the House. Of slightly greater numerical significance was the passing into Opposition of Samuel and his Liberal followers in November 1933.[1] From the point

[1] For some time after the 1931 election, many Liberals were unwilling to give up the hope of reunion with the National Liberals. The resignation of 10 Liberal ministers at the end of September 1932 over the free-trade issue leaving the Liberal Nationals in the government made the gulf almost unbridgeable. In May 1933 the Liberal Assembly called upon the party to cross the floor and the final move came after several votes in the House of Commons in which the Liberals had joined the Opposition. Four Liberals failed to follow Samuel's lead. The decline of

of view of the future of the Labour Party, its record in local elections was more encouraging. The municipal elections of November 1931 were as disastrous as the general election had been, but November 1932 saw a reversal of the downward slide with results slightly better than those of 1929. In 1933 an even better result was obtained, and in 1934 Morrison at last achieved his objective of capturing the LCC for Labour, in a year which also saw good results in the provinces.

But although these were pointers to the future and indicated the extent to which the continued slump contributed to tightening Labour's grip on its natural clientele, the major issues of policy were largely decided by debate and trials of strength within the government majority; protection and imperial preference, the constitutional future of India, the proper reaction in terms of foreign policy and armaments to the darkening international scene in Europe and East Asia – these were the matters which made up the stuff of politics but to which the Opposition could make little contribution. On the domestic front on the issues surrounding the treatment of the unemployed and the 'depressed' areas where the decline of staple industries seemed to offer no hope even in the event of general recovery, Labour clearly had more to say, particularly when its powerful trade union voice is taken into account as well as its strong presence in local government. Here there was once again a challenge from the extra-parliamentary Left undaunted by the rout of Communist candidates in the 1931 election. Although neither 'hunger marches' nor other demonstrations severely threatened the ability of the government to preserve order and although the Labour leadership stood firm against Communist infiltration, continental experience where left-wing violence had been the prelude to dangerous movements on the far Right were bound to cause some concern.[2] And this became the more obvious when Mosley after the debacle of the New Party went on to found the British Union of Fascists in October 1932 – a body which appeared a more formidable challenge to constitutional government than the earlier small fascist groups of the 1920s.[3]

the Liberal Party in the 1930s is chronicled in Roy Douglas, *The History of the Liberal Party 1895–1970* (London, 1977) and Chris Cook, *A Short History of the Liberal Party 1900–1976* (London, 1975).

[2] The history of the extreme left in the early 1930s is usefully summarized in John Stevenson and Chris Cook, *The Slump: Society and Politics during the Depression* (London, 1977), chaps. 9, 10, 11.

[3] There is a useful summary of the considerable literature on the British fascists in Stevenson and Cook, *The Slump*, chap. 12. The biography of *Oswald Mosley* by Robert Skidelsky (London, 1975) goes in considerable detail into the rôle of Mosley himself, but his effort to minimise the anti-semitic aspect of Mosley's campaign has been demolished by G.C. Lebzelter in *Political Anti-Semitism in England 1918–1939* (London, 1978).

The 1930s in Britain have not been treated kindly by historians; a contrast is often drawn and was at the time between the rather pedestrian policies of the National Government and the excitements of Roosevelt's New Deal. Yet a more proper comparison would be with Britain's continental neighbours. Britain did not follow the German course through dictatorship to totalitarianism; there was also nothing corresponding to the February 1934 riots in Paris and to the deepening social and political tensions to which they were a prelude. It may be that British society showed a greater resilience because its structures and institutions had survived the post-war upheavals in better shape than those of other countries; but something should perhaps be put to the credit of MacDonald and his colleagues.

The election and the evidence that it provided that the National Government was no mere emergency improvisation but had come to stay for a considerable period produced a return to ordinary cabinet government; the changes made on 5 November brought the number up again to 20. The principal changes in the senior posts were the replacement of Snowden (who had not stood in the election) as Chancellor by Neville Chamberlain, and of Reading at the Foreign Office by Simon. Snowden, transferred to the Upper House, remained in the cabinet as Lord Privy Seal; Thomas gave up the Colonial Office to Cunliffe-Lister but remained in the cabinet as Dominions Secretary. At the War Office, Crewe gave way to Hailsham whose inclusion in the original National Government had been objected to by the National Labour leaders, and at the Admiralty, Austen Chamberlain gave way to Sir Bolton Eyres Monsell. The new cabinet was heavily dominated by its Conservative members and particularly the inner group, Baldwin, Neville Chamberlain, Hoare and Cunliffe-Lister. With them must be counted Simon since the Liberal Nationals were increasingly identified with the Conservatives. The weakness of the Samuelite Liberals was further illustrated when on the death of Sir Donald Maclean in June 1932, his replacement was the Conservative ex-Viceroy Lord Irwin who had refused the Foreign Secretaryship when the National Government was formed on the ground that his unpopularity with many Conservatives would damage the new administration. Irwin who became Viscount Halifax in January 1934 must also be regarded, after his return to office, as one of the inner circle.

In some respects there was a degree of continuity in British policy surviving even the great upheaval of 1931. The new constitutional rôle of the Dominions agreed to at the Imperial Conference of 1930 had to be translated into statutory form and when Parliament reassembled, Thomas piloted through the bill that became the Statute of Westminster; though Baldwin's support was required to fend off an attack by the Conservative die-hards led by Churchill. The opposition to the bill – 50 members voted against it on second reading – was not of course motivated by any desire to deny the recognition of full autonomy to the old Dominions; what was worrying was the impact that this might have on the reluctant Dominion, Ireland, and above all on India to which Dominion status had been held out as a goal.

In the case of Ireland, the anxieties of the critics were soon shown to be not unfounded. De Valera who became Prime Minister of the Irish Free State in March 1932 made it clear that he intended to transform the position of his country into that of an independent republic in association with the Commonwealth, and treating the monarch merely as the head of that association having no claim to Irish allegiance. The theoretical assertion of Ireland's right to amend the Statute of Westminster unilaterally and the constitutional steps taken towards that end were the subject of much legal argument between the two governments. Of more practical concern was de Valera's discontinuance of the land annuities which were a relic of the financial transactions through which the Irish peasantry had become a class of owner-occupiers, rather than tenants. The move was bound up with a general effort to make the Irish economy a more independent one along the protectionist lines that were typical of most European countries at the time. The British government was not minded to take any sanctions against Ireland to secure repayment and Thomas's failure to bring about an agreement did not enhance his authority within the cabinet.[4]

India remained a more serious matter since the divisions in the Conservative party were by no means at an end; nor was Baldwin unaware of the widespread suspicion that Churchill's motive in upholding the cause of the die-hards on India was to substitute himself for Baldwin in the leadership. The Round Table Conference on the future constitution began in November 1930, though without Congress being represented. After its conclusion in January 1931 the Viceroy made an agreement with Gandhi which enabled Congress to be represented, though by Gandhi alone, when it reassembled in London in the autumn of 1931. With Hoare as Secretary of State the new government seemed determined to follow its predecessor in

[4] Although written before the opening of the archives, the account of the new phase in Anglo-Irish relations by Sir Keith Hancock shows great insight into the nature of the controversies. See W.K. Hancock, *Survey of British Commonwealth Affairs*. Vol. I: *Problems of Nationality 1918–1936* (London, 1937), chapter 6 'Ireland Unappeased'. For an account from the Irish point of view see F.S. L. Lyons, *Ireland since the Famine* (London, 1971), part IV, chaps. 2, 3, 4.

seeking for an all-India federation with full self-government in the
provinces and defined safeguards for minorities and imperial
interests including defence. When Hoare presented the results of the
Conference to the House of Commons on 2 December, Churchill
insisted on dividing the House but was defeated by 369 to 43. It was
the beginning of a long parliamentary battle carried on also in the
country and which did not end until the Royal Assent was given to the
Government of India Act in July 1935.[5]

If Conservatives might fear that on Ireland and India they were
being made to give way to the views of their new partners, in handling
the economy and above all in bringing about a regime of protection
and imperial preference they found themselves virtually unimpeded.
The general financial climate remained difficult and the burden that
fell on the new Chancellor, Neville Chamberlain, considerable.
Emergency measures were taken in respect of manufactured imports
to prevent abnormal levels pending the imposition of a general tariff;
and provisional measures were taken in respect of some agricultural
commodities leaving a more permanent system to await agreement
with the Dominions. In December Chamberlain secured the
appointment of a committee on the balance of trade in which all
three government parties were represented. Its recommendations
amounted to a general tariff (except for certain foods and raw
materials) with an independent tariff board to advise on further duties
on non-essentials. There was to be colonial preference and provisions
for retaliation against foreign discrimination and for negotiations for
reciprocal tariff reductions. Quite apart from being a major departure
from Britain's historic commitment to free trade, the proposals were
also notable for involving a breach with the constitutional practice of
collective cabinet responsibility, since it was agreed that Snowden
and the Liberal ministers would be able to adhere to their personal
policy commitments by being left free to speak and vote against the
government's policy.

The Ottawa conference was long in the making.[6] At previous
imperial conferences in 1926 and 1930 the British had fought shy of
the economic issues since unless they were prepared to contemplate
important measures of protection, little could be offered to the

---

[5] Accounts of the struggle over the India bill can be found from the point of view of the
opposing camps in J.A. Cross, *Sir Samuel Hoare: a Political Biography* (London, 1977), chap. 4
and Martin Gilbert, *Winston S. Churchill.* Vol. v: *1922–1939* (London, 1976), chaps. 20, 25, 28,
30, 31. One can judge from the correspondence on the matter in the 'Companion' volumes to
the *Churchill* how much the campaign depended on Churchill's own efforts and the extent to
which he had to rely on very second-rate figures to support his cause. No other statesman of the
first rank was prepared to fight against the government's Indian policy.

[6] On the Ottawa conference and its preparation, see Ian M. Drummond, *Imperial Economic
Policy 1917–1939: Studies in Expansion and Protection* (London, 1974), chaps. 5 and 6.

Dominions. After the 1930 conference a cabinet committee was set up to consider what might be done to meet the impatience of some Dominions but little progress had been made by the time the National Government was set up. The interim measures of protection in the winter of 1931–2 were accompanied by soundings of the Dominion governments. The incorporation of the various proposals in the agenda of the conference was a matter for the Canadian government as host of the meeting and the agenda was received on 7 July, less than two weeks before its opening. There was even at this stage no agreement in British government circles on several important matters including the question of the relations between the currencies of Commonwealth members.

The conference itself lasted for a month and dealt with most aspects of the Commonwealth's economic relations. The British team was led by Baldwin and included Chamberlain, Hailsham, Gilmour, Thomas, Runciman and Cunliffe-Lister; with so many of the principal ministers in Ottawa there was little supervision from London, and Chamberlain and Thomas who had done most of the preliminary work had a fairly free hand. What they were aiming for was that in return for some concessions giving preferences to Dominion-produced foodstuffs, British manufacturers should be in a position to compete with domestic producers in Dominion markets more effectively than their foreign competitors. Any institution-alizing of economic links was effectively prevented by Dominion sensitivity to any notion of centralization in Whitehall, a sensitivity particularly strong where Canada was concerned.

In the end everything depended upon bilateral agreements between Britain and the Dominions, all of which had their own particular problems and requirements. The idea that had fuelled Beaverbrook's Empire Crusade, that of a largely self-sufficient Empire–Commonwealth in which Britain would supply the manufactures and the Dominions and colonies the foodstuffs and raw materials was shown to be wholly impracticable in the light of the determination of the Dominions themselves to diversify their own economies. Even the notion of assisting British industry to compete on equal terms was difficult to apply in practice. What arose out of Ottawa was a series of preferential tariffs and some quantitative restrictions on foreign goods. Monetary arrangements which might have been more effective were not attempted. The economists' general conclusion that the agreements themselves did little to achieve their object of increasing trade and so employment can be accepted, as also the indications that what did happen was some diversion of trade, so that more of Britain's imports came from the Dominions and more of her exports went in that direction. But the

extent to which this increase in economic interdependence was due to
the agreements themselves and not to other changes in the economic
climate remains controversial.

The British Conservative ministers were perhaps more pleased to
have secured an agreement at all than they were about its actual
contents. But the achievement by his younger son of a diluted version
of Joseph Chamberlain's vision went too far for the free-traders in the
Cabinet. The agreement to differ could not encompass this overt and
seemingly permanent departure of Britain from free trade principles.
The Liberal ministers and Snowden resigned at the end of September
and were replaced by Conservatives and Liberal Nationals. The
distinction between the latter and the Conservatives was now hard to
perceive, and the National Government was now more than ever a
Conservative administration presided over by an increasingly solitary
and less effective MacDonald. Of his National Labour followers in
August 1931, Snowden had become an embittered critic of the
government, Sankey remained as Lord Chancellor for the remainder
of MacDonald's premiership but without exercising any important
political influence, and Thomas while retained at the Dominions
Office as another symbol of the government's national credentials,
was a much less serious and effective figure than during his earlier
union-based career.

The tasks of the government of which Baldwin and Chamberlain
were clearly the two dominant members were seen by them as
primarily domestic. As they saw it their business was to restore
confidence in the nation's finances through governmental frugality
and in so far as they were saddled with the social burdens arising from
the depression to meet these at minimum cost so as not to confront
industry with heavier taxation and thus impede recovery. While
making what it could of its protected markets British industry would
benefit even more by a return to a more stable world economy and
some hopes were therefore invested in the world economic conference
that met in June 1933. Since its outcome would clearly depend very
largely on what the new Roosevelt administration in the United
States would do, Chamberlain wished it to meet in Washington. But
MacDonald seeking an outlet on the world scene for his frustrations at
home, had spent some time in Washington in the spring and
preferred the conference to meet in London where he would be the
chairman. But any possibility of a final triumph to crown his career
came to nothing when it became clear that Roosevelt put the
stimulation of domestic recovery through devaluation ahead of world
stabilization. With the United States refusing to enter a system of
fixed exchange rates, the other policy advocated by the experts, tariff
reduction, also proved unattainable, and the conference broke up

early in July with nothing achieved.

Henceforward the National Government in Britain like other governments pursued its own course.[7] Unemployment, the most important indicator of the economic situation, had reached its peak in 1932 at 2,745,00; it fell until 1934–5 when it rose again, falling once more till 1937 when the unemployment figure was 1,484,000. But in dealing with both unemployment and its social consequences, the government had to take into account more than the brute figures. The recovery was not due in any large measure to an improvement in the depressed trades but rather to the development of new industries, particularly in the area of consumer durables, and these in turn depended for their profitability largely upon access to large markets and found their main area of expansion to be in the London area and the midlands. It was the safety valve of internal migration that reduced unemployment but this in turn threw into even greater relief the regions and even individual cities or districts which did not share in the recovery.

By 1934 this aspect of the problem was recognized in official circles and despite the general reluctance to intervene in the economy, the Special Areas Act of 1934 did give some limited assistance to investment in the areas of particular distress. The composition of the workforce by age and sex also changed and there remained as a hard core of long-term unemployed, the former male bread-winners in the mining and other heavy industries. The contrast between the areas of large-scale unemployment and the rest of the country was made sharper by the growth of real incomes where employed persons were concerned. Yet the attempt to capitalize on this fact by making the unemployed a political force on their own, made largely under communist auspices, did not get very far. The demonstrations and 'hunger marches' of 1932–3 attracted much public attention and sympathy but made no permanent mark.

Government policy towards the unemployed preserved as did social policy generally a marked continuity with the policies of the 1920s; perhaps not surprisingly given the domination of Neville Chamberlain in this field.[8] The main difficulty seemed to be that the insurance schemes designed to meet spells of short-term unemployment due to the ups and downs of the economy could not cope with the large numbers of unemployed whose insurance entitlements were rapidly exhausted. In 1930 the Labour government had made benefits for those no longer entitled to a return on their

[7] See H.W. Richardson, *Economic Recovery in Britain 1932–1939 (London, 1967)*.

[8] For a summary of social policy in this period, see Derek Fraser, *The Evolution of the British Welfare State: a History of Social Policy since the Industrial Revolution* (London, 1973), chap. 8 'The Inter-War Years', and B.B. Gilbert, *British Social Policy 1914–1939* (London, 1970).

contributions a charge on the Treasury rather than the unemployment fund but at the same time made them easier to obtain. The
resultant burden on the Treasury had been a prime cause of the
appointment of the May Committee and a principal reason why a
reduction in unemployment benefit had seemed so essential a part of
restoring financial confidence. The National Government both
reduced the insurance benefits and limited their duration. Beyond
that the unemployed person had to apply to the Public Assistance
Committees of the Local Authorities who operated a family means
test, the source of much of the bitterness of these years. The system
also had the demerit of being administered differently in different
regions and with different scales of benefit. This position which
reproduced some of the weaknesses of the old Poor Law could hardly
provide a long-term solution.

The Labour government had set up a royal commission on
unemployment insurance in 1930 but by the time its final report
appeared in December 1932, its deliberations had been overtaken by
the measures taken after the crisis of 1931. It however confirmed
Chamberlain in his view that unemployment insurance must be
insulated from politics and that all relief measures must be subject to a
measure of central control. The 1934 Unemployment Act confirmed
the division between insurance and assistance to those whose
insurance benefits had come to an end. The insurance scheme was
extended to new categories of workers; contributions were to be equal
as between employer, employee and the State and the 1931 cuts were
restored. Workers would be entitled to benefits under the scheme only
for the first 26 weeks of unemployment. The Minister of Labour was
to be advised on running the scheme in such a way as to maintain its
solvency by a new Unemployment Insurance Statutory Committee.

Another independent statutory body the Unemployment Assistance Board took over the remaining responsibilities from the Public
Assistance Committees and was charged with providing relief from
destitution from central funds.

The new system came in amidst fierce objections, partly because
the scales of benefit operated by the Board when it started its
operations in January 1935 were lower than those of the more
generous local Public Assistance Committees. Now the marches and
demonstrations which had revived in the previous autumn were
largely led by trade union and labour figures although the TUC
nationally did its best to prevent co-operation with the National
Unemployed Workers' Movement, the Communist Party's
preferred instrument. The degree of opposition reflected in
Parliament and attracting much middle opinion obliged the
government to revise its plans. Applicants were temporarily allowed

to claim the old scales where these were preferable to those of the UAB. It was not until April 1937 that the new system came fully into operation.

The Public Assistance Committees relieved of their obligations to the able-bodied unemployed henceforth were concerned with other specialized categories of the needy; particularly institutional care for the aged, the sick and homeless children; some categories also received cash relief. The aged were further assisted by extension in 1937 of the provisions for old-age pensions in the Acts of 1925 and 1929 – another example of the continuity of Chamberlain's policies. The shift from local to central provision for the needy had thus gone some way but by no means all the way.

In other areas of social policy the tasks before the National Government seemed less urgent. One result of the movement of population to new areas of employment was a boom in private house-building, the 'ribbon development' so much the target of social satirists and later planners. By the end of the 1930s the shortage of housing so prominent a feature of public discussion in the 1920s seemed to be over; but this focussed interest on the quality of the housing provided. The 1930 Housing Act had included provisions for slum clearance and the rehousing of the families affected; and in further Acts of 1933 and 1935, new programmes of slum clearance and new definitions of overcrowding further stimulated local action.

While there were criticisms of the health insurance provisions still based on the 1911 Act, there were no important changes at this time. The Public Health Act of 1936 was a consolidating measure as was the Factories Act of 1937. In education there were no important developments; there was indeed no major piece of legislation on this subject between Fisher's Act of 1918 and the Butler Act of 1944. A Children and Young Persons Act of 1933 building on the 1908 Act was concerned with the rehabilitation of children in need and with the handling of juvenile delinquents.

By the standards applied by critics in the next decade when war had once again called attention to the 'condition of the people' problem, the National Government's social record seemed characterized by parsimony and lack of imagination; yet in more distant retrospect and particularly taking the international dimension into account it is hard to reconcile this view with the fact that the country's democratic institutions survived the depression and continued to receive the assent of the vast majority of the citizens.

Apart from the challenge to public order occasionally posed by demonstrations on the Left, there was as elsewhere in Europe a challenge from the Right. Mosley launched the British Union of Fascists in October 1932, recruiting largely from earlier fascist-type groups founded in the 1920s. The British Fascists modelled themselves upon the Italians who helped Mosley financially and relied upon uniforms, marches and other visible signs of the possible use of force, not indeed against the established order but to forestall an alleged danger from the Left. Meetings were held by the BUF in different parts of the country in the autumn of 1933 and early in 1934; some were attended with disorders; others were peaceful. Early in 1934 the newspapers controlled by Lord Rothermere took up Mosley's cause rather as a potential source of resistance to communism than for the sake of any ideology. But relations between Rothermere and Mosley soon cooled down. The turning point came with the meeting at Olympia in June 1934 when fascist violence against interruptors caused anxiety in circles no longer exclusively on the Left and led to a final breach between Mosley and Rothermere in July. Mosley now increasingly identified his opponents as Jewish-inspired and this move towards Nazi ideas was unwelcome at a time when suspicion of Hitler was growing. The BUF's anti-semitism ceased to have a purely theoretical aspect when Mosley increasingly concentrated on organizing demonstrations in the East End of London where there had been trouble on a lesser scale since 1933. His hope was to exploit latent working-class anti-semitism by arguing that the effect of the depression was being made worse because of the competition for jobs by Jews whose numbers had increased in Britain with the recent arrival of refugees from Europe.

The Government which had hitherto concentrated on subversive movements on the Left now felt impelled to act. The Incitement to Disaffection Act of November 1934 had been modified during its passage to meet the objections to the wide powers it was proposed to confer on magistrates and the police. After the Olympia meeting a bill had also been proposed to the cabinet by the Home Secretary, Sir John Gilmour, which would have given him powers to ban open-air meetings and marches likely to provoke breaches of the peace and which would make the wearing of political uniforms illegal. Once again, there were objections partly from the same quarters and partly from those who argued that it was better not to drive dangerous movements underground. It was not until further disturbances in 1936 caused renewed disquiet that the cabinet decided to move; the new Public Order Act was introduced in November and passed through all its stages by Christmas. Its main provisions were directed against the wearing of political uniforms and meetings and marches likely to create disorder. It did not have the effect of stopping trouble altogether and sporadic incidents occurred well into 1939. But the main danger had now passed and to that the Act had undoubtedly contributed, despite the left-wing claims that the police unduly favoured the fascists and were more concerned to use their new powers against the Left.

To put this accusation into context, it must be observed that the National Unemployed Workers' Movement and the Communist Party were openly committed to a revolutionary creed and enjoyed the patronage of the Soviet Union about whose intentions suspicions remained very much alive. Mosley claimed to be a British patriot ready to help in resisting the forces of subversion and to co-operate with rather than defy the police.[9] It was only when the European fascist powers and particularly Nazi Germany came to be regarded as potential enemies and when Mosley seemed to be identified with a favourable stance towards them, that the parallels with the tactics which had brought these regimes to power became alarming.[10] In dealing with the challenge to public order as with so much else in the 1930s, the international context of British politics can never be out of mind.

The period between the election of 1931 and MacDonald's super-session as premier by Baldwin in June 1935 saw major changes in the international scene and a watershed in British perceptions of its problems. From a decade in which the victors of the First World War still held a dominant position, one passes into one in which their security was increasingly under threat. From a concern with disarmament one passes to the beginnings of a general acceptance of the need to strengthen the country's and the Empire's defences, from attempting to liquidate the consequences of the World War to efforts to find ways of averting its repetition. In this process many of the assumptions of the 1920s were put to the test and found wanting. Because the policies of other powers were in flux and because their intentions were hard to assess, the course of diplomacy was marked by unusually frequent changes of direction and this was true also of defence policy. It is not difficult to see why public opinion found it difficult to keep up with what was happening and remained much influenced by ideas and prejudices formed under very different circumstances. This failure was most marked in the Opposition which had lost in MacDonald and Henderson the only two Labour leaders of the 1920s with serious interests in the international scene. The influence of pacifism in the Labour Party had been considerable since the fall of the first Labour government. At the Party's annual conference at Margate in 1926 an unequivocal motion in favour of non-resistance sponsored by Ponsonby and Fenner Brockway was

[9] See Stevenson and Cook, *The Slump,* chap. 11 'The Government and Public Order'.
[10] On British sympathizers with Nazi Germany and their political activities, see Richard Griffiths, *Fellow Travellers of the Right: British Enthusiasts for Nazi Germany 1933–1939* (London, 1980).

carried by acclamation, though this did not prevent Ponsonby from becoming a minister in the 1929 government and accepting that government's arms estimates. In the House of Commons itself there were between 1924 and 1931 10 occasions when motions pressing for unilateral disarmament were pressed to the vote; 76 MP's voted for them at one time or another.[11]

The gulf of suspicion between government and the Opposition created by the events of 1931 made it difficult to visualize a national consensus and helps to explain the government's failure to take the nation fully into its confidence, and to try to drive home the lesson that influence depends ultimately upon power.

It was not in the Labour Party alone that the twenties and early thirties were marked by a strong wave of pacifism. The Churches, particularly the Anglican Church after the failure of any follow-up of the COPEC's 1924 initiative as far as domestic action was concerned, also gave room for much propaganda favour of pacifism.[12] And a specifically Christian Pacifism achieved further recognition when Lansbury became leader of the Labour Party after the 1931 election. Until some time after Hitler's assumption of power in January 1933 which brought new urgency into the whole issue, pacifism in many people's minds managed to co-exist more or less happily alongside a belief in the League of Nations and other methods of collective action for the prevention of war.[13] This overlap is illustrated by the celebrated Oxford Union debate of 9 February 1933 when the House carried the motion that it would 'in no circumstances fight for king and country'. While the impetus to hold such a debate was a pacifist one and while its passage owed much to the pacifist eloquence of the popular philosopher C.E.M. Joad, many of its supporters thought they were merely repudiating the unthinking jingoism of the First World War and believed that their position was not incompatible with support for the League of Nations.[14]

In addition to the overlap between 'collective security' and pacifism, there was of course the exploitation of anti-war feeling in the interests of revolutionary politics – an exploitation made easier by the impact of many novels about the First World War in which

[11] Martin Ceadel, *Pacifism in Britain 1914-1945: The Defining of a Faith* (Oxford, 1980), p. 75.
[12] Ceadel, *Pacifism*, p. 67. COPEC was the Conference on Politics, Economics and Citizenship held at Birmingham in April 1924 on the initiative of William Temple, then bishop of Manchester. See E.R. Norman, *Church and Society in England 1770-1970* (Oxford, 1976), chap. 7.
[13] Those who find it hard to understand how ideas themselves contradictory can be held simultaneously should consider the claims by Labour spokesmen, 50 years later that they stood for both 'unilateral' and 'multilateral' disarmament.
[14] The national and international repercussions of this overblown episode which owed its notoriety to the press comment it aroused are fully and definitively treated by M. Ceadal, 'The King and Country debate', *Historical Journal XXII (1979)*.

ordinary soldiers and civilians were depicted as victims of foolish statesmen and uncaring brasshats. But such exploitation depended on the vicissitudes in the Soviet Union's own position and policies. And it was already noticeable at the World Anti-War Congress held at Amsterdam in August 1932 that the need to protect the Soviet Union against Japan was given priority over anti-war sentiment in general and that for most delegates 'pacifism' as most British pacifists conceived of it was anathema.[15]

The Soviet Union's own change of course in 1934–6 to a fully collective security stance put an end to the rôle of the Communist dominated 'No More War Movement'. It also assisted in the gradual evolution of the official policy of the Labour Party – although as late as the spring of 1935, the Labour Party voted against the air estimates. It was the crisis over Abyssinia later in the year that enabled Bevin and Citrine to bring round first the Trade Union Congress and then in October, the Labour Party to favour the 'collective security' aspects of the League of Nations.[16]

Nevertheless these years also witnessed the building up of the pacifist campaign on a non-party basis, chiefly throught the work of Canon H.R.L. Sheppard as leader of the Peace Pledge Union, a movement of largely though not exclusively Christian inspiration. The moral case was powerfully reinforced by the simple emotion of fear. Although the outcome of the 1914–18 war had not been significantly affected by air power and although casualties in air raids had been minor compared with the horrors of the battlefields, it was by now commonly accepted that any future conflict would be dominated by the air arm and that once hostilities began bombs would rain down upon the heads of defenceless civilians. While possibilities of defence against air attack clearly existed, no one could know how effective they would be. When Baldwin told the House of Commons on 10 November 1932 that the bomber would 'always get through' he was echoing a wide stratum of opinion as well as voicing his own belief.[17] While this attitude helped to keep alive attempts at reaching agreements on disarmament even after the virtual collapse of the Disarmament Conference with Germany's final withdrawal in October 1933, it also made it more difficult to persuade the public that the new dangers required some measure of British rearmament. In dealing with British decisions over armaments and the connected problems of foreign policy between 1931 and 1939, it is therefore

[15] Ceadel, *Pacifism*, p. 114.
[16] See the account of the struggle within the Labour movement in Alan Bullock, *The Life of Ernest Bevin* (London, 1960) I, chaps. 19–20.
[17] For a full account of Baldwin's attitude which was crucial to the government's policy see Keith Middlemas and John Barnes, *Baldwin: a Biography* (London, 1969), chap. 27.

necessary to remember that at no point was the government being
urged from outside the political arena to go faster with re-armament
than it was itself prepared to advocate; and even in the House of
Commons while Churchill spoke in favour of strengthening air
defence in February 1934, it was only after 1935 that his tireless
energies were directed away from India and towards the burning
problems of Europe.

It is true of course that popular hatred of war and suspicion of
armaments was not the only obstacle in the government's way. It had
to contend even after 1935 with the view powerfully entrenched in the
Treasury that Britain must never face a war with her financial
strength impaired and that this prescribed limits to the possibilities of
peacetime expenditure on armaments.[18] It was also a Treasury view
which had strong support in industrial and City circles that an
excessive concentration on re-armament would damage the rest of
industry and hence the exports on which national solvency depended,
nor was government organized for direct intervention in industrial
matters.[19] Finally there was the belief powerful in service circles and
in Whitehall, that Britain's prime duty in matters of defence was to
safeguard the Empire and its lines of communication and that these
commitments might be impaired if attention was concentrated upon
the possibility of a European war in which Britain would be expected
to take part in operations on the continent.[20] Sir Maurice Hankey was
the most effective exponent of this general point of view. The most
important consequence of its appeal combined with public aversion to
any form of compulsory military training was to make the army the
cinderella of the services when it came to additional expenditure.[21]

Naval preparations had been limited by the London Treaty of 1930
which put an end to some of the long-standing arguments with the
Americans but at a price it was feared in some quarters of making
Britain in the Far East even more dependent upon them.[22] Nor did it
prevent the feelings in some American naval circles of the desirability
of being able to challenge Britain's world position in the interests of
American commercial aims. While logic might seem to suggest that
the *status quo* powers should pool their naval resources, the navies

[18] See G.C. Peden, *British Rearmament and the Treasury 1932–1939* (Edinburgh, 1979). See
also, Max Beloff, 'The Whitehall Factor: the Rôle of the Higher Civil Service 1919–1939', in
Gillian Peele and Chris Cook, *The Politics of Reappraisal 1918–1939* (London, 1975).

[19] See R.P. Shay, jr., *British Rearmament in the Thirties: Politics and Profits* (Princeton, 1977)
which does bring in the industrial aspects of the problem though the author is not impeccable in
his understanding of British politics.

[20] See Stephen Roskill, *Hankey, Man of Secrets*. Vol. III: *1931–1963* (London, 1974).

[21] On the rôle of the army in British defence policy see Brian Bond, *British Military Policy
between the Two World Wars* (Oxford, 1980).

[22] On the naval aspects of the period, see Stephen Roskill, *Naval Policy between the Wars*. Vol.
II: *1930–1939* (London, 1976).

themselves – British, American, French and even Dutch – were unprepared for such intimate co-operation.[23]

The National Government had inherited from its predecessor a position in European affairs largely opposed to that of France. One issue of disagreement had been over the complex problems relating to reparations and inter-allied debts. Where reparations were concerned, any prospect of collecting further sums were ended by the Hoover moratorium proposals of June 1931 and the whole issue was buried at the Lausanne Conference a year later. Henceforth the debts question was primarily of importance in connection with Anglo-American relations. After making a token payment in 1933, Britain followed the example of the other European debtors and defaulted.

The ending of reparations had come without any concessions on the political side from Germany so that when the Disarmament Conference opened in February 1932, there was a straight conflict between Germany's claim to equality of treatment and France's insistence that this would only be accorded if new guarantees could be found for her security. British policy was at first unsympathetic to the French claims, partly because of pressure at home for ending the discriminatory provisions of the Versailles Treaty and partly because what further guarantees seemed to mean in practice was the extension of Britain's commitment under Locarno to embrace the French alliances in Eastern Europe.

The first challenge to the *status quo* came however not in Europe but in the Far East with the invasion of Manchuria by the Japanese in September 1931 and the subsequent setting up of the puppet state of Manchukuo and the two months' fighting between Chinese and Japanese around Shanghai from January to March 1932. The British attitude to these events was coloured both by some sympathy for Japanese complaints about the Chinese handling of foreign interests and by an unwillingness to push Japan into a general position of hostility towards the West. On the other hand, to some people, the occasion appeared as one of clear-cut aggression and thus a challenge to the League's authority. Britain also felt the need not to go beyond what Dominion opinion would countenance and thus held aloof from suggestions of invoking the sanctions provisions of the Covenant. The situation was clearly one in which no serious move to restrain the Japanese could be undertaken without a guarantee that the United States would go along with such action and help defend European interest against any Japanese reprisals. But the Americans confined

---

[23] The relations between opinion and policy and departmental and service attitudes in the major countries in the period are examined with particular reference to the Far East in Christopher Thorne, *The Limits of Foreign Policy: the West, the League and the Far Eastern Crisis of 1931–1933* (London, 1972).

themselves to stating their objection in principle to the use of force to change the *status quo*, notably in Secretary of State Stimson's pronouncement on 'non-recognition' of 7 January 1932. The very cautious actions and pronouncements of the League were too much for the Japanese to swallow and on 27 March 1933 they gave notice of their intention to terminate their membership.

Although there was something of a lull in Far Eastern affairs as Japan consolidated her new positions, the events of 1931–3 had important repercussions. Britain's unwillingness, as the Americans saw it, to follow their lead led to irritation and to misleading assertions that a stiffer attitude by Britain might have deterred the Japanese. If the United States felt let down by Britain, British statesmen felt that the episode showed both the weakness of relying on world opinion in the face of a power determined to promote its own interests and more specifically that the United States could not be relied upon for more than words. Individuals in the British government, notably Neville Chamberlain, had all along been reluctant to confront Japan and in the autumn of 1934 Chamberlain and Simon made an attempt at a rapprochement with the Japanese despite warnings that to do this would risk alienating the Americans whose support in the long run was more important. What the episode did not do was clear up the question of the utility of economic sanctions.

Between April and July 1933 the British government successfully used economic pressure against the Soviet Union to secure the release of British engineers convicted of espionage in a Moscow 'show trial'. But the Soviet Union at a time of great economic weakness and dependence could be made to give way while the Japanese it was thought might retaliate by military measures in a part of the world where their local superiority was manifest and where the Singapore base intended to be the fulcrum of the British naval response to them was still far from complete.[24] Only gradually did considerations arising from Britain's weakness in the Far East come to affect the government's attitude towards rearmament and for this to happen anxiety needed to be felt about the situation in Europe.

The European situation, as it happened, rapidly gave signs of being even more immediately threatening than the position in the Far East. Even before Hitler came into power, Germany as we have seen was making demands for full equality in armaments and was known to be secretly going ahead with her preparations. This together with an increasingly erratic foreign policy on the part of Mussolini set the scene for what was to be the primary issue of national policy from

[24] See Paul Haggie, *Britannia at Bay: the Defence of the British Empire against Japan* (Oxford, 1981) and J. Neidpath, *The Singapore Naval Base and the Defence of Britain's Eastern Empire 1919–1941* (Oxford, 1981).

1931 until the outbreak of war. The *status quo* in Europe, Africa, the Middle East and the Far East was being threatened by three revisionist powers against whom Britain or even Britain and France combined could scarcely hope to provide a sufficient counterweight. Only two powers existed whose strength if mobilized could suffice to turn the scales; the United States dedicated to an isolationism reinforced by its New Deal commitment and the Soviet Union whose designs were bound in the long run to be revisionist also and whose strength was very difficult to assess.

British defence policy had to do the best it could to provide against a series of possible eventualities, always bearing in mind the security demands of the Dominions and in particular of Australia and New Zealand, and diplomacy was given the task of seeing whether one or other member of the possibly hostile coalition could be browbeaten or cajoled into abandoning its partners, actual or potential. In considering the various often apparently contradictory phases through which British policy passed, it is essential to note that these guiding threads were never repudiated, even if rarely articulated in a way that might command public understanding and assent. Instead both the public and some future historians were confused by the continued use of what was thought to be the more appealing phraseology of 'collective security'.

The first decision of the cabinet to revoke the '10 year rule' which was made on 23 March 1932 did little in itself except free the experts to plan for what had previously been ruled out, a war against a major power, but it was made clear that this change did not itself imply more money for arms, and that in making plans the financial limits on what could be done would have to be taken into account. The first fruit of the decision was in fact the setting up of the powerful Defence Requirements Committee of civil servants and military chiefs which held its initial meeting on 14 November 1933. The prominence of the Japanese threat and hence of the issue of strengthening the Singapore base was evident from the strong plea made by Warren Fisher for concentrating on the naval needs as measured against Japan in order to persuade Japan to come to a peaceful resolution of her differences with Britain and thus enable Britain to concentrate upon the threat nearer home. The idea that Japan need not be an enemy made a considerable appeal in some quarters in the Foreign Office and also to Neville Chamberlain. The overlap between the period of disarmament and that of at least prospective rearmament was shown when the DRC report was passed on for consideration to the cabinet committee on the disarmament conference. After much discussion the committee and the cabinet took the view that the German threat was the more dangerous one and that priority should be given to deterring

Germany by a rapid building up of bomber squadrons with the other services having to make do with what could be spared when the needs of the air force were met.

☞ Since the expansion could be met financially without too much trouble owing to an improvement in the economy and greater yields from taxation, it was not at this stage thought necessary to put rearmament in the forefront of the government's programme. Hopes of reaching some kind of agreement with Germany were not abandoned. It was certainly the view of ministers that any great emphasis on rearmament would in the pacifist climate of the day be counter-productive; and the strength of this current of feeling seemed confirmed by the East Fulham by-election on 25 October 1933 when the Conservative candidate was defeated and the seat lost to a Labour candidate – a by-election in which accusations of war-mongering against the government contender were thought to have played an important part, and in which the government was often taken to task for being responsible for Germany's quitting the Disarmament Conference.[25]

Although there would be renewed efforts later on to find a way of coming to an agreement with Japan, the immediate question was as between trying to decide whether Germany or Italy would be the easier to appease. Clearly, Germany was or soon would be the more formidable opponent; on the other hand, there were rather strong currents of opinion favourable to trying to find an accommodation with the Germans. Pro-Italian sentiment was not very widespread and was on the whole limited to certain Catholic circles. Pro-German sentiment took many forms. The most familiar was that on the Left where sentiments of guilt about the alleged injustices of the Versailles Treaty were still strong and where little was altered in the argument by the coming into power of Hitler. The willingness to give Hitler the benefit of the doubt and to discount the reports coming from within Germany was not fully dispelled until much later in the decade. In addition, there were those on the Right (including Mosley) whose sympathies were evoked by what they saw as the positive social and political achievements of the Nazi regime and felt drawn towards it in

[25] See Martin Ceadel, 'Interpreting East Fulham', in C. Cook and J.A. Ramsden, eds., *By-Elections in British Politics* (London, 1973). Ceadel shows that though the peace issue did figure largely in the campaign as in other by-elections at this time where the government did badly though without losing a seat, it is hard to distinguish this factor from a general mood of disillusion with the National Government, and that the most important aspect of the issue in Fulham may have been its appeal to the Liberal vote since no Liberal was standing. In the 1935 general election the Conservatives on a higher turnout won back the seat. Ceadel disposes of the recurrent myth that when Baldwin referred to the East Fulham election in the House of Commons on 12 November 1936, he was using it to explain equivocations over rearmament in the general election campaign of 1935; it was the difficulty of beginning rearmament in 1933–4 which was clearly what he had in mind.

various degrees. If the government wished to seek to come to terms with Germany neither the press nor the public nor indeed Parliament was likely to create obstacles.[26] On the other hand, there were clear limits to what Britain could concede and in official circles, particularly in the Foreign Office, a continued scepticism about the genuineness of Hitler's professions of peaceful intentions which seemed to accord ill with his actual policies. It was known that pro-German feeling was stimulated by Nazi propaganda and it was feared that the degree of acquiescence in German demands might be exaggerated in the reports on the British scene ultimately reaching Hitler.

In such circumstances, direct contact between British statesmen and the German leaders always seemed desirable if only to avoid the possibility of misunderstanding. MacDonald himself showed considerable sympathy for the German position in 1933–4; Baldwin however, the key figure in the cabinet, succeeded in spite of pressure from pro-German quarters in holding himself aloof from direct participation in Anglo-German exchanges and left formal talks to the Foreign Office.[27]

The lead in finding a policy to deal with German revisionism and rearmament was however taken by the French after the breakdown of the disarmament conference, and in July 1934, Simon accepted with some reserve the idea of a so-called Eastern Locarno being mooted by the French foreign minister Louis Barthou; Eden who as Lord Privy Seal was also involved in the work of the Foreign Office failed to persuade Simon to insist upon French concessions on disarmament as the price of British support.[28]

The murder of Barthou and of King Alexander of Yugoslavia on 9 October brought about a change in the attitude of France which under Flandin and Laval showed a distinct disposition to bring about a rapprochment with Italy, while still pursuing the attempt made by Barthou to bring Russia into the French security system through a Franco-Soviet pact which was eventually concluded in May 1935. In the previous month, alarmed at the German threat to Austrian independence, MacDonald and Simon had met Mussolini and the French ministers at Stresa where assurances were received from the French that the French agreement with the Russians would not involve Britain in a conflict with Germany by virtue of her Locarno obligations. Simon and Eden had already tried and failed to involve Germany in a wider system of security pacts during a visit to Berlin in

---

[26] For early British opinion in the rise of Hitler, see B. Granzow, *A Mirror of Nazism: British Opinion and the Emergence of Hitler 1929–1933* (London, 1964).

[27] Griffiths, *Fellow Travellers*, pp. 116ff.

[28] David Carlton, *Anthony Eden: Biography* (London, 1981), pp. 50–1.

March. It was increasingly evident that the main concern of German diplomacy was to retain a free hand while rearmament proceeded, and that although British statesmen and other visitors might be given encouragement to believe that Germany would accept some new security system, precision as to what this might entail would not be forthcoming. Meanwhile, the likelihood that Italy would invade Abyssinia had been growing since December 1934 when a frontier incident took place on the border between Abyssinia and Italian Somaliland.

The consequences of this possible conflict and the policy to be adopted were however matters which would concern a new phase in the life of the National Government. On 7 June 1935 Baldwin succeeded MacDonald as Prime Minister; the latter though now clearly ageing remained in the cabinet as Lord President until his death almost two years later, but his serious involvement in politics was now at an end. Sankey now retired, and was succeeded on the woolsack by Hailsham, leaving Thomas as the only other cabinet survivor of the original National Labour group; though the numbers were brought up by the inclusion of MacDonald's son Malcolm as Colonial Secretary. At the Foreign Office, Sir Samuel Hoare replaced Simon who went to the Home Office while Eden became Minister without portfolio for League of Nations Affairs and entered the cabinet for the first time. Changes also took place in the sphere of defence; at the Air Ministry, Lord Londonderry who had seen the first steps taken towards expansion was replaced by Sir Philip Cunliffe-Lister who went to the Lords as Viscount Swinton, and Halifax moved to the War Office. Neville Chamberlain, remaining at the Exchequer, was clearly Baldwin's intended successor and in many ways already the key figure in the government.

Eden's curious appointment which again suggested that foreign policy was one thing and the League of Nations another, illustrated both the ambiguities in the public mind about the rôle of the League and Eden's success in identifying himself with the ideology of collective security to which in fact his allegiance was far from total. But in the middle of 1935, enthusiasm for the League as the way to avoid war reached new heights, as was shown in the apparent success of the so-called Peace Ballot.

The Peace Ballot was the most dramatic achievement of the League of Nations Union. This body had been founded in October 1918 by a merger of two earlier societies working to eliminate war. After the mid 1920s with the decline of the Union of Democratic Control (which had no fewer than 15 of its members holding office in the first Labour government), the LNU became the most important and active of the peace societies. It reached its peak in 1931 when 406,868 subscriptions were collected.[29] In 1933 it claimed a membership of almost a million organized in 3,000 branches.[30] Its moving spirit Viscount Cecil of Chelwood was himself a believer in the force of 'public opinion' as the main deterrent to war. But the ballot itself was intended to demonstrate the public's willingness to support a policy of sanctions against an aggressor. The votes were collected by a house to house canvass between June 1934 and June 1935 and the astonishing number of $11\frac{1}{2}$ millions actually took part – more than half of the active electorate. Over 90 per cent voted that Britain should remain a member of the League, for negotiated all-round disarmament and for the abolition of the private manufacture of arms. Over 80 per cent voted for the abolition of all national air forces. On the crucial question of sanctions, 85 per cent voted in favour of economic sanctions and 74 per cent in favour of military measures if necessary. Only a few thousand answered this question by expressing the full Christian pacifist position.

It was clear that the experience over the Japanese seizure of Manchuria had not been of much effect, and that there were a large number of voters who did not accept the fact that economic sanctions might prove powerless if there was no military force to back them up. The government had both to take this element of unreality into account and yet make use, if it was to retain support, of the language of disarmament and collective security.

By this time Baldwin's government had already one achievement to its credit in the field of disarmament though an equivocal one. In announcing on 22 May 1935 his repudiation of the disarmament clauses of the Versailles Treaty, Hitler had offered to conclude with Britain a treaty of naval limitation. Negotiations were begun on 4 June and concluded on 18 June; Britain's principal negotiator was Hoare whose translation from the Admiralty to the Foreign Office took place during these proceedings. The German undertaking not to build a fleet more than 35 per cent of Britain's and to limit the ratio of German submarines to only 45 per cent (or in exceptional circumstances 100 per cent) could be regarded as satisfactory.

But this optimistic view took little account of the changes in Britain's world position since the last age of Anglo-German naval rivalry. The diplomatic consequences were the first to be felt. The idea that the treaty might be the precursor of an air pact including France was shown to be illusory and Britain's willingness to deal with Germany on her own was a setback to the recent improvement in

[29] Ceadel, *Pacifism,* pp. 75 and 317.
[30] Daniel Waley, *British Public Opinion and the Abyssinian War 1935–1936* (London, 1975), chap. 4.

Anglo-French relations. The most convincing argument in favour of the treaty was that it recognized the realities of the situation. If Germany was going to rearm, Britain was not going to war to stop her and it might therefore be thought marginally preferable that this should be done within the limits of a freely accepted treaty. In any event, it did not damage the government's standing in the eyes of the electorate.

In October, Baldwin was able to use the Party Conference to announce a dual policy based upon some measures of rearmament combined with firm support for the League. With the India Bill out of the way – the royal assent had been given on 2 August – the prime source of intra-party conflict had been removed and Churchill and the die-hards were safely back in the fold. The main cloud on the horizon was the apparent unwillingness of the Italians to curb their demands on Abyssinia; an attempt together with the French to find a solution to the problem had broken down in mid August and the only option seemingly open was the mobilizing of the power of the League. On 11 September, in a speech to the League of Nations Assembly, Hoare had enunciated what appeared to be a strong collective security position, even though it was clear to those with an inside knowledge of the situation that Britain would not take any risks that France would not share, and that France was unwilling to jeopardize her European diplomacy in an African colonial quarrel.

Baldwin's decision to dissolve Parliament announced on 19 October was influenced by the uncertainties of the international situation and the wish to face the coming crisis with a government not seen to be in the last year of its life.[31] MacDonald's fears that the Conservatives would profit by the country's mood to entrench their power still further were no doubt justified, but he was in no position to strike a new bargain. Polling day was to be on 14 November and Baldwin was thus able to use the foreign affairs debate in the House of Commons on 21 and 22 October to open the election campaign by playing on the discrepancy between the Labour Party's vote against the defence estimates in the spring and their current demand for more vigorous pre-emptive action against Mussolini. The Samuelite Liberals had taken much the same line.

Despite the fact that the Conservative Party machine was not particularly well prepared for an election called at short notice, the outlook seemed not unfavourable. While a number of seats had been lost to Labour in by-elections in 1933 and 1934 – though only East Fulham was a traditional Conservative seat – by mid 1935 a recovery

---

[31] See C.T. (Tom) Stannage, *Baldwin Thwarts the Opposition: the British General Election of 1935* (London, 1980).

in the government's standing was becoming obvious. Economic recovery which had begun in 1933 was now clearly in progress and was assisted by a general upswing in the world economy. There was no danger of any split in the Conservative vote; by standing at Wavertree, Liverpool, as an independent Conservative in February 1935, Randolph Churchill had enabled Labour to win the seat but he stood as an official candidate in another Liverpool constituency in the general election. On the evidence of by-elections generally, what seemed to be happening was that traditional Labour voters were swinging back to their own party, in so far as they had deserted it in 1931, while the Conservatives were holding their own. The Liberals were in no position to mount a major challenge. They put up a mere 161 candidates and fought an uninspired campaign.

Baldwin's campaign began by emphasizing the dual commitment to the League of Nations and to rearmament but there was some shift away from the original position later on; more was made of the commitment to peace and more stress was laid on the dangers of socialism should the government be defeated. The results suggested that such a defeat had never been likely. The Conservatives and their allies won 53.7 per cent of the total vote (as against 59.5 per cent in 1931), while the Labour share rose from 30.8 per cent to 40.3 per cent, above the 1929 figure. The Liberal share remained almost the same as in 1931, with however a marked decline in their average votes for Liberal candidates. Translated into seats, these results gave the Conservatives 386 seats with 45 more going to their Liberal National and National Labour allies. The Labour recovery produced only 154 seats, roughly their figure for the 1924–9 Parliament, while the Liberals retained only 21 seats with two of their elected members crossing the floor immediately after the election. Among Liberals who lost their seats was Sir Herbert Samuel who was succeeded as leader by Sir Archibald Sinclair. In the new Parliament the Lloyd George group returned to the Liberal fold. A government majority of about 200 seemed to provide Baldwin with more than adequate support.

MacDonald's forebodings were proved to have been fully justified. The Labour faithful attacked their former leader for his abandonment of the socialist cause. After bitter campaigns both he and his son Malcolm were unseated; since without them, the National label looked almost devoid of content, both were found Conservative seats, MacDonald for the Scottish Universities and Malcolm for Ross and Cromarty – very different constituencies from Seaham Harbour and Bassetlaw. The recovery of the hold of the Labour Party on the traditional areas of working-class concentration was shown by the fact that the Labour gains were heavily concentrated in London, the north of England and Scotland. Some Conservative seats were lost in the midlands but there as over the south of England outside London, the Conservative predominance was still overwhelming. After the patent artificiality of the 1931 election, that of 1935 seemed to indicate the beginning of a new period of stabilization – a basically two-party system with class and region - the two often interlocking – as the main determinants of political allegiance. From that point of view, the subsequent arguments as to whether Baldwin had asked for or been given a mandate for re-armament would seem largely irrelevant; indeed it would be hard to prove that matters of foreign and defence policy were particularly important in deciding the outcome of the election. In domestic affairs, as already noted, 1935 marks no real break in the carrying through of the government's social programme – what was to create the atmosphere of crisis which persisted from 1935 until the outbreak of war was externally generated; the questions to be answered were not merely in the industrial and financial spheres – it was also questionable whether a country so seemingly divided could stand up to the new strains and come through.

9 Appeasement and Rearmament (1935–1939)

The period between the general election of 1935 and the outbreak of war in 1939 was dominated by problems of foreign policy, the accelerating pace of rearmament and other preparations for the coming struggle. The high tide of pacifism had passed, but public opinion was slower than inside opinion to perceive the magnitude of the threat. The cabinet continued in office after the election much as Baldwin had reconstructed it in June; the only important change was the advent of Lord Halifax to the office of Lord Privy Seal, replacing Lord Londonderry who became out of office a strong advocate of appeasing Germany. Malcolm MacDonald and Thomas exchanged offices, the former now taking over the Dominions Office with Thomas becoming Colonial Secretary. On the opposite side, Attlee originally regarded as an interim leader held on against the competition of Herbert Morrison and Arthur Greenwood, both now back in the House of Commons. But the defeat of Lansbury although it meant a victory for 'collective security' over pacifism was not sufficient to bring the Labour Party round to endorsing rearmament whatever its growing antipathy to the European dictators. It was not until July 1937, largely under trade union pressure, that the Party agreed to abstain on the defence estimates rather than vote against them as had been normal; and Attlee himself voted against the change.[1] He did not accept the case for rearmament until after the Munich conference in September 1938 and in the following April he still objected to the introduction of compulsory military service. Archibald Sinclair, the new Liberal leader, became an important advocate of increased preparedness particularly in the air – working increasingly in close concert with Churchill.

The weakness of the Labour Party not only in parliamentary terms, but in the contradictions of its attitude towards the major issue of the day, meant that the real decisions depended upon the currents of opinion in the Conservative Party and their reflection in the

[1] For Attlee's rôle in the 1930s, see Kenneth Harris, *Attlee* (London, 1982).

cabinet.[2] As the documents of the period become more readily available, and are subject to closer scrutiny, two other aspects of these years claim attention. In the first place it was not politicians merely who took part in decision making. Both in the Foreign Office and the Treasury, senior officials argued their case on equal footing with ministers and in the committees set up to discuss and plan rearmament, ministers and officials sat side by side. In these areas at any rate the traditional picture of the constitutional position of civil servants hardly holds good. The historian must take account of the views of Warren Fisher, Maurice Hankey, Richard Hopkins, Robert Vansittart, Horace Wilson and Alexander Cadogan as much as of those of Baldwin, Chamberlain, Halifax, Hoare and Eden. On the service side, the rôle of individuals is less easily assessed and may have been less important. The successive chiefs of the Imperial General Staff were not particularly distinguished and none of the chiefs of the air staff after Trenchard retired in 1930 carried the same authority. On the other hand, Chatfield, the First Sea Lord from 1933 to 1938, was clearly an influential figure, a fact recognized when he was brought back to the centre of affairs as Minister for the Co-ordination of Defence in January 1939.

The rôle of the senior officials reflected in some degree the growth during the period since 1914 of the civil service as a whole which in turn arose out of the increased scale of government intervention in all aspects of economic and social affairs. The measurement of this growth is to some extent complicated by the different definitions adopted for the non-industrial civil service. It is clear that the major period of expansion had been during the was itself; according to official figures from over 282,000 civil servants in August 1914 to over 380,000 in April 1920. Thereafter there was a slight decline to about 307,000 in 1929. But the depression and the increased activities of central government that this entailed as well as the beginnings of rearmament drove the figure up to over 376,000 by 1938.[3]

From the figures collected by the May Committee in 1931, it is clear that the major area of growth had been in the lower ranks of the service, particularly in the executive and clerical grades.[4] The officials who occupied posts involved in policy-making through advice to ministers – the administrative class – had also grown in numbers

---

[2] A highly idiosyncratic but suggestive treatment of the period laying emphasis on domestic politics and the rôle in particular of Halifax is to be found in Maurice Cowling, *The Impact of Hitler: British Politics and British Policy 1933–1940* (Cambridge, 1975). A study of the divisions in the Conservative Party in a more prosaic vein is Neville Thompson, *The Anti-Appeasers: Conservative Opposition to Appeasement in the 1930s* (Oxford, 1971).

[3] Emmeline Cohen, *The Growth of the British Civil Service 1780–1939* (London, 1941), p. 164.

[4] K.B. Smellie, *A Hundred Years of English Government* (London, 1937), p. 455.

though less steeply. A contemporary and well-informed study put the number of these (outside the diplomatic and consular services) at 1,430 at the beginning of 1939.[5]

A service as small as this was obviously hard pressed when work expanded as was inevitably the case when re-armament and other preparations for war began to loom larger among the government's preoccupations.[6] On the other hand, its influence was enhanced by its relative compactness, the similarity in its methods of recruitment and training and the unquestioned dominance of the senior department, the Treasury. While there were important divergences between members of the Foreign Office as to the relative importance of the different threats to the nation's security and as to the fields in which appeasement might be most rewarding, the Treasury and the other domestic departments were of a like mind, emphasizing the importance of classical economic teaching and the continued desirability of preventing extravagance and of husbanding the nation's economic resources against future calls upon them.[7] Ministers without external sources of information or advice were inevitably dependent upon their officials and could make decisions only within the narrow boundaries of what the official mind considered feasible. Scientists worried about the need to keep abreast of advancing technology – radar is the conspicuous and all-important example – and industrialists worried about a repetition of the bottlenecks in supplies, so notorious in the war of 1914–18, required a good deal of persistence and political acumen if they were to make the necessary headway against entrenched opinions and entrenched interests. Nor were the senior ministers of a competent but uninspired administration likely to be of any great help.

The difficulty of dealing with the issues in such a way as to carry opinion along was a real one; for several reasons the inward thinking of the government could not easily be made public. There is therefore perhaps no period of British history to which contemporary debate is so poor a guide.[8] Decisions were made on the basis of military and naval weaknesses that could not be made public without further encouraging aggression, and they had therefore to be defended on different grounds, thus making it harder to use these experiences to create assent to further effort. An element of bluff went into the discussions with the Pacific Dominions where assurances had to be

---

[5] H.E. Dale, *The Higher Civil Service of Great Britain* (London, 1941), p. 3.

[6] See R.P. Shay, jr., *British Rearmament in the Thirties: Politics and Profits* (Princeton, 1977).

[7] For the rôle of the Treasury see G.C. Peden, *British Rearmament and the Treasury 1932–1939* (Edinburgh, 1979).

[8] For important summaries of subsequent research see Wolfgang J. Mommsen and Lothar Kettenacker, eds., *The Fascist Challenge and the Policy of Appeasement* (London, 1983).

given that Britain could still make provision for their defence –
assurances which were belied by the facts of Britain's capabilities;
but the alternative would have been still further Dominion pressure
for appeasement at all costs. A similar degree of bluff had to exercised
at times towards Britain's potential allies. In the same way, it could
not easily or openly be stated that the decisions made to restrain
expenditure on armaments arose primarily from economic and financial conditions, and did not reflect a real confidence that the threats
to Britain's position could somehow be conjured away by 'appeasement'. The ministers themselves, their Treasury advisers and financial circles in the City were all convinced that there were strict limits
to the country's ability to pay for greater armaments. It was held that
attempts to pay for them out of taxation would impede economic
recovery and contribute to inflation and social unrest; even more
inflationary would be any attempt to deal with the matter by extensive
borrowing since it was held that any borrowing exceeding the rate of
savings was bound to be inflationary, even if unused capacity could
be shown to exist. Any signs of financial overstrain would, it was
feared, lead to a flight from sterling and a weakening of the reserve
position, upon which both prosperity at home and the ability to fight
a long war in the future appeared to depend. But to confess that
Britain could not afford to do what she needed to do, was again something that could only be stated publicly at the price of creating precisely those conditions of financial uncertainty which it was the object
of the government's policy to avoid.

On the industrial side, arguing out the country's needs in public
was also a difficult task. The government itself did not wish to see too
great a switch from peacetime production to the provision of
armaments because of the fears that a consequent fall in exports
would produce heavy pressure upon the balance of payments. The
firms themselves, other than those used to providing for the services,
were reluctant to switch their efforts, partly because of the
uncertainties that rearmament in general seemed to create for the
future, and partly because of the fact that the rather rapid rate of
technological change, for instance in relation to aircraft, meant a
series of interruptions to the course of production as service
requirements were revised. Compulsion in peacetime seemed out of
the question and to provide sufficient financial incentives would lay
open the government to the charges of conniving at 'profiteering' – a
word which had since the war carried with it serious social and
political overtones. What was true of capital was no less true of
labour. Bevin and Citrine awakened by their European labour and
socialist contacts to the need for re-armament were prepared to
discuss what might be done; but they also suffered from the

inhibitions of their own constituency – industrial conscription, dilution, limitations on the right of workers to get the highest return for their skills were unacceptable. Much was made by the government's critics of the need for a ministry of supply, but the government were right in thinking that the question of such a ministry was more than a matter of Whitehall mechanics, a technical issue in respect of the machinery of government; it was bound up with the question as to whether the new international environment made it possible for Britain to retain its commitment to an open voluntarist society, moving by broad consensus, or whether it would need to go some way towards creating wartime controls in what was still a period of peace. The decisions in the spring and early summer of 1939 to go ahead with conscription and to create a ministry of supply were indications that hopes of preserving the peace were rapidly fading away.

If neither finance nor industrial preparedness easily or safely lent themselves to public debate, scientific developments were even less susceptible of open discussion; yet opinions as to the likely outcome of particular avenues of research were of great importance for deciding where, within the general financial constraint, the weight of expenditure should fall. If as was the current doctrine in the early 1930s there was truly no defence against the bombing aircraft, it was natural to rely upon 'deterrence', that is to say upon bombers of one's own and, given their relatively short range, upon arrangements to make available forward bases on the continent. But if, as it began to appear, radar made the detection and interception of hostile aircraft a practical possibility, home defence, fighter planes, anti-aircraft guns and other devices might take priority. Because the implications of conclusions that would, in default of experience, always have some element of the speculative were so great, the rôle of the government's scientific advisers, and indeed the arguments and rivalries between them, were an important, and at the time largely unrevealed aspect, of the government's preparations.[9]

The Baldwin government, like the Chamberlain government which succeeded it, was thus faced with a complex of issues of very grave importance a full understanding of which could not be expected of the public at large, or even of members of Parliament except for Churchill whose own sources of information were important, and whose experience made it impossible to treat him as an outsider, however unwilling the Conservative hierarchy may have been to see

---

[9] The changing course of British rearmament can be followed in N.H. Gibbs's *Rearmament Policy*, being volume I of the official series *Grand Strategy* (London, 1976). On the scientists see Ronald W. Clark, *Tizard* (London, 1965) and the Earl of Birkenhead [F.W.F. Smith] *The Prof. in Two Worlds: the Official Life of Professor F.A. Lindemann, Viscount Cherwell* (London, 1961).

him back in office. Yet there were some aspects of the situation upon which on the government side of the House at least there was or could have been general. agreement. If one looked merely at generally available statistics of population, industrial strength and basic military resources, it was clear that once Germany had repudiated the limitations placed on her armaments and was in a position, if she wished, to circumvent other restrictions freely negotiated, her power together with that of Italy and Japan presented a greater threat to the interests of Britain and France than those two powers, with any lesser allies they might acquire, could possibly hope to resist, unless, as seemed improbable in the short run, Russia and the United States could be brought into play to redress the balance. It was thus perfectly reasonable for any British (or for that matter French) government to try to prevent the coalescence of these prospective enemies, either through appeasement of one or more of them, or through a knock-out blow at the most vulnerable of them. Such calculations would have seemed natural to past practioners of international statecraft and did figure in the internal debate within government.

There were however two obstacles to the successful practice of *realpolitik* by British governments in the 1930s. The pursuit of such policies clearly depended upon being able to assess with accuracy the true objectives and policy preferences of the countries it was sought to appease. Since all three regimes with which it was necessary to deal were in a sense revolutionary this task was peculiarly difficult, even though in the Nazi case, the long-term aspects of policy were quite public and never repudiated. It was on the whole the view of the Foreign Office – though individuals differed – that in fact there was no point at which Hitler would stop short that was compatible with Britain's interests and that appeasement would therefore merely have the effect of making Germany stronger, so that the inevitable conflict would be waged when she was in a better position to win it. Against this view, other elements within government, notably in the Treasury, supported in this by large sections of public opinion, particularly after the first shock of the establishment of the dictatorship had worn off, were convinced of the contrary. Since they looked with the utmost apprehension on the likely consequences of another war against the Germans, and saw no other way of avoiding it, it is perhaps not surprising that they did their best to put the most favourable possible construction upon Germany's deeds and words and were prone to treat as 'war-mongers' those who questioned the soundness of their analysis. Differences over the respective intentions of Italy and Japan were less acute among the general public, though at times of crucial importance to policy-makers.

The second difficulty was that much of the public – particularly its

Liberal and Labour elements – refused to accept this approach. As the Peace Ballot had shown, the ideology of the League of Nations and of collective security still commanded in 1935 a powerful degree of allegiance. What was needed, it was argued in such quarters, was to demonstrate that aggression would be dealt with through the machinery of 'collective security'. When this lesson had been brought home to the dictators, they would accept the need to limit their demands to what the international community might reasonably accept. The failure to handle Japan by this method during the Manchurian crisis was put down to distance, and to the lack of will of the United States. The invasion of Abyssinia by Italy on 3 October 1935 seemed to provide a much better terrain for the testing of these assumptions.[10]

The dilemma with which such action would confront Britain had been foreseen for some time. Although Hoare had made a strong speech in favour of the general principle of collective security at the League Assembly on 11 September, the cabinet had all along been conscious of the damage that would be done to Britain's world position if Italy responded to sanctions by attacking the Mediterranean fleet, and the need therefore to take no action which the French would not support. But discussions with the French had revealed that Laval was very unwilling to forfeit Italian support against the more immediate dangers from Germany in Europe. By the time the election campaign was being fought, the League had indeed undertaken a programme of sanctions to which Britain adhered but this had not prevented a rapid advance by the Italian forces against the under-equipped Abyssinians.[11] In order to avoid the necessity of considering further sanctions, such as an embargo on oil, that would confront Mussolini with the alternative of giving way or going to war with the powers imposing them, of which Britain would be the principal one, the government began, immediately after the election, to seek through Laval's contacts with Mussolini some compromise solution to the conflict which might give Mussolini enough of a grip on Abyssinia to enable him to accept the nominal survival of the empire.[12] But the Italians were in Laval's view unlikely

---

[10] See Norton Medlicott, 'The Hoare–Laval Pact Reconsidered', in David Dilks, ed., *Retreat from Power: Studies in Britain's Foreign Policy of the Twentieth Century.* Vol. I: *1906–1939* (London, 1981).

[11] A narrative account of the crisis is to be found in Frank Hardie, *The Abyssinian Crisis* (London, 1974). It is written from a strong 'collective security' point of view: e.g. 'the effective ending of the League of Nations was perhaps a more decisive turning-point in the road to the Second World War than the Anglo-French surrender of Czechoslovakia to Nazi Germany' (p. 3).

[12] See J.A. Cross, *Sir Samuel Hoare: a Political Biography* (London, 1977), chap. 6 'The Hoare–Laval Pact'.

to accept what the British thought the League could be expected to swallow.

In order to expedite matters a meeting was arranged between Hoare and Laval in Paris on 7 December, when Hoare would be on his way to a Swiss holiday, in the hope of coming to an agreement which would prevent the League committee on sanctions due to meet five days later from coming to decisions that might lead to a wider war. The cabinet seemed to have hoped, though with differences of individual emphasis, that some peaceful way out of the situation might still be found; most of its members accepted the view that Britain's state of preparedness did not enable her to contemplate a war though some felt that the danger of Italy using the oil sanction (which itself would depend upon American concurrence) as a *casus belli* might have been exaggerated. The discussions in Paris which revolved round territorial acquisitions by Italy and economic concessions to her to be compensated for by an Abyssinian outlet to the sea, made it clear that Laval was far keener on finding something that Mussolini would accept than on planning for Anglo-French military co-operation and the imposition of further sanctions. On the following day agreement was reached on a projected solution which was to be submitted first to the British cabinet, and then to Italy and the other governments involved in the League's deliberations.

Hoare having departed for Switzerland, it was left to officials to take the proposals to London where they were approved by the cabinet on the evening of 9 December. The only proviso was that Abyssinia should be informed simultaneously with Italy about the contents of the proposals. Laval agreed to this procedure but asked for assurances that the oil sanction would not be pressed if Italy accepted the proposals and Abyssinia rejected them. Vansittart who had remained in Paris as the contact with the French premier strongly urged the cabinet to agree; but at its meeting on 10 December it refused to give such an undertaking. Nevertheless a further cabinet on 11 December made it clear that most members thought that the lagging response from other League members and the uncertainty as to America's position made immediate recourse to the oil sanction a highly unpalatable idea.

By now however these discussions, necessitated by the need to brief Eden on how to present the issue at Geneva, were increasingly irrelevant to the political situation that was developing in the country at large. Instead of the orderly but secret set of initiatives contemplated at the Paris meeting, most of the contents of the Hoare–Laval proposals had been leaked to the French press and repeated in the British press. Most British press comment – apart from the Beaverbrook and Rothermere papers – was hostile and that the public reaction was similar seemed to be the lesson from MPs postbags. On 16 December *The Times* in an editorial headed 'A corridor for camels' declared that British opinion would never support 'an unjust peace'. Although Hoare (who returned to England a sick man after a skating accident) pointed out that there was no indication that any other League member had made preparations to back sanctions with force, the cabinet were not prepared to go through with the proposals. Eden was to make it clear at Geneva that since they did not command general agreement, the British government would not press them.

Nevertheless it was still expected that the attempt Hoare had made to find a peaceful settlement would be defended when an Opposition motion of censure was debated in the House of Commons on 19 December. But a meeting of the Conservative Foreign Affairs Committee under the chairmanship of Austen Chamberlain on 17 December proved so hostile that the cabinet decided in Hoare's absence that it would have to repudiate him altogether as having exceeded his authority. Since Hoare continued to hold that he had got the best terms available for the Abyssinians, the cabinet's decision involved his own resignation which was announced shortly before the debate. In the new circumstances, the Conservative Party fell into line behind the government and the censure motion was defeated by 232 votes. Eden took over the Foreign Office and the immediate political crisis appeared to be at an end.

The crisis was however significant for two reasons. It was widely believed that it showed the force that public opinion could exert over government on a major issue of foreign policy. There was indeed a good deal of pressure on the government from such quarters as the League of Nations Union, identified with the idea of collective security. Private individuals who joined in the protests were also affected in some cases by the characteristic British sympathy with the underdog, now personified by the Abyssinians. Such opinions received more support in the press than journals like the *Daily Mail* could muster for the Italians both on isolationist grounds and because of the feeling that the white empires should stand together and that an Italian defeat might produce problems for Britain in her own African colonies. On the Left also, the upholders of collective security who had won a major victory at the Labour Party conference just prior to the outbreak of the war were more effective than either the pacifists or the left-wingers of the Socialist League and the ILP who regarded opposition to Italian imperialism as a mask for the prosecution of Britain's own imperialist aims. But later research suggests that contemporaries may have overestimated the rôle of external pressure and that the real weakness in Hoare's position was the conviction of a great majority of MPs on the government side that (despite some ambiguity in Baldwin's own pronouncements) they had gone to the country, and been elected, on a collective security platform which they could not in decency now repudiate. It was parliamentary opinion not public opinion that was decisive.[13]

The second significant fact is that Hoare's fall made no difference to the realities of the situation. The war continued, and no further and more far-reaching sanctions were initiated. In February 1936 the cabinet accepted the idea of an oil sanction in principle, but there was still no likelihood of French consent being forthcoming for harsher measures. Indeed the Rhineland crisis in early March, and the emergence in a new form of the problem of containing Nazi Germany, made it more than ever unlikely that the French would proceed further to alienate Italy, a consideration never absent in fact from British calculations. The enthusiasm of the advocates of further action against Italy did not however diminish in the League of Nations Union and similar quarters. On the contrary the revelations that Italy which had based its case on Abyssinian 'barbarism' was now using poison gas stimulated a new wave of protest. But with the massive defeat of the Abyssinian forces on 31 March and the occupation early in May of Addis Ababa, the raison d'être of sanctions had disappeared; it was only a matter of time before they were formally abandoned. On 18 June the government announced that they were being lifted, and five days later only two Conservative MPs went into the lobby in support of a censure motion.

It has been suggested that public opinion was hostile to even this acceptance of the inevitable, partly perhaps because the idea of Britain being unable to exert its will against Italy was an affront to national feeling. But the argument that the loss of J.H. Thomas's seat at Derby in a by-election caused by his resignation from the government after being involved in a budget-leak scandal and his replacement by Philip Noel-Baker a leading Labour apostle of collective security, coming as it did two days after the League itself had lifted sanctions, can be regarded as a verdict on the government's handling of the Abyssinian crisis does not carry conviction. Five previous by-elections had shown anti-government swings and two other seats had been lost. It is hard to resist the conclusion that many other factors played their part.

Germany and problems of rearmament were bound to dominate political discussion from after the fiasco of the Hoare–Laval proposals. Domestically, there were the questions raised particularly

[13] Daniel Waley, *British Public Opinion and the Abyssinian War 1935–1936* (London, 1975) provides much useful material.

for the Prime Minister by the beginning of a new reign. George V whose health had given cause for concern for some time was taken ill after Christmas and died on 20 January. It was a low point in the nation's morale and in Baldwin's.

The pressure on the government took two forms; a demand for a more effective machinery for re-armament and for a speeding up of the arms programme and, from rather different quarters, for a renewed commitment to collective security to meet future attempts to alter by force the *status quo* both in Europe and overseas. The creation of a ministry of defence, advocated for its own reasons by the Air Ministry but opposed by the War Office and with even more conviction by the Admiralty, also faced powerful political objections. It implied a derogation from the co-ordinating functions of the Prime Minister and was a threat to Treasury control of expenditure. The furthest the government would go to meet its critics was the appointment of a Minister for the Co-ordination of Defence who could, as deputy for the Prime Minister, follow in greater detail the allocation of funds to the service ministries, and intervene to mitigate the industrial obstacles to the carrying out of their programmes. The announcement on 13 March 1936 that the post would go not to Churchill but to the Attorney-General Sir Thomas Inskip seemed to indicate the restricted nature of the innovation, though Inskip's record suggests that within the assigned limits he was probably as successful as anyone was likely to be.

The task could not be an easy one, not simply because of the financial restrictions imposed upon the armaments programme, but also because of the uncertainties of strategic doctrine as between deterrence and defence in the air and as between the demands of imperial defence and the possible need to intervene on the European continent. Inskip made some progress in dealing with the employers' organizations in order to avoid some of the problems that had faced the expansion of the munitions programme in the war, but given the hostile attitude of labour to any interference with the free market in skills and traditional industrial structures, no serious attempts were made to bring its representatives into the planning process before the spring of 1938. Whether this could have been done at an earlier date, as has been argued, must be regarded as an open question. It would have involved treating the TUC as distinct entirely from the Labour Party which was clearly and vocally hostile to the government's policy and not simply to the methods by which it was implemented.

The dangers in Britain's military and diplomatic situation as the Abyssinian war drew to its inevitable conclusion were forcibly brought home when on 7 March 1936 Hitler ordered German troops to begin the reoccupation of the demilitarized zone of the Rhineland,

thus tearing up not merely the 'imposed' treaty of Versailles but also
the freely negotiated treaty of Locarno. In practical terms the damage
was greater to French than to British interests. France's network of
alliances in eastern Europe had been predicated on her ability to come
to the aid of her allies by invading Germany across an undefended
western border. Once that border was fortified doubts as to the utility
of France's guarantees were bound to multiply. Yet as the diplomacy
of subsequent days and weeks was to show, France was not prepared
to make a counter-move even in the face of an eventuality long-
predicted. The strain of general mobilization which her military
chiefs declared needful was thought too great to be sustained. But it
was also the case that Germany could only be successfully opposed if
British and French policies were successfully co-ordinated, and the
crisis found the two countries far apart in their assessment of the
situation. Relations between the two governments were not happy.
The French resented the Anglo-German naval treaty of June 1935 in
which it was felt that Britain had sacrificed the general interest in
order to secure narrow objectives of her own. Even though Laval had
left office, the Hoare–Laval affair and the further alienation of Italy
had adversely affected French opinion. On the other hand, the British
government had no troops to offer for operations on the continent,
and British public opinion seemed prepared to accept the view that
Germany's action within her own boundaries was not any kind of
aggression, and that Hitler's protestations of a willingness to discuss
possible new guarantees for peace could be taken at face value.

Except in circles where the internal repressiveness of the Nazi
regime was a factor in their outlook on foreign policy, the public
attitude to the Rhineland crisis was in stark contrast to the outburst of
emotion over the Abyssinian war and sanctions. Germany excited
both more fear and more sympathy than Mussolini's Italy. And the
fact that it was the ratification of a pact between France and Soviet
Russia that was Hitler's pretext for the timing of his action was bound
to weigh with people who were understandably sceptical about the
degree to which the Soviet Union had genuinely undergone a conversion to the doctrines of collective security, and abandoned its more
natural role of *tertius gaudens*.

For the rest of 1936 and in 1937, Germany was able to count on a
good deal of sympathy in Britain which was only finally dissipated in
the following year. Yet if one looks at government policy one can see
in retrospect that the Rhineland crisis does in fact mark a watershed in
the official outlook. There could now be no going back on the drive
towards rearmament whatever brakes might be placed upon it by
financial prudence. And Germany was clearly the country against
which the major preparations were directed. Furthermore the diver-

gences of policy with France could not conceal the fact that a war with Germany if one became inevitable could only be contemplated in alliance with her. From the spring of 1936 onwards contacts with the French at both the diplomatic and military levels became more regular and more intimate, though as 1940 was to show hardly intimate enough. In that sense there are important resemblances between the period 1936–9 and the years immediately before the outbreak of war in 1914.

The essentials of the British attitude were highlighted by the handling of the problems created by the Spanish Civil War which began in July 1936. It confirmed British suspicions of both Italy and Russia while less was made of German intervention; it illustrated France's inability to pursue a wholly independent policy; but above all it highlighted the extent to which Britain was a divided country.[14]

The attitude of the government was throughout a negative one, in the sense that it could neither wish for communism to triumph nor see with equanimity a regime sympathetic to fascism establish itself on France's south-western border and athwart British communications in the Mediterranean; on the other hand it did not want to take any action that might further envenom the general situation and make war in the near future more likely. As in the Rhineland crisis it seemed that decision was primarily one for France. In France Léon Blum's 'popular front' government newly in power presided over a country which was even more sharply divided over the merits of the rising. Hence the proposal for 'non-intervention' while it might seem to question the normal right of a sovereign government to purchase arms abroad suited both France and Britain so long as it was observed. But British opinion was not wholly behind this prudent course.

On the Right, there were sections of opinion notably among Catholics for whom Franco's war was being waged against godless communism, even before the communists established their domination on the Republican side. Support also came from elements in

[14] The international as well as the domestic aspects of the Spanish conflict are fully dealt with in Hugh Thomas, *The Spanish Civil War* (London, 1961). Its impact on British politics is dealt with in K.W. Watkins, *Britain Divided: the Effect of the Spanish Civil War on British Political Opinion* (London, 1963). Peter Stansky and William Abrahams, *Journey to the Frontier. Julian Bell and John Cornford: their Lives and the 1930s* (London, 1966) which deals with the scions of two noted intellectual families killed in Spain gives an account of how fighting or ambulance driving on the Republican side appeared to offer an escape from the political and moral frustrations of the Left at home, and is perhaps the most successful effort at recreating the impact upon 'Bloomsbury' of the advent of European fascism. The celebrated poet W.H. Auden (who was to spend the years of Britain's own war in self-imposed exile in America) played a briefer and less heroic part in the Spanish conflict. For a general view of the impact of the politics of the 1930s upon the English literary scene see Samuel Hynes, *The Auden Generation: Literature and Politics in England in the 1930s* (London, 1976).

British opinion sympathetic to either Mussolini or Nazi Germany. Other figures on the Right, notably though not altogether consistently Churchill, were by now so suspicious of the fascist powers as to prefer the risk of backing the Republicans. On the Left, the matter was simpler in that apart from some Catholics and the pacifists there was naturally general sympathy for the Republican cause. But there were divisions over how far to go. Originally, the right wing of the Labour Party and most of the leading trade union figures supported non-intervention provided it could be made to work, while clamouring for more positive action were the Left in both the Party and the trade unions, the Communist Party (which organized the recruiting for the so-called international brigade), the Independent Labour Party and some smaller groups. It was the identification of the Communists with a more active policy of support for the Republic that persuaded Bevin to use his influence to make the TUC support non-intervention. But as evidence of active assistance from Italy and Germany to the insurgents (and Soviet support for the Republic) became evident, this position became harder to maintain. Yet criticism that called for an active anti-fascist foreign policy when combined with continued hostility to the re-armament programme was not easy to advance convincingly.

In this situation of divided counsels and general uncertainty, Churchill found a new opportunity, after his defeat over the India bill, to come back into the forefront of politics as the exponent of a robust policy of collective security through the League combined with more active measures of re-armament.[15] The movement known as 'Arms and the Covenant' took shape in the latter part of 1936 when Churchill's assertions that the government was underestimating the extent and speed of Germany's re-armament in the air began to win him support beyond the ranks of the Conservative Party. The campaign culminated in a meeting at the Albert Hall on 3 December when Churchill was supported on the platform by a distinguished all-party grouping, presided over by Citrine. Messages in support of Churchill's campaign came from three elder statesmen, Austen Chamberlain, J.R. Clynes and Herbert Samuel.

In the last few months of 1936 while the international scene darkened, the energies of the Prime Minister and of some of his senior colleagues were distracted by the sequence of events leading to the abdication on 10 December of King Edward VIII in favour of his brother the Duke of York, who took the title of George VI. Despite subsequent revelations of the way in which the Germans hoped to exploit the King's friendly feelings towards Germany, and his public

---

[15] See Martin Gilbert, *Winston S. Churchill*. Vol. v: *1922–1939* (London, 1976), chap. 40.

sympathy for close ties between the ex-servicemen of the two countries, and despite the rumours at the time that his overt sympathy with the plight of the long-term unemployed was irritating to ministers whose policies he might seem to be criticizing by implication, it is abundantly clear that the abdication was not itself a political question.[16] The reason for the abdication was the obvious and overt one, namely that the King wished to marry a woman twice-divorced whom public opinion neither in Britain, nor in the Dominions, now necessarily involved in consultations, were prepared to accept as Queen. The only possible compromise between the King's determination to marry the woman of his choice and the position taken by the cabinet was a 'morganatic' marriage; but this demanded legislation which it was clear that Parliament would not pass, nor the Dominions accept.

The wide measure of agreement in the country and the Commonwealth became clear as events developed. In Britain itself, this seems to have been independent of class and party. The inner group of cabinet ministers who acted with Baldwin, MacDonald, Chamberlain, Halifax, Simon and Runciman represented all three strands in the government's majority; also consulted were Attlee and Citrine. In the cabinet only Duff Cooper the Secretary of State for War, a personal friend of the King's, was an advocate of temporization. In the final days, what appeared to be a move towards a 'King's party' developed among a few figures who thought that any opportunity of getting rid of Baldwin was too good to miss – the press Lords Beaverbrook and Rothermere and to his own ultimate discomfiture Churchill. But they received no encouragement from either King or people.

The importance attached to the question of the King's proposed marriage and his abdication illuminates the new significance attached to the monarchy in the inter-war years. In part this was due to the fact that with completion of the progress of the Dominions towards total independence, the Crown seemed to be the only common element in their constitutions. And this Commonwealth rôle had been enhanced by King Edward VIII himself as Prince of Wales, during his lengthy visits to the Dominions, India and parts of the colonial empire in the 1920s. But there was also a domestic side to the new rôle of the monarchy as was revealed during the celebrations in May 1935 of King George V's jubilee.

After surmounting the problems of the early years of the reign, George V had played an important rôle as a rallying point for public steadfastness during the war years and had helped as has been seen to

---

[16] The case for taking this view emerges persuasively from the best of the many works on the subject: Frances Donaldson, *Edward VIII* (London, 1974).

bring about a settlement in Ireland. Although without particular political flair, he had developed a pattern of conduct appropriate in a democratic age to what was expected of him, and accepted without complaint the burdens that fulfilling this rôle implied for himself and his family.[17] Despite mutterings on the Left about his rôle in the 1931 crisis, there was no serious questioning of the value of the monarchy as the keystone of the British constitutional arch. No doubt George V was much assisted by the holders of the office so important for a constitutional monarch, that of his private secretary: Lord Stamfordham from his accession until his own death in March 1931, and subsequently Lord Wigram.

It also became clear during the reign of George V that under the new conditions, it was not enough that a monarch should fulfil his constitutional duties which only very intermittently could involve personal judgement and maintain the contacts necessary for their performance, or involve himself and his family in various aspects of the country's life – particularly in the work of the various voluntary and philanthropic bodies which still played so important a rôle in providing services and relieving distress. It was also desirable that the monarch and his family should be seen and heard by members of the public on a much greater variety of occasions if they were to fulfil the rôle expected of them. Towards the end of his reign George V became the first British sovereign to have at his disposal the new instrument of radio; the first royal broadcast was on Christmas Day 1932.

The dual rôle of head of State and national symbol was not an easy one and it was clear to many people in public life, including George V himself, that it was not one that would altogether suit his heir. Edward was not well-educated politically and held opinions often based on little more than personal prejudice; at the same time he had a high opinion of his own prerogatives. Again, although capable of filling with ease and charm the rôle of national symbol, and vastly popular, the Prince of Wales clearly resented some of the obligations that royalty imposed, particularly where these might impinge upon his private pursuits and pleasures. The degree of self-discipline now required by the people of their monarch was not at his disposal. And although the abdication came as a great shock to the general public – where the self-censorship of the British press had prevented most people from knowing about aspects of the King's life familiar to American newspaper readers – the dénouement can hardly have been surprising to the initiated. Yet by a stroke of good fortune, Edward VIII was succeeded by a monarch George VI who, despite a

---

[17] See Harold Nicolson, *King George V: his Life and Reign* (London, 1952); Kenneth Rose, *King George V* (London, 1983).

nervous and shy disposition, was fully determined to carry on his father's work and whose rôle during the war that was already looming was to be even more important for national morale than his father's between 1914 and 1918. By 1945 the monarchy was established in popular esteem to a degree unprecedented, except perhaps in the years of Queen Victoria's two jubilees.[18]

The immediate political effects of the abdication crisis were considerable. It gave Baldwin a chance to show his political skill and his capacity for representing a national consensus. A serious challenge to his leadership in the early months of the new reign was out of the question and it remained open to him to choose the moment for handing over the premiership to his clearly designated successor, Neville Chamberlain. If Baldwin's stock rose, Churchill's collapsed even more dramatically. His standing in the country sharply declined and he was for the moment not a leader around whom the government's critics could easily rally; the movement he had initiated could make no further progress. The government's Conservative critics in the House of Commons were a group of backbenchers lacking a recognized leader or a unifying doctrine. Labour's leaders were still caught in the dilemma of preaching the Covenant without Arms.

The Spanish War continued to add to Labour discomfiture. In March 1937 the Republicans' victory at Guadalajara revealed the degree of armed intervention by the Italians; the bombing of Guernica by German planes on 26 April (while denied by some of Franco's more enthusiastic partisans in Britain) made the illusion of non-intervention even harder to maintain. On 27 July the National Council of Labour finally committed the Labour Party to opposing the non-intervention policy as such. The internal history of the Labour Party between the general election of 1935 and the outbreak of war was powerfully influenced by the prominence of issues of foreign and defence policy and by the relative quiescence of domestic strife at a time of modest economic recovery. Believing as many Labour supporters did that the government's policy was based upon an ideological hostility to the Left, sympathy for all defenders of the capitalist structure of society irrespective of their methods, and a determination to allow Soviet Russia no say in the affairs of the rest of Europe, two alternative currents of thought manifested themselves; though their consequences are often hard to portray schematically, in the light of the changing positions held by prominent individuals, and the groups with which they were identified.

For some people on the Left, the lesson of events at home and

---

[18] See John W. Wheeler-Bennett, *King George VI: his Life and Reign* (London, 1958).

abroad was that the reformism of the dominant leaders in the parliamentary party, Attlee, Morrison, Greenwood, Dalton, and in the trade unions, Bevin and Citrine was inappropriate. What was needed was a Marxist or near-Marxist analysis of the whole situation and this in turn would suggest pacts with other parties or groups not affiliated to the Labour Party but sharing in a common 'socialism'. Perhaps the chief effect of this general approach was to give respectability to the Communist Party, and to make possible the fashionable admiration for communism among some British intellectuals which if never as important as the corresponding mood in the United States, did have the practical consequence of preparing the way for Soviet penetration of the British intelligence and foreign services whose full ramifications only became apparent very much later.[19]

The alternative argument which was particularly affected by the war in Spain and later on by the threat to Czechoslovakia in 1938 was to the effect that any movement based solely upon 'socialism' would remain the affair of a minority, with no hope of attaining power. What was needed was a wider gathering of forces which should embrace all those who were opposed to the European dictatorships and wished to see British policy based upon this opposition. It was to be a British version of the 'Popular Front'.

Neither alternative possessed much appeal for the Labour leadership, though individual members of Parliament or trade unionists might be attracted by the latter. With only a few years separating the Labour leaders from the debacle of 1931, the importance of party unity was bound to figure largely in their outlook. On the one side, there had been the persistent struggle to prevent communist penetration of the trade unions, and to resist the Communist Party's demand for affiliation to the Labour Party itself. On the other side, the Liberals were the obvious target for such an alliance but the whole course of the Labour Party's history had been dominated by the determination to eliminate the Liberals as a political force, and to leave Labour as the sole alternative to Tory rule. Could an alliance at the national level be compatible with continuing the struggle in the constituencies? Would not such a movement provide an occasion for Lloyd George to step once more onto the centre of the stage – a prospect no more palatable to Attlee than to Baldwin? Lloyd George had indeed launched in 1935 a 'new deal' of his own and had founded in the same year 'A Council of

---

[19] One immediate result was to have the Communist version of the internal affairs of the Spanish Republic accepted by the entire Left. A principal vehicle of 'Popular Front', i.e. Communist, propaganda was the Left Book Club with its 65,000 members. See Iain Hamilton, *Koestler: a Biography* (London, 1982), pp. 44–5.

Action for Peace and Reconstruction' in an attempt to capitalize on the support for the League of Nations revealed in the Peace Ballot; and while this had now faded away, and Lloyd George in his mid seventies seemed at last reconciled to private life, no one felt that this absence from the arena could be relied upon to endure.

Meanwhile in the Labour Party there were also difficulties, since there was considerable frustration on the Left at its failure to affect the course of government policy in either domestic or foreign affairs.[20] It was felt in some quarters that the new leadership was too ready to fall into an acceptance of the old conventions of parliamentary government which it was argued had been the root cause of MacDonald's failure and ultimate treachery. The historic Left represented by the ILP had begun to move away from Labour orthodoxy during the lifetime of the second Labour government and although still nominally affiliated to the Party in fact fought the 1931 election independently. Having failed to get the Labour Party standing orders amended so as to give it full freedom to advocate its own policies, the ILP formally disaffiliated itself in July 1932.

In the 1935 election it put up 17 candidates – only four of whom, all in Glasgow, were successful. Henceforward it became little more than a localized sect. The Communists were by 1935 moving towards a United Front of socialist parties under the impulse of the changing position of the Comintern. In 1935 it put up only two candidates of its own – one of whom was elected.

The main focus of left-wing activity was by now the Socialist League which was formed in 1932 by members of the ILP who had not wished to follow their leaders into the wilderness and remained individual members of the Labour Party; they linked up in order to form the League with a Society for Socialist Inquiry and Propaganda of which Bevin was chairman and G.D.H. Cole, the former guild socialist, vice-chairman. Cole who, with Professors H.J. Laski and R.H. Tawney – the one increasingly drawn towards marxism and the other an egalitarian socialist of Christian inspiration – was one of the three dominant intellectual figures in the Labour Party at this time, was also secretary of the newly founded New Fabian Research Bureau (which was to amalgamate with and virtually take over the now somewhat moribund but historic Fabian Society in 1939). Bevin was however unacceptable as chairman of the Socialist League itself to the ex-ILP element who preferred one of their own number, Frank

[20] The standard (though by no means objective) account of the party's history remains that by G.D.H. Cole, *A History of the Labour Party from 1914* (London, 1948). From a still more left-wing viewpoint there is also Ralph Milliband, *Parliamentary Socialism* (London, 1961). The impact of external events is brought out in John F. Naylor, *Labour's International Policy: the Labour Party in the 1930s.* (London, 1969).

Wise. On his premature death in 1933, he was succeeded by Stafford Cripps.

Cripps an eminent barrister and the son of Lord Parmoor, who had been a member of both MacDonald's Labour cabinets, had only recently become a member of the Labour Party when MacDonald made him Solicitor-General in 1930. He now rapidly became the hero of the non-communist Left through his advocacy not only of an advanced socialist programme, but of an all-embracing emergency powers act that would permit an incoming Labour government to circumvent the delays of the parliamentary timetable, and preclude the expected attempts by financial interests to sabotage its programme. Unable to secure a majority within the Party for his views, and taking advantage of the increasing opposition to the foreign policy of the Baldwin government, Cripps came out in 1936 in favour of a United Front to link the Labour Party with the Communists, the ILP and the Opposition Liberals. The Communists had not yet gone beyond appealing to the unity of the working class, and the ILP were and remained hostile to any combinations including non-socialist elements, but Cripps pressed on, and in 1937 founded a journal *The Tribune* to serve as a platform for his views.

Neither the trade union nor the parliamentary leaders of the Party were well disposed towards such initiatives, and the Party insisted on taking a hard line against Labour Party members appearing on the same platform as members of the ILP or Communists. In January 1937 it was agreed that members of the Socialist League who did not accept this position should lose their party membership, and in March the Socialist League dissolved itself. At the Labour Party Conference in October 1937, the Party's position was reaffirmed, although paradoxically, Cripps himself was re-elected to the NEC.

By the winter of 1937 the Communists for their part were prepared to link up with any party or grouping opposed to 'appeasement' and by the autumn of 1938 Cripps was advocating an even wider coalition than previously, to include anti-Chamberlain Tories as well as other parties. It was this that led to his expulsion from the Labour Party in January 1939. He was not readmitted till 1945. The contempt that Chamberlain displayed for the Opposition and its leaders which was to prevent him from becoming an accepted wartime national leader, was thus in his own terms justified by their inability either to support his own diplomacy and policies of re-armament, or to produce an agreed and plausible alternative to them.

The Conservative Party also had its dissidents and not only on the issue of re-armament which Churchill had made peculiarly his own; there were also a number of younger Tories who felt that there was room in the Party's policy for more radical attacks upon social evils and that Treasury orthodoxy should not be allowed to diminish the Party's commitment to reform. Harold Macmillan, MP for the industrial constituency of Stockton-on-Tees from 1924 to 1929 and again since 1931, was the leading figure in this group and had published a number of books setting out the Tory reform case.[21] But the Baldwin–Chamberlain combination had proved able to hold all its critics at bay. Despite important issues arising in the re-armament programme from which the Prime Minister could not altogether hold aloof, the last months of Baldwin's premiership were those of a caretaker. The coronation of the new monarch took place on 12 May, and on 27 May, Baldwin resigned in accordance with a pre-arranged timetable made public some time previously.

When Chamberlain became Prime Minister his preparations were complete and the changes from the cabinet he inherited not very numerous. MacDonald took the occasion to end his ministerial career – his health was failing – and was replaced as Lord President by Halifax who was to be the key figure until the outbreak of war. Simon moved to the Exchequer and was succeeded at the Home Office by Samuel Hoare. Duff Cooper replaced Hoare at the Admiralty and was replaced at the War Office by Hore-Belisha. At the Board of Trade one of the rising hopes of the Conservative Party, Oliver Stanley, replaced the veteran National Liberal Runciman. With the departures of MacDonald and Runciman the overwhelmingly Conservative character of the cabinet was further accentuated and though the label 'National' was retained, the justification for its use was increasingly difficult to find. Much more important was the change in the style of leadership from Baldwin who had been content to act as an arbitrator between the departments and to leave initiatives to his colleagues, to Chamberlain who was convinced both that the country's situation was very serious and that it was up to him to find solutions to its problems. What was ironical was that someone whose reputation rested upon his achievements in domestic reform, and as an administrator, should find that these problems were essentially those created by forces outside this country and to a large extent outside his experience.

The substance of policy was determined by circumstances; it was the mode of operation that changed. Chamberlain had always been convinced that it was essential to prevent Britain and France facing a grand alliance, and had been a partisan of detaching Japan by timely

[21] The appendices to the first volume of Harold Macmillan's memoirs, *Winds of Change 1914–1939* (London, 1966) include the preface to *Planning for Employment* published in 1935 by 14 MPs, including Macmillan himself. The overlap in membership between this group and those who emerged later as critics of Chamberlain's foreign policy is not very considerable.

concessions. But the refusal of Japan to adhere to the London Naval Treaty of March 1936 had indicated how determined she was to pre-serve a free hand, and although exploratory talks began soon after Chamberlain's assumption of the premiership, the renewal on 7 July of fighting in China on a large scale destroyed any hopes of progress along these lines. Chamberlain thus fell back on the hope that Italy at least might still be brought to loosen its ties with Germany, and was to make this the principal object of his diplomacy until the following year. Since he believed that the Foreign Office were unwilling to pursue so active a policy, the use of means that by-passed the official channels made an obvious appeal and for advice Chamberlain fell back on Sir Horace Wilson who had been seconded from the Treasury as the government's Chief Industrial Adviser.

Nevertheless it was never overlooked by Chamberlain nor indeed by those who doubted the wisdom of his tactics, that ultimately it was Germany not Italy that was at the heart of Britain's problem. It was Germany alone that presented a direct threat to the United Kingdom and no system of peaceful relations could be established in Europe without her.[22] The argument popular on the Left at the time, and among Soviet historians ever since, that Chamberlain was actively working to divert German expansionism eastwards and that he would have looked with equanimity at annexations at Russia's expense does not correspond to the facts. Chamberlain was no less an adherent of the balance of power theory than his critics; and the more Germany came to dominate central and eastern Europe the more the balance would shift in her favour, quite apart from the impact of her economic policies upon Britain's own trade in that area. The underlying rationale of British policy was that Germany should be brought to accept some self-limitation of her ambitions in Europe and a com-mitment to the peaceful settlement of any disputes with her neigh-bours and that in return her economic difficulties might be attended to, and in particular that concessions in the colonial sphere might be found acceptable.

A good deal of the behind-the-scenes diplomacy of the period was concerned with the colonial issue but it was not one which could figure prominently in public discussion. While the Imperial Conference that took place at the time of the Coronation guaranteed general Dominion support for what was coming to be known as the policy of 'appeasement', individual Dominions and notably South Africa were unlikely to favour any alteration in the disposition of colonial

---

[22] For the view that British policy towards Germany was essentially consistent and that divisions between 'hawks' and 'doves' have been exaggerated in retrospect see Norton Medlicott, 'Britain and Germany, the search for agreement 1930–1937', in Dilks, ed., *Retreat from Power* I.

territories. It was also the case that quite apart from imperialists of the 'what we have we hold' school who were liable to be critics of appeasement, elements on the liberal Left upon whose sympathies Chamberlain originally felt he could rely, were by now sensitive to using colonial peoples as chattels to be disposed of in the interests of distant rulers and who, in particular, felt that Nazi racialism made the Third Reich an unsuitable regime to rule over non-European peoples.

As far as the Soviet Union was concerned two arguments could be used in favour of the policy of excluding her from participation in the process of trying to create a new European system to replace that of the League of Nations, which after its failure to prevent the conquest of Abyssinia was held to be unable to play more than the most subsidiary rôle. Chamberlain himself strongly mistrusted the Russians, as not sharing for ideological reasons in the idea of general security but as deviously seeking to promote their own revolutionary ends. And to those who felt that by now the Soviet Union was at a distance from its revolutionary origins, it could be pointed out that its military capacity was very doubtful, and actually in process of being weakened by the internal purges that reached their peak at this time. The argument put forward by Lloyd George and others that no combination excluding the Soviet Union had a chance of success seemed to depend more on faith than on evidence.

The other unknown quantity was the United States. Chamberlain had derived from the Far Eastern crisis of 1931–2 the conviction that the United States was not to be relied upon for resistance to aggression, even where its own interests were involved, still less where, as in Europe, they were seen as rather remote. Neither he nor his cabinet could be unaware of the fact that isolationism in the United States had received new accessions of strength and that the neutrality legislation imposed by Congress upon the President might make it impossible in the event of war for the United States to provide the assistance that had been so vital to Britain in the earlier world conflict. The British government was prepared to go some way with the Americans in their belief that economic cures could be found for political ills and to assist in negotiations directed towards the freeing of trade, though not without concern for the effect of these upon the Ottawa system of imperial preferences; but it was perceived more clearly in London than in Washington that Germany's aims were essentially political, and that economic policy was being used to promote political objectives rather than vice-versa. Furthermore the United States had an indirect hold over British policy in that Chamberlain had no intention of separating Britain from the Dominions in pursuit of his European policies and the Dominion leaders, in particular Mackenzie King of Canada, were increasingly affected by their sense of ultimate dependence upon the power of the United States. While Roosevelt's habit of using a multiplicity of agents made his embassy in London of only secondary importance, it was not wholly without significance that the ambassador from early in 1938 to after the end of Chamberlain's term of office, Joseph Kennedy, was a strong supporter of the Prime Minister's policies of appeasement and mixed socially with even more fervent advocates of seeking for an accommodation with Hitler at almost any price.[23]

The twin themes of Chamberlain's premiership until the outbreak of war in September 1939 are thus abundantly clear. On the one hand, there was the effort to pursue the objectives of British diplomacy against a background, punctuated by successive events on the continent and in the Far East, that made its success less and less likely: the increasing intervention of Germany and Italy in the Spanish Civil War only partially checked by the firm stand against allegedly unknown but actually Italian submarine activities in the Mediterranean taken by Britain and France at the Nyon Conference in September 1937, and the final collapse of the Republic at the end of March 1939 leaving in power in Spain a government likely in the event of war to prove sympathetic to Britain's enemies; the outbreak of further fighting in China in July 1937 and the evidence of a rapprochement between Japan and Britain's European antagonists already initiated by the German–Japanese 'anti-Comintern Pact' in November 1936 which Italy adhered to in November 1937, followed by her withdrawal from the League of Nations; Germany's annexation of Austria, the long-expected '*Anschluss*' on 12 March 1938; the growing pressure on Czechoslovakia culminating in the Munich agreement on 29 September – an agreement which removed the strongest element of resistance to German designs in eastern Europe; the destruction of the false sense of security engendered by the apparent completion of Hitler's plans for the unification of the German elements in Europe's populations when on 15 March 1939 Hitler abolished what was left of Czechoslovak autonomy, followed on 22 March by the seizure of Memel which turned attention to the vulnerability of Poland, now the only east European country except for the Soviet Union outside the range of Germany's economic and political hegemony; the apparent reversal of British policy that followed and the attempt to build up some kind of security system that might still give Hitler cause to hold his hand; Mussolini's annexation of Albania on 7 April and the clear evidence that his assistance in bringing about

---

[23] See C.A. MacDonald, *The United States, Britain and Appeasement 1936–1939* (London, 1981) and Michael R. Beschloss, *Kennedy and Roosevelt: the Uneasy Alliance* (New York, 1980).

the Munich Conference did not mean that he could be relied upon as a partisan of the *status quo*; finally, the German diplomatic triumph in the Nazi–Soviet pact of 23 August, the proximate cause of the Second World War.

The other theme is of course the growing pace of British rearmament, the changes in the direction of Britain's military effort as the likelihood of fighting on the continent increased, and the preparation of the measures that would be required should war break out, on the industrial side and in respect of civil defence. The attention of the public and of most of those in politics was concentrated on the diplomatic scene; and historians during and immediately after the war tended to ask two questions of their material; first, whether Chamberlain continued to believe that an accommodation with Hitler was possible and accepted the need for rearmament as a bargaining factor, or whether knowing that an ultimate showdown was inevitable he pursued the diplomacy of appeasement in order to gain time for Britain's rearmament to make up for past deficiencies and give a reasonable chance of victory; second, whether any alternative policy might have built up such resistance in Europe to Hitler that he would have been discredited at home and replaced by a government with which an acceptable new settlement could have been reached. More recent historians would appear to take the view that the first question is of biographical rather than historical interest, and that it may be as impossible to disentangle these threads in Chamberlain's thinking as it is to isolate individual convictions in the changes of outlook and mood generally. On the latter question, opinion would seem to be converging towards the view that given the nature of the Nazi regime and the fragmentation and uncertainties of the opposition to it, war at some point with Germany was hardly avoidable, and that given the nature of the Soviet regime and the attitudes of other countries towards it, the creation of a Grand Alliance was probably out of reach even of the most skilful diplomacy.

The steps in Britain's own preparedness can be listed briefly.[24] The position that Chamberlain inherited was dominated by two facts, the priority given to imperial defence in the allocation of resources and the assumed vulnerability to air attack of the home islands. But there had already been a movement towards accepting the view that an expeditionary force might have to be mounted for the continent and that this would entail a more active policy in respect of reserves, notably in the expansion and training of the territorial army. Even before he became Prime Minister, Chamberlain was applying his

[24] See Michael Howard, 'British Military Preparations for the Second World War', in Dilks, ed., *Retreat from Power* I.

mind to the military as well as the financial implications of this
development, as well as to the problem in respect of the RAF as to
whether to concentrate resources on bombers to deter attack or on
fighters to defeat an attack if it came.[25] As Prime Minister,
Chamberlain appointed Inskip to review the entire rearmament
programme with the aid of three senior officials, Horace Wilson,
Hankey and the head of the Supply Board of the CID, Sir Arthur
Robinson. Its interim report was available to the government in
December 1937 and its final report, containing concrete recommendations, in February 1938. The report emphasized the importance of maintaining financial solvency and not diminishing the
country's credit which would be necessary for the purchase of supplies
in a prolonged conflict such as that of 1914–18. It adhered to the existing priorities of expenditure, putting the provision of a force required
to act alongside continental allies after the claims of home and
imperial defence.[26]

Indeed the pressure to economize on the army was such as to justify
the view that in fact the whole idea of Britain ever fighting in a
continental war of the 1914–18 kind was alien to the government's
thinking, and this was reinforced by the insistence of the new
Chancellor, Sir John Simon, that there must be an absolute
maximum on armaments expenditure over the next five years, the
sum chosen being the *minimum* prescribed in the government's own
white paper of February 1937. The new Secretary of State for War,
Hore-Belisha, was thus obliged to abandon Duff Cooper's plans for
expanding the territorial army. He continued to press the case for
expansion but his energies were largely diverted to a reshaping of the
army high command, leading to bitter disputes with the General
Staff. It was perhaps important that Hore-Belisha was advised during
his first year in office by the military correspondent Basil Liddell Hart
whose own attitudes had been powerfully affected by the losses of the
First World War, and whose own strategic doctrines would seem to
have ruled out a comparably massive military involvement.[27]

The first important policy decision of a positive kind was made
when Inskip, strongly supported by the Treasury, came out against
the air staff's preference for bombers and switched resources to the
production of the newly devised radar chain and the modernized
fighter force to go with it. The general thrust of Inskip's thinking was

[25] The personal impact of Chamberlain's thinking can be followed in Peden, *British
Rearmament*.
[26] See Shay, *British Rearmament*, pp. 159ff.
[27] See Brian Bond, *British Military Policy between the Two World Wars* (Oxford, 1980),
chaps. 9–11, for the evolution of army preparedness between May 1937 and the outbreak of
war.

accepted by the cabinet at the end of 1937. In the final report, Inskip himself however came out for accelerated defence spending, on the ground that a concentration of the proposed five-year programme into two years would give the best opportunity to negotiate with Britain's prospective antagonists from a position of strength. Britain therefore entered upon the fateful year 1938 with no settled plans for intervention on the Continent; the need to cover forward bases for the RAF in the Low Countries seemed to have been dropped. Although Inskip and others noted the risks that were being taken, and the degree to which policy was being based upon assumptions of France's defensive strength, there was at this point no 'continental commitment'.

Hopes that this posture could be maintained were partially dispelled by the *Anschluss* and all three services began once more to press for added expenditure. For the moment however both the navy and the air force found their requests turned down, as was Duff Cooper's criticism of the Treasury's rationing of the services. The question of air defence was more complicated, in part because of the friction between the industry and the Secretary of State, Lord Swinton.

Nevertheless some acceleration of the air defence programme was contemplated; at the beginning of the year it had been decided to approach the TUC about the provision of labour; contacts with the employers were also strengthened although it was clear that with compulsion ruled out, there were severe limitations on what could be done. On the question of cost, there was renewed argument between Swinton and the Treasury but on this occasion Swinton was supported by Inskip, and the Air Ministry was empowered to order 12,000 planes to be completed by May 1940 in place of the 7,500 under the existing programme. It was at this point that the shift in Labour Party policy brought about by Bevin and Dalton at the October 1937 Conference became important since the Opposition now joined Churchill and his friends in their attacks upon the Air Ministry. Swinton's known preference for some measures of compulsion to meet the labour shortage did not endear him to Chamberlain who requested Swinton's resignation on 13 May, replacing him by Kingsley Wood who had attracted Chamberlain's favourable attention at his own former ministry, Health. Lord Weir who felt that Swinton had been wrongly sacrificed resigned as the Air Ministry's industrial adviser.

But it was the situation not the men who determined policy. Kingsley Wood himself soon began to press the Treasury for further expenditure, using arguments about the need to keep pace with the Germans that as Simon pointed out were incompatible with the

Treasury's commitment to rationing. The arguments between the Treasury and the Air Ministry took place against the background of the Czech crisis which was the central preoccupation of the government in the summer of 1938. The diplomacy of the crisis was governed on the British side by the clear warnings of the Chiefs of Staff that Britain and France did not possess the means of coming to the aid of the Czechs, and that if war came the only hope was that, after a long conflict in which Japan and Italy might well also be involved, the Western allies might emerge victorious and so restore Czech sovereignty. But if there was to be a general war, the arguments for postponing it until some of the new defence arrangements were ready was a powerful one. While Munich was the logical culmination of such thinking, its revelation of the country's weakness inaugurated a year in which the priorities of defence policy because once more subject to radical revision.

One result of Munich was further changes in personnel. Duff Cooper resigned as First Lord, and was replaced by Lord Stanhope who was content to accept Chamberlain's continued adherence to the need for economy with the result that the Admiralty played little part in the pressure for swifter measures of rearmament. This situation was unaltered when, on 29 January, Inskip was succeeded as Minister for the Co-Ordination of Defence by Lord Chatfield, the recently retired First Sea Lord and Beatty's successor as the most influential sailor in the country. (Inskip himself, elevated to the House of Lords as Viscount Caldecote, became Dominions Secretary, a not unimportant position given Chamberlain's determination not to take action which did not carry with it the assent of the Dominions.) The case of the army was different from that of the navy. Indeed before the immediate crisis was resolved at the Munich Conference, the cabinet had on 13 September reversed itself by restoring the army's continental rôle, directing that preparations should be made for an expeditionary force to be sent to the Continent within a short time after the outbreak of war. It had however, neither upgraded the army's scale of equipment to meet this requirement nor added to the funds available. After Munich, debate ensued between the War Office and the Treasury as to the financing of the new measures.

To the pressure from the War Ministry on the cabinet was added the knowledge that the French were expressing growing unease at the possibility that they would be asked to carry the major burden of a land war with only token British support. On the other hand the Treasury stuck to their view that the ordinary course of business should not be impeded, and successfully averted demands for a Ministry of Supply of which Hore-Belisha and before his dismissal

Inskip had become the advocates, and for which the argument was enhanced by the fear of profiteering in the armaments industry, and by the continued friction between the Air Ministry and its suppliers.

Resistance to the demands of the service ministries was further weakened by Hitler's Prague coup in March 1939. Opinion in the country now shifted so strongly in favour of greater preparedness that Chamberlain, while not abandoning his diplomatic objectives, had no option but to go along with parliamentary and cabinet views. New and far-reaching demands in respect of the regular army, the territorials and supplies were presented by the War Office in April. At the end of the month, Chamberlain accepted what the French had been urging since January, a measure of compulsory service – conscription – the first in Britain's peacetime history. Here it was political rather than service opinion that got its way, since it would be some time before this measure could strengthen the forces actually available, while the training of recruits would impose an immediate burden upon the already hard-pressed army. By now also, Chatfield had come round to Inskip's view that a Ministry of Supply was essential to meet the new needs The bill creating such a ministry was passed in May though the first holder of the new office, Leslie Burgin, a not very eminent National Liberal who had been serving as Minister of Transport, was only appointed in July.

Almost until the outbreak of war, the Treasury maintained its commitment to giving priority to financial stability and to the minimum interference with normal business against the pleadings of successive service ministers. Chamberlain's idea of a National Defence Loan was foiled in 1937 in the face of industrial and City opposition, and it was not until July 1939 that the Treasury accepted the need for higher direct taxation, government direction of savings and the other financial instruments of a nation at war. It has been argued that the failure to deal more effectively with the profits being made out of rearmament as well as the unpopularity with the Left of Chamberlain's foreign policy help to explain the slow progress of talks with the unions about the measures that were becoming necessary to make certain that armament production would not be hampered by labour shortages. In March 1938 a voluntary compact was entered into with the TUC by which the unions agreed to help get skilled men into the defence industries and accept a degree of dilution. Even these mild measures evoked some criticism from more militant trade unionists than Citrine and the General Council; and relations between the government and the trade union movement as a whole remained at arm's length.[28]

[28] On these aspects of pre-war policy see Keith Middlemas, *Politics in Industrial Society: the Experience of the British System since 1911* (London, 1979), chap. 9.

For the general public these moves, however modest, towards preparation for war, even accompanied as they were by preparations for dealing with the likelihood of assault from the air – Air Raid Precautions as they were known, civil defence in modern terminology – made less impact than the successive crises in diplomacy and their political consequences. The string of defeats sustained by Chamberlain in pursuit of 'appeasement' added new figures to the ranks of the anti-appeasers and diminished pro-German feeling until it embraced only those prepared to go a long way with Nazism itself. Yet although the repercussions of the divisions within the Conservative Party arising from different views over appeasement were to be felt both during and after the war, few of its opponents adopted the full critical stance of Churchill; and he was more closely in touch with the official world and was listened to with more attention than appeared at the time.

The first crisis came when Chamberlain, convinced that Eden was proving an obstacle to his approaches to Mussolini, put his Foreign Secretary in a position which he felt left him no alternative to resignation. On 20 February 1938 Eden who had found himself isolated in the cabinet left office and was replaced by Halifax who was henceforward to be the key figure in the administration since without his support Chamberlain's position would have become untenable. It was afterwards claimed that Eden had taken into account Chamberlain's original reluctance to take up with enthusiasm a rather vague suggestion of Roosevelt's for an international conference to seek an economic solution to the world's ills which Chamberlain felt might cut across his own more precise formulation of offers that could be made to Germany and Italy. In fact Chamberlain did come round to Eden's view that the Roosevelt initiative should be explored, but by this time Roosevelt himself had thought better of it. It is therefore clear that Eden's sticking point was his conviction that Mussolini was not to be trusted, and that the Italian dictator no matter what promises he might make, would not disengage from his Spanish commitments. Eden, while possessing some following on the back benches, did not seek to lead a 'cave' and remained available for office should the situation change.[29]

The inability of Mussolini to dissociate himself from Hitler was shortly to be demonstrated when on 12 March Germany brought about the *Anschluss* after obtaining Italy's consent. The event strengthened the arguments of Eden's partisans, but did not have a massive impact upon opinion generally. Austria which had excited

---

[29] Eden's own account in his *Facing the Dictators* (London, 1962) is subject to critical analysis in David Carlton, *Anthony Eden: a Biography* (London, 1981), chap. 4 'Chamberlain's Foreign Secretary'.

much sympathy on the Left in the 1920s had been written off since the destruction of the republic by indigenous right-wing forces in 1934. Although the seven by-elections of the summer produced two Labour gains there was little evidence of a massive swing against the government.

The annexation of Austria brought the question of Czechoslovakia into the foreground and presented Chamberlain with a serious dilemma. On the face of things the claims of the Sudeten Germans to some form of self-determination, provided it was brought about by peaceful means, were not outrageous; and even Hitler's declared interest in their fate could be squared with his claim that it was only the fate of the Germans in Europe that concerned him. On the other hand, Czechoslovakia was the principal beneficiary of the Franco-Soviet pact; her elimination as a military and political factor which would be the consequence of any redrawing of her boundaries would call into question the whole of France's policy in eastern Europe. As was shown by a preliminary alarm in late May, based upon a misreading of Germany's readiness to intervene, there was no issue more likely to bring about a European war in which Britain's ties with France would almost inevitably force her to take part. And for reasons, related to the state of Britain's rearmament programme, particularly in the air, even those who would favour resistance at some point would have preferred to postpone the trial of strength.

Chamberlain now thought it desirable to put an end to the strained relationship that existed with Eire and an agreement with De Valera on 25 April included among its provisions the abandonment of the treaty right for Britain to use in wartime the Southern Irish ports of Berehaven, Queenstown and Lough Swilly. Although many people at the time accepted the Admiralty view that without a friendly hinterland the ports would be of little use, and condemned Churchill's attack upon the decision as another example of 'appeasement', wartime experience suggests that Churchill may have been right in his estimate of the strategic sacrifice that had been made.[30]

Of more far-reaching importance was Chamberlain's persistence in seeking some accommodation with Japan despite her undeclared war against China and her signature of the anti-Comintern Pact with Germany on 25 November 1936. The ability to meet Japan's demands that Britain should abandon her support of the Chinese government and abandon her special privileges in China, was limited by the unwillingness to alienate American opinion. On the other hand, the growing danger in Europe meant that the guarantee to the

[30] Stephen Roskill, *Naval Policy between the Wars.* Vol. II: *1930–1939* (London, 1976), pp. 446–7.

Dominions that in the event of war a major fleet could be sent to Singapore was clearly impossible to fulfil in the light of threats nearer home. In the end the balance struck in the Craigie–Arita agreement of 24 July 1939 seemed for the time being to have averted the danger that Britain might be distracted from her European and Mediterranean tasks by the demands of the Far East.

But the main energies of Chamberlain were concentrated upon Europe. The first British effort at defusing the Czech situation was the sending of Runciman as a kind of mediator between the Sudeten German leaders and the Prague government.[31] The Runciman mission, meticulously prepared, lasted from the beginning of August 1938 to 16 September, but by the beginning of that month Hitler's determination to detach the Sudetenland altogether, irrespective of any changes in the policy of the Czech government and to use force to do so if at all necessary, was becoming increasingly evident.

The possibility of a peaceful solution to the crisis at the expense of Czechoslovakia's territorial integrity was clearly not excluded from the government's thinking, although a leading article in *The Times* on 7 September advocating such a course produced a prompt denial from the Foreign Office that this was contemplated. Indeed general opinion in the country seemed to be hardening. But pressure from the French to find a way out fortified Chamberlain's own convictions. Chamberlain now decided that only a personal approach to Hitler could avert catastrophe and on 15 September he flew to meet Hitler at his mountain retreat, Berchtesgaden. Hitler made it plain that he would be satisfied with nothing less than major territorial concessions, and these immediately. He gave little encouragement to Chamberlain's hopes that the Czech territories proper would remain independent, and that if a peaceful solution to the crisis could be reached a general Anglo-German understanding might follow.

The cabinet with the somewhat hesitant exception of Duff Cooper decided that it would be wrong to fight to prevent the application of the principle of self-determination to the Sudeten Germans. Runciman's final report in which he had recommended cession was published on 21 September, and the French joined the British in persuading the reluctant Czechs to go along with these proposals. But when Chamberlain met Hitler on 22 September at Godesberg, ostensibly to finalize the agreement, he found the German dictator angry at being baulked of a military triumph and demanding a speeding up of the timetable and much harsher conditions eliminating any kind of international supervision of the transfer. Further discussions pro-

---

[31] For a very unfriendly account of Chamberlain's diplomacy see Keith Middlemas, *The Diplomacy of Illusion: the British Government and Germany 1937–1939* (London, 1972).

duced no softening in the German attitude despite the fact that the new proposals, amounting to a virtual ultimatum, would obviously be more difficult for Chamberlain to commend to opinion at home.

Three indecisive cabinet meetings were held during which both Duff Cooper and Hore-Belisha pressed unsuccessfully for measures of mobilization. Military advice remained the same. Nothing could prevent the Germans from overrunning Czechoslovakia in a short campaign, and the only course that would then be open to Britain and France would be to attack Germany's western frontier, a task which experience suggested would not be easy. Anglo-French discussions on 25 September showed that the French also objected to Hitler's new terms; on the other hand their account of their own military situation was not encouraging. In the end Chamberlain got the French to agree to a last offer to Hitler – a negotiated transfer of territory with a measure of international supervision and some minimum safeguards for the unfortunate Czech inhabitants of the territories to be ceded. Hitler showed little enthusiasm for these ideas, and agreed to see the Czechs for detailed discussions only if they came to Berlin on 28 September and accepted 1 October as the date for completing the German takeover.

The bellicosity of Hitler's demeanour, both public and private, now made it look probable that efforts to resolve the crisis would be overtaken by events. On 27 September Chamberlain agreed to mobilize the fleet, but did not make this public in his broadcast that evening in which he spoke to the nation of the nightmarish preparations for war. Further negotiations suggested that if Hitler could get his way without war he would be prepared to accept minor modifications in his proposals, and these hints proved sufficient to persuade Chamberlain that a third meeting with Hitler might yet bring about the desired result. He was successful in enlisting the collaboration of Mussolini, unwilling to see war come at this juncture. The result was the arrangement for a conference at Munich in which Chamberlain would be joined by Daladier and Hitler by Mussolini. The announcement that the conference would take place was made to the House of Commons by Chamberlain at the end of an account of his efforts to reach a peaceful settlement, and was greeted with unfeigned relief by the great majority of members.

The Munich Conference on 29 September produced a programme for the handing over of the Sudetenland which was sufficiently different from that demanded at Godesberg to enable Chamberlain to present it as a diplomatic success; although in the upshot the concessions made were proved to be of no great assistance to the Czechs; all the matters left open for negotiation ended up by being settled in Germany's favour. The way was opened for further territorial cessions by Czechoslovakia to her other neighbours, Poland and Hungary; and the idea that the rump of Czechoslovakia should be guaranteed by the Four Munich Powers never materialized. The other outcome of the conference, a declaration on Anglo-German relations looking to a peaceful settlement of all outstanding questions, was however available to Chamberlain as an additional argument in favour of his Munich venture. Parliamentary and public support was in any event assured for the moment; only Duff Cooper resigned and he over the detailed provisions of the handover which he felt were humiliating for the Czechs, not over the principle of the cession. Duff Cooper was succeeded by Earl Stanhope; a more significant appointment was that of Sir John Anderson as Lord Privy Seal to succeed Earl De La Warr who had taken Stanhope's place at the Board of Education. Anderson who had been Permanent Secretary at the Home Office in the 1920s and then much concerned with emergency arrangements including air raid precautions, and who had subsequently made a reputation for toughness as Governor of Bengal, was given responsibility for both manpower problems and civil defence. By contrast, Runciman, who had become something of a symbol for appeasement, re-entered the cabinet as Lord President of the Council.

These cabinet changes came only at the end of October; meanwhile Parliament had been recalled to debate the Munich agreement which it did over four days beginning on 3 October. Apart from Duff Cooper's explanation of his resignation and a speech from Eden on a less forthright note, the criticism of Chamberlain's action came largely from the familiar group of dissident Tories and from Labour. The most powerful indictment of the whole conduct of British policy and an assessment of the weakening of Britain's position in Europe came, as was to be expected, from Churchill. The degree of opposition among the Conservatives was now such that some ministers advocated an immediate general election in which those Conservatives who opposed the government would not receive official support. It was thus assumed that the country as a whole was strongly behind Chamberlain. Some Conservatives attempted to avoid the problem by persuading the Opposition to table a motion in terms that would not amount to a vote of censure. There was even a question of Labour support for dissident Tories should an election be called. But nothing came of these approaches, and the opponents of the government on the Conservative side could not agree on common action. In the event 30 Conservatives abstained including Eden, Duff Cooper, Amery and Harold Macmillan. Churchill and a dozen others remained seated in their places, the most demonstrative form of abstention. On the other hand, two holders of junior posts who had resigned with Eden (as had his under-secretary Viscount Cranborne) voted with the government.[32]

Chamberlain felt sufficiently strong, when Parliament reassembled at the beginning of November, to declare his intention of pursuing talks with Germany on the basis of the Anglo-German agreement. But by now there were growing doubts as to the possibility of coming to terms with Germany so long as the Nazi regime persisted; and Halifax in particular, who had been appalled by Hitler's Godesberg terms, began to move into the camp of the doubtful.[33] The acceleration of German rearmament, the anti-Jewish rioting and measures against the Jewish community in November following the murder of a German diplomat in Paris were having their effect on both ministerial and public opinion. The degree of support for Chamberlain in the country was tested in several by-elections. In the first of these at Oxford, the Labour and Liberal Parties combined to support the candidature of the Master of Balliol as an independent anti-appeasement candidate.[34] In the upshot, Quintin Hogg, son of the former Lord Chancellor, retained the seat though with some falling off in the Conservative vote. At Dartford on 7 November, Labour won a fairly marginal seat from the Conservatives. But in the most spectacular though not much reported of these by-elections at Bridgwater in Somerset on 17 November, Vernon Bartlett, a well-known Liberal journalist standing as an Independent Progressive, captured what had seemed to be a safe Tory seat, though one with a strong nonconformist Liberal tradition for him to build on.

Yet an analysis of these and the other post-Munich by-elections makes it very difficult to assert that even at this juncture, foreign affairs exerted a more than usually significant impact upon the electorate. It does look as though the government would not have gained the unequivocal triumph expected by some ministers if Chamberlain had in fact gone to the country after Munich; but equally there is no great evidence for an erosion of public support as successive events abroad cast doubt upon the effectiveness of the 'appeasement' policy. Single-issue elections are notably hard to mount in British conditions. When the Duchess of Atholl, formerly a right-wing Conservative figure who had been alienated from the government by its handling of the Spanish Civil War, resigned her seat and stood as an anti-appeasement candidate she lost the by-

[32] See Thompson, *The Anti-Appeasers*, chap. 10 and Gilbert, *Churchill* v, chap. 48. There is some discrepancy in the figures for abstentions; those given here are from Gilbert.

[33] See S. Newman, *March 1939, the British Guarantee to Poland: a Study in the Continuity of British Foreign Policy* (Oxford, 1976), pp. 53ff.

[34] See Iain McLean, 'Oxford and Bridgwater', in C. Cook and J.A. Ramsden, eds., *By-Elections in British Politics* (London, 1973).

election on 21 December to a pro-Chamberlain candidate. While the government was losing ground, it had after all been long in office, and faced many problems at home as well as abroad.

More significant was the evolution of the government's own policy which followed a double track. On the side of trying to find an accommodation with Germany a good deal was made of contacts between the industrialists of the two countries and those ministers and officials concerned with trade. These contacts continued up till the following summer. On the other hand, attempts were made to counter German influence in south-eastern Europe including Turkey through financial assistance. The objective in both cases was a Europe in which freedom of trade might break down German autarky and bring both Germany and the Balkan countries into a closer economic relationship with the western powers. On the political side the idea of a trade-off between colonial concessions and some limitation of German armaments remained alive. But the further development of such policies was affected by events. In January 1939 came reports of German preparations for an attack on Holland, and an agreement with the French that both Holland and Switzerland would have to be defended if attacked. It was the threat to Holland which finally brought about the return to the idea of an expeditionary force as an essential part of the country's military preparations.

Of even greater importance than the rumours about Holland (which proved to be premature) was the bare fact of Hitler's seizure of the remainder of Czechoslovakia on 15 March 1939. It came at a time when there was some optimism about the future in government circles. But after Chamberlain's first somewhat cool reaction, it became evident that, even for previous supporters of the government's policy, a new situation had to be faced.[35] It could no longer be claimed by the Germans that they were interested only in national unification. Hitler's pledges seemed worthless, and in so far as the government still hoped to avert war, it was not in the belief that mere paper agreements would suffice.

To some extent the next steps were an improvisation based upon the rumour that the Germans would follow up their action by further advances. On 22 March Lithuania ceded Memel to Germany. The next target appeared to be Rumania, and the only way to save it some combination involving the two surviving east European powers of military significance, Poland and Russia. The difficulty was that neither Rumania nor Poland was keen on any arrangement that would open the way for the Red Army to operate on their territory.

[35] The period between March and September 1939 is covered in some detail in Sidney Aster, *1939: the Making of the Second World War* (London, 1973).

Yet it was felt that some immediate step was necessary and on 31 March an Anglo-French guarantee was given to Poland. Two days earlier as a further demonstration, Hore-Belisha had announced the doubling of the territorial army.

Mussolini's annexation of Albania on 7 April turned attention to the Balkans and the Mediterranean. The country most immediately affected was Greece, where Britain had been trying to use its political influence to counter the strong German economic penetration.[36] Greece had since Munich been pressing the British for a formal alliance but there had been some division of opinion in Whitehall. The Chiefs of Staff worrying about Italian naval power had argued against undertakings to Greece or Turkey as likely to make any rapprochement with Italy even more difficult. The Foreign Office feared that any signs of such a rapprochement would alienate not only Greece and Turkey but also Yugoslavia. Furthermore, reminiscent of Grey's dilemma, there was the hostility between Greece and Bulgaria and a desire in some British quarters not to offend the latter. Nevertheless on 13 April, Anglo-French guarantees were given to Greece as well as Rumania. Ideas that Hitler and Mussolini could somehow be separated received a further blow with the signature on 22 May of the 'Pact of Steel' between them. By now the concentration of British resources seemed all important and the drain of the military presence in Palestine no longer tolerable. On 19 May in what Churchill and others regarded as a culminating act of appeasement government policy on Palestine was restated in a White Paper conceding to the Arabs their main demand, a slowing down and eventual termination of Jewish immigration.

These swiftly moving events had their repercussions on party politics. After Hitler's seizure of Prague, there was a demand from some of Chamberlain's critics in the Party for a National Government which could ease the task of putting the country on a war footing. Indeed pressure to form such a government in which Eden would have been a key figure may explain the hardening of Chamberlain's position. For a three-party government led by or even including Chamberlain seemed ruled out by the hostility to him personally of the Labour leaders.

But once the guarantee to Poland had been given – it was made reciprocal on 5 April to satisfy Poland's *armour propre* – the criticism from the Eden group was muted, since Eden did not want to prejudice his chances of returning to office. Halifax while sympathetic to broadening the government's base was still prepared to go along with

[36] For relations with Greece see John S. Koliopoulos, *Greece and the British Connection 1935–1941* (Oxford, 1977).

the existing administration. The difficulties that would have faced a three-party government in deciding upon policy may be judged from the fact that when Chamberlain for political and diplomatic reasons did in fact introduce a compulsory service measure on 20 April, it was opposed by both the Labour Party and the Liberals.

Political pressure from several quarters was now exerted on the government to find a way of associating the Russians with the embryonic combination now being built up to contain further German expansion. In the cabinet itself it was held by some – notably the very anti-communist Hoare – that without the Soviet Union the combination would be too weak to deter Hitler if not to defeat him. But the powerful military arguments in favour of such an arrangement were bolstered by others which were predicated on the assumption that only ideological prejudice prevented it from coming about. And these views were played upon in influential social and political quarters by the highly activist Soviet ambassador, Maisky. From communist and fellow-traveller sources had all along come the view that the purpose of 'appeasement' was to bring about a clash between Nazi Germany and Soviet Russia from which the West could stay aloof.

Once the guarantees to Poland and Rumania had been given there was no way in which Germany could attack Russia without bringing them into play. But equally Russia's own bargaining position was much strengthened. Soviet policy was the reverse of the one attributed to it by the admirers of the Soviet Union in the West; it was if possible to avoid war with Germany at least until that country had been weakened by what everyone assumed might be a long and exhausting war against France and Britain. Since Hitler's own intentions were still indecipherable in the short run, it was necessary for Russian diplomacy to hold the British and French in play until these doubts could be cleared up. While by the end of May Chamberlain had come round to the view that an agreement with the Russians must be attempted, the long negotiations of the summer culminating in the military mission in August were compounded of a double unreality. The demands made by the Soviet Union as the price of an arrangement would have put an end to the independence of the Baltic states and were as has been seen unacceptable to the Poles. It was hardly in the power of the British or French government to offer the Russians the territorial buffer in eastern Europe which appeared to be the price of their collaboration. Hitler however, once he had decided to swallow his ideological prejudices in an agreement with the Soviet Union which might either bring about a Polish capitulation or enable the Polish campaign to be won with the minimum of loss, was in a position to offer the Russians exactly what the Western powers were refusing. The possibility of being trumped by Hitler was not over-looked in British official circles, although the government's critics did not appreciate the extent to which the overt pressure on ministers to produce results weakened their negotiating hand. In the end the speed of the dénouement caught both government and critics by surprise. On 24 August the announcement of the Nazi–Soviet pact put an end to speculation and in the opinion of most people made war inevitable.

Neither the British nor the French viewed the prospect with exhilaration although British preparations were much further advanced than a year earlier. The only way of avoiding the fulfilment of the guarantee to Poland seemed to be some readiness by the Poles to follow the Czech example at the time of Munich and accept Hitler's demands should these prove to be compatible with the nation's continued existence. Various moves through official and unofficial channels continued for a few days but Hitler had no intention of being baulked of his conquest and Parliament would not tolerate any equivocation about Britain's pledged word. By now Dominion assent to resistance had been obtained. On 3 September Britain went to war; an hour later, the French (having failed to get assistance this time from Mussolini) delivered their own ultimatum. Chamberlain remained Prime Minister and the main group of ministers who had implemented the policy of appeasement (except for Runciman) remained in place. But Anthony Eden entered the cabinet as Secretary for the Dominions, and Winston Churchill found himself back at the Admiralty as in that far off August of 1914.

10 Epilogue: Britain and the Second World War

The war upon which Britain entered in 1939 appeared at first sight to be a resumption of the conflict of 1914–18 – the second German war, or as francophiles remembering 1870 sometimes styled it, the third German war. The enemy was the same; the principal ally was the same; it had begun ostensibly once more out of an east European quarrel; the generals were regimental officers who had survived the earlier struggle. At the Admiralty, Winston Churchill, recalled with Eden to office as soon as war broke out, once again occupied his old and favoured rôle. Hankey, the pivotal civil servant in the earlier war, entered the cabinet. Once more the fleet took up its stations for the protection of the home islands and the enforcement of the blockade. Once more an expeditionary force took up its position alongside the French.

The outcome was however to be very different. While, as had been foreseen, the advent of the bomber aircraft (and towards the end, of pilotless aircraft and rockets) meant that British civilian casualties were heavier than those of the First World War, and while British servicemen fought and died in many parts of the world, there was nothing that corresponded to the long drawn out agony of the efforts to break through on the western front in 1914–18 and the toll of casualties that accompanied them. Whatever reasons or excuses might be adduced for Britain's faltering performance in the post-1945 world, it could not again claim to have lost a generation. In both military and civilian terms, it was in this war the eastern front that was to see the major sacrifices of human life.

The material losses were heavy. In addition to the renewal of the submarine campaign against British merchant shipping there was the destruction wrought upon ports, industrial installations and the homes of the people by the assault from the air. The 'home front' now meant more than belt-tightening or unfamiliar conditions of work. The word 'blitz' passed into the language. Yet great as was the destruction, it was less than that ultimately inflicted upon Germany's cities by Britain's bomber command and Britain's American allies, let alone the final horrors of Hiroshima and Nagasaki. And although the degree to which the country was ultimately mobilized for war was unparalleled, the machinery by which this was effected bore many similarities to that of the earlier conflict, and was in many respects built upon that experience, avoiding many of the former errors.

The higher direction of the war and the political framework that sustained it were also in large part the products of the earlier struggle, and in many respects an improvement upon the earlier improvisations. On this occasion, the conduct of the war by the Prime Minister who had entered upon it was of much shorter duration. By the time the critical operations in the West began, the Chamberlain government, discredited by the unsuccessful campaign in Norway, had given way to a national coalition under Churchill in which the Labour Party was a full partner.[1] A small war cabinet – though a little larger than the Lloyd George model – was the supreme political authority; but the civilian–military lines of demarcation were much more clearly drawn with the Chiefs of Staff committee acting as the source of military advice to the war cabinet and to the Prime Minister in his capacity as Minister of Defence. Churchill himself although far more prone than Lloyd George had ever been to intervene in the choice of individual commanders (and more qualified to do so) and in actual operations, did in the end invariably accept the professional advice he was offered. The supply side took a little longer to settle down, but here also after some improvisation in the early part of the war the machine worked to very great effect. Parliament was again reduced to a subordinate rôle and although discontent with the way things were going was occasionally vocal, as in the dreadful early months of 1942, Churchill's authority was never seriously impaired. Parliament's own life was prolonged with the result that there was no general election between 1935 and 1945, the longest such gap in modern British history. And the party truce again made the testing of opinion at by-elections a matter for independent candidatures or new and ephemeral groupings.

But the sense of the familiar proved to be an illusion. Although it was not perhaps fully perceived until a few years after the end of the war, the position of Britain had changed much more drastically than as between 1914 and 1918. From the point of view of the international system, the First World War began with an admitted constellation of eight Great Powers – six in Europe, with the United States and Japan outside it. The war eliminated one of them – the Austro-Hungarian Empire – and temporarily weakened Germany and Russia. But in 1939 the British Empire was still a Great Power, in a

---

[1] For Churchill's return to office and for the early part of his wartime premiership, see Martin Gilbert, *Winston S. Churchill*. Vol. VI: *1939–1941* (London, 1983).

world of Great Powers. The course of the war destroyed that status in the sense that Britain could no longer play a wholly independent rôle in matters of the first importance. The world was now dominated by two 'Super Powers' and Britain's security and for a time her very existence as a functioning democracy depended on her alignment with one of them – the United States. From one point of view, the drama of the war years is the gradual revelation of the extent to which this was now ineluctably the case. It was also the personal tragedy of Winston Churchill who fought consistently and stubbornly for a continued place at the 'top table' even after it became clear that the top table had been laid for only two.

The successive phases of the war which from the point of view of the military historian are those of early defeats followed by the gradual wearing down and ultimate victory over Italy, Germany and ultimately Japan, are from the narrower British angle to be seen as marking stages in the erosion of Britain's own power and influence which the skills of her commanders, the bravery of her troops and the endurance of her civilians could do little to check. As the struggle widened it became less and less a British war, but rather the war of an alliance in which Britain was not the leading member and whose purpose was not the recovery of Britain's lost imperial territories nor a re-establishment of the system which had made their retention and security possible.

It must not be forgotten that as in 1914 so in 1939, it was not just the United Kingdom but the British Empire as a whole that went to war. It is true that the Dominions did so through their own political processes, and in the case of South Africa not without an internal political upheaval; it is true that the taking of India into the war by imperial fiat added to the alienation of the nationalist movement and confronted British power in the sub-continent with a much greater problem of internal security than in the First World War – a problem frightening in its implications when the Japanese seemed poised for a large-scale invasion; it is true that the Irish Free State adopted a sullen neutrality of considerable benefit to the enemy cause; yet by and large the resources of the Empire and Commonwealth in men and materials were at the disposition of the Imperial power. But those who had seen that Britain's resources were overstretched for the extent of her responsibilities and had forecast that the financial burden of maintaining a world-wide war effort would prove too great were in the event to be justified.

It is perhaps not surprising that after the predictable and speedy elimination of Poland, and the partition of that country with his Soviet accomplice, Hitler should have thought it possible that Britain might yet accept some form of German hegemony in Europe in return for a guarantee of her overseas possessions. In fact the months of the 'phoney war' so different from the dramatic military events of August–September 1914 were occupied in building up Britain's strength, in tightening the links with France, in trying by diplomacy to keep Italy, Spain and other potential allies of Germany out of the war, and were marked by some hesitation between accepting the fact of Russian hostility and a lingering expectation that in the end events would bring Russia in as an ally. It was hoped that means would be found to deny to the Germans the raw materials its war effort required, and that military activity, as was unsuccessfully attempted in Norway, could be used to give teeth to the economic arm.

All this was shattered with the collapse of France in May–June 1940, the failure of the attempt by offering an organic union with that country to keep at least part of her forces and her colonial empire in the war,[2] and the loss of much of Britain's military equipment through the evacuation of her army from France, though much of its manpower was saved. Although there were those who felt that Britain had no option but to follow the French example and seek what terms she could get from the conqueror, Churchill's determined leadership ensured that such voices would be muffled. Instead in a remarkable exercise in morale building, Britain's isolation and weakness was made to appear a source of strength. Britain was alone, and Britain would show the world what she could do when wholly the master of her fate.

What had from September 1939 been an Anglo-French war against the Axis – though Italy only became a belligerent when France was on the verge of total defeat – became Britain's war against Germany and against a German-dominated and largely German-occupied Europe. Two controversial decisions by Churchill mark the transition: first the refusal to throw in Britain's last reserves of fighter aircraft to support the beaten French armies, thus making possible what became the 'battle of Britain' and second, the even more difficult and ruthless decision to destroy major units of the French fleet at Oran rather than risk their falling into German hands. Perhaps Oran should be taken as the true end of 'appeasement'. After it no one would be likely to doubt Britain's resolution.

From the fall of France to Hitler's attack on Russia in June 1941, the war was almost Britain's alone – whether beating off the enemy air attack and thus frustrating German plans for an invasion or defending Egypt and the Middle East. London became the capital of

[2] See Max Beloff, 'The Anglo-French Union Project of June 1940', in *The Intellectual in Politics, and other Essays* (London, 1970). A vivid though by no means definitive study of the Anglo-French relationship in the early part of the war is Eleanor M. Gates, *End of the Affair: the Collapse of the Anglo-French Alliance 1939–1940* (London, 1981).

all those fighting to end the Nazi grip on continental Europe, becoming the seat of the Dutch, Norwegian and Belgian governments in exile and of General de Gaulle's 'Free French'. A Polish government in exile was also constituted and many Poles fought alongside the British. Much effort was devoted to intelligence about enemy operations and plans, and British academics from various disciplines were recruited for the code-breaking operations including those now generally referred to as 'ultra'. Contacts were built up with the resistance movements on the continent and agents were parachuted in to join them. Propaganda which had got off to a bad start with leaflet raids on the Germans in the early weeks of the war was now refined and extended. Above all the external services of the BBC became for much of Europe the only reliable source of information, even though listening to them was dangerous. All the constituted bodies in British society from the trade unions and employers organizations to the universities found themselves drawn into the war effort, though not, as in 1914–16, the political parties.

Nevertheless the exhilaration of self-sufficiency was to some extent based upon illusion. In neither productive resources nor manpower could Britain match what was available in Hitler's Europe. Britain's dwindling financial resources and the United States' neutrality laws made it impossible to make full use of American capacity without seeking new financial and legal methods of operation. Apart from waging war, the principal early activity of the Churchill government was the building up of a new relationship with the Americans, relying on President Roosevelt's growing perception of the danger to the United States itself inherent in the challenge of the European dictators and the threat from Japan. The deal by which American destroyers were acquired in exchange for bases in the western hemisphere, and the 'lend-lease' agreement by which the financial veto on the transfer of weapons of war was lifted, were symptoms of a more intimate relationship which in the unspoken thoughts of some looked towards eventual American belligerency. The experiences of the overlapping missions to America in the First World War were taken into account, and Lord Halifax succeeding Lord Lothian as Ambassador found himself at the head of a vast bureaucratic empire which mirrored the organization of Whitehall itself.

The mixing-up of British and American concerns and efforts on which Churchill set such store was not without its costs. It was clear that while there was agreement on the need to defeat the Nazis and to restore the independence of the countries they had overrun, the mere restoration of the pre-war European empires was not the long-term objective that the Americans had in mind. On the contrary, they wished to see the Wilsonian principle of national self-determination applied to the rest of the world, while continuing at the same time the drive for universal non-discrimination in trade and payments. The agreement reached between Churchill and Roosevelt in the Atlantic Charter of 12 August 1941 did not conceal profound differences that later revealed themselves more clearly.

Hitler's attack upon the Soviet Union was another mixed blessing. It diverted Germany's major military resources to a front which would not directly threaten British interests unless the German advance took them through the Caucasus and so into the Middle East. While there was originally some scepticism about the Soviet powers of long-term resistance, it was clearly in Britain's interest to give the maximum assistance possible to the Soviet armies; and despite Churchill's long anti-communist record, his willingness to accept the Soviet Union as an ally was never seriously in doubt. But help to Russia and the naval strain of convoying supplies to Russia's northern ports were additional burdens on Britain's resources. Furthermore the nature of the Soviet system made it impossible for there ever to be the frank exchange of ideas and plans that went on with the United States, even when the United States was formally speaking a neutral power. At no point did the Russians take their allies into their confidence or admit to their own people the importance of external aid. Furthermore, the Russians inevitably concerned to relieve the pressure on their own front, constantly harangued the British (and later the Americans also) to speed up the re-invasion of western Europe, and attributed the delay to political ill will rather than to the manifest difficulties of such an amphibious operation of which they lacked direct experience. British communists who while the Nazi-Soviet pact remained in being had shown no enthusiasm for the 'imperialist' war, suddenly became the main advocates of further effort, and began a clamour for a 'second front' in which they were joined by other elements on the Left susceptible to Soviet influence and even by some far from left-wing personalities like Lord Beaverbrook, who were now ready to overlook the Russians' earlier complicity with the aggressor. Finally, the Russians having made considerable territorial gains in eastern Europe – including the annexation of the Baltic states – were clearly determined not to sacrifice these gains but rather to extend them in the new diplomatic situation. And it was difficult, as Russia's own conduct made it clear, to see how these objectives could be reconciled with the restoration of Poland for which Britain had gone to war. Defeat for the Russians would be a catastrophe; victory for the Russians would bring its own problems, not least because the British and the Americans did not see these problems in the same way.

The months between the German invasion of Russia and the

Japanese attack on Pearl Harbor, followed by the German and Italian declarations of war against the United States, were a phase during which Britain benefited from the increasing involvement of the United States in the guarding of the Atlantic sea-routes but was itself preoccupied with the defence of the Middle East, and with its offshoot – the unsuccessful campaign in Greece which left Germany in control of the Balkans. Never in the long history of Britain's involvement in the politics of the Mediterranean had the inland sea and its littoral so dominated her military thinking. The Western Desert replaced Flanders' fields in the imagery of British warfare.

It was events following Pearl Harbor that inaugurated the new and final phase of the war. Britain was now part of an alliance which could scarcely be thought of as not being victorious in the long run. But the conquest by the Japanese of Britain's Far Eastern empire, of which the fall of Singapore was the symbol, marked the end of the period in which the Empire–Commonwealth could sustain itself through its own might. While in the First World War troops from India, Australia and New Zealand could safely be used as far from home as imperial necessities might dictate, all three countries were themselves now liable to invasion. India despite the opposition of the Congress leaders to the war effort was defended by British and Indian forces; the pressure from the Americans and their favoured allies the Chinese Nationalists for radical political change which might have impeded successful defence was held in check, but that the days of the Raj were numbered was now apparent in a way not previously the case. Australia and New Zealand, without any weakening of commercial and cultural ties with Britain, could only look to the United States for their security, and Australia itself became the base for the American counter-offensive.

Once the American capacity for mass-production was put fully at the disposal of the war effort, and once American manpower could be called upon to swell America's armed forces, it was obvious that in respect of divisions in the field, ships at sea and supplies of all kinds, America would become the major partner in the Alliance even though her leaders were less experienced and her organization less stream-lined than their British counterparts. It took some time before the strategic and political implications of this fact fully sank in, but when an American was appointed to command the long-postponed reinvasion of Europe, which only came in June 1944, America's senior status was amply confirmed.[3]

---

[3] Sir David Fraser's biography of the British Chief of the General Staff from 1941 to 1946, *Alanbrooke* (London, 1982), provides a masterly account of these developments and indeed of the whole strategic problem as seen by Churchill's principal military adviser.

Britain was fortunate in that Roosevelt had from the beginning accepted the single most important strategic decision of the war, that the defeat of the Nazis must be given priority over the defeat of Japan, despite the contrary view held by the US navy and the strong pressure from American public opinion in the opposite direction. But this did not prevent the diversion of some effort to the Pacific war, notably in the production and deployment of landing craft which came to represent the principal bottle-neck on the allied side. Nor did it prevent the Americans making use in arguments over the form that the anti-German strategy might take of the knowledge on the part of the British that if they pressed disagreement too far, the result might be that further resources would be switched to the Pacific war where the Americans could be certain of having their own way.

The war in and around Europe was directed by the Combined Chiefs of Staff meeting in Washington – the Americans had been obliged to create a parallel machinery of planning and decision-taking to match the British contribution to the organization. On the political side Roosevelt and Churchill gave ultimate guidance through their series of summit meetings and other contacts. But the symmetry was largely one of appearance. On the British side, it was clear that military action was at the service of policy, that operations had to be judged in the light of the political ends it was hoped to achieve. On the American side, Roosevelt allowed greater latitude to the military, and their instinct was to avoid any considerations that looked towards an ultimate political objective, and to seek only the quickest and least costly victory over the enemy. In particular, the Americans were very reluctant to see the Russians as anything but full and committed partners in a common aim or to share the growing British view that eastern Europe ought not to be rescued from the Nazis merely in order to have communist governments imposed upon it. The British intervention in Greece at the end of 1944 was the only case where Britain was in a position to carry this determination into effect, and it did so at the price of alienating much American opinion.

On the basic military strategy of how to defeat the Axis there was in fact no real disagreement. In 1942 there was nowhere except North Africa where the enemy could be engaged. In 1943 the invasion of Italy was a possible option, whereas the build-up of American forces in Britain had not reached the point at which a cross-Channel invasion could safely be contemplated. Disagreements of a serious kind only arose over the relation of the Italian campaign to the cross-Channel invasion and over the way in which victory in the West should be exploited. But there were suspicions on the American side that arguments based upon purely military considerations were a cover either for British unwillingness to tackle the hazards of reinvasion or for a preference for using the strength built up in the Mediterranean to challenge the Russians for mastery in south-eastern Europe.

The period between the landings in North Africa in November 1942 and the liberation of France in the summer of 1944 was also marked by important differences between Britain and the United States over that country's future. Difficult as was General de Gaulle to handle, the British went along with him in seeing the importance of France's playing a part in her own liberation, and being treated as soon as possible as an equal member of the victorious alliance. Fearful that Russia had succeeded Germany as a threat to the equilibrium of the continent, and unwilling to trust the Americans to provide a counterweight once they had dealt with Hitler, Britain had little option but to place its hopes in a regenerated France which with Belgium and Holland, cured of the illusions of neutrality, might form the nucleus of a non-communist European bloc. The disaster of 1940 could not be allowed to dominate the future of Anglo-French relations.

The same line of reasoning impelled the British to see the reconquest of their own Far Eastern possessions and of those of France and Holland as a prime objective in the war against Japan. The United States, dubious about the restoration of the European empires, and convinced that Japan could only be defeated by an assault on the home islands as the culmination of a long maritime campaign in the south-west Pacific, was averse to such a dispersion of effort. For the Americans the only point in recovering Burma was to make it easier to send supplies to the Chinese who would, it was hoped, tie down Japanese forces on the mainland, as would the Russians when they intervened as promised after the German collapse.[4]

In the end these arguments were found to be based on false expectations. Japan was indeed driven out of her conquests, but neither the British nor the Dutch nor the French could restore for good their pristine authority whose psychological foundations had been destroyed by the Japanese victories and occupation. Japan itself was never invaded, since the hitherto unknown factor of the atomic bomb forced her to sue for peace. Yet this invention also illustrates the passing of power across the Atlantic. The basic discoveries leading to the making and utilization of the atomic bomb had largely been made in Britain, partly by refugee scientists from Europe. But the exploitation of these theoretical discoveries for practical purposes could only

[4] For a masterly analysis of the wartime relationship between the British and the Americans in respect of the Asian theatre of war, see Christopher Thorne, *Allies of a Kind: the United States, Britain and the War against Japan 1941–1945* (London, 1978).

be made on the necessary scale in the United States (where British and refugee European scientists also played their part). It was only the most spectacular of the instances of largely or wholly British discoveries ultimately being turned to profit by a country enjoying much greater resources, including empty space. Where could one have put a British Los Alamos?[5]

By the time that Japan surrendered, the Churchill government was no longer in office. Assuming that the war with Japan would be prolonged for 18 months after the defeat of Germany, Churchill had offered his Labour colleagues a choice between continuing the wartime coalition until then, or an immediate winding-up of the coalition and an election fought in conditions of party independence. Although Attlee had put the former proposal to the National Executive it found only a little support and that exclusively from the trade union element. The government resigned; Churchill formed a caretaker National government to fight the election. After a three weeks' delay to enable the service votes to be counted, the result came in the middle of the Potsdam Conference with the Americans and Russians; Churchill had been massively defeated. Attlee and Bevin, his unexpected choice as Foreign Secretary, now represented Britain in her new position of material inferiority to her fellow-victors. The contrast with Lloyd George's personal triumph in 1918 could not have been greater; yet the historian is likely to agree that Churchill's achievement as war leader was the more remarkable of the two. Why then had he been repudiated?[6]

It would not appear to be the case that Churchill himself had been found wanting, or that his war leadership was underestimated. It was rather that, unlike Lloyd George, he had found himself unable to personify or become the spokesman of the feeling that if such a war as had taken place was to be justified, it must lead not merely to a restoration of the *status quo* but to material improvements in the condition of the people. Despite his brushes with organized labour, Lloyd George had retained enough of the reputation of his radical past to be a plausible leader of a government devoted to internal reconstruction as well as international peacemaking. Churchill's radicalism was further behind him nor indeed was he willing to encourage the belief that the economic losses of war were a possible

[5] For Anglo-American relations in the atomic field see Margaret Gowing, *Britain and Atomic Energy 1939–1945* (London, 1964).

[6] The most satisfactory attempt to explain the wartime evolution of British politics remains Paul Addison, *The Road to 1945: British Politics and the Second World War* (London, 1975); for a picture of the impact of the war upon the civilian population written from a radical populist viewpoint see Angus Calder, *The People's War: Britain 1939–1945* (London, 1969). See also the extracts from the archives of mass-observation in Tom Harrisson, *Living Through the Blitz* (London, 1976).

foundation for massive new forms of public expenditure on social betterment. He had consistently taken the view that victory was its own reward; that to free the world from the tyranny of Nazism was sufficient in itself. He had not encouraged post-war planning on a large scale, and was known to be sceptical of the proposals for economic and social change now widely in circulation.

Furthermore although only reluctantly accepted as leader of the Conservative Party, Churchill had made his own rôle inseparable from it. The election was fought on party lines and Labour defeated the Conservatives. Put in this way, it is not so surprising nor should those who had followed the by-elections or the now newly developing opinion polls have been taken aback by the result. It could indeed be argued on the normal principle of the swing of the pendulum in what was once again a virtually two-party system that Labour was likely to do better the next election after 1935, though there is evidence to suggest it would not have won a 1940 election if the country had been able to hold one. But developments during the war had made such a victory more likely in a number of ways.

The social historian is likely to attach most importance to a change in the public temper brought about by the impact of the war on the home front – the revelation during the evacuation from London of mothers and children for fear of air raids early in the war, of the degree of poverty and slumdom still persisting even in the more prosperous parts of the country; the breaking down of class barriers when urban communities were faced with the perils of the blitz and the work of fire-fighting and other remedial measures; a system of rationing for food and clothing much more far-reaching than anything attempted in the First War, and appealing to some as indicating the possibilities of a much more egalitarian society. It could be argued that the need for change had been demonstrated and the possibilities for change made to appear less remote.

Yet the translation of social experience into political behaviour must be undertaken with caution. The war gave the Labour Party an opportunity of which its leaders made the fullest use. The very concentration of Churchill and most of his Conservative colleagues upon matters directly concerned with the war effort or with the international aspects of the conflict left the home front ministries largely in Labour hands, and with a major voice in planning for post-war reconstruction, once this was on the agenda. Most important of all, Ernest Bevin's presence in the war cabinet as Minister for Labour, made it clear that without the co-operation of organized labour war production could not be brought to the required level but also that the price for this was the taking into partnership of the trade union movement in the person of its dominant representative figure. Herbert Morrison at the Home Office with responsibilities for 'home security' became a figure of national importance; as did through a somewhat meteoric series of arrivals and departures, the erstwhile leader of the extreme Left, Sir Stafford Cripps. Above all perhaps, Attlee, as Churchill's deputy and in a variety of behind-the-scenes rôles, displayed administrative and political qualities that made it reasonable to regard him as a possible alternative Prime Minister.[7] While no single figure on the Labour side could match Churchill in the breadth of his appeal, Labour could in 1945, as it could hardly in 1918, present itself as at least equal and perhaps superior in the quality of its alternative governmental team.

Furthermore, the war not only demonstrated the possibilities of collectivism through its apparatus of controls, it also brought into government service at various levels the intellectual proponents of collectivist philosophies, both those of an overtly socialist nature and those of a more Liberal hue such as had been expounded by Keynes and Beveridge. The Beveridge Report of December 1942 encapsulated the belief that building on the foundations of the Lloyd George welfare state, society could protect its members against all the ills that flesh is heir to, and the vast publicity it enjoyed made it, as Churchill rightly feared, an unparalleled weapon against the Conservatives, although it was Labour rather than Beveridge's own Liberals who were to reap the electoral benefit. Beveridge's later and personal report on full employment, published in 1944, gave popular form to the Keynesian view that the correct management of the economy by government could conquer the scourge of unemployment. But it was not merely the more prominent exponents of collectivism who were of importance; at lower levels within the departments, enthusiastic young socialists were giving their energies to planning the economic and social future. In all this there was much that was agreeable to younger Conservatives in the ministry; indeed the main piece of social legislation passed during the period of the coalition was the Conservative R.A. Butler's Education Act of 1944. Much that was to be the basis of the Attlee government's legislative programme from 1945 to 1951 was fairly common form in wartime Whitehall.

Even more important as an explanation of the 1945 election was however the political use made of the new respectability of collectivist ideas. It could be and was freely argued that it had now been intellectually demonstrated that the hardships of pre-war unemployment, and its concomitant social evils, could have been avoided by a more intelligent or more caring government. The

---

[7] For a sympathetic account of Attlee, see Kenneth Harris, *Attlee* (London, 1982).

Conservatives were thus pictured as the party of unemployment and deprivation. By an even more daring transposition of the truth, the Conservatives were now blamed for having made the war itself inevitable by their appeasement of the dictators, despite the fact that the parties to which the individuals now expressing such views belonged had themselves opposed almost to the end the development of the military means by which resistance could have been made meaningful. Churchill, then, paid in 1945 for the sins or alleged sins of Baldwin and Chamberlain.

Such propaganda undoubtedly fell on willing ears. The popularity quite early in the war of the broadcasts of such left-wing partisans as J.B. Priestley, the startling by-election victories of the 'Commonwealth Party' – a grouping set up to enable a socialist banner to be carried while the official Labour Party observed the agreed truce – the material circulated by the Army Bureau of Current Affairs – the first gesture towards politicizing a British army since Cromwell's day – and at a popular level the highly partisan treatment of such issues by the *Daily Mirror* – all these must have had a cumulative effect upon the political stance in 1945 of servicemen and civilians alike. While between 1914 and 1918 the left-wing activists faced some repressive measures, and while the left-wing intelligentsia was an important minority on the fringe of society, between 1940 and 1945 left-wing activists formed most of what there was of a parliamentary Opposition and the left-wing intelligentsia was clasped to the bosom of the Establishment.

It would however be wrong to isolate the development of political opinion from the progress of the war and the increasing prominence of the Americans and the Russians. The contrast in the British reaction to the two major allies is significant. The nineteenth-century reputation of the United States as the home of true democracy which had made it popular with the British working class had disappeared. It was now much easier for Conservatives like Churchill to welcome the mixing up of the two countries' affairs. On the other hand, in the latter part of the war the stationing in Britain of large numbers of American servicemen meant that there was now a good deal of actual acquaintance for good or ill with Americans, their ways and their beliefs.

With the Russians, the case was very different. For knowledge of what the Russians were like the public had to rely on the media and it was felt for obvious reasons desirable to present them in as good a light as possible – the easier while they were clearly bearing the brunt of the Nazi onslaught. And this understandable admiration for Russian courage and endurance was exploited not only by communists, but by the newly powerful intellectuals of the Left. Perhaps among the factors to be taken into account in dealing with the election of 1945 should be British admiration for the Red Army.

After their election defeat many Conservatives pointed to the fact that much of the propaganda that had helped to bring it about had been the work of government-sponsored agencies, the Ministry of Information, the BBC, the Army Bureau of Current Affairs. Churchill himself was alert to such possibilities but unable to do much about them amid the more pressing aspects of the war effort that fell upon his shoulders. It may be argued however, that when some fairly large and easily grasped general ideas begin to circulate in a society, transmission belts will always be found. Only the most rigorous civil censorship could be a barrier and this did not exist in wartime Britain. The message was more important than the medium.

The pre-war governments were condemned for the failure of 'appeasement' without any suggestions of what alternative policy there might have been for a country whose commitments outran the resources the electorate was prepared to offer for their defence. It was equally true that on matters of domestic policy, the pre-war years were depicted in terms that omitted the brighter side.[8] And this fact was to be significant later on. For while it was not difficult to pinpoint the social evils of period – unemployment, slumdom, lack of proper health care, restricted educational provision – the belief that simple remedies might have removed them was bound to create difficulties for subsequent governments.

Nevertheless the Labour Party went into the election intent on reviving memories of the disillusion that had followed the victory of 1918, and promising that this time the promises of social betterment would all be fulfilled if a Labour government were returned to power. On foreign affairs, the campaign also took up the popular theme of the need for better relations with the Soviet Union by asserting that 'Left' would be able to speak to 'Left'.

In the event the Labour government that took office under Attlee in 1945 had an easier task in some respects that the Coalition had had between 1918 and 1922. There was no immediate outcry for the abolition of 'controls' – that was to be delayed for a quinquennium – and although much of the government's attention had to be focused on immediate issues of policy at home and abroad, it could with its unassailable majority, secure the enactment of the vast bulk of its legislative programme. It was later administrations that would have to cope with the deficiencies of wartime intellectual preparedness.

[8] Left-wing intellectuals were themselves to come round to see that the inter-war period had not been one of total gloom: 'this was the best time, mankind, or at any rate, Englishmen had known: more considerate with more welfare for the mass of the people packed into a few years than into the whole of previous history'. A.J.P. Taylor, *English History 1914–1945* (Oxford, 1965), p. 180.

The nationalization of the Bank of England was intended to symbolize the importance now attached to macro-economic controls for avoiding what seemed to be the outstanding paradox of the inter-war period, large-scale unemployment while many obvious national tasks awaited attention. Could a combination of directed investment and demand management achieve the full employment in a free society that was the core of the Beveridge–Keynes approach? To what extent was it possible to use the Keynesian techniques successfully in a country so dependent upon foreign commerce and hence needing to watch the balance of payments? Above all, could the injection of demand into the economy be combined with avoiding inflation if there was no parallel ability to control incomes – would the answer to greater demand mean higher prices rather than increased production and hence more employment? Neither Beveridge nor Keynes were unaware of these problems. It may be for this reason that both men remained Liberals rather than give their adherence to the Labour Party. But what they and those who accepted their basic teachings had not taken into account was that the trade unions whose assent was required for any form of incomes restraint had by no means accepted, and perhaps could not accept, a theoretical analysis that deprived them of their main *raison d'être*, the pursuit of their members' interests through 'free collective bargaining'. One result of the war and of the Labour victory had been further to entrench the position of the unions as major partners in the framing and conduct of public policy. In that sense the new economic orthodoxy was politically less firmly based than might in 1945 have seemed the case.

In respect of the other part of the Beveridge gospel, generalized welfare provisions, the key problem had been foreseen by the Webbs and others during the great debates on social policy in Edwardian England. If you mitigate the hardships of unemployment do you not also thereby diminish the incentive to work – and if you diminish this incentive will you get the production you need in order to fulfil the commitments to welfare? To ask such questions by now was to call into question the most powerful of public sentiments. It is perhaps not surprising that the problem was to continue to haunt future governments.

More novel was the intellectual difficulty of coping with the desire to make direct public provision in kind and without demanding payment in return in important areas in which it was now agreed that the inter-war period had fallen short of what a civilized society might expect to do for its citizens. Health and education were to be the two fields in which the failure to apply a rigorous theoretical analysis were to become most apparent. The creation of a National Health Service was from one point of view the most striking achievement of the post-war government; the provision made for every citizen could be contrasted with the way in which in some other countries and notably the United States, the costs of medical care could break a family's financial back. Yet no one had paused to think that medical care was in its nature infinitely extensible – could every citizen expect the kind of medical attention that pulled Churchill through his wartime illnesses? Would not the success of the application of greater medical care itself aggravate the problem of resources by weighting the population towards the upper age limits where ill-health was more common and its treatment more expensive. Did anyone believe in 1942 that 40 years later, about one person in 30 in the United Kingdom would be employed by the National Health Service and that even then it would be spoken of as woefully under-financed?

In education, the Butler Act made secondary education a universal right just as primary education had been regarded for a long time. But if secondary education, then why not higher education? Was there no limit to the resources that the community should be prepared to spend upon education – and if there was a limit who should decide where entitlement to its various levels should lie?

In these fields and in others, the position was once again complicated by the fact that it was not simply a matter of the State and the individual – patient or child or young person. Powerful vested interests existed in the unions and these were likely to grow in strength in a political environment on the whole favourable to their claims. The repeal of the 1927 Trade Disputes Act showed how committed the Labour Party was to using legislative power to enhance trade union immunities and privileges. In the case of education, the position was further complicated in that at the school level and in respect of much technical education, the operating agents were organs of local and not central government.

Lastly one might point to the problems created by 'nationalization'. The nationalization programme of the post-war government sprang from many different sources – the doctrinal belief in the virtues of public ownership enshrined in clause IV of the Labour Party's constitution; the belief that ownership of major sectors of the economy would enable their policies to be based on 'use not profit' so that they would better serve the needs of the community, the desire as in the mining industry to end once for all the sad history of industrial relations that had bedevilled it since its beginnings. But while the purposes might be various the arrangements to be made were dominated by the single 'Morrisonian' model.

It is true that in the legislation as ultimately enacted by the 1945–51 Labour government, the degree of ministerial control over the new public corporations was much greater than that envisaged in the pre-war discussions about the subject.[9] Yet it does not appear that there was any serious consideration of the central economic issue that subsequently emerged, namely the extent to which the 'independence' of the corporations could be meaningful, if the industries concerned needed to be subsidized out of the public purse so as to enable them to meet the financial claims of their work-force, and their requirements for investment.

The programme envisaged for post-war Britain which was in the event largely implemented, was then primarily based upon an emotional reaction against the hardships of much of the working population and above all of the unemployed in the inter-war period. It was however sustained by the other element in the situation already mentioned, an unreasoning and wholly ill-informed admiration for the Soviet Union. The resistance of the Soviet armies and people – the more remarkable for having been largely discounted in many quarters – was taken as evidence for the fact that the British people had all along been deceived as to the nature of the Soviet regime. Since what was wrong with Britain and the West in general was 'capitalism', the answer must be sought in 'socialism' – and of socialism the Soviet Union was or claimed to be the exemplar. What had become known about the darker side of the Soviet experience was put out of mind or explained away as necessary to prepare the country for the experiences it was now facing with such fortitude. Forced industrialization, the collectivization of agriculture and the deportations and famine that were its accompaniment, the state trials and the purges – all could be explained and excused or merely overlooked. Within Britain itself, the zigzags of communist policy, the Communist Party's record of infiltration and subversion could not now act as a barrier against the sentiment that those who admired the Soviet Union were united in the cause of anti-fascism and 'progress'.

For leading intellectuals not directly involved in the war effort – and for some of those who were – the justification for the war must be seen to lie in its potentiality for changing the world through international action directed by socialist principles and in harmony with the Soviet government. Professor Harold Laski, E.H. Carr, a powerful influence with *The Times* of the war years, appealed to strata in the population for whom J.B. Priestley was too folksy and the *Daily Mirror* too vulgar. For others for whom animosity towards the Germans and scepticism about the existence of any barrier to their ultimate domi-

---

[9] On the post-war legislation and its antecedents, see Sir Norman Chester, *The Nationalization of British Industry 1945–1951* (London, 1975).

nation in Europe other than the Soviet Union were more important than their own anti-socialism, collaboration with the Soviet Union was justified in terms of national self-interest without ideological overtones; the historian Lewis Namier may be taken as a representative of this viewpoint.

The fashionable political outlook on the international future was summarized in two books of considerable influence in their day – Carr's *Conditions of Peace* published in 1942 and Laski's *Reflections on the Revolution of our Times* published in 1943. Yet it was not in the international sphere that the influence of pro-Soviet thinking was to be most effective. For while as has been seen, the Labour government entered upon office in 1945 with some illusions about 'Left speaking to Left', it did not long retain them. In the face of Soviet policy towards the large part of Europe occupied by the Red Army, its stance changed to one of resistance to any further extensions of Soviet power. But the Soviet myth went on playing its rôle as a buttress for domestic socialism. How, it was asked, could socialism be a utopian creed when one of the two Great Powers now dominating the world scene was itself a socialist country? Only rare intellectuals, such as George Orwell, pointed out that if the Soviet Union was what was meant by a socialist country, then socialism left much to be desired; the difficulties of finding a publisher for his satire *Animal Farm*, eventually published in 1945, illustrate the difficulties of resisting the tide of opinion in favour of a vital ally. It was of course even rarer to find writers prepared to argue that the extension of the scope of the State common to all western industrialized countries might ultimately endanger freedom almost as much as the imposition of communist control by force. Friedrich von Hayek's *The Road to Serfdom* published in 1944 received recognition only retrospectively.

The British people entered upon the post-war world in an atmosphere of elevated utopianism more pronounced than had been the case in 1918. Indeed the comparison between Britain's experience in the two wars shows more differences than similarities. The First World War with its mass armies pitted against each other was a common European experience in which Britain had shared. In the Second World War, Britain's experience was different. The geographical barrier of the sea, the belated but ultimately correct concentration in rearmament upon fighter aircraft and radar, Churchill's insistence on not further depleting the air force in order to sustain a foredoomed French defence, the crowning miracle of the evacuation from Dunkirk – all these meant that Britain almost alone in Europe escaped invasion and occupation. Sorely tried physically as were her people, they did not have to face the moral dilemmas of resistance and collaboration which confronted so many European nations – we shall never know if there could have been a British Quisling.[10]

In some respects the similarities would be with an earlier conflict in which struggles for power and rival ideologies brought Britain into a European war with repercussions far outside Europe – the war against Revolutionary France and Napoleon. Lloyd George and Churchill would seem to form a natural pair for a latter day Plutarch; yet on closer inspection the parallels fade. If in the seamless webb of English history we are to seek for a forerunner of Churchill as a war leader, should it not be found rather in the dedicated figure of the younger Pitt? Was not his proud boast 'England has saved herself by her exertions and Europe by her example' something that Churchill could have repeated without hyperbole when he met with President Truman and Stalin in the ruins of Berlin? What happened thereafter is another story.

[10] There is a vast and growing literature upon the problems confronting the occupied countries which British opinion at the time tended not unnaturally to simplify. See the treatment of the subject in W. Rings, *Life with the Enemy: Collaboration and Resistance in Hitler's Europe 1939-1945* (London, 1982). The Resistance was also a seedbed for ideas about European unity which did not make the same impact in Britain.

Bibliography

The monographs on particular topics upon which this book is mainly based are referred to in the relevant footnotes and need not be listed here. The same is true of the memoirs and biographies of the period, but these should of course be supplemented by the appropriate volumes of the indispensable *Dictionary of National Biography*. There is no general bibliography of British History for the post-1914 decades comparable to those available for earlier centuries. The best served bibliographically are the military historians. See the later chapters of R. Higham, ed., *A Guide to the Sources of British Military History* (London, 1972) and A.G.S. Enser, ed., *A Subject Bibliography of the First World War: Books in English 1914–1978* (London, 1979) and *A Subject Bibliography of the Second World War: Books in English 1939–1974* (1977). For those wishing to pursue the general subject in primary sources, there are the four volumes of Chris Cook, *Sources in British Political History 1900–1951* (London, 1975–7).

The work most often consulted during the writing of this book was D.H.E. Butler and J. Freeman, *British Political Facts 1900–1960* (London, 1963 and subsequent editions). For details of election results see F.W.S. Craig, *British Parliamentary Election Results 1918–1949* (London, 1969; revised edn 1977) and for information on the parties' platforms see F.W.S. Craig, *British General Election Manifestoes 1900–1945* (London, 1975). The Reports of Royal Commissions and similar documents are usefully grouped and summarized in the three volumes by P. and G. Ford each entitled *A Breviate of Parliamentary Papers: 1900–1916* (Oxford, 1957); *1917–1939* (Oxford, 1951); *1940–1954* (Oxford, 1961). Foreign policy did not come within their purview but is for the inter-war period exhaustively covered in *British Documents on Foreign Policy 1919–1939* (London, 1947–) – a series which is still to be completed. Official documents for the diplomacy of the two world wars has not been similarly made available, but for the second world war, there is the five volume official history based on the foreign office archives: Sir Llewellyn Woodward, *British Foreign Policy in the Second World War* (London, 1970–6); a shortened version had been published in 1962.

For students wishing for an alternative approach to the period from that provided by the present volume, there are three previous books that cover roughly the same years: C.L. Mowat, *Britain Between the Wars 1918–1940* (London, 1955); A.J.P. Taylor, *English History 1914–1945* (Oxford, 1965) and Robert Rhodes James, *The British Revolution*, vol. II: *1914–1939* (London, 1977). All three works contain bibliographies, that in the volume by Taylor being the most thorough and wide-ranging; but a glance at it will show how much the literature of the subject has been enriched in the last 20 years.

While as the bibliographies already cited make clear there are massive official histories of the campaigns of the First World War, there is nothing comparable to the series on *Grand Strategy* in the official history of the Second World War; the six volumes which were completed with the appearance of vol. I in 1976 present a unique conspectus of the inter-relations between political and military considerations in the making of British policy. Important also is another official history, F.H. Hinsley, *British Intelligence in the Second World War: its Influence on Strategy and Operations*. The first two of three projected volumes appeared in London in 1979 and 1981. The civil aspects of the war effort were also the subject of a series of official histories; particularly important are W.K. Hancock and M.M. Gowing, *British War Economy* (London, 1949) and R.M. Titmuss, *Problems of Social Policy* (London, 1950), a key document in the development of the welfare state.

The richness of the literature on the whole period to some extent conceals its uneven distribution. The development of the Constitution itself has not so far found an authoritative historian, though the most important of British institutions receives detailed treatment in S.A. Walkland, ed., *The House of Commons in the Twentieth Century* (Oxford, 1979). Useful also is G.H.L. Le May, *British Government 1914–1953: Select Documents* (London, 1955). Administrative history both central and local is another area in which much remains to be done. While the history of the economy in general terms has been much studied, the evolution of British business is still only beginning to be recognized as a suitable field for historical inquiry despite some thorough histories of individual firms, such as C.H. Wilson, *The History of Unilever: a Study in Economic Growth and Social Change* (2 vols., London, 1954).

The trade union movement also lacks a proper history for this period since the work by H.A. Clegg, Alan Fox and A.F. Thomson, *A History of British Trade Unions since 1889*, vol. I: *1889–1910* (Oxford, 1964) stops short – a sequel is promised. This gap may explain why the history of both the Conservative and Liberal Parties during this period has been the subject of more scholarly inquiry than that of the Labour Party. Much new light on all three parties has been thrown by a monograph which appeared just as the present work was being completed: Michael Pinto-Duschinsky, *British Political Finance 1830–1980* (Washington D.C., 1981). The atmosphere of politics may be better recorded by diarists and letter writers not themselves politically of the first rank; mention should be made of two for this period: Harold Nicolson, *Diaries and Letters*, ed. Nigel Nicolson, vol. I *1930–1939* (London, 1966) and vol. II *1939–1945* (London, 1967); *Chips: the Diaries of Sir Henry Channon*, ed. Robert Rhodes James (London, 1967).

Index

(Battles, Conferences, Government Departments, Legislation, and Treaties are listed under these general heads)